HISTORY
of
LEXINGTON
KENTUCKY

Its Early Annals
and Recent Progress

INCLUDING

BIOGRAPHICAL SKETCHES AND PERSONAL REMINISCENCES OF THE PIONEER SETTLERS, NOTICES OF PROMINENT CITIZENS, ETC., ETC.

BY

George W. Ranck

HERITAGE BOOKS
2012

HERITAGE BOOKS
AN IMPRINT OF HERITAGE BOOKS, INC.

Books, CDs, and more—Worldwide

For our listing of thousands of titles see our website
at
www.HeritageBooks.com

A Facsimile Reprint
Published 2012 by
HERITAGE BOOKS, INC.
Publishing Division
100 Railroad Ave. #104
Westminster, Maryland 21157

Entered according to Act of Congress,
In the year one thousand eight hundred and seventy-two,
By G. W. Ranck,
In the office of the Librarian of Congress, at Washington.

— Publisher's Notice —
In reprints such as this, it is often not possible to remove blemishes from the original. We feel the contents of this book warrant its reissue despite these blemishes and hope you will agree and read it with pleasure.

International Standard Book Numbers
Paperbound: 978-1-55613-193-6
Clothbound: 978-0-7884-9307-2

TO MY WIFE

Helen Carty Ranck

A DESCENDANT OF EARLY SETTLERS OF LEXINGTON AND FAYETTE
COUNTY, AND THE ONE WHO SUGGESTED THIS WORK
AND WAS THE CAUSE OF ITS COMPLETION

THESE PAGES ARE

AFFECTIONATELY INSCRIBED

PREFACE.

No American city of its age has clustering around it more interesting associations than Lexington. Founded in the midst of a great revolution; built up by daring men in the heart of an almost boundless wilderness, and nurtured and protected through years of hardship and Indian warfare, she played the most prominent part in the early and tragic days of the Dark and Bloody Ground. Lexington then was substantially Kentucky herself. She was more. She was the Jamestown of the West; the advance-guard of civilization; the center from which went forth the conquerors of a savage empire.

During another long and eventful era, she was the political, literary, and commercial metropolis of "the great Northwest." She was crowded with men who made her famous.

She has now entered upon the third epoch of her existence, an epoch material, during which steam will give her an industrial prosperity proportionate to her great natural advantages.

Very much of the rich past of Lexington has died with her founders. Even the traditions of her pioneer days are dim, and the old landmarks are being rapidly obliterated. Realizing these sad truths, and appreciating Lexington's history, the author of this book resolved to save for those who will come after us all that could be gathered from this wreck of time. These pages are the result of his efforts. If he has preserved something which ought not to have been lost, or if his work will encourage some abler hand to gather and perpetuate other annals of our city which he overlooked or slighted, he will have attained his object.

The author has used every means to make his work accurate. If it is not entirely so, the fault is to be attributed to the peculiar disadvantages which always surround the local historian. In the preparation of these pages, he has consulted many of the oldest and best-informed inhabitants of Lexington and Fayette county, and also every other attainable authority considered reliable. For reasons obvious to every fair-minded person, he has ignored the many exciting events which occurred in Lexington during the late war between the States. It is to be hoped that they will receive attention of a chronicler in the unprejudiced future. As propriety required as little extended mention of the *living* as possible, the writer confined himself, in that respect, to sketches of a few aged citizens, and brief notices of ministers of the gospel and persons in some official connection.

As it is the work of the *local* historian to furnish the first elements of *general* history, to record facts rather than deductions from facts, the author has contented himself with a plain statement of past events, to the neglect of ornamental rhetoric and romantic conclusions.

LEXINGTON, KY., *August*, 1872.

HISTORY OF LEXINGTON.

CHAPTER I.

Ancient Lexington.

THE city now known as Lexington, Kentucky, is built of the dust of a dead metropolis of a lost race, of whose name, and language, and history not a vestige is left. Even the bare fact of the existence of such a city, and such a people, on the site of the present Lexington, would never have been known but for the rapidly decaying remnants of ruins found by early pioneers and adventurers to the "Elkhorn lands."

But that these remains of a great city and a mighty people did exist, there can be not the shadow of a doubt. The somewhat notorious Ashe, who published a volume of travels in 1806, says: "Lexington stands on the site of an old Indian town, which must have been of great extent and magnificence, as is amply evinced by the wide range of its circumvallatory works and the quantity of ground it once occupied." These works he declares were, at the time he saw them (1806), nearly leveled with the earth by the ravages of time and the improvements that had been made by the settlers. The testimony of the learned Prof. C. S. Rafinesque,* of Transylvania University, fully corresponds with this, and proves the former existence in and about the present Lexington of a powerful and somewhat enlightened ante-Indian nation. Other proofs are not wanting.

---

* Western Review, 1820.

The first settlers of Lexington found here a well, regularly and artificially built with stone,* a domestic convenience unknown among the American Indians, and they plowed up curious earthen vessels,† such as could only have been manufactured by at least a semi-civilized people. In 1790, an old lead mine, which had every appearance of having been once worked and abandoned, was opened near this city.‡ Kentucky's first historian¶ tells us of stone sepulchres, at Lexington, built in pyramid shape, and still tenanted by human skeletons, as late as two years after the siege of Bryant's Station. "They are built," says he, "in a way totally different from that of the Indians." Early in this century, a large circular earthen mound, about six feet in height, occupied a part of what is now called Spring street, between Hill and Maxwell. It was located between the property of Dr. Bell and the rear outbuildings of Mr. P. Yeiser. In course of time it was leveled, and was found to consist of layers of earth of three different colors. In the center was discovered an earthen vessel of curious form and a quantity of half-burnt wood.§ The mound is supposed to have served the purpose of a sacrificial altar. A stone mound, which stood not far from Russell's cave, in this county, was opened about 1815 and found to contain human bones.*

These well-attested facts, together with the tradition related to this day of an extensive cave existing under the city of Lexington, relieve of its improbable air the statement that a subterranean cemetery of the original inhabitants of this place was discovered here nearly a century ago.† In 1776, three years before the first permanent *white* settlement was made at Lexington, some venturesome hunters, most probably from Boonesborough, had their curiosity excited by the strange appearance of some stones they saw in the woods where our city now stands. They removed these stones, and came to others of peculiar workmanship,

---

* Morse.   † Imlay, page 369.   ‡ Old Kentucky Gazette, 1790.
¶ John Filson.   § Benj. Keiser.   * Prof. Rafinesque.
† Letter to Robt. Todd, published in 1809.

which, upon examination, they found had been placed there to conceal the entrance to an ancient catacomb, formed in the solid rock, fifteen feet below the surface of the earth. They discovered that a gradual descent from the opening brought them to a passage, four feet wide and seven feet high, leading into a spacious apartment, in which were numerous niches, which they were amazed to find occupied by bodies which, from their perfect state of preservation, had evidently been embalmed. For six years succeeding this discovery, the region in which this catacomb was located, was visited by bands of raging Indians and avenging whites; and during this period of blood and passion, the catacomb was dispoiled, and its ancient mummies, probably the rarest remains of a forgotten era that man has ever seen, were well nigh swept out of existence. But not entirely. Some years after the red men and the settlers had ceased hostilities, the old sepulchre was again visited and inspected.* It was found to be three hundred feet long, one hundred feet wide, and eighteen feet high. The floor was covered with rubbish and fine dust, from which was extracted several sound fragments of human limbs. At this time the entrance to this underground cemetery of Ancient Lexington is totally unknown. For nearly three-quarters of a century, its silent chamber has not echoed to a human footfall. It is hidden from sight, as effectually as was once buried Pompeii, and even the idea that it ever existed is laughed at by those who walk over it, as heedless of its near presence as were the generations of incredulous peasants who unconsciously danced above the long lost villa of Diomedes,

That Lexington is built upon the site of an ancient walled city of vast extent and population, is not only evident from the facts here detailed, but the opinion becomes almost a certainty when viewed in the light of the historic proofs that can be produced to support the claim, that all

---

* Ashe.

the region round about her was at a distant period in the past the permanent seat of a comparatively enlightened people. As early as 1794,* it was well and widely known that in the neighborhood of Lexington there existed two distinctly defined fortifications furnished with ditches and bastions. One of these ancient monuments was visited in 1820 by Rafinesque, the celebrated professor of natural history in Transylvania University, a gentleman whose opinions on the subject of the ancient remains in the Mississippi Valley are so often quoted by historians and so much respected. His map and plate of the remains near Lexington constitute one of the most valuable features of the "Smithsonian Contributions."† He says‡ of the fortification already named:

"I have visited, with a friend, the ancient monument or fortification situated about two and a half miles from Lexington, in an easterly direction, and above the head of Hickman creek; and we have ascertained that it is formed by an irregular circumvallation of earth, surrounded by an outside ditch.

"The shape of this monument is an irregular polygon of seven equal sides. The whole circumference measures about sixteen hundred of my steps, which I calculate at nearly a yard, or three feet each; or, altogether, four thousand eight hundred feet—(less than a mile.) The different sides measure as follows: west side, three hundred and sixty feet; southwest side, seven hundred and fifty feet; south side, seven hundred and fifty feet; east-southeast side, six hundred and sixty feet; east-northeast side, one thousand and eighty feet; northeast side, six hundred feet; northwest side, six hundred feet. Total, 4,800 feet.

"The angles are rather blunt. Two of the angles have deep ravines; one lies at the angle between the west and the southwest sides, and the other between the east-southeast and the east-northeast sides. This last is the largest and deepest—it reaches to the limestone, and had water in

---

* Imlay's Western Territory, page 368. † Vol. I, page 27.
‡ Western Review, April,

it. It forms a brook running easterly, and is formed by two rills meeting near the angle and nearly surrounding the central. Another ravine comes out near the north corner. All these originate within the circumvallation, which incloses one of the highest grounds near Lexington, and particularly a large, level hill which is higher than any in the immediate neighborhood, and stretches, in part, toward the northwest.

"The sides are straight. The earthen walls are raised upon a level or raised ground, and are nowhere lower than the outside ground, except for a few rods toward the northeast side. The situation is, therefore, very well calculated for defense, and it is very probable that there were formerly springs within the walls.

"The whole surface is covered with trees of a large growth, growing even on the walls and in the ditch; excepting, however, a small corner toward the northwest, which is now a corn-field. It may include from five to six hundred acres.

"At present the heighth and breadth of the wall and ditch are variable—from eight to sixteen feet in breadth, and from two to four in depth, the average being twelve in breadth and three in depth; but these dimensions must have been greater formerly. The wall was probably sixteen feet broad throughout, and four feet high, while the ditch was rather narrower, but deeper. The walls are made of the loose earth taken from the ditch. There is only one large distinct gateway, on the northeast side, where there is no ditch and hardly any wall."

After this survey some little interest was excited in the subject, and other remains were visited and inspected. Several in the vicinity of the one described; another, a square inclosure, west of Lexington, "near the northern Frankfort road;" many mounds and graves south of the city, and two groups lying on the south side of North Elkhorn, about a mile from each other. Extraordinary as it may appear, these monuments, though so near our city, and as singular as any on this continent, were never surveyed till as late as 1820. Some months after he had examined and described the fortification at the head of Hickman creek, Prof. Rafinesque surveyed the upper group on North Elkhorn, near Russell's cave, or what is now known as the West place. We quote his description of it, which will be read with more and more interest and wonder as time passes, and slowly but surely levels with the earth and blots out forever all that is left to remind us of a lost race, whose stupendous structures covered the fertile tract which afterward became the favorite hunting ground of savage tribes. He says :*

"I visited this upper group of monuments, a few days ago, in company with two gentlemen of Lexington. They are situated about six miles from this town, in a north-northeast direction, on the west and back part of Colonel Russell's farm, which stands on the road leading from Lexington to Cynthiana.

"The ground on which they stand is a beautiful level spot, covered with young trees and short grass, or fine turf, on the south side of a bend of North Elkhorn creek, nearly opposite the mouth of Opossum run, and close by Hamilton's farm and spring, which lie west of them. They extend as far as Russell's cave, on the east side of the Cynthiana road.

"No. 1, which stands nearly in the center, is a circular inclosure, six hundred feet in circumference, formed of four parts: 1. A broad circular parapet, now about twenty feet broad, and two feet high. 2. An inward ditch, now very shallow and nearly on a level with the outward ground. 3. A gateway, lying due north, raised above the ditch, about fifteen feet broad, and leading to the central area. 4. A square central area, raised nearly three feet above the ditch, perfectly square and level, each side seventy feet long and facing the four cardinal points.

"No. 2 lies northeast of No. 1, at about two hundred and fifty feet distance; it is a regular, circular, convex mound, one hundred and seventy-five feet in circumference, and nearly four feet high, surrounded by a small outward ditch.

---

*Western Review, 1820, page 53.

"No. 3 lies nearly north of No. 1, and at about two hundred and fifty feet distance from No. 2. It is a singular and complicated monument, of an irregular square form, nearly conical, or narrower at the upper end, facing the creek. It consists: 1. Of a high and broad parapet, about one hundred feet long and more than five feet high, as yet, above the inward ditch on the south base, which is about seventy-five feet long. 2. Of an inside ditch. 3. Of an area of the same form with the outward parapet, but rather uneven. 4. Of an obsolete broad gateway at the upper west side. 5. Of an irregular raised platform, connected with the outward parapet, and extending toward the north to connect it with several mounds. 6. Of three small mounds, about fifty feet in circumference, and two feet high, standing irregularly around that platform, two on the west side and one on the east.

"No. 4. These are two large *sunken mounds*, connected with No. 3. One of them stands at the upper end of the platform, and is sunk in an outward circular ditch, about two hundred and fifty feet in circumference, and two feet deep. The mound, which is perfectly round and convex, is only two feet high, and appears sunk in the ditch. Another similar mound stands in a corn-field, connected by a long raised way to the upper east end of the parapet in No. 3.

"No. 5 is a monument of an oblong square form, consisting of the four usual parts of a parapet, an inward ditch, a central area, and a gateway. This last stands nearly opposite the gateway of No. 3, at about one hundred and twenty-five feet distance, and leads over the ditch to the central area. The whole outward circumference of the parapet is about four hundred and forty feet. The longest side fronts the southwest and northeast, and is one hundred and twenty feet long, while the shortest is one hundred feet long. The central area is level, and has exactly half the dimensions of the parapet, being sixty feet long and fifty wide. It is raised two or three feet as well as the parapet. The end opposite the gateway is not far from Hamilton's spring.

"No. 6 is a mound without a ditch, one hundred and ninety feet in circumference, and five feet high. It lies nearly west from No. 1.

"No. 7 is a *stone mound*, on the east side of Russell's spring, and on the brim of the gulley. It lies east from the other monuments and more than half a mile distant. It is ten feet high and one hundred and seventy-five feet in circumference, being formed altogether by loose stones heaped together, but now covered with a thin soil of stone and grass.

"No. 8 is a similar *stone mound*, but rather smaller, lying north of No. 7, at the confluence of Russell's spring with North Elkhorn.

"Among the principal peculiarities, which I have noticed in this group of monuments, the square area of No. 1, inclosed within a circular ditch and parapet, is very interesting, since it exhibits a new compound geometrical form of building. The ditch must have been much deeper once, and the parapet, with the area, much higher; since, during the many centuries which have elapsed over these monuments, the rains, dust, decayed plants, and trees must have gradually filled the ditch, etc. I was told by Mr. Martin that within his recollection, or about twenty-five years ago, the ditch in the monument at the head of Hickman's creek was at least one foot deeper. Whenever we find central and separated areas in the Alleghawian monuments, we must suppose they were intended for the real places of worship and sacrifices, where only the priests and chiefs were admitted, while the crowd stood probably on the parapet to look on; and, in fact, these parapets are generally convex and sloping inward or toward the central area.

"The ditched mound, No. 2, is remarkable, and must have had a peculiar destination, like the sunken mounds, No. 4, which differ from No. 2 merely by being much lower, and appearing, therefore, almost sunk in the ditch.

"The stone mounds, Nos. 7 and 8, are also peculiar and evidently sepulchral. But why were the dead bodies covered here with stone instead of earth? Perhaps these mounds belonged to different tribes, or the conveniency of finding stones, in the rocky neighborhood of Russell's cave and spring, may have been an inducement for employing them."

Some of these mounds described by Rafinesque were visited in 1846, and found to be nearly obliterated; others, however, near the dividing line between the old military survey of Dandridge and Meredith, were still distinct, and were described in 1847* as follows, viz: "The most easterly work is on the estate of C. C. Moore. It is on the top of a high bluff, on the west side of North Elkhorn, in the midst of a very thick growth, mostly of sugar trees, the area within a deep and broad circular ditch is about a quarter of an acre of land. The ditch is still deep enough in some places to hide a man on horseback. The dirt taken from the ditch is thrown outward; and there is a gateway where the ditch was never dug, some ten feet wide on the north side of the circle. Trees several hundred years old are growing on the bank and in the bottom of the ditch and over the area which it incloses, and the whole region about it. There is another work a quarter of a mile west of the above one. It commences on the Meredith estate and runs over on the Cabells' Dale property, and contains about ten acres of land. The shape of the area is not unlike that of the moon when about two-thirds full. The dirt from the ditch inclosing this area is thrown sometimes out, sometimes in, and sometimes both ways. An ash tree was cut down in the summer of 1845, which stood upon the brink of this ditch, which, upon being examined, proved to be four hundred years old. The ditch is still perfectly distinct throughout its whole extent, and in some places is so deep and steep as to be dangerous to pass with a carriage.

A mound connected with this same chain of works was opened in the summer of 1871. It is situated about half a mile west of the earthwork already described as on top of the bluff, and about a quarter of a mile north of the larger oval one. It is on the farm of Mr. James Fisher, adjoining the

---
* Collins.

plantation on which Dr. Robert Peter at present resides, and is part of the old Meredith property before mentioned.* The mound has a diameter of about seventy feet, and rises with a regular swell in the center to the height of three and a half to four feet above the general level of the valley pasture on which it is located, only about fifteen feet above low water in the North Elkhorn creek, and about three hundred and twenty-five feet south from its margin. Mr. Fisher made an excavation into the center of this mound about four to five feet in diameter and about three and a half feet deep, in which, in a bed of wood-ashes containing charred fragments of small wood, he found a number of interesting copper, flint, bone, and other relics of the ancient Mound Builders, which were carefully packed by Dr. Robert Peter (who resides on the adjoining Meredith farm), and transmitted to the Smithsonian Institute, at Washington, for preservation.

The copper articles were five in number; three of which were irregularly oblong-square implements or ornaments, about four inches in length and two and one-eighth to three and three-quarter inches wide and one-quarter inch thick at lower end (varying somewhat in size, shape, and thickness); each with two curved horns attached to the corners of one end, which is wider and thinner than the other end. These were evidently made of native copper, by hammering, are irregular in thickness and rude in workmanship, and have been greatly corroded in the lapse of time, so that they not only have upon them a thick coating of green carbonate and red oxide of copper, but the carbonate had cemented these articles, with adjoining flint arrow-heads, pieces of charcoal, etc., into one cohering mass, in the bed of ashes, etc., in which they were found lying irregularly one upon the other.

The other two copper implements were axes or hatchets; one nearly six inches long, the other nearly four inches; each somewhat adze-shaped wider at one end, which end had a sharp cutting edge.

---

* Description by Dr. Peter.

With these were found nearly a peck of flint arrow-heads, all splintered and broken, as by the action of fire; also, three hemispherical polished pieces of red hematitic iron ore about two inches in diameter; some door-button shaped pieces of limestone, each perforated with two holes; several pieces of sandstone, which seemed to have been used for grinding and polishing purposes; and many fragments of bones of animals, mostly parts of ribs, which appeared to have been ground or shaped; among which was one, blackened by fire, which seemed to have been part of a handle of a dagger; also, some fragments of pottery, etc. The fragments of charcoal, lying near the copper articles, were saturated with carbonate of copper, resulting from the oxidation of the copper articles, parts of which were oxidized to the center, although a quarter of an inch in thickness; and many pieces of this coal and portions of flint arrow-heads remain strongly cemented to the copper implements by this carbonate.

To what uses these rude, oblong-square horned copper articles were put, except for ornament, can not be conjectured. No inscription or significant mark was found on any of them.

No human bones could be distinguished among the fragments found, but only the immediate center of the mound was opened.

The citizens of Lexington may, in truth, muse among the ancient ruins and awe-inspiring relics of a once mighty people. Who and what were the beings who fought with these weapons, ate from these vessels, built these tombs and mounds and altars, and slept at last in this now concealed catacomb? Where existed that strange nation, whose grand chain of works seemed to have Lexington for its nucleus and center? We can only speculate! One* inclines to the opinion that they were contemporaries of the hardy Picts. Another† declares them identical with the Alleghawians or progenitors of the Aztecs, and cites as proof, the remains of their temples, which are declared to be wonder-

---

* Imlay, page 369.   † Rafinesque.

fully similar to those of the ancient Mexicans described by
Baron Humboldt. The earthen vessels here plowed up
from the virgin soil, he says, were like those used by the
Alleghawians for cooking purposes. Still another writer,*
dwelling upon the mummies here discovered, sees in the
original inhabitants of Lexington, a people descended from
the Egyptians. Other authors, eminent and learned, almost
without number, have discussed this subject, but their
views are as conflicting as those already mentioned, and
nothing is satisfactory, except the negative assurance that
the real first settlers of Lexington, the State of Kentucky,
and the entire Mississippi valley, were not the American
Indians, as no Indian nation has ever built walled cities,
defended by entrenchments, or buried their dead in sepulchres hewn in the solid rock.

Who, then, were these mysterious beings? from
whence did they come? what were the forms of their
religion and government? are questions that will probably
never be solved by mortal man; but that they lived and
flourished centuries before the Indian who can doubt?
Here they erected their Cyclopean temples and cities, with
no vision of the red men who would come after them, and
chase the deer and the buffalo over their leveled and grass
covered walls. Here they lived, and labored, and died, before Columbus had planted the standard of old Spain upon
the shores of a new world; while Gaul, and Britain, and
Germany were occupied by roving tribes of barbarians,
and, it may be, long before imperial Rome had reached the
height of her glory and splendor. But they had no literature, and when they died they were utterly forgotten.
They may have been a great people, but it is all the same
to those who came if they were not, for their greatness
was never recorded. Their history was never written—
not a letter of their language remains, and even their name
is forgotten. They trusted in the mighty works of their
hands, and now, indeed, are they a dead nation and a lost
race. The ancient city which stood where Lexington now

---

*Josiah Priest's "American Antiquities."

stands, has vanished like a dream, and vanished forever. Another has well said: "Hector and Achilles, though mere barbarians, live because sung by Homer. Germanicus lives as the historian himself said, because narrated by Tacitus; but these builders of mounds perish because no Homer and no Tacitus has told of them. It is the spirit only, which, by the pen, can build immortal monuments."

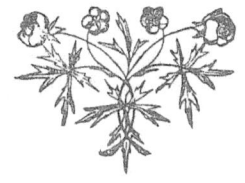

CHAPTER II.

The Indian Occupation.

It is a favorite theory of many that the Indians of North America migrated from Asia; that the once noble race, which has almost melted away, was descended from the ten tribes of Israel* which were driven from Palestine seven hundred years before the birth of Christ. But this is a theory only. The advent of the Indians and the stock from which they sprung will never be determined; but that they came *after* the "Mound Builders" is evident. The appearance of the Indians was the death-knell of that doomed race whose rich and beautiful lands and spoil-gorged cities inflamed the desperate and destitute invaders. The numerous tumuli which yet remain attest the fierceness of the conflict which ensued. A great people were swept out of existence, their cities disappeared, the grass grew above them, and in time the canebrakes and the forests. Out of all this vast extent of conquered territory, the Indians selected a portion as a hunting-ground and called it "Kantuckee," because it had been in truth to them a "dark and bloody ground." It was a shadow-land to the Indians. In 1800, some Sacs who were in St. Louis said of Kentucky that it was full of the souls of a strange race which their people had long ago exterminated.† They regarded this land with superstitious awe. Here they hunted and here they fought, but no tribe was ever known to settle permanently in it.‡ And while they hunted and roamed and paddled here their bark canoes, unknown centuries rolled away. Jamestown, the germ and herald of a

---

* Roger Williams, Dr. Boudinot. and others.   †Priest's Antiquities.
‡ Hall's Sketches.

mighty empire was building, and royal colonies of their future enemies waxed strong, while they sported and slept; and even when their brethren " across the mountains " were falling like ripe grain before the reaper, while forests were disappearing, and villages, and towns, and churches, and mills, and colleges were multiplying, they built their camp-fires undisturbed where Lexington now stands—for even to Virginia, the vast area since called the Northwestern Territory was then an unexplored and unknown country. But the handwriting was upon the wall, and the same fate to which the Red Men had consigned the Mound Builders was in waiting for them also.

CHAPTER III.

Coming of the White Man.

THE genius of civilization pointed out to her chosen pioneer a savage land to be reclaimed; and on the ever memorable 7th of June, 1769,* Daniel Boone, the "Columbus of the land," stood upon a lofty cliff which towered above a branch of the Kentucky river, and gazed enraptured upon the Italy of America, and feasted his eyes upon the beauty and fatness of a country celebrated now the wide world over in story and in song. The conqueror of the wilderness had come, a vast army was following at his back, and the future of the Dark and Bloody Ground was decided. In 1770,† the Long Hunters crossed the rocky barrier which shut out the old settlement from the wilderness, and penetrated the fabled region, and in 1773 they were followed by a band of Virginia surveyors appointed by Lord Dunmore.‡ Parties of colonial soldiers from the Old Dominion came out in search of homes. Cabins were erected and corn raised at Old Town, now Harrodsburg, in 1774,§ and the spring of the year following found Boone building on the Kentucky river the log fort and capital of the famous Transylvania Colony. "With this year," (1775,) says Marshall, "begins the first permanent and real settlement of Kentucky," an event which filled the Indians with rage. To them the white men were invaders and robbers. From their first appearance they had tracked them with torch and tomahawk and scalping knife, never doubting but that by bloodshed and cruelty they would be able to drive them from their hunting-ground; and now when they saw them

---
* Filson. † Annals of the West, 119.
‡ Marshall. § Butler.

deliberately preparing permanent settlements, their indignation and mortification knew no bounds. They resolved to utterly exterminate their persistent foes, to repossess every foot of soil so daringly appropriated—and from this time for many a long year after were enacted scenes of blood and horror, the recital of which is enough to sicken the stoutest soul.

2

CHAPTER IV.

Discovery and Naming of Lexington.

UNTIL the year 1775, no white man is positively known to have visited the place now called Lexington, but in that year, says General Robert McAfee, in his history of the war of 1812, "Robert Patterson, Simon Kenton, Michael Stoner, John Haggin, John and Levi Todd, and many others took possession of the north side of the Kentucky river, including Lexington." Fortunately the names of a few of those included in the indefinite phrase, "many others" are preserved. They were John Maxwell, Hugh Shannon, James Masterson, William McConnell, Isaac Greer, and James Dunkin.* They were sent out from the fort at Harrodsburg. Clothed in their quaint pioneer style of buckskin pantaloons, deerskin leggins, linsey hunting-shirt, and peltry cap, and armed each with a trusty flint-lock rifle, a hatchet and scalping-knife, they toiled through the trackless woods and almost impenetrable cane-brakes in the direction of the future Lexington. On or about the 5th of June, the approach of night ended one of their solitary and dangerous marches; and glad to rest, the tired hunters camped on a spot afterward known successively as McConnell's Station, Royal's Spring, and the Headly distillery property. It is only a few steps from the present "Old Frankfort road," and is nearly opposite the beautiful Lexington Cemetery.† The spring from which the pioneers drank and watered their horses still exists, with a stream as cool, clear, and grateful as then. After posting one of their number on the "look out" for the "redskin varmints," who were ever on the alert to slay the "pale-face," the rest seated themselves around a blazing brush-heap on logs

---

*Bradford's Notes.
†Bradford's Notes, and Observer and Reporter of July 29, 1809.

and buffalo hides, and, with hunger for sauce, supped with gusto upon the then inevitable "jerk" and parched corn. While eating their simple meal, they talked with enthusiasm of the beautiful country they had just traveled over, and surprised and delighted with the prospect about them, they determined that their place of settlement should be around the very spot where they were then encamped. And no wonder they were delighted with their new-found home, for of all the broad rich acres they had seen in all "Kan-tuck-ee," these were the fattest and most fertile. Never before had their eyes feasted on such an untold wealth of blue grass pasture. The deer, the elk, the bear, and buffalo crowded the woods with juicy food. They forgot the skulking savage and the dangers on every hand, and glowed with the excitement which only a hunter can feel, as they surveyed the virgin glories of the red man's most cherished hunting-grounds, and realized the full truth of the wondrous tales they had heard of a distant El Dorado.

The hunters assisted William McConnell to build a rude little cabin on their camping-ground as the foundation for a title, for Virginia as early as the year 1774, had offered four hundred acres of land to each person who cleared a piece of land, built a cabin, and raised a crop of Indian corn.* The name of the settlement that was to be, was discussed with animation. One suggested "York," another "Lancaster," but both were dropped with a shout for "Lexington!"† as the conversation turned to the strange news that had slowly crept through the wilderness, and which, after being weeks on the way, they had just heard, of how "King George's troops, on the 19th of April, had called American 'rebels,' and shot them down like dogs at Lexington, in Massachusetts colony." The story of Lexington's christening—the historic fact of how she got her name, is as romantic as the legend of the beautiful Princess Pocahontas, and is an incident far more interesting, because more true than the fabulous one told of the founding of ancient Rome.

---

*Imley. †Bradford's Notes.

So the hunters called the new settlement Lexington, in memory of that bloody field hundreds of miles away, and some of them soon after joined the Continental army, and fought long and bravely to avenge the minute men who fell that day. How strange the story of that pioneer camp! Here almost a hundred years ago, when Kentucky was a wilderness territory of the royal province of Virginia; here, far away from civilized life, in the heart of an unbroken forest, at the dead of night, a little band of adventurers erected the *first monument* ever raised on this continent in honor of the *first dead* of the revolution! It is true, the ceremonies of its dedication were not attended with glittering pomp or show, for the officials were only clad in buckskin and honest home-spun, and the music of their choir naught but the scream of the panther, the howl of the wolf, or the far-off yell of the savage! But it was consecrated by the strictest virtue and truest patriotism, and nature smiled benignantly upon it from an Eden of luxuriant beauty. Those pioneers have long since passed away, and some of their graves are still to be seen not far from the spot where they encamped on that memorable occasion.

CHAPTER V.

Lexington an Indian Camping Ground.

THE frail and hastily-built little hut of McConnell gave Lexington her name, and that was all, for no settlement was effected until four years after its erection. The summer of 1776 found no white man in all the length and breadth of the present Fayette county. McConnell's cabin was deserted and falling to pieces, and the would-be settlers of Lexington had all retired to the much needed protection of the few log forts then in existence. The American Revolution had now fairly opened. Ticonderoga had been captured, the battle of Bunker's Hill had been fought, and one of the saddest tragedies of that eventful struggle had been enacted upon the Plains of Abraham. The Indians, consistent with the policy they ever pursued of leaguing with the strongest, had early enlisted on the side of England, and the northwestern tribes in particular were not slow to act. They came to Kentucky with the buds of spring, and summer had not commenced before all Fayette county and the adjoining region were filled with roaming bands of angry Shawanese, Cherokees and their associates.* All ideas of attempting to make new settlements were abandoned by the whites, personal safety was the one thing thought of, and fear and anxiety prevailed, for the savages clearly indicated that they had not abandoned their cherished desire of driving their enemies from the country. Settlers were killed every few days ; on the 14th of July two of Colonel Calloway's daughters and one of Daniel Boone's were captured within rifle shot of Boonesborough, and about the same time Hinkston's settlement on

---
* Western Annals, 154.

Licking creek was broken up. Dark days had come and still darker were ahead, and many even of the stoutest-hearted settlers left the country entirely.*

The wilderness country heretofore a part of Fincastle county, Virginia, was formed into "Kentucky county," on December 7, 1776,† but the protection of the "Old Dominion," whose forces were needed to lead the van of the continential army was barely felt in the newly-created department. The handful of brave pioneers struggled with their savage foes alone and unaided, and to their sufferings were added the horrors of the winter of starvation, which marked the opening of the year 1777. The succeeding spring and summer gave them as little encouragement. To attempt to raise corn was certain death, game was shot at the peril of the hunter's life. Harrodsburg, Boonesborough, and Logan's fort were constantly watched, and each in succession attacked by the Indians; and at this time the whole military force of the newly-made Kentucky county amounted to only one hundred and two men.‡ Fortunately Colonel Bowman arrived from Virginia *early* in he fall with a hundred men, and hope rose again in the hearts of the almost despairing settlers. The prospect continued to brighten during the year 1778. The well-planned and swiftly-executed movements of that brilliant soldier and remarkable man, Colonel George Rogers Clark, against the British posts of Kaskaskia and Vincennes, met with wonderful success; the grand attack of an overwhelming force of Indians and Canadians, under Du Quesne, upon the heroic little garrison of Boonesborough, signally failed, confidence was restored, immigration again commenced, and the settlers once more ventured out to "possess the land."

---

*Col. Floyd's Letter.   †Morehead's Address.   ‡Butler and Marshall.

CHAPTER VI.

*Settlement of Lexington—The Block-House—The Settlers—
Col. Robert Patterson—John Maxwell—James Masterson—
The McConnells and Lindsays—John Morrison—Lexington Fort—McConnell's Station—Bryant's Station—Its Settlers—Grant's Station—Col. John Grant and Capt. William Ellis—Natural Features about Lexington Station—
Soil, Forests, Game, and Flowers.*

IN the latter part of March, 1779, Col. Robert Patterson, since distinguished as the founder of two cities, was again ordered from the fort at Harrodsburg, to establish a garrison north of the Kentucky river,* and this time he was successful. At the head of twenty-five men he commenced his march for the beautiful and fertile garden spot he had visited four years before, and which he had never forgotten. The party reached its destination the last day of the month, and encamped, for rest and refreshment, at a magnificent spring, whose grateful waters, in an unusual volume, emptied into a stream near by, whose green banks were gemmed with the brightest flowers. The discovery of this spring determined the location of the little garrison, and bright and early on the morning of the next day, the 1st of April,† the axes of the stout pioneers were at work; trees were felled, a space cleared, and a block-house, surrounded by a stockade, and commanding the spring, was soon under headway. This rude but powerful defense was quickly completed, as no unnecessary labor was spent upon it. The logs for the walls were chopped out, provided with ports, and "raised;" the long and wide clapboards, rough

---
* McAfee. † Butler and Marshall.

from the ax and firmly secured by wooden pins, formed the roof; trees split in two, and cut to the proper length, made the floor; a substantial slab door was provided, and these, together with openings to admit the light and carry off the smoke, constituted the block-house.

The ground upon which this block-house was erected, and which is now so rich in historic associations, is at present occupied by the "Carty Building," on the corner of Main and Mill streets, and upon no other spot has the progress of Lexington been more distinctly indicated. The infancy of our city was here shown, in 1779, by the rude block-house; this was succeeded, in 1788, by a frame one; in 1807, what was then called "a splendid two-story brick," was erected, and in 1871, this gave place to the four-story iron front which now marks the spot where the settlement of Lexington commenced, and is, at the same time, an appropriate monument to commemorate the beautiful character of one of her greatly beloved and respected citizens— the lamented John Carty. The spring near the block-house was the principal one of the series of springs now concealed by a number of buildings on Main street, which have been erected over them. When Lexington grew to be a "station," the spring was embraced within the walls of the stockade, and supplied the entire garrison with water, and when the fort was removed, the spring was deepened and walled up for the benefit of the whole town,* a large tank for horses was made to receive its surplus water, and for many years, under the familiar name, "the public spring," it was known far and wide.

As soon as the block-house was completed, it was occupied by Col. Robert Patterson, John Maxwell, James Masterson, William and Alexander McConnell, and James and Joseph Lindsay, who proceeded to raise a crop of corn on the ground now covered by Cheapside, the court-house, and a part of Main street, and all other necessary preparations were made to insure a permanent settlement.† The year 1779, thanks to the pioneer successes we have men-

---

* City Records. † Butler, Marshall, and old documents.

tioned, was one of comparative peace. Immigrants came to Kentucky in increasing numbers, eager to be in time to get the benefit of the "settlement right," under which Virginia guaranteed them a magnificent estate, which "right" was to cease in 1780.* A few of the bolder of these new comers ventured, during the summer, to the solitary blockhouse at Lexington, "the forlorn hope of advancing civilization," and built cabins adjoining its protecting walls. In the autumn, a little company, of which John Morrison and his wife were a part, removed from Harrodsburg, and still further additions were made to the defenses of the settlement. The fort, which had by this time become a place of some importance, had assumed the shape of a parallelogram, two sides of which were formed by the exposed walls of two rows of cabins, the extreme ends of the fort being defended by stockades of sharpened posts fixed securely in the ground, and furnished with ports. The pickets and walls were about ten feet high.

Another row of cabins stood in the center of the inclosed place, which was large enough to shelter, not only the settlers and new comers, but also all the live stock which might, at any time, have to be driven in from the reach of their destroying foe. The fort had but one gate, a large slab one, and it was on the side of the station which extended from the block-house, on Carty's corner, to about the center of West Main street, near or on the site of the building now occupied by Celia Allen, between Mill and Broadway, where James Masterson's house once stood.† The station embraced and inclosed a part of Main street between the two streets just named, and a good portion of the ground now covered by business houses on East Main, included between the same streets. While this little outpost was being established on the extreme frontier of Virginia, a large part of her territory, nearer home, was being devastated by an enemy but little less savage than those who were the terror of her distant county of Kentucky, and great events, brilliant, disastrous, and moment-

---

* Filson, 1784.   † Butler and old inhabitants.

ous, were rapidly occurring and shaping the destiny of a nation, of whose future greatness no mind was so daring as to dream.

Lexington was founded in the midst of a mighty revolution, and her founder was a man suited to the time and born for the purpose. Col. Robert Patterson was of Irish parentage, and was born March 15, 1753, near Cove Mountain, Pennsylvania. He came to Kentucky in 1775, and settled at Harrodsburg, and in that year, as we have already related, he visited Fayette county. In 1776, he assisted in building a fort at Georgetown. During the years which intervened between this time and the settlement of Lexington, he figured conspicuously as a gallant Indian fighter. As Captain Patterson, he served under Clark in his expedition against the Shawanese, on the Little Miami. He was promoted to a colonelcy for important services, and was second in command in the terrible battle of Blue Licks. He was badly wounded in 1786, while with General Logan, in his expedition against the Shawanese towns. Subsequently, he became the owner of a third of the original town plot of Cincinnati, and may be called the founder of that city also. In 1783, Col. Patterson built him a log house, on the southwest corner of Hill and Lower streets, near or on the site of the present residence of S. T. Hayes. The large tract of land owned by Col. Patterson in that part of the city, included the present property of M. C. Johnson. The log house was, in course of time, succeeded by a substantial two-story stone one, which stood there for many years. In 1804, Col. Patterson removed to Dayton, Ohio, where he died, August 5, 1827. In person, Col. Patterson was tall and handsome. He was gifted with a fine mind, but like Boone, Kenton, and many others of his simple-hearted pioneer companions, was indulgent and negligent in business matters, and, like them, lost most of his extensive landed property by shrewd rascals.

Those who aided Col. Patterson in founding Lexington are not to be forgotten; and of these, none are more worthy of mention than John Maxwell. He was born in Scotland, in 1747, and was brought to America by his parents while in the fourth year of his age. He was one of the early adventurers in the wilds of Kentucky, arriving before a solitary station or even a cabin existed within its limits. In pioneer days, he owned a large part of the land now included in the city limits of Lexington, but, true to the old hunter nature, it rapidly slipped from his grasp. He and Sarah, his wife, were the first persons married within "the fort." John Maxwell was the first coroner of Fayette county; was one of the original members of Dr. Rankin's Presbyterian church; was one of the founders of the old St. Andrew's Society, and from him "Maxwell's spring" gets its name. This useful and greatly respected citizen died in 1819, and was buried in what was then "Maxwell's Graveyard," but which now forms part of the neglected old City Cemetery, on Bolivar street, in which stands the "Mission Church."

James Masterson, after whom "Masterson's station," five miles west of this city was named, was a genuine specimen of the pioneer type. He was straight as an Indian, and devoted to the woods and the excitements of a woodman's life. Long after Lexington had become an important town, he continued to dress in the primitive hunter style, and invariably wore his powder-horn and carried his rifle. He loved to tell of the dangers which threatened " the fort" when he was married in it, and the number of deer and buffalo he had killed between it and the present " Ashland."* His walking ability and powers of endurance may be inferred, from the fact that he undertook to go to a point considerably below the falls of the Ohio and return, in " a day or so," with a big bag of salt. He returned in the time specified with the bag of salt on his back. It was the first used in the fort,† and was welcomed with a shout. He lived to a green old age.

The McConnells and Lindsays were among the first adventurers who followed Boone out into "the wilderness." They assisted Col. Patterson in several dangerous enterprises, and shared in the perils of the Blue Licks disaster.

---

* McCullough, S. D.   † McCabe.

William McConnell established "McConnell's station," at "Royal's spring," in 1783, but it was soon merged in Lexington station. McConnell's station stood on the ground lately occupied by Headley's distillery,* on the old Frankfort road, and the fine spring there ("Royal's") was, at an early day, the favorite resort of the people of Lexington on public occasions. Alexander, the brother of William McConnell, was the hero of the thrilling adventure narrated in another chapter, in which he proved himself, unaided, a match for five Indians. The McConnells and Lindsays were buried in the "Station Graveyard," opposite the present Lexington Cemetery. The wife of Major Morrison, already mentioned was the first white female that settled in "the fort," and her son, Capt. John Morrison, who fell at Dudley's defeat, in 1813, was the first native of Lexington.†

One of the results of the increased immigration to Kentucky, in the fall of 1779, was a settlement, made at a point about five miles northeast of the Lexington "fort," and known as "Bryant's station."‡ The immigrants were principally from North Carolina, the most conspicuous of whom were the family of Bryants, from whom the place took its name. There were four brothers, viz.: Morgan, James, William, and Joseph, all respectable men, in easy circumstances, with large families of children, and mostly grown. William, though not the eldest brother, was the most active, and considered their leader. His wife was a sister of Col. Daniel Boone, as was also the wife of Mr. William Grant, who likewise settled in Bryant's station, in 1779. The death of William Bryant, who died of a wound received near the mouth of Cane run, so discouraged his friends that they returned to North Carolina, and the greater part of the population from that State left the fort about the same time, which would have so reduced the strength, as to compel the remainder also to remove, if the fort had not acquired new strength, in a number of families from Virginia. Robert Johnson (the father of the Hon.

---

*F. McCallie.   †McCabe, page 6.   ‡Bradford's Notes.

Richard M. Johnson), the Craigs, Stuckers, Hendersons, and Mitchells were among the number who removed to Bryant's station, and kept up the strength of the place at what it had been, if not greater than at any former period. A buffalo "trace" fortunately ran from this station close to Lexington, and the settlers of both places joined forces in clearing it of logs, undergrowth, and other obstructions; a wise measure, as subsequent events proved, for, owing to it, the troops from Lexington that went to the assistance of the besieged station, in 1782, were enabled to reach it much sooner than they could otherwise have done.

One day, late in September, 1779, a little caravan of armed and watchful hunters, leading their loaded and tired pack-horses, stopped for a night's rest at Lexington fort. They were all up and moving bright and early the next morning, and before the week closed had established Grant's station, in what is now called the Huffman, Ingels, and Hardesty neighborhood, five miles from Bryant's, in the direction of the present town of Paris. The settlement was made under the direction and leadership of Col. John Grant, of North Carolina, and Capt. William Ellis, a native of Spottsylvania county, Virginia, and grandfather of Mrs. John Carty, of Lexington. The station was, subsequently, greatly harassed by the Indians; in 1780, they made pioneer life such a burden to the settlers, that they returned to Virginia. Capt. Ellis entered the Continental army, and commanded a company until the close of the Revolutionary war, when he and Col. Grant came again to Kentucky, and Col. Grant settled permanently at the old station. Capt. Ellis, Timothy and James Parrish, and a number of other Virginians, settled a fertile tract of country on the head waters of Boone's creek, in Fayette county, near their old neighbor from Spottsylvania, the Rev. Lewis Craig, the most prominent of the early Baptist preachers in Kentucky. In 1786, Capt. Ellis married Elizabeth Shipp. Subsequently, he was with St. Clair in the terrible "defeat," of November 4, 1791. After arriving at an advanced age, the old pioneer died, and was buried in the county he had helped to settle. He was a man of great energy, liberality, and hospitality. The strength of his mind and the integrity of his character gained for him the respect and esteem of all who knew him.

With the building of "the fort," at Lexington, came also the cutting of the cane, the girdling of the trees, and the opening of the land for cultivation; and civilization had never before demanded the sacrifice of the primeval glories and wild beauties of such a region as that of which Lexington was the center. Boone styled Kentucky "a second paradise," and if its general characteristics merited such a eulogy, what must have been the virgin charms of the country around Lexington, which is conceded by all to be the finest in the State. John Filson, the biographer of Boone, and who was himself one of the early settlers and residents of Lexington, refers to it as the most luxuriant portion of "the most extraordinary country on which the sun has ever shone." The black and deep vegetable mold, which had been accumulating for untold centuries, made it "a hot-bed of fertility," and an early traveler says of it,* "in the spring no leaves are found under the trees, for the ground is so rich and damp that they rot and disappear during the winter." It was in such a soil as this that the founders of our city raised their first crop of corn, the only grain cultivated at that time. The surrounding forests abounded in game, and it was an unusual thing for the fort not to be well stocked with the meat of the deer, buffalo, bear, elk, and minor animals. The thick canebrakes, though the chosen retreat of the panther and the wildcat, were thronged with birds prized by the hunters. Provender for the horses and cattle was not wanting. They waded, up to their knees, in native clover; they reveled in waving oceans of wild rye and buffalo grass, and grew fat upon the young shoots of the nourishing cane. The earth glowed with the beauty of numberless natural flowers, many of which are now rarely, if ever, seen here. Lilies, daisies, pinks, wild tulips, and columbines delighted the eye; beds of sweet violets and fragrant wild hyacinths perfumed

---

*American Museum.

the air, and the brilliant cardinal flower and the admired crown imperial grew spontaneously here, in greater beauty than in any other part of the world.* A scene of wild and picturesque loveliness, such as is rarely accorded to men, must have greeted the eyes of the settlers of Lexington; and it had not lost all of its natural charms, even as late as 1794, when visited by Captain Imlay, an officer of the Revolutionary army, if his florid language is an indication. He says, "Lexington is nearly central of the finest and most luxuriant country, perhaps, on earth. Here, an eternal verdure reigns, and the brilliant sun, piercing through the azure heavens, produces in this prolific soil an early maturity, which is truly astonishing. Flowers, full and perfect as if they had been cultivated by the hand of a florist, with all their captivating odors, and with all the variegated charms which color and nature can produce, here, in the lap of elegance and beauty, decorate the smiling groves. Soft zephyrs gently breathe on sweets, and the inhaled air gives a voluptuous glow of health and vigor, that seems to ravish the intoxicated senses. The sweet songsters of the forest appear to feel the influence of the genial clime, and in more soft and modulated tones, warble their tender notes, in unison with love and nature. Everything here gives delight, and in that wild effulgency which beams around us, we feel a glow of gratitude for the elevation which our all-bountiful Creator has bestowed upon us."

Fortunately for the settlers at Lexington, the winter succeeding their arrival was a peaceful one,† and they took advantage of it. They strengthened the fort and increased its comforts, with the wise design of attracting settlers, and their efforts were rewarded.

---

*Imlay. †Collins, page 388.

CHAPTER VII.

The Indians—John and Levi Todd—Life in the Fort—Incidents and Tragedies—A Terrible Winter—Fayette County Formed—Early Cemeteries—First Schools—Transylvania University—Its Origin—Incidents—George Nicholas—Presidents Moore, Blythe, Holley, Woods, Peers, Coit, Davidson, Bascom, Green—Professors of the Academical, Medical, and Law Colleges—Fires, Buildings, Donations, Sectarian Contention—James Morrison, Peter, Hunt, and others—Normal School—Decline of the University—Consolidation—Kentucky University—Origin—Removal to Lexington—Regent Bowman—Organization of Various Colleges—Presidents, Professors, and Officers, Milligan, Johnson, Harrison, Gratz, Beck, and others.

THE spring which succeeded the peaceful winter of 1780 as usual brought with it the Indians, small parties of whom almost constantly watched the traces leading to Lexington station, and the settlers were frequently fired upon. At this time game, and particularly the buffalo, was the chief dependence of the garrison for food, bread being a rare luxury until corn was fit to make meal of; and in order to get the much-needed game, and at the same time escape the Indians, the hunters found it necessary to start early enough to get out in the woods three or four miles before day, and on their return, to travel a like distance after night.*

Colonel John and Levi Todd came to Lexington this year, where they had located large tracts of land some time before. Colonel Todd was at this time military governor

---
*Bradford's Notes.

of Illinois, and although he settled his newly married wife in the fort here, he was soon compelled to leave her, to attended to the affairs of that new county of Virginia. He managed, however, to pass a good part of his time at Lexington, and in 1781, made it his permanent home, and was one of its most prominent and highly esteemed citizens. He commanded the Lexington militia in the battle of the Blue Licks, 1782, and died gallantly fighting at their head, leaving his wife and one child (a daughter), who afterward became the wife of Robert Wickliffe, Sen.*

Levi Todd came from Virginia to Harrodsburg, in 1775, and some years after attempted to settle a station in Fayette county, but being compelled by the Indians to abandon it, he came to Lexington. He was the first county clerk of Fayette; represented her in conventions and in the legislature, and was long one of her most useful and respected citizens.†

Life in the fort in 1780 was more picturesque than easy and delightful. The men "by turns" stood guard, and kept up a sharp lookout for the enemy; while those off guard risked their lives in hunting to supply the garrison with food, cleared the land, planted, plowed, brought in the cows, and did mending, patching, and all manner of work. The women milked the cows, cooked the mess, prepared the flax, spun, wove, and made the garment of linen or linsey, and when corn could be had, ground it into meal at the hand-mill, or pounded it into hominy in the mortar. Wild game was the principal food, and that was eaten most of the time without salt, which was seldom made at the "licks" without loss of life. Sugar was made from the maple trees, coffee was unknown, but fine milk supplied its place as long as the Indians spared the cows.

Wooden vessels,‡ either turned or coopered, were in common use as table furniture. A tin cup was an article of delicate luxury, almost as rare as an iron fork. Every hunter carried his knife; it was no less the implement of a warrior. Not unfrequently the rest of the family was left

---

*Collins, 536. †Collins, page 274. ‡Marshall.

with but one or two for the use of all. The cradle was a small rolling trough. A like workmanship composed the table and the stool—a slab hewn with the ax, and sticks of a similar manufacture set in for legs supported both. Buffalo and bear-skins were frequently consigned to the floor for beds and covering. When the bed was by chance or refinement elevated above the floor and given a fixed place, it was often laid on slabs placed across poles, supported on forks set in the earthen floor; or, where the floor was puncheons, the bedstead was hewn pieces pinned on upright posts, or let into them by auger holes. Other utensils and furniture were of a corresponding description, applicable to the time. The now famous Kentucky hunting-shirt was universally worn by the settlers. It was made either of linsey or dressed deerskin, and provided with a pocket in the bosom for tow used in cleaning the rifle. Every hunter carried a tomahawk and scalping-knife, wore deer-skin breeches, moccasins of the same material, and generally a bear-skin hat. The little money in circulation was depreciated Continental paper.

The spring of 1780 marked the beginning of an era in the history of Lexington, so rich in deeds of daring, and so fraught with thrilling adventures, experiences of intense suffering, and incidents of danger and of blood as to rival in romantic interest the days of Wallace, or the times of the hunted Huguenots. Could a record of all the forgotten events of this eventful period be gathered and combined with those that are preserved, Lexington, and the region round about it, would in time become as favorite a theme for the poet and the novelist as are now some of the story-lands of the old world.

As the spring advanced, the number of the Indians increased, and several parties of hunters pursued by them were compelled to take refuge in the fort. One of the settlers named Wymore, having ventured out alone, was killed and scalped by the Indians near where the Masonic Hall, on Walnut street, now stands, and another barely escaped a like fate near the present residence of Mr. F. K. Hunt,

INCIDENTS AND TRAGEDIES.

where he had been waylaid by an Indian, who was quietly awaiting his chance to slay him. He discovered his foe barely in time to save his life; shot him just as he was preparing to throw his tomahawk, and carried his reeking scalp in triumph to the station.* One of the saddest tragedies of the year took place about the first of May. A very young man, brave as he was handsome, and greatly beloved by the settlers, was mortally wounded by a band of the savages, who fired upon him while he was driving up the cows, and pursued him nearly to the fort. He staggered up to the gate, which a pitying and courageous woman who loved him unbarred with her own hands, and covered with blood, he died a few minutes after, clasped in her last fond embrace.† Closely following this was the attack on Strode's station, near the present town of Winchester, by a large body of Indians,‡ and the news of this event increased the gloom at Lexington, caused by anxiety and anticipations of evil. These forebodings were not without foundation, and were only providentially kept from being realized. Suddenly, in June, the settlers discovered the woods about the station swarming with Indians, who destroyed their corn, drove off all the horses that were not hurriedly sheltered within the walls of the fort, and then without doing further damage, disappeared as quickly as they had come. The astonishment of the alarmed garrison at this unaccountable proceeding was increased ten-fold on hearing faint but unmistakable reports of distant artillery, the first sounds of that kind which had ever awakened the echoes of the dark and bloody ground. Anxious but determined, the little force remained closely within the stockades, with ready rifles, watching and wondering day and night until all was explained, and the dark cloud lifted by the arrival, foot sore and hungry, of the brave Captain John Hinkston, who had just escaped from the retreating Indians, who constituted a large part of the formidable force under Colonel Byrd, during this, his celebrated invasion of Kentucky. Captain Hinkston gave the settlers the

---
*Old Journal. †Tradition. ‡Collins, 234.

first news of the capture of Ruddell's and Martin's stations,* both of which were distant only a few hours march from Lexington. The discouraged inmates of Grant's station, which was between Bryant's and the present town of Paris, dreading a like fate, abandoned it and sought refuge in the more secure fort at Lexington, where some of them remained during the winter. But the immediate danger was now over. Colonel Byrd, either from disgust and indignation at the barbarous conduct of his savage allies, or through fear of the sudden falling of the waters of the Licking, hastily retreated without an attempt at the capture of Lexington and Bryant's stations, though strongly urged by the elated Indians to move against them.† The effect of this invasion was the rapid formation of another expedition of retaliation by the Indian's dreaded foe, Colonel G. Rogers Clarke, who again swooped down upon them like an eagle. Lexington was largely represented in this campaign, which was made against the Indians of Ohio. It was secret, short, and so decisive, that no *large* bodies of the enemy invaded Kentucky during the whole of the next year.

The hardships and sufferings of the Puritans, in the two first years of the Plymouth settlement, were not greater than those of the founders of Lexington for a like period in her infancy. To the wearing anxieties, constant alarms, and bloody afflictions, endured by the inmates of the fort, must be added the privations of the terrible winter which followed Byrd's invasion.‡ It was a season not only of intense sufferings, but of protracted suffering. The pioneers had never known a winter in Kentucky to set in so early, and to continue so long. Snow and ice were on the ground without a thaw from November to the succeeding March. The small streams were solid ice. Snow fell repeatedly, but as it did not melt it became almost impassible for man or beast, and it was only with the greatest difficulty that the hunters were able to find such of the wild animals as had not been starved or frozen to death.§ As the corn had been

---

*Collins, 343.   †Id. 342.   ‡Boone's Nar.   §Marshall.

destroyed in the summer, bread was rarely seen in the fort, and when it was, a single johnnie-cake was divided into a dozen parts, distributed and made to serve for two meals.* The use of bread ceased entirely, long before the winter was over. On one occasion when Colonel Todd returned to the fort almost famished, the provisions were so nearly exhausted that his wife could offer him nothing but a gill of milk and a little piece of hard bread two inches square, and this was turned over in silence to his starving servant.† The cattle, after starving to death for want of fodder, were devoured by the inmates of the station, and from the time the cattle died until spring the settlers subsisted upon venison carefully distributed, and water; clothing was insufficient, the roughly-built cabins let in the piercing cold, and the firewood was chopped from trees incased in walls of snow and ice. Freezing and starving—such was the condition of the heroic settlers of Lexington, through this long and fearful winter of suffering.

In the month of November of this year (1780), Virginia formed Kentucky county into a district, composed of the three counties of Fayette, Lincoln, and Jefferson.‡ The new county of Fayette was given the name of that distinguished friend of Washington, General Gilbert Mortier de La Fayette, and was defined as " all that part of the said county of Kentucky which lies north of the line, beginning at the mouth of the Kentucky river, and up the same and its middle fork to the head, and thence south to the Washington line."‖ Fayette then included more than a third of the present State of Kentucky, and since that time she has enjoyed the proud distinction of being the mother of great counties and populous cities, and her sons have helped to lay the foundations of many of the empire states of the mighty West. The organization of the county was not completed until the next year (1781).§

The settlers killed by the Indians, in the summer of 1780, were sadly and reverently carried, by an armed band of

---
*Davidson, 62. †Collins, 536. ‡Collins, 24. ‖Marshall. §Butler.

their surviving companions, along the cow-path which extended by the side of the fort, on to what the garrison called the "first hill," now known as the Baptist churchyard, on Main street.* A small space on this hill was cleared of cane, and here, after a silent prayer, the earliest settlers of Lexington were buried. This ground was afterward set aside by the trustees of the town for religious purposes.† This was the first cemetery used, and was for a long time the only one. During the fatal cholera season of 1833, when the citizens of Lexington were swept off by the hundreds, tier upon tier of bodies were buried in this graveyard, and it ceased to be used after that terrible time. The next earliest graveyard established was that of the McConnells, opposite the present Lexington cemetery, and between Main street and the track of the Louisville, Lexington and Cincinnati Railroad, and there many of the pioneers of the city and county rest in obliterated graves. The Maxwell burying-ground, on Bolivar street, was used shortly after that of the McConnells. In 1834, the city bought the ground adjoining the Maxwell graveyard, and the two were merged in what is now called the "Old City Graveyard." Here the mother of John Maxwell was buried in 1804, his wife in 1811, and the old pioneer himself in 1819. In this neglected spot the ancient tablets are broken and crumbling, and upon one of them can scarcely be made out the inscription:

John Maxwell, sr.,
Died July 13th, 1819.
Aged 72 years.
Emigrated from Scotland to the United States in 1751, and to the wilds of Kentucky in 1774.

The Catholic cemetery, on Winchester street, was consecrated about forty years ago. Dr. Samuel Brown, Judge Hickey, Annie Spalding, the first superioress of St. Catharine's Academy, are among the sleepers in this last resting place. The Episcopal cemetery had its origin in 1837. Many prominent persons are buried there, and there are few Lex-

---

*Old Journals. †City Records.

ington families that have not a sad interest in its sacred ground. The same can be said of the Presbyterian burying-ground established shortly after the last mentioned. The large trees which now throw so grateful a shade over it, owe their presence to the mournful interest of Dr. Daniel Drake, whose wife was buried there. He raised the means to pay both for the ᴕees and their planting. For history of Lexington cemetery, see year 1849.

The history of education, in Lexington, dates from the commencement of the city itself; and the germ of that which afterward made her the literary and intellectual center of the state was laid with her foundation. Because the settlers of Lexington were out on "the frontier," because their life was one of hardships, and because their rude huts were destitute of costly adornments, did not prevent many of them from being what they certainly were, men of culture, education, and refinement, and endowed with all the ease and polished manners of the best society of Virginia, North Carolina, and Pennsylvania. The fort had its little school as early as 1780, taught by John McKinney, who had settled at Lexington the year before, at the solicitation of Colonel Patterson; and Transylvania Seminary, which was subsequently located here, was chartered by the legislature of Virginia the same year. After the close of the Revolutionary war, when the British and Indians ceased to annoy and distress the settlers, McKinney moved out of the fort, and taught in a log school-house, erected on the site of the pump on the present Cheapside.* It was in this house that his famous fight with the wildcat took place, an account of which will be found in the chapter on 1783. The first trustees of the town took an early opportunity to lay off and reserve ground for "Latin and English schools,"† and this encouragement brought to Lexington, in 1787,‡ Mr. Isaac Wilson, of Philadelphia College, who established the "Lexington Grammar School." He informs the citizens, in his advertisement, that "Latin, Greek, and the different branches of science will be carefully taught. Price of

---

*McCabe, 9. †City Records. ‡Old Gazette.

tuition four pounds, payable in cash or produce, and boarding on as reasonable terms as any in the district." The following spring "John Davenport" opened in what was then known as Captain Young's house, which stood on part of the ground now occupied by Jordan's Row,* the first dancing school Lexington ever had, and from that day to this the saltatory art has had a host of admirers in this city. In 1788, Transylvania Seminary was opened in Lexington, and from this day forward schools accumulated, and the love of literature grew, gaining for the city an enviable fame throughout the country.

Transylvania University was the *first* regular institution of learning founded in the mighty West. The influence it has exerted, both morally and intellectually, has been immense, and its name is not only venerated and respected in all civilized America, but is well known in Europe. Its history begins with the history of Lexington, and its establishment has been attributed to the enlightened exertions of Colonel John Todd, then a delegate from the county of Kentucky in the Virginia General Assembly—the same Colonel Todd who soon afterward fell at the disastrous battle of Blue Licks. In 1780, nearly twelve years before Kentucky became a member of the Union, the legislature of Virginia passed a law to vest eight thousand acres of escheated lands, formerly belonging to British subjects, in the county of Kentucky, in trustees for a public school; in order, says the preamble of the bill, " to promote the diffusion of useful knowledge even among its *remote* citizens, whose situation in a barbarous neighborhood and savage intercourse might otherwise render unfriendly to science."†

In 1783, the school was incorporated, and styled Transylvania Seminary; the name " Transylvania "—a classical rendering of " the backwoods "—being the same that Colonel Richard Henderson & Co. applied to the proprietary government they attempted to establish in Kentucky, in 1775, regardless of the authority of Virginia. The teachers and pupils were exempt from military service. At the

---

*McCabe, 8. †Acts Virginia Assembly.

time of its incorporation, the seminary was endowed with twelve thousand additional acres of land. After Kentucky was erected into a state, laws were passed exempting lands from escheat, the effect of which was to deprive Transylvania Seminary of all the escheated lands with which she had been endowed by the State of Virginia, except eight thousand acres, from the sale of which she received thirty thousand dollars. This sum of money was afterward invested in the stock of the Bank of Kentucky. The legislature repealed the charter of that bank, by which a loss is alleged to have been subsequently sustained by the "university" of twenty thousand dollars.

The trustees of the seminary met at Crow's station, in Lincoln county, November 10, 1783, when the Rev. David Rice was elected chairman, and the enterprise was encouraged by the donation of a library (the nucleus of the present one), from the Rev. John Todd, the first Professor of Sacred Literature in the seminary, and uncle of the above-named Colonel Todd.

In February, 1785, the seminary was opened, in the house of Mr. Rice, near Danville, and that gentleman became its first teacher, the endowment being too unproductive to afford more than a scanty salary for one professor. "Old Father Rice," who was one of the very first pioneer Presbyterian ministers who emigrated to Kentucky, was born in Hanover county, Virginia, December 20, 1733, and was educated at "Nassau Hall," now Princeton College. He was ordained in 1763, and came to Kentucky in 1783. He was largely instrumental in raising up both Transylvania Seminary and its subsequent rival, Kentucky Academy. After a long life of ministerial usefulness, he died, June 18, 1816, in Green county, Kentucky.*

In 1787, Virginia further endowed the seminary with one-sixth of the surveyor's fees in the District of Kentucky, formerly given to William and Mary College. This law was repealed by the legislature of Kentucky in 1802.

In 1788, the school was located in Lexington. "Tuition,

---

*Davidson.

five pounds a year, one-half cash, the other in *property*. Boarding, nine pounds a year, in *property*, pork, corn, tobacco, etc." John Filson, to whom Daniel Boone dictated a memoir of his life, was a zealous friend and advocate of the school. Being a northern man, he favored the employment of teachers from that section, which caused a correspondent of the old Kentucky Gazette to ask him the very sensible question: "What peculiar charm have northern teachers to inspire virtue and suppress vice that southern teachers do not possess?"*

The first building used by Transylvania Seminary, in Lexington, was a plain two-story brick one. It stood on the north end of the "college lawn," facing Second street, and with the present Third street in its rear. The lot on which it was erected, was donated† by a number of citizens of Lexington, who were anxious to have the school in their midst. Isaac Wilson, of Philadelphia, was a teacher in the seminary at this time.

Another teacher was added to the seminary upon its removal to Lexington, its course was extended, and nothing occurred to mar its prosperity until 1794, when the trustees, with John Bradford as chairman, elected as principal Harry Toulmin, a talented Baptist minister, with strong inclinations to the priestly school of theology, and who subsequently became secretary of state under Governor Garrard. Sectarian jealousy was at once developed. The Baptists claimed equal rights in the seminary, as a state institution. The Presbyterians claimed control, on the ground that its endowment was due to their exertions, and they finally withdrew their patronage from the school, and, in 1796, established and supported "Kentucky Academy," at Pisgah, near Lexington.

Fortunately, the troubles between the rival institutions were adjusted, and, in 1798, both schools were merged in one, under the name of "Transylvania University," with Lexington as its seat. But one department of the university, the academical, was in existence in 1798. The first

---

*Old Gazette.   †President's Report.

president of the united institutions was the Rev. James Moore,* noticed at length in the chapter, in this volume, on Christ Church. His colleagues were the Rev. Robert Stuart and the Rev. James Blythe.

In 1799, the institution was given the appearance of a regular university, by the addition of law and medical departments.

Colonel George Nicholas,† who became the first professor in the law department, was an eminent lawyer of Virginia, who had served as colonel in the Revolutionary war, and came to Kentucky at an early day. He was an influential member of the Virginia Convention which adopted the Federal constitution, and was one of the most prominent spirits in the convention which framed the first constitution of Kentucky. This able man, whose statesmanship was long prominent in this commonwealth, was for many years a citizen of Lexington. His residence was on the site of the present Sayre Institute. He died at about the age of fifty-five, shortly after he accepted the law professorship in Transylvania University.

Colonel Nicholas was succeeded in the chair of law by Henry Clay, James Brown, John Pope, and William T. Barry (of whom see biographical sketches in this volume). In 1819, when Dr. Holley became president of the university, the law college was regularly organized with three professors, and it soon attained a reputation co-extensive with the country, and no similar college in the United States was considered its superior in reputation, the ability of its teachers, and the number of its students. Its law society was noted. Its library, donated by the city of Lexington, was, at that time, the best one of the kind in the West. The following professors have adorned the law department since the incumbency of those already named, viz: Jesse Bledsoe, John Boyle, Daniel Mayer, Charles Humphreys, George Robertson, Thomas A. Marshall, and A. K. Woolley. (See biograpical sketches in this book.)

The earliest professor of medicine in Transylvania and

---

*Davidson. †Collins.

in the West was the distinguished Dr. Samuel Brown,* who was born, January 30, 1769, and was a son of the Rev. John Brown, and Margaret, his wife, residents of Rockbridge county, Virginia. After graduating at Carlisle College (Pa.), he spent two years studying medicine in Edinburg, after which he removed to Lexington. He was professor of medicine in the university until 1806, when he resigned, but was again appointed in 1819. He died in Huntsville, Alabama, January 12, 1830. Dr. Brown was a man of unusual learning and scientific attainments.

His name appears among those of the contributors to the American Philosophical Transactions, and to the medical and scientific periodicals of the day, in this country and in Europe. He is specially noted as the first introducer of vaccination into the United States.†

The first place where medical instruction is believed to have been given to students, in Lexington, was in the original old University building.

Dr. Frederick Ridgely, who was appointed a medical professor very shortly after Dr. Brown, was the first who taught medicine by *lectures* in the West. He was appointed surgeon to a Virginia rifle corps in the Revolutionary army, when nineteen years old, removed to Kentucky in 1780, was one of the founders of the medical college, and was one of the early preceptors of the distinguished surgeon, Dr. Ben. W. Dudley. Dr. Ridgely lectured his class at one time in a room in "Trotter's warehouse," which stood on the site of the present china store, on the corner of Mill and Main.

The first president of Transylvania University, Rev. James Moore, was succeeded, in 1804, by Dr. James Blythe. Rev. James Blythe, M. D., was born in North Carolina, in 1765, and was educated for the Presbyterian pulpit at Hampden-Sidney College. He came to Kentucky in 1791, and two years after was ordained pastor of Pisgah and Clear Creek churches. He continued to preach up to the time of his death. For six years before his accession to the

---

*Annals of Transylvania University.   †Michaux, 1802.

presidency of the university, he was professor of mathematics and natural philosophy, and often supplied the pulpit of the First Presbyterian church. He was president for nearly fifteen years, and after his resignation, filled the chair of chemistry in the medical college until 1831, when he accepted the presidency of Hanover College (Indiana), which prospered greatly under his charge. He was a faithful and animated preacher and fine debater. He died in 1842.

The first academical degree was conferred in 1802.

In the spring of 1804, a party of Shawanese Indians placed their children at Transylvania University to be instructed.

In 1805, Rev. James Fishback, M. D., was appointed to the chair of the Theory and Practice of Medicine. It was in the office of Dr. F., that Dr. Ben. Dudley studied the rudiments of physic. At this early period, the medical department met with but small success, and in 1806,* the professors resigned.

An effort was made to organize a full faculty and establish a medical school in our university, in the year 1809. Dr. B. W. Dudley was appointed to the chair of Anatomy and Surgery; Dr. Elisha Warfield, to that of Surgery and Obstetrics; the noted Joseph Buchanan, referred to in another chapter, to that of the Institutes of Medicine, and Dr. James Overton, to that of the Theory and Practice of Medicine.

It does not appear, however, that any lectures were delivered at this time. In 1815, Dr. William H. Richardson was added to the medical faculty, and his connection with the school continued until his death in 1835. Dr. Daniel Drake was appointed to the chair of Materia Medica in 1817. Dr. Drake resigned in a short time, and afterward became a professor in the Cincinnati Medical College. He died in 1852. The class of 1817 numbered twenty pupils.

The degree of M. D. was conferred, at the end of this course, in 1818, for the first time in the West, perhaps, on a

---

*Dr. Peters' Lecture.

citizen of Lexington, one of this class, John Lawson McCullough, brother of our worthy fellow-citizen, Samuel D. McCullough.*

In 1817, a large and handsome college building was erected in the college lawn and in front of the old edifice. The house and lot known as the Blythe property was bought and donated to the university by a number of liberal gentlemen, Mr. Clay being among the number. The grounds of the institution were beautified with trees, flowers, and shrubbery, and a determined effort was made to greatly increase the usefulness of the university. The trustees of the institution and the citizens of Lexington labored together in the work of its up-building, and Dr. Horace Holley, then of Boston, was invited to the presidency, which he accepted, and was inducted into office, December 19, 1818, and voted a salary of three thousand dollars.

Dr. Holley, the third president of Transylvania University, was born in Salisbury, Connecticut, February 13, 1781.† He assisted in the store of his father (who was a self-taught and self-made man) until he was sixteen, when he was sent to Yale College, where he graduated, in 1803, with a high reputation for talents and learning. Soon after, he studied theology with Dr. Dwight, and, in 1809, accepted the pastorate of the Hollis-street church, in Boston, and such was his popularity that a larger and more elegant edifice was soon rendered necessary. In this charge he remained nine years, greatly admired and beloved. To a remarkably fine person was added fascinating manners and brilliant oratory. His eloquence may be inferred from the fact that, during one of his sermons delivered before the ancient artillery company of Boston, he extorted a noisy demonstration of applause, the only instance known of a staid New England audience being betrayed into forgetfulness of their wonted propriety.‡

Dr. Holley was welcomed to Lexington with the most flattering attentions, and immediately set to work to make the university a success. The institution was at once thor-

---
*Peters' Lecture. †Caldwell's Memoir. ‡Pierpont.

oughly reorganized, and the medical school in particular dates its astonishing progress from this time, when the eminent surgeon, Dr. B. W. Dudley, the apostle of phrenology in the West, Dr. Charles Caldwell, and the learned antiquarian, Dr. C. S. Rafinesque, were called to its chairs. These gentlemen are specially mentioned in other chapters of this book. At this time, lectures were delivered to the medical class in a large room in the upper story of a then tavern building, on Short street, between Upper and Market, now occupied by banks.

The events which took place during Dr. Holley's presidency are full of interest.

In the year 1819, the legislature of Kentucky appropriated the bonus of the Farmers and Mechanics' Bank at Lexington, for two years, to the use and benefit of Transylvania University, which amounted to the sum of $3,000. In 1820 the sum of $5,000 was appropriated to the medical department.

In the year 1821, an act was passed appropriating onehalf of the clear profits of the Branch Bank of the Commonwealth of Kentucky at Lexington to the university, from which it is stated the sum of $20,000, in the paper of the said bank, was received—equal to $10,000 in specie —and there was a grant of twenty thousand dollars from the state treasury in 1824. All of which sums of money were expended in the purchase of books, philosophical apparatus, and in the payment of the debts of the institution.

There was probably no college library in the United States superior to that of Transylvania University in 1825. In addition to the books purchased through the liberality of Lexington and the State, the library had been enriched by a handsome donation from the British government, and by contributions from many private individuals, among whom may be named Edward Everett, who presented a collection of fine classical works which he had personally selected in Europe. The medical library selected by Professor Caldwell, in France and England, was the best in the country at that time. The university was visited by President Monroe, General Jackson, Governor Shelby, and others, in 1819. In 1825 it was visited by Marquis de Lafayette, at which time it was the center of attraction in the entire West to all scholars and eminent characters, both native and foreign. About this time, also, Lord Stanley, afterward Earl of Derby, made a personal examination of the institution. At the time of his visit, Judge Barry, one of the law professors, was absent. Dr. Holley, in addition to his regular duties, temporarily filled the judge's chair, and lectured the class before the distinguished visitor, on the subject of the similarity of the governments of the United States and England as regards the responsibility of public agents to the people.*

The rise and prosperity of the medical college of the university was remarkable. In 1818, the class numbered twenty, with one graduate, and in 1826, it numbered two hundred and eighty-one, with fifty-three graduates.† In 1827, the medical college had attained such a position and celebrity as to be regarded as second only to the University of Pennsylvania. It was complete in its corps of eminent professors, and in its magnificent library and chemical and anatomical apparatus. In addition to the distinguished men already mentioned, the following professors had been connected with the medical college up to 1827, and some of them remained in it for years after, viz: Dr. John Estin Cooke, of Virginia, author of the celebrated congestive theory of fevers; Dr. Lunsford P. Yandell, editor of the Transylvania Journal of Medicine, founded in 1827; Dr. H. H. Eaton, of New York, who greatly improved the chemical department, and Dr. Charles W. Short, who resigned in 1838.

In 1823, the "Morrison Professorship," in the academical department, was endowed and established by a bequest of twenty thousand dollars from Colonel James Morrison, of whom mention will again be made in this chapter.

The grand design of Dr. Holley was to make Transylvania a genuine university, complete in every college, and

---

*Observer and Reporter. †College Records.

liberally sustained by a great endowment. Under great disadvantages he accomplished much of his work, but his own imprudent conduct and Unitarian sentiments, together with prejudice and sectarian animosity, prevented its completion. His religious opinions and his love of amusements were unceasingly discussed and denounced by sectarians, who were disappointed in obtaining control of the institution. Finally, a storm of opposition was raised, which was continued with great bitterness by ministers of all denominations,* until Dr. Holley was forced to resign the presidency, which he did in 1827, to the great regret of a majority of the citizens of Lexington, and the sorrow of his pupils, a large number of whom immediately left the university. Two facts speak volumes for Dr. Holley's administration. When he came to the university, it was comparatively little known—when he left it, it was celebrated all over this country and Europe. During the sixteen years before he came, twenty-two students had graduated in it—in the nine years of his presidency, the institution turned out six hundred and sixty-six graduates.†

Immediately after his resignation, Dr. Holley was engaged as president of the College of New Orleans, and was meeting with the most flattering success when he was prostrated by fever. Upon his recovery he embarked for the North, in hopes that the sea air would benefit him. On the voyage he was seized with yellow fever, and, after suffering intensely for five days, he died, and on the 31st of July, 1827, the body of this distinguished man was committed to the deep. The scholar's cloak was his winding sheet, the ocean is his grave, and the towering rocks of the Tortugas are his monument.

The academical department, or college of arts, of Transylvania University was crowded with students during Dr. Holley's administration. Its corps of instructors, near the close of his term, were: President Holley, Professor of Philology, Belles-lettres, and Mental Philosophy; John Roche, Professor of Greek and Latin Languages; Rev.

---

*Flint's Mississippi Valley, 1826. †Caldwell's Memoir.

George T. Chapman, Professor of History and Antiquity; Thomas J. Matthews, Morrison Professor of Mathematics; Rev. Benjamin O. Peers, Professor of Moral Philosophy.

The resignation of Dr. Holley was a heavy blow to the university; but the trustees were not idle. On the 16th of April, 1827, the corner-stone of a new medical hall was laid by the Masonic fraternity, on the site of the present City Library, on the corner of Market and Church streets. The eloquent William T. Barry delivered an appropriate oration before the immense crowd assembled. The trustees of the university, at that time, were John Bradford, Thomas Bodley, Charles Humphreys, Benjamin Gratz, Elisha Warfield, James Fishback, John W. Hunt, James Trotter, Elisha I. Winter, George T. Chapman, William Leavy, Charles Wilkins, and George C. Light.

In June, 1828, the trustees called to the presidency of the university the Rev. Alva Woods, D. D.,* who was then at the head of Brown Univiversity. Dr. Woods was a Baptist clergyman, and the oldest child of Rev. Abel Woods, of Massachusetts, and had a high reputation for learning and liberality. He was president of Transylvania for but two years, when he resigned, and accepted the presidency of the University of Alabama. A few years ago he was still alive and residing at Providence, Rhode Island.

On the night of May 9, 1829, during Dr. Woods' administration, the principal building of the university, together with the law and societies' libraries, was destroyed by fire. The exercises of the institution were not interrupted a single day, nor did a solitary student leave in consequence of the disaster.

The Transylvania Literary Journal, Professor T. J. Matthews, Editor, was established in 1829.

In 1832, Dr. Robert Peter, the present able and noted Professor of Chemistry, became connected with the university, and has continued to reflect honor upon it for forty years. Dr. Peter was born in England, in 1805. He is a graduate of the Transylvania Medical College.

---

*Observer and Reporter.

The fifth president of Transylvania was the Rev. Benjamin O. Peers, an Episcopal minister, who was born in Loudon county, Virginia, in 1800, and brought to Kentucky in 1803. After graduating at Transylvania, he studied theology at Princeton, after which he joined the Episcopal Church, and located in Lexington, where he established the Eclectic Institute, which soon became one of the most valuable educational establishments in the West. He did much to bring about the present common school system of Kentucky, for which, together with his sound learning and ardent piety, he will long be remembered. Mr. Peers was president of Transylvania about two years. He died in Louisville, in 1842. The assistants of President Peers, in the academical department of the university, were Professor S. Hebard, of Amherst College, and Professor John Lutz, of the University of Gottingen.

During the Peers term, the present Morrison College building was completed, and on the 14th of November, 1833, it was thrown open, with appropriate inauguration ceremonies, at which time the oath of office was administered to Mr. Peers by the chairman of the university board of trustees. While Mr. Peers was president, a theological department, under the auspices of the Episcopal Church, was opened in the university.

Morrison College was founded through the liberality of Colonel James Morrison, who was born in Cumberland county, Pennsylvania, in 1775, and was the son of an humble Irish immigrant. After serving in the war of the Revolution, he came to Kentucky, and settled in Lexington, in 1792. Possessed of strong sense, energy, and decision of character, he rapidly elevated himself. He became, in succession, state representative from Fayette, quartermaster-general, president of the branch of the United States Bank, and chairman of the board of trustees of Transylvania University. He acquired immense wealth, much of which he used in the promotion of letters. He died, in Washington, D. C., April 23, 1823. Whether he was a Unitarian or a Presbyterian is undecided. He bequeathed twenty thousand dollars to establish a professorship in

Transylvania University, and a residuary legacy of forty thousand dollars, with which the present Morrison College edifice was established.*

The societies flourishing in the University, in 1833, were the Union Philosophical, the Whig, and the Adelphi Alpha.

The public exercises of the institution, at this time, were always conducted with much dignity and state. Probably no state governor in this country has ever been inducted into office with more imposing and impressive ceremonies than those formerly attending the inauguration of a Transylvania president. The long procession, composed of students, alumni, college societies, city associations and orders, members of the bar, members of Congress, governor and staff, banners and music, the immense crowd of eager citizens, strangers, and beautiful women, the solemn oath of office, delivery of university keys, address to the president and his reply, all made up a scene of surpassing interest and brilliancy.

Among the number of those who have acted as tutors in the university, we find the names of Jesse Bledsoe, Daniel Bradford, Mann Butler, C. S. Morehead, and James McChord.

Rev. Thomas W. Coit, D. D., another Episcopalian divine, became the sixth president of the university, in 1835. Dr. Coit came from New England, in 1834, to fill a professorship in the Episcopal Theological Seminary, in Lexington. He acquired some celebrity for his writings in favor of Trinitarianism, and for his pungent essays on the history of the American Puritans. He presided over Transylvania for nearly three years. At present, he is rector of St. Paul's church, Troy, New York.

In 1837, an effort was made by a majority of the faculty of the medical college, to remove it bodily to Louisville. They were unsuccessful, and such was the public indignation, that the enemies of the Lexington College found it convenient to resign.

---
*Davidson's History.

The Medical College suffered by the treachery of pretended friends and open enemies, but it speedily recovered. The faculty was at once reorganized, and the following gentlemen were elected:

To the chair of Anatomy and Surgery, B. W. Dudley, M. D., Professor, and J. M. Bush, M. D., Adjunct Professor; Institutes of Medicine and Medical Jurisprudence, James C. Cross, M. D.; Theory and Practice of Medicine, John Eberle, M. D.; Obstetrics and Diseases of Women and Children, William H. Richardson, M. D.; Materia Medica and Therapeutics, Thomas D. Mitchell, M. D.; Chemistry and Pharmacy, Robert Peter, M. D.

The interest of the entire community was strongly awakened, and a united effort made to increase the endowment of the university. In 1838-39, the city of Lexington donated $70,000; seventy gentlemen, incorporated February 20, 1839, by the name of the Transylvania Institute, contributed $35,000, out of part of which fund the present dormitory building was erected; and the professors of the medical department, by private contributions, purchased the lot of ground on which a new medical hall was soon built. These gentlemen also paid, out of their own funds, residuary debt on that building to the amount of more than $15,000.

The libraries, museums, chemical and philosophical apparatus, and the means of instruction generally, were greatly increased, and the university was put on a more favorable footing than it had ever been. The new medical hall referred to was built on the corner of Second and Broadway, and occupied the site of the present residence of Dr. Bush. The corner-stone was laid July 4, 1839, and the oration was delivered by Robert Wickliffe, Jr.

In 1838, after the resignation of Dr. Coit, the Academical Faculty consisted of Dr. Louis Marshall, President *pro tem.*, and Professor of Ancient Languages; Rev. Robert Davidson, Professor of Moral and Mental Philosophy; Dr. Arthur J. Dumont (who succeeded Mr. Priczminski), Professor of Mathematics; Robert Peter, M. D., Professor of Natural

History and Experimental Philosophy; Rev. Charles Crow, Principal of Preparatory Department.

Rev. Robert Davidson, D. D., a Presbyterian minister, referred to more especially in the chapter in this volume on the Second Presbyterian Church, was the seventh regular president of Transylvania University, and was inaugurated in November, 1840.

In the fall of 1842, the Methodist Church was given the control of the university, which by this time had become considerably prostrated, particularly in the literary and academical department. The eloquent and untiring bishop, Henry B. Bascom, D. D. (see chapter on First Methodist Church), was made president of the institution, and it soon prospered as it had not done for years. There were four times as many students in it two years after the Methodists obtained control than there was the year before they took possession. Bishop Bascom resigned in 1849, and the university again reverted to the state.

Professor J. B. Dodd, well known as the author of a number of mathematical works, succeeded Dr. Bascom, and acted as president *pro tem.* up to the reorganization of the university in 1856. Professor Dodd died in Greensburg, Kentucky, March 27, 1872, aged sixty-five.

In 1855, the chairs of the Law College were filled by Professors George Robertson (see chapter on year 1835); George B. Kinkead, a native of Woodford county, Kentucky, Secretary of State under Governor Owsley, and distinguished both for his high-toned character and legal ability; and Francis K. Hunt, born in Lexington, a graduate of Transylvania Law School, a gentleman of rare graces and culture, and one of the first lawyers in Kentucky.

The university was reorganized in 1856,* and in connection with it, a normal school, for the education of teachers, was established, under the patronage of the state, as an indispensable aid to the common school system of Kentucky. The scheme was a noble one; the legislature appropriated $12,000 per annum to its support, and the cause of popular

---

*Acts Legislature.

education in Kentucky never looked more promising. Rev. Lewis W. Green, D. D., was called to the presidency, and the university opened March 4, 1856, with eighty pupils. Dr. Green, the ninth and last regular president of Transylvania University, was the son of Willis and Sarah Reed Green, and was born near Danville, Kentucky, January 28, 1806.* He was a student at Transylvania for some time, but graduated at Centre College, in 1824, after which he entered the Theological Seminary at Princeton, studied for the Presbyterian ministry, and was finally ordained. He spent two years in Europe, at the Universities of Bonn and Halle, and while studying biblical literature and the oriental languages, enjoyed the instructions of Neander, Hengstenberg, and other distinguished scholars. When called to Transylvania, he was president of Hampden Sidney College, Virginia. He labored, with satisfaction and success, at Lexington, for two years, at the end of which time, for some reason, the legislature withdrew the yearly appropriation for the normal school, and abandoned the project. Dr. Green accepted the presidency of Centre College, entered upon his duties there in January, 1858, and filled the position up to the time of his death, which occurred May 26, 1863. He was buried in the Danville cemetery. Dr. Green was an eloquent divine, and, in point of learning, had few equals in the Presbyterian Church in the West. His fine character and amiable disposition always gained for him the sincere love of his pupils.

The Medical School continued to exist with varying success up to the commencement of the late war between the States. In 1859, its faculty was composed of Drs. Ethelbert L. Dudley (see year 1862), S. L. Adams (see First Methodist Church), W. S. Chipley (see Lunatic Asylum), B. P. Drake, S. M. Letcher, H. M. Skillman, and J. M. Bush.

Dr. Drake is a graduate of this school, and now lives in Mt. Sterling, Kentucky.

Dr. Letcher, a native of Lancaster, Kentucky, was also a graduate of the Transylvania Medical College. He is well

---
*Biography.

remembered, not only as a fine physician, but as a fine instructor in his department. He died in Lexington, in 1862. Dr. Bush, born in Frankfort, Kentucky, and Dr. Skillman, a native of Lexington, are both graduates of the school in which they were teachers, and both now stand in the front rank of their profession in Kentucky.

From its founding up to its dissolution, at the beginning of the late war, the Medical College had conferred the degree of M. D. upon nearly two thousand graduates.*

The university, which had been declining for years, sunk hopelessly after the failure of the normal school. The academical department struggled on for a few years, owing its existence mainly to that superior instructor, Mr. Abram Drake. It settled into a grammar school, during the late war, under whose depressing influences all educational institutions languished, and through that period its principal was Professor J. K. Patterson, the present accomplished presiding officer of the Agricultural and Mechanical College of Kentucky University.

In January, 1865, the trustees of Transylvania, desiring to perpetuate for Lexington her character and usefulness as an educational center, conveyed the entire property of the institution to, and consolidated it with Kentucky University, on the condition of its removal to Lexington. From 1865, the history of Transylvania University blends with that of Kentucky University, of which it now forms a part.

The record of Transylvania, both at home and abroad is a proud one. Among the names of her thousands of graduates, appear those of Jefferson Davis, Thomas F. Marshall, Dr. B. W. Dudley, Richard H. Menifee, John Boyle, James McChord, Dr. Joseph Buchanan, Richard M. Johnson, John Rowan, W. T. Barry, Jesse Bledsoe, C. S. Morehead, Elijah Hise, "Duke" Gwin, C. A. Wickliffe, and a host of others—with cabinet officers, foreign ministers, governors, generals, physicians, divines, and men of every grade and business of life. There is scarcely a town

---

*Biography.

of any size in all the West and South that does not contain one or more of her graduates.

The power that Transylvania has exerted will be felt for generations to come.

Kentucky University, the successor and perpetuator of Transylvania, was incorporated in February, 1858, and located in Harrodsburg, Kentucky. Its endowment then consisted of $150,000, obtained by Mr. John B. Bowman, from members of the Christian Church and other liberal friends of education. At the same time, it received the funds and property of Bacon College, an institution founded by the Christian Church in 1836, in Georgetown, but which was removed to Harrodsburg in 1840, and finally failed for want of a sufficient endowment.*

John B. Bowman, the founder of Kentucky University, its present regent, and the one to whom its efficiency and prosperity is so largely due, was born at Bowman's station, near Harrodsburg, Kentucky, October 18, 1824. His grandparents were among the first settlers of Mercer county. His father, born near Lexington, is probably the oldest living native of Fayette county. Regent Bowman graduated at Bacon College under President Shannon, and in February, 1846, married Mary D., daughter of Dr. Charles Williams, of Montgomery county, Kentucky. The accomplishments and self-sacrifice of Mrs. Bowman have had no little to do with the success of Kentucky University. From the time he left college, up to the year 1855, Mr. Bowman was occupied in farming, but ever since that year, his life has been devoted to the up-building of the great institution of which he is the head. He is a man of extraordinary energy, executive ability, and financial sagacity.

"Taylor Academy," a preparatory school of the university, was opened in the old Bacon College building, at Harrodsburg, in September, 1858, with nearly one hundred students in attendance.

The College of Arts, the first regular department of the university to go into operation, was opened in September,

---
*University Records.

1859, under the presidency of Robert Milligan. Pesident Milligan is a native of Ireland, and is now in the fifty-ninth year of his age. He is a graduate of Washington College, Pennsylvania, and was at one time Professor of Mathematics in Bethany College. His colleagues at Harrodsburg were Professors R. Richardson, Robert Graham, L. L. Pinkerton, Henry White, and J. H. Neville. All of the professors with one exception (Professor Richardson) subsequently taught in the university after its removal to Lexington. There were about two hundred students in the university during its first session.*

In February, 1864, the old edifice of Bacon College, used by the university at Harrodsburg, was destroyed by fire, together with its apparatus and library. At this juncture, it was found that the trustees of Transylvania University were willing to convey the gounds and buildings of that institution to the curators of Kentucky University, on the condition of its removal to Lexington. The board left the whole question of removal and location to a committee, of whom Mr. Bowman was chairman.†

Accordingly, Mr. Bowman called the committee to meet at Frankfort, in January, 1865; but an expected *denouement* followed. While there, the proposition of Congress to donate to Kentucky 330,000 acres of land, for the purpose of agricultural and mechanical education, came up for consideration. The state was not prepared to accept the grant with the conditions imposed, and the munificent provision of Congress seemed likely to be lost to the state. Mr. Bowman proposed to make the State Agricultural College a department of Kentucky University, and to consolidate into the great institution the University of Harrodsburg, Transylvania, and the Agricultural College, and the whole to be located at Lexington. He further proposed, if this should be done, to provide an experimental farm, and all the requisite buildings, and to give gratuitous instruction to three hundred students, to be selected by the state; and he furthermore pledged, that the board of curators would

---

*University Records.   †Id.

carry out, in the agricultural department, the spirit and intent of the act of Congress encouraging the education of the industrial classes.

A bill to this effect was accordingly drawn up, and, after long and animated discussion in the General Assembly, it was passed by a large majority, and Kentucky University was removed from Harrodsburg, the grounds and buildings and endowment of Transylvania were transferred, and the State Agricultural College was made a part of the university, with an aggregate capital of more than one-half million of dollars. As a condition of this removal, the curators of Kentucky University bound themselves to refund to citizens of Mercer county $30,000 which they had contributed to the institution, and also furnish $100,000 more, to be invested in an experimental farm and buildings. Mr. Bowman set to work at once to secure the amounts needed, and the following gentlemen, in a printed address,* strongly urged the people of Lexington to assist him, viz: M. C. Johnson, John Carty, Benj. Gratz, J. G. Chinn, John B. Tilford, J. G. Allen, H. T. Duncan, Jr., John B. Payne, Jr. In three months the money was obtained by subscription, principally from the citizens of Lexington and vicinity, of all creeds and denominations.

The first session of Kentucky University, at Lexington, commenced on Monday, October 2, 1865,* with formal and appropriate exercises, in the chapel of Morrison College. Four other departments, in addition to the College of Arts, had, in the meanwhile been created, and went at once into active operation. At its opening in Lexington, therefore, the university consisted of the College of Arts, the Law College, the Agricultural and Mechanical College, the Bible College, and the Academy.

The college of arts, up to the present time, has had four presidents, viz: R. Milligan, 1859; R. Graham, 1865; J. Aug. Williams, 1868; Henry H. White, 1870. The old Morrison College building is used by the college of arts. Henry H. White, Professor of Mathematics, and John H.

---

*Observer and Reporter. †Id.

Neville, Professor of Greek Language and Literature, have long reflected credit upon this ably conducted college of the university. Dr. Peter, so long associated with Transylvania, is the distinguished Professor of Chemistry in this college.

The organization of the Agricultural and Mechanical College was the work, to a very great extent, of its thoroughly accomplished first president, John Augustus Williams, now the head of Daughter's College, at Harrodsburg, and noted as having few equals in the West as an educator. His successors were J. D. Pickett, 1867; Henry H. White, 1868, and J. K. Patterson, 1870. This department enjoyed for some time the services of Professor A. Winchell, now the well-known geologist of Michigan University. The seat of the Agricultural and Mechanical College was purchased in 1866, and cost one hundred and thirty thousand dollars. It consists of "Ashland," the homestead of Henry Clay, and the adjoining estate of "Woodlands," which extends within the limits of the city of Lexington. The entire tract contains four hundred and thirty-three acres of land, unsurpassed for beauty and fertility. Four brick buildings, for the use of officers and students, were erected at "Woodlands," during the year 1867. The large and handsome edifice, used by the mechanical department, at "Ashland," was built in 1868.

The Law College is the full equal of its famous Transylvania predecessor. Madison C. Johnson was elected its president in 1868, and still occupies that position. Major Johnson is a graduate of the Transylvania Law College, and was one of its professors in 1850. His strong mind and laborious application have placed him in the front rank at the Kentucky bar.

Of Judge W. C. Goodloe, professor in 1865, see chapter on year 1863.

Judge R. A. Buckner, also a professor in 1865, is a native of Green county, Kentucky. He was circuit judge by appointment of Governor Letcher; speaker of the Kentucky House of Representatives in 1859, and is at present engaged as one of the commissioners appointed by Governor Leslie and the Supreme Court to revise the Kentucky Code of Practice. Judge Buckner's legal attainments are of the first order.

General John B. Huston, who succeeded Judge Buckner as professor, in 1865, and who still retains the position, is a native of Nelson county, Kentucky, and a graduate of Center College. He represented Clark county in the legislature, and was speaker of the house. He removed to Lexington in 1863. General Huston is greatly gifted, both as a lawyer and a speaker.

James O. Harrison, elected professor in 1870, was born in Mount Sterling, Kentucky, in 1804, and, after graduating at the Transylvania Law College, settled in Lexington, in 1824. Though he has, at different times, been tendered high official appointments by the general government, Mr. Harrison has confined himself strictly to his professional duties. He is distinguished for his integrity, literary culture, and superior legal attainments.

The Bible College has had but one president, viz: Robert Milligan, from its organization, in 1865, to the present time.

The academy had three principals during its existence, viz: A. R. Milligan, 1866; G. W. Ranck, 1867; D. G. Herron, 1869. This department was discontinued in 1870.

The principals of the commercial department, since its organization in 1867, are named in the order of their succession, viz: J. P. Marquam, W. H. Marquam, A. Hollingsworth, H. P. Perrin.

The societies of the university, viz: the Periclean, Cecropian, Union Literary, Christomathean, and Philothean, have reflected no little honor upon the institution, and are rapidly attaining literary efficiency and celebrity.

In 1870, Congress appropriated twenty-five thousand dollars to the university, to compensate for the destruction, by fire, of the Transylvania Medical College building, while in the possession of Federal troops, during the late war.

The present executive committee of the university is composed of J. B. Bowman, Benjamin Gratz, Joseph Wasson, Joseph Smith, and Joseph S. Woolfolk. The oldest member of the committee, Mr. Gratz, was born in Philadelphia, September 4, 1792, and settled in Lexington in 1819. He became a trustee of Transylvania in the distinguished Dr. Holley's time, and has been connected with that institution and its successor, Kentucky University, for nearly half a century, and has always been known as one of the firmest and most influential friends of education and public improvement in Lexington.

James B. Beck, the present distinguished congressional representative from the "Ashland district," is a member of the board of curators of the university. Mr. Beck is a native of Dumfriesshire, Scotland, but came to the United States at the age of sixteen, and settled in Lexington, where he graduated at the Transylvania Law College. He was elected to Congress in 1867, and has been returned at every succeeding election. Mr. Beck overcame many very discouraging obstacles in early life, and is a self-made man of the best type. His mind is of extraordinary strength and clearness, and is only matched by his energy and industry.

The various libraries of Kentucky University comprise about ten thousand volumes, and the anatomical museum, the museum of natural philosophy, and the collections of chemical, astronomical, and philosophical apparatus are large and valuable. In June, of the present year, appeared the first number of "The Collegian," a monthly, established and ably supported by the literary societies of the university. The endowment and real estate of the institution now amount to eight hundred thousand dollars; and as many as seven hundred and seventy-two matriculates have attended its various colleges in one session.

The States of Virginia and Kentucky, the city of Lexington, individual members of all parties and sects, and the United States Government, have all contributed, at various times, to this consolidated fund and this great success; and if the institution is governed and directed as it should be, in accordance with these facts; if its economy is liberal and generous, and free from sectarian bigotry and shortsightedness, it will continue to grow, and will become the full equal of any institution of learning in this country.

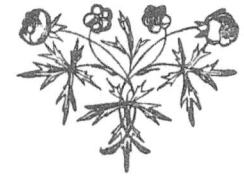

CHAPTER VIII.

First Trustees of Lexington—Adventures of McConnell, Bryant, and Hogan—County Government—List of Clerks and Sheriffs—Charles Carr—Court-Houses—Town of Lexington Laid off—First Lot Owners.

THE blow given by Clarke to the Miami Indians prevented any formidable invasion during this year (1781), but it could not keep out *small* bands of the enemy, who constantly hung upon the outskirts of the settlements, and captured or killed many of the pioneers. But, despite their savage enemies and all other drawbacks, the inhabitants of Lexington station persisted in the up-building of their village. The terrible winter gave place to a delightful spring; game for the settlers and food for the live stock were abundant, and energy came with renewed hope. Early in the spring more land was cleared; planting was commenced as soon as possible; a road (Main street) was cut, cleared, and extended some distance from the gate of the fort, and the settlers assembled and elected their first board of trustees, composed of Robert Patterson, Levi Todd, Henry McDonald, David Mitchell, and Michael Warnock.* The trustees held their first meeting, March 26, in one of the log cabins of the fort, and, with an eye to the growth and prosperity of Lexington, acted with a most commendable spirit of enterprise and liberality. By this time, the first court of Fayette county had been formed, and one of the first resolutions of the trustees was, "To inform the court of Fayette county that, if they should deem Lexington a proper place for holding courts in the future, the sum of £30 in gold or silver, or the value thereof in continental

*City Records.

currency, will be granted by the trustees for public buildings."* At this meeting it was also, " Ordered that the town land be laid off in lots, the in-lots to contain one-third part of an acre each; and that they be granted to each free male person above the age of twenty-one years, and each widow; every young man who can make it appear he acts in his own behalf, and not under the immediate control and jurisdiction of some other person, who, at the time of laying them off and distributing them, appears to be an actual resident within the place, subject to such conditions and penalties as shall be hereafter required; that a number of lots, not less than thirty, be reserved for public uses, and such other purposes as may hereafter be requisite."† Proper persons were selected for the work of laying off the town, but the plan was not adopted for nine months after this meeting. Whether the Indians were the cause of the delay or not, we can not speak positively; but that they continually harassed the settlers of all the stations in Fayette county during the entire spring and summer, we know.

One charming day in April, Alexander McConnell took his rifle and went out from the fort to hunt deer, in the woods near where Mr. Frank McCallie now lives, on the Versailles turnpike. He soon killed a large buck, and returned to the station for a horse, in order to bring it in. During his absence, a party of five Indians, on one of their usual skulking expeditions, accidently stumbled on the body of the deer, and perceiving it had been recently killed, they naturally supposed that the hunter would speedily return to secure it. Three of them, therefore, took their station within close rifle shot of the deer, while the other two followed the trail of the hunter, and waylaid the path by which he was expected to return. McConnell, suspecting no danger, rode carelessly along the path which the two scouts were watching, until he had come within view of the deer, when he was fired upon by the whole party, and his horse killed. While laboring to extricate

---

*City Records. †Ib.

himself from the dying animal, he was seized by his enemies, instantly overpowered, and borne off a prisoner. His captors, however, seemed to be a merry, good-natured set of fellows, and permitted him to accompany them unbound; and, what was rather extraordinary, allowed him to retain his gun and hunting accoutrements. He accompanied them with great apparent cheerfulness through the day, and displayed his dexterity in shooting deer for the use of the company, until they began to regard him with great partiality. Having traveled with them in this manner for several days, they at length reached the banks of the Ohio river. Heretofore, the Indians had taken the precaution to bind him at night, although not very securely; but on that evening he remonstrated with them on the subject, and complained so strongly of the pain which the cords gave him, that they merely wrapped the buffalo tug loosely around his wrists, and having tied it in an easy knot, and attached the extremities of the rope to their own bodies, in order to prevent his moving without awakening them, they very composedly went to sleep, leaving the prisoner to follow their example or not, as he pleased.

McConnell determined to effect his escape that night, if possible, as on the following night they would cross the river, which would render it much more difficult. He therefore lay quietly until near midnight, anxiously ruminating upon the best means of effecting his object. Accidentally casting his eyes in the direction of his feet, they fell upon the glittering blade of a knife, which had escaped its sheath, and was now lying near the feet of one of the Indians. To reach it with his hands, without disturbing the two Indians to whom he was fastened, was impossible, and it was very hazardous to attempt to draw it up with his feet. This, however, he attempted. With much difficulty he grasped the blade between his toes, and, after repeated and long-continued efforts, succeeded at length in bringing it within reach of his hands.

To cut his cords was then but the work of a moment, and gradually and silently extricating his person from the arms of the Indians, he walked to the fire and sat down.

He saw that his work was but half done. That if he should attempt to return home, without destroying his enemies, he would be pursued and probably overtaken, when his fate would be certain. On the other hand, it seemed almost impossible for a single man to succeed in a conflict with five Indians, even although unarmed and asleep. He could not hope to deal a blow with his knife so silently and fatally, as to destroy each one of his enemies in turn, without awakening the rest. Their slumbers were proverbially light and restless; and if he failed with a single one, he must instantly be overpowered by the survivers. The knife, therefore, was out of the question.

After anxious reflection for a few minutes, he formed his plan. The guns of the Indians were stacked near the fire; their knives and tomahawks were in sheaths by their sides. The latter he dared not touch for fear of awakening their owners; but the former he carefully removed, with the exception of two, and hid them in the woods, where he knew the Indians would not readily find them. He then returned to the spot where the Indians were still sleeping, perfectly ignorant of the fate preparing for them, and taking a gun in each hand, he rested the muzzles upon a log within six feet of his victims, and having taken deliberate aim at the head of one and the heart of another, he pulled both triggers at the same moment.

Both shots were fatal. At the report of their guns, the others sprang to their feet, and stared wildly around them. McConnell, who had run instantly to the spot where the other rifles were hid, hastily seized one of them and fired at two of his enemies, who happened to stand in a line with each other. The nearest fell dead, being shot through the center of the body; the second fell also, bellowing loudly, but quickly recovering, limped off into the woods as fast as possible. The fifth, and only one who remained unhurt, darted off like a deer, with a yell which announced equal terror and astonishment. McConnell, not wishing to fight any more such battles, selected his own rifle from the stack, and made the best of his way to Lexington, where he arrived safely within two days.

Shortly afterward, Mrs. Eve Dunlap, who had been several months a prisoner among the Indians on Mad river, made her escape, and returned to her home at Lexington station. She reported that the survivor returned to his tribe with a lamentable tale. He relates that they had taken a fine young hunter near Lexington, and had brought him safely as far as the Ohio; that while encamped upon the bank of the river, a large party of white men had fallen upon them in the night and killed all his companions, together with the poor defenseless prisoner, who lay bound hand and foot, unable to either escape or resist.*

A large pignut tree, under which McConnell was captured by the Indians, was carefully preserved for a long time by the father of Mr. Frank McCallie, who subsequently owned the land upon which it grew.†

After the capture of McConnell, the Indians annoyed the stations in Fayette county greatly. They lurked in the canebrakes, waylaid the traces, stole horses, butchered cattle, and not unfrequently killed and scalped indiscreet settlers. Finally, the Indians became so bold and harassing, that it became necessary for hunters to go out in bands so as to be able to repel attacks.

One afternoon, about the 20th of May, William Bryant, at the head of twenty men, left Bryant's station on a hunting expedition. They moved with caution, until they had passed all the points where ambuscades had generally been formed, when, seeing no enemy, they became more bold, and determined, in order to sweep a large extent of country, to divide their company into two parties. One of them, conducted by Bryant in person, was to descend the Elkhorn on its southern bank, flanking out largely, and occupy as much ground as possible. The other, under the orders of James Hogan, a young farmer in good circumstances, was to move down in a parallel line upon the north bank. The two parties were to meet at night, and encamp together at the mouth of Cane run.

Each punctually performed the first part of their plans.

---

*McClung's Sketches.   †McCallie, F.

Hogan, however, had traveled but a few hundred yards, when he heard a loud voice behind him exclaim in very good English, "stop, boys!" Hastily looking back, they saw several Indians on foot, pursuing them as rapidly as possible. Without halting to count numbers, the party put spurs to their horses, and dashed through the woods at full speed, the Indians keeping close behind them, and at times gaining upon them. There was a led horse in company, which had been brought with them for the purpose of packing game. This was instantly abandoned, and fell into the hands of the Indians. Several of them lost their hats in the eagerness of flight; but quickly getting into the open woods, they left their pursuers so far behind that they had leisure to breathe and inquire of each other, whether it was worth while to kill their horses before they had ascertained the number of the enemy.

They quickly determined to cross the creek, and await the approach of the Indians. If they found them superior to their own and Bryant's party united, they would immediately return to the fort; as, by continuing their march to the mouth of Cane run, they would bring a superior enemy upon their friends, and endanger the lives of the whole party. They accordingly crossed the creek, dismounted, and awaited the approach of the enemy. By this time it had become dark. The Indians were distinctly heard approaching the creek upon the opposite side, and after a short halt, a solitary warrior descended the bank and began to wade through the stream.

Hogan waited until they had emerged from the gloom of the trees which grew upon the bank, and as soon as he had reached the middle of the stream, where the light was more distinct, he took deliberate aim and fired. A great splashing in the water was heard, but presently all became quiet. The pursuit was discontinued, and the party, remounting their horses, returned home. Anxious, however, to apprise Bryant's party of their danger, they left the fort before daylight on the ensuing morning, and rode rapidly down the creek, in the direction of the mouth of Cane run. When within a few hundred yards of the spot where they supposed the encampment to be, they heard the report of many guns in quick succession. Supposing that Bryant had fallen in with a herd of buffalo, they quickened their march in order to take part in the sport.

The morning was foggy, and the smoke of the guns lay so heavily upon the ground that they could see nothing until they had approached within twenty yards of the creek, when they suddenly found themselves within pistol shot of a party of Indians, very composedly seated upon their packs, and preparing their pipes. Both parties were much startled, but quickly recovering, they sheltered themselves as usual, and the action opened with great vivacity. The Indians maintained their ground for half an hour with some firmness, but being hard pressed in front, and turned in flank, they at length gave way, and being closely pursued, were ultimately routed with considerable loss, which, however could not be distinctly ascertained. Of Hogan's party, one man was killed on the spot, and three others wounded, but none mortally.

It happened that Bryant's company had encamped at the mouth of Cane, as had been agreed upon, and were unable to account for Hogan's absence. That, about daylight they had heard a bell at a distance, which they immediately recognized as the one belonging to the led horse which had accompanied Hogan's party, and which, as we have seen, had been abandoned to the enemy the evening before. Supposing their friends to be bewildered in the fog, and unable to find their camp, Bryant accompanied by Grant, one of his men, mounted a horse and rode to the spot where the bell was still ringing. They quickly fell into an ambuscade and were fired upon. Bryant was mortally, and Grant severely wounded; the first being shot through the hip and both knees, the latter through the back. Both being able to keep the saddle however, they set spurs to their horses and arrived at the station shortly after breakfast. The Indians, in the meantime, had fallen upon the encampment and instantly dispersed it, and, while preparing to regale themselves after their victory, were suddenly attacked, as we have seen, by Hogan. The timidity of Hogan's party at the first appearance of the Indians, was the cause of Bryant's death. The same men who fled so hastily in the evening were able the next morning, by a little firmness, to vanquish the same party of Indians. Had they stood at first, an equal success would probably have attended them, and the life of their leader would have been preserved.*

During the summer, and in the midst of trials and bloodshed the organization of the government of Fayette county was completed. Governor Jefferson, of Virginia, appointed John Todd colonel, Daniel Boone lieutenant-colonel, and Thomas Marshall surveyor of the county.† John Maxwell was made coroner.‡ Levi Todd was chosen as clerk of the county court, and held the office for twenty-five years after.|| The successors of Todd were John D. Young, 1807; James C. Rhodes, 1817; James A. Grinstead, 1845; Sanders D. Bruce, 1849; Joseph R. Gross, 1862; Ernest Brennan, 1863; Allie G. Hunt, 1866.

The justices of the county court were successively sheriffs of the county until the law was changed in 1792.§ The first sheriff under the succession rule was Charles Carr. Mr. Carr was a native of Virginia, and emigrated to this state when he was but ten years of age. He was a private soldier in the American army, under General Anthony Wayne, in 1794, and took an active part in his celebrated campaign against the Indians.

In the war of 1812 he served as captain, and was at one time a prisoner. Subsequently he was a member of the state legislature. He died in Fayette county, at an advanced age. His successors as sheriffs were Thomas Clarke, J. C. Richardson, Leonard Young, A. Young, James Wood, W. R. Morton, Edward Payne, John Bradford, G. W. Morton, Waller Bullock, A. Thomson, Oliver Keene, T. S. Redd, R. S. Todd, T. A. Russell, M. Flournoy, J. R. Sloan, Moses Ellis, J. B. O'Bannon, Waller Rhodes, Abraham Dudley, Joseph Gross, C. S. Bodley, Thomas Nichols, W. W. Dowden, R. S. Bullock.

---

*McClung's Sketches. †Marshall, 140. ‡Ky. Gazette.
||County records. §Marshall.

The proposition of the trustees of Lexington to the county court was accepted, and in December, 1781, "the trustees agreed to pay the commissioners appointed by the court a sum sufficient to build a court-house, prison, and office to answer the present necessity, and grant one square for that purpose."*

But the "present necessity" was such that the court could not wait until buildings were erected, and its sessions for some time were held in one of the cabins within the station. The next house used was a log one, erected about two years after this, on the corner of Main and Broadway, now known as "Yeiser's corner." It was still standing in 1796, and was used at that time by William McBean, as a dry goods store.† A small stone court-house was erected about the year 1788, on the square granted by the trustees, and where the present one stands. Levi Todd, the first county clerk, had his office separate from this building, and used a little 12 by 15 one which stood on what is now called the Wickliffe farm, on the Richmond turnpike. This was destroyed by fire on the night of January 31, 1803, and with it most of the records of the county.‡ The following commissioners were appointed by the governor, " with full powers and authority, to meet at some convenient place, and adjourn from time to time, as they shall think fit, and to summons, hear, and examine witnesses, at the instance of any person who has been or may be injured by the destruction of the records of county courts," viz: Thomas Lewis, Robert Todd, Henry Payne, Thomas Bodley, James Trotter, John A. Seitz, Walker Baylor, John Bradford, John Richardson. This calamity, and the rapid growth of the city, now necessitated the erection of a larger building, and in 1806 the present brick court-house was built. About the year 1814 it was remodeled and the town clock was put up, and now altogether constitutes the venerable disfigurement at present so unpleasantly prominent upon the public square and so disgraceful to the county. The court-house can boast of nothing but its associations. Its walls

---

*City records.   †Old Gazette.   ‡Gazette.

have echoed to the voices of Clay, Barry, Bledsoe, Crittenden, the Wickliffes, Menifee, R. J. and John C. Breckinridge, Thomas F. Marshall, and a host of other distinguished men both living and dead.

On the 26th of December, 1781,* the trustees of Lexington station adopted a plan for the town, and the lots defined in it were disposed of by them to the inhabitants, who " were required to pay a proportionable part of the money necessary to build the public houses and expenses arising toward good order and regularity in the town."

The names of those who secured lots at that time are recorded as follows in "the Trustees' Book:" James Masterson, William McDonald, Henry McDonald, Samuel McMullins, David Mitchell, Thornton Farrow, Nicholas Brobston, James McBride, William Henderson, Samuel Martin, John Torrence, William Martin, Sen., John Clark, William Niblick, Francis McDonald, Francis McConnell, Daniel McClain, Robert Stanhope, John Wymore, Hugh Martin, David Vance, William Mitchell, Timothy Payton, Elisha Collins, John Morrison, Stephen Collins, Levi Todd, Ephraim January, Alexander McClain, Caleb Masterson, Samuel Kelly, Joseph Turner, Samuel Kelly, John Wymore, William McConnell, John McDonald, Joseph Lindsey, Jane Thompson, John Todd, James Lindsay, Alexander McConnell, Hugh Thompson, James Morrow, Robert Thompson, Hugh McDonald, James McGinty, John Martin, Samuel Johnson, James January, James Wason, William Haydon, Josiah Collins, Matthew Walker, James McConnell, John M. McDonald, Michael Warnock, William Martin, James McDonald, Alexander McConnell, William McConnell, a clergyman, John Williams, Peter January, Joseph Waller, John Niblick, Charles Seaman, Francis McDermid.

---

*City Records.

CHAPTER IX.

Trouble with the Indians—Incidents—The War Closed—Lexington Incorporated—The Great Invasion—Siege of Bryant's Station—Aaron Reynolds—Battle of the Blue Licks—Benjamin Netherland—The Terrible Defeat—Burial of the Dead—Sorrow and Gloom—The Women of Lexington—James Morgan—Clark's Expedition—John Filson—Thomas Marshall.

THE year 1782 was one of excitements, stirring events, and mournful disasters to Lexington and Fayette county. The outlook, so bright with hope to others, was gloomy indeed to them. Far across the Atlantic, even from the commencement of the year, the British House of Commons had been ringing with eloquent demands for a termination of the war against the American colonies; but here, on this side of the great ocean, even while those cries for peace were going up, the tribes of the great Northwest were gathering their incensed and desperate warriors, to strike what they hoped would be a final and crushing blow at the frontier settlements. Numerous small scouting parties of Indians were ordered to Kentucky, and soon the woods teemed with savages, and no one was safe beyond the walls of a station. Late in March, a hunter from the fort at Lexington was killed by some Indians in ambuscade near the present Lexington Cemetery,* and a few weeks after, another settler was shot and dangerously wounded in a field where the jail now stands, and his savage foe was running, knife in hand, to scalp him, when he was himself shot by a skillful marksman then on watch in the block-house, and

---

*Tradition.

fell dead upon the body of his wounded enemy.* It is strongly intimated by one historian† that the marksman who made this famous shot was the celebrated Daniel Boone himself. Certainly, the "picking off" of an Indian at such a distance, while he was kneeling above the fallen settler, and a shot so directed as to kill the one without injury to the other, was a feat not unworthy the grand old pioneer. In May, a courier brought the news to Lexington of Estell's defeat, a calamity which made a profound sensation in every settlement, and the more because the bold and masterly movement of the Indians which decided the fate of the day, indicated an advance in military science, which presaged no good to the settlers. Lexington and Bryant's stations were now the most exposed points in Kentucky, and as Estell's defeat confirmed the general impression that another Indian invasion was imminent, the settlers were weighed down with anticipations of evil.

At this gloomy juncture, the second board of trustees of Lexington received a copy of the law passed by the Virginia Assembly, at Richmond, on the 6th of May, incorporating Lexington.‡ The law was entitled, "An act to establish a town at the court-house, in the county of Fayette," and was worded as follows, viz:

"WHEREAS, It is represented to this assembly that six hundred and forty acres of unappropriated land in the county of Fayette, whereon the court-house of said county stands, has been by the settlers thereon laid out into lots and streets for a town; and that the said settlers have purchased seventy acres of land lying contagious to the said six hundred and forty acres, being part of a survey made for John Floyd; and whereas, it would tend greatly to the improvement and settling of the same if the titles of settlers on the lots were confirmed, and a town established thereon:

Be it therefore enacted, That the said seven hundred and acres of land be and the same is hereby vested in fee simple in John Todd, Robert Patterson, William Mitchell, Andrew Steele, William Henderson, William McConnell, and Will-

---

*Boone's Narrative.   †Bogart, 226.   ‡Trustees' Book.

iam Steele, gentlemen trustees, and established by the name of LEXINGTON.

And be it further enacted, That the said trustees, or any four of them, shall, and they are hereby empowered and required to make conveyance to those persons who have already settled on the said lots, as also to the purchasers of lots heretofore sold, agreeable to the condition of the contracts, and may also proceed to lay off such other parts of the said land as is not yet laid off and settled into lots and streets; and such lots shall be by the trustees sold or otherwise disposed of for the benefit of the inhabitants of the said town, and convey the same in fee simple agreeable to the condition of the contract: *Provided,* always, that the lots in the said town which have been laid off and set apart for erecting thereon the public buildings of the said county shall be and remain to and for that use and purpose, and no other whatever.

And be it further enacted, That the said trustees, or the major part of them, shall have power from time to time to settle and determine all disputes concerning the bounds of the said lots, and to settle such rules and orders for the regular building of houses thereon as to them shall seem best and most convenient. And in case of the death, removal out of the county, or other legal disability of any of the said trustees, it shall and may be lawful for the remaining trustees to elect and choose so many other persons in place of those deceased, removed, or disabled, as shall make up the number; which trustees so chosen shall be, to all intents and purposes, individually vested with the same power and authority as any one in this act particularly mentioned.

And be it further enacted, That the settlers, as well as purchasers of lots, in the said town, so soon as they shall have saved the same according to the conditions of their respective deeds of conveyance, shall be entitled to have and enjoy all the rights, privileges, and immunities which the freeholders and inhabitants of other towns in this state not incorporated by charter or act of assembly have and enjoy.

And be it further enacted, That the said trustees shall cause the survey and plat of the said town to be recorded in the court of the said county of Fayette, leaving to all persons all such right, title, and interest which they, or any of them, could or might have to the lands, or any part thereof, hereby vested in the said trustees as if this act had never been made."

The Indian invasion, so dreaded by the infant settlements, was now near at hand. Most of the summer following Estell's defeat had been spent by the savages in perfecting a plan by which they hoped to regain for themselves the possession of their lost hunting grounds in the West.

Early in August, detachments of Indian warriors from the Cherokee, Wyandot, Tawa, and Pottowatomie nations, as well as from several other tribes bordering on the lakes, assembled in grand council at Chillicothe, where they were met by Simon Girty, James Girty, and M'Kee, three renegade white men, who urged them to proceed at once to the step they so much desired to take.

The advice of the white savages was quickly acceded to, the council ended with a war whoop, and the Indians, with a few Canadian allies, took up the line of march for Kentucky, with the understanding that Bryant's station should be taken first, and then Lexington station, after which they were to act as circumstances should direct. The force in this noted expedition has been variously estimated from six hundred to one thousand.

Of the two stations marked out for destruction, Lexington was the strongest. Its garrison consisted of about sixty effective men,* and it enjoyed the very superior advantage of an abundant and never-failing supply of water *inside* its walls. Bryant's station stood on a gentle rise on the southern bank of the Elkhorn, a few paces to the right of the road from Maysville to Lexington, and consisted at this time of about forty cabins, was built in the usual parallelogram shape, was about two hundred yards long by fifty wide, strengthened with block-houses at the angles, and where the

---

*Bradford's Notes.

cabins did not join, the vacancies were filled with strong pickets. The garrison consisted of forty-four men. Unfortunately, there was no supply of water within the fort, and the only dependence was a spring on its northwestern side. The station was situated on a tract of land admired by all the settlers for its natural beauty, and it doubtless merited the glowing praise of the poet*, who speaks of

> " A picketed station on fair Elkhorn,
> Surrounded by groves of the milk-white thorn,
> And paw-paw, with long and silvery stem,
> And dogwood of beautiful diadem;
> Green meadows with antlered deer yet dotted,
> And lawns with flowers the loveliest spotted."

The savage army entered Kentucky, and penetrated with celerity and great secrecy into the very heart of the district. A party was at once sent out to demonstrate against McGee's and Strodes' stations, with the object of drawing away from their posts the garrisons of Bryant and Lexington stations. On the morning of the 14th of August, this party defeated Captain Holder, and the stratagem of the wily red men barely escaped being crowned with complete success, as subsequent events will show. The main body of the Indians moved carefully forward, and on the night of the 14th gathered as silent as the shadows around Bryant's station†. The great body of Indians placed themselves in ambush in some high weeds, within pistol shot of the spring, while one hundred select men were placed near the spot where the road now runs after passing the creek. Providentially for the garrison, a messenger had arrived just before night with the intelligence of Holder's defeat, and they set to work immediately to prepare for an early march in the morning to the general rendezvous at Hoy's station. The Indians seeing the lights glancing from block-houses and cabins, and hearing the bustle of preparation, believed that their approach had been discovered, though the settlers were utterly unconscious of their presence. Under the impression that their stratagem to decoy the garrison from the

---

*W. D. Gallagher.   †McClung's Sketches.

fort had failed, the band of a hundred men was ordered to open a brisk fire early in the morning, and show themselves to the garrison on that side of the station, for the purpose of drawing them out, while the main body held themselves in readiness to rush upon the opposite gate of the fort, hew it down with their tomahawks, and force their way into the midst of the cabins. Day stole through the forest, the settlers rose from their brief slumbers, took their arms, and were on the point of opening the gates to march, under the command of Captain Elijah Craig, to the assistance of their friends, when the crack of rifles, mingled with yells and howls, told them in an instant how narrowly they had escaped captivity or death. The former practice of this fort was known, and the Indians expected every man to run to the spot where the firing commenced, which would leave it undefended on the side where the main body lay; but the number of guns discharged, and the near approach of the party, convinced the people of the fort that it was a plan to draw the men out; and, instead of falling into this trap, the opposite side of the fort was instantly manned, and several breaches in the picketing at once repaired.* Their greatest distress rose from the prospect of suffering for water.

The more experienced of the garrison felt satisfied that a powerful party was in ambuscade near the spring, but at the same time they supposed that the Indians would not unmask themselves until the firing upon the opposite side of the fort was returned with such warmth as to induce the belief that the feint had succeeded.

Acting upon this impression, and yielding to the urgent necessity of the case, they summoned all the women, without exception, and explaining to them the circumstances in which they were placed, and the improbability that any injury would be offered them until the firing had been returned from the opposite side of the fort, they urged them to go in a body to the spring, and each to bring up a bucketful of water. Some of the ladies, as was natural, had no relish for the undertaking, and asked why the men could

---

*Bradford's Notes.

not bring water as well as themselves, observing that *they* were not bullet-proof, and that the Indians made no distinction between male and female scalps!

To this it was answered that women were in the habit of bringing water every morning to the fort, and that if the Indians saw them engaged as usual, it would induce them to believe that their ambuscade was undiscovered, and that they would not unmask themselves for the sake of firing at a few women, when they hoped, by remaining concealed a few moments longer, to obtain complete possession of the fort; that if *men* should go down to the spring, the Indians would immediately suspect that something was wrong, would despair of succeeding by ambuscade, and would instantly rush upon them, follow them into the fort, or shoot them down at the spring. The decision was soon made.

A few of the boldest declared their readiness to brave the danger, and the younger and more timid rallying in the rear of these veterans, they all marched down in a body to the spring, within point-blank shot of more than five hundred Indian warriors! Some of the girls could not help betraying symptoms of terror, but the married women, in general, moved with a steadiness and composure which completely deceived the Indians. Not a shot was fired. The party were permitted to fill their buckets, one after another, without interruption, and although their steps became quicker and quicker on their return, and when near the gate of the fort degenerated into a rather unmilitary celerity, attended with some little crowding in passing the gate, yet not more than one-fifth of the water was spilled, and the eyes of the youngest had not dilated to more than double their ordinary size.*

Being now amply supplied with water, they sent out thirteen young men to attack the decoy party, with orders to fire with great rapidity, and make as much noise as possible, but not to pursue the enemy too far, while the rest of the garrison took post on the opposite side of the fort, cocked their guns, and stood in readiness to receive the ambuscade

---

*McClung and Bradford.

as soon as it was unmasked. The firing of the light parties on the Lexington road was soon heard, and quickly became sharp and serious, gradually becoming more distant from the fort. Instantly, Girty sprung up at the head of his five hundred warriors, and rushed rapidly upon the western gate, ready to force his way over the undefended palisades. A small body of the most daring reached the fort, and set fire to a few houses and stables, which were consumed; but the rest of the fort and the lives of the people were saved by an easterly wind, which drove the flames from the houses. Into the immense mass of dusky bodies the garrison poured several rapid volleys of rifle balls with destructive effect. Their consternation may be imagined. With wild cries they dispersed on the right and left, and in two minutes not an Indian was to be seen. At the same time, the party who had sallied out on the Lexington road, came running into the fort at the opposite gate, in high spirits, and laughing heartily at the success of their maneuver.

A regular attack, in the usual manner, then commenced, without much effect on either side, until two o'clock in the afternoon, when a new scene presented itself. Upon the first appearance of the Indians in the morning, two of the garrison, Tomlinson and Bell, had been mounted upon fleet horses, and sent at full speed to Lexington, announcing the arrival of the Indians, and demanding reinforcements.

Upon their arrival, a little after sunrise, they found the station occupied only by some women and children and a few old men, the rest having marched to the assistance of Holder. The two couriers instantly followed at a gallop, and, overtaking them on the road, informed them of the danger to which Bryant's station and Lexington were exposed during their absence. The whole party, with some volunteers from Boone's station, instantly countermarched, and repaired, with all possible dispatch, to Bryant's station. They were entirely ignorant of the overwhelming numbers opposed to them, or they would have proceeded with more caution. The couriers had only informed them that the station was surrounded, being themselves ignorant of the numbers of the enemy. At about two P. M. the men from Lexington and Boone's station arrived in sight of the fort, at the moment the firing had ceased, and no indications of danger appeared. The reinforcement believed it had been the victim of a false alarm, and the sixteen mounted men approached the fort the usual route along a narrow lane, which was lined for more than one hundred yards by the enemy on both sides, who commenced a fire unperceived at a few feet distance. It is believed the great dust which was raised by the horses' feet in a considerable degree protected the party; they got safely into the fort without the slightest wound on man or horse.* The men on foot were less fortunate. They were advancing through a corn-field, to the left of what is now the Maysville and Lexington road, and might have reached the fort in safety but for their eagerness to succor their friends. Without reflecting that, from the weight and extent of the fire, the enemy must have been ten times their number, they ran up, with inconsiderate courage, to the spot where the firing was heard, and there found themselves cut off from the fort, and within pistol shot of more than three hundred savages.

Fortunately the Indian guns had just been discharged, and they had not yet had leisure to reload. At the sight of this brave body of footmen, however, they raised a hideous yell, and rushed upon the Lexington infantry, tomahawk in hand. Nothing but the high corn and their loaded rifles could have saved them from destruction. The Indians were cautious in rushing upon a loaded rifle, with only a tomahawk, and when they halted to load their pieces, the Kentuckians ran with great rapidity, turning and dodging through the corn in every direction. Some entered the wood and escaped through the thickets of cane, some were shot down in the corn-field, others maintained a running fight, halting occasionally behind trees and keeping the enemy at bay with their rifles; for, of all men, the Indians are generally the most cautious in exposing themselves to danger.† A stout, active young fellow was so hard

---

*Bradford's Notes. †Id.

pressed by Girty and several savages, that he was compelled to discharge his rifle (however unwilling, having no time to reload it), and Girty fell.

It happened, however, that a piece of thick sole-leather was in his shot-pouch at the time, which received the ball, and preserved his life, although the force of the blow felled him to the ground. The savages halted upon his fall, and the young man escaped. Although the skirmish and the race lasted for more than an hour, during which the cornfield presented a scene of turmoil and bustle which can scarcely be conceived, yet very few lives were lost. Only six of the white men from Lexington were killed and wounded, and probably still fewer of the enemy, as the whites never fired until absolutely necessary, but reserved their loads as a check upon the enemy. Had the Indians pursued them to Lexington, they might have possessed themselves of it without resistance, as there was no force there to oppose them; but after following the fugitives for a few hundred yards, they returned to the hopeless siege of the fort.

It was now near sunset, and the cattle and stock, while attempting to return, as usual, to the fort, were mostly killed; the few sheep were totally destroyed.

By this time the fire on both sides had slackened. The Indians had become discouraged. Their loss in the morning had been heavy, and the country was evidently arming, and would soon be upon them. They had made no impression upon the fort, and without artillery could hope to make none. The chiefs spoke of raising the siege, but Girty determined, since his arms had been unavailing, to try the efficacy of negotiation. He approached, under cover of a thick growth of hemp, to a large stump of a tree, which stood not far from the spot where the dwelling-house of Mr. Rogers was afterward erected, and hailed the fort, demanding a surrender, stating that the forces were commanded by him, and inquired if he was known to the people of the fort. He declared that the prisoners should be protected if they would surrender, which was out of his power if the place was taken by storm, as it would be that night, on the arrival of his cannon and strong reinforcements, which were hourly expected.* This language from Girty, and the recollections by the people in the fort, that cannon were employed in the reduction of Ruddle's and Martin's stations, was calculated to create considerable alarm. But one of the garrison, a young man by the name of Aaron Reynolds, remarkable both for wit and courage, and afterward distinguished for a noble act at the battle of the Blue Licks, perceiving the effect of Girty's speech, took upon himself to reply to it. To Girty's inquiry, "whether the garrison knew him," Reynolds replied "that he was very well known; that he himself had a worthless dog to which he had given the name of 'Simon Girty,' in consequence of his striking resemblance to the man of that name; that if he had either artillery or reinforcements, he might bring them up and be d—d; that if either himself or any of the naked rascals with him found their way into the fort, they would disdain to use their guns against them, but would drive them out again with switches, of which they had collected a great number for that purpose alone; and, finally, he declared that *they* also expected reinforcements; that the whole country was marching to their assistance; and that if Girty and his gang of murderers remained twenty-four hours longer before the fort, their scalps would be found drying in the sun upon the roofs of their cabins."

Girty took great offense at the tone and language of the young Kentuckian, and retired with an expression of sorrow for the inevitable destruction which awaited them on the following morning. He quickly rejoined the chiefs; and instant preparations were made for raising the siege. The night passed away in uninterrupted tranquillity, and at daylight in the morning the Indian camp was found deserted. Fires were still burning brightly, and several pieces of meat were left upon their roasting-sticks, from which it was inferred that they had retreated a short time before daylight.†

---

*Bradford's Notes. †McClung.

And thus ended one of the most remarkable and celebrated sieges known in the history of Indian warfare, and one crowded, brief as it was, with strange and thrilling events. The firing in the morning was in time to prevent the march of nearly all the men to a distant point, and the enemy so far overrated their plan, that instead of drawing the men out, every one prepared for a siege. Then there was the providential circumstance of the wind springing up from the east, and saving the place from the flames. Add to this, the almost miraculous escape of the two couriers to Lexington, the daring charge of the sixteen death-defying heroes from Lexington through a cross-fire of hundreds of Indians, and their entrance into the fort unhurt, and the escape of their gallant comrades on foot, with a loss of only six killed and wounded, when all of them seemed doomed to utter destruction, and we have a chapter of truths stranger far than many a page of highly-wrought fiction. Only two persons, Mitchell and Atkinson, were killed in the fort. One of the most heroic of the brave little garrison, Nicholas Tomlinson, was slightly wounded in the arm. He was one of the most active defenders of his country, and was employed in Harmer's expedition, in 1790, as a spy. At the defeat of a detachment of the army under Colonel John Hardin, on the Oglaze, the daring Tomlinson, being in advance, was literally shot to pieces by an ambuscade of more than one thousand Indians.*

The loss of the Indians in the seige of Bryant's station has never been accurately ascertained, but it is known to have been very considerable. The residence and improvements of Mr. Charlton Rogers now (1872) cover part of the ground upon which the fort stood. The famous spring, from which the heroic women of the garrison drew water, still pours forth a grateful stream.

Swift couriers carried the news of the presence of the Indian army to the various stations, and while the savages were retreating, the hunters were rapidly gathering at Bryant's station, to pursue them. Colonel Daniel Boone ac-

---

*Bradford's Notes.

companied by his youngest son, Isaac, and Samuel, the brave brother of the old pioneer, headed a strong party from Boonesborough. Colonel Stephen Trigg brought up the force from Harrodsburg, and Colonel John Todd commanded the Lexington garrison. Todd and Trigg, as senior colonels, took command.*

Dispatches had been sent to Colonel Benj. Logan, in Lincoln county, during the seige, and he had hastily collected about three hundred men, and started upon his march, but before he was able to reach Bryant's station, the Indians had raised the seige and gone. Colonel Logan followed as fast as possible, in the hope of coming up with those who marched from the neighborhood of Lexington before they overtook the Indians, but met them not far from Bryant's on their return. In the midst of trying scenes of tears and sadness, the misgivings of the wife, and the forebodings of the mother, the brave men made every preparation for the march. On the morning of the 18th of August, their force amounted to one hundred and eighty-two men,† and though it was well-known that the numbers of the enemy were overwhelmingly superior to this, the pursuit was urged with that precipitate courage which has so often been fatal to Kentuckians, and on the afternoon of the same day, the march was commenced.‡

The Indians had followed the buffalo trace, and the Kentuckians had not proceeded more than nine or ten miles, before the lynx-eyed Boone discovered certain signs on the route indicating a willingness on the part of the Indians to be pursued, which was plainly evinced by their leaving a plain trail. Notwithstanding, they evidently used all the means in their power, to conceal their number, for which purpose they marched in single file, treading in each other's footsteps.

The pursuing force, after a hard march, camped that night in the woods only a few miles distant from the now sadly famous battle-gound, the appearance of which, at that time, is thus quaintly described by one§ who fought

---
*G. Rogers Clark.   †Bradford's Notes.   ‡McClung.   §Bradford.

upon its sanguinary soil: "The Blue Licks are situated about forty miles from Lexington, and about thirty-five from Bryant's station. The Licking river at this place is about three hundred feet wide at common water, and forms a semi-elipsis, which embraces on its northeast side, toward Limestone, a great ridge of rocks which had been made bare by the stamping of buffalo and other game, drawn together from time immemorial to drink the water and lick the clay. Two deep ravines, heading in this ridge near each other, and extending in opposite directions, formed the longest diameter of this elipsis. This ridge had very little timber on it, and what it had was very indifferent, and exhibited a very dreary appearance; but the ravines were furnished not only plentifully with timber, but with a thick brushwood also."

On the following day, by an easy march, the Kentuckians reached the lower Blue Licks, where for the first time since the pursuit commenced, they came within view of an enemy. As the miscellaneous crowd of horse and foot reached the southern bank of Licking, they saw a number of Indians ascending the rocky ridge on the other side.

They halted upon the appearance of the Kentuckians, gazed at them for a few moments in silence, and then calmly and leisurely disappeared over the top of the hill. A halt immediately ensued. A dozen or twenty officers met in front of the ranks, and entered into consultation. The wild and lonely aspect of the country around them, their distance from any point of support, with the certainty of their being in the presence of a superior enemy, seems to have inspired a portion of seriousness, bordering upon awe. All eyes were now turned upon Boone, and Colonel Todd asked his opinion as to what should be done. The veteran woodsman, with his usual unmoved gravity, replied:

"That their situation was critical and delicate; that the force opposed to them was undoubtedly numerous and ready for battle, as might readily be seen from the leisurely retreat of the few Indians who had appeared upon the crest of the hill; that he was well acquainted with the ground in the neighborhood of the lick, and was apprehensive that an ambuscade was formed at the distance of a mile in advance, where two ravines, one upon each side of the ridge, ran in such a manner, that a concealed enemy might assail them at once, both in front and flank, before they were apprised of the danger.

"It would be proper, therefore, to do one of two things. Either to await the arrival of Logan, who was now undoubtedly on his march to join them, or if it was determined to attack without delay, that one-half of their number should march up the river, which there bends in an elliptical form, cross at the rapids, and fall upon the rear of the enemy, while the other division attacked in front. At any rate, he strongly urged the necessity of reconnoitering the ground carefully before the main body crossed the river."*

Such was the counsel of Boone. And although no measure could have been much more disastrous than that which was adopted, yet it may be doubted if anything short of an immediate retreat upon Logan, could have saved this gallant body of men from the fate which they encountered. If they divided their force, the enemy, as in Estill's case, might have overwhelmed them in detail; if they remained where they were, without advancing, the enemy would certainly have attacked them, probably in the night, and with a certainty of success. They had committed a great error at first, in not waiting for Logan, and nothing short of a retreat, which would have been considered disgraceful, could now repair it.

Boone was heard in silence and with deep attention. Some wished to adopt the first plan; others preferred the second; and the discussion threatened to be drawn out to some length, when the boiling ardor of McGary, who could never endure the presence of an enemy without instant battle, stimulated him to an act, which had nearly proved distructive to all. He suddenly interrupted the consultation with an Indian war whoop, spurred his horse into the

---

*Bradford and McClung.

stream, and shouted aloud, "Let all who are not cowards, follow me."

The rashness of McGary was contagious. He was followed in quick succession by the whole party, who crossed the river in great disorder and confusion, whilst the officers were reluctantly borne along in the tumult. After crossing the river, no authority was exercised, nor any order observed in the line of march, but every one rushed forward, tumultuously pursuing the road over the rocks to the end of the ridge of hills, where a forest of oaks and deep ravines, with underwood, concealed the enemy from view, who awaited in their ambuscade to receive them.

McGary lead the van of the army, closely followed by Major Harlan and Captain William McBride, supported by the men on horseback. They reached the spot mentioned by Boone, where the two ravines head on each side of the ridge, when Girty, with a chosen part of his tawny host, rushed forward from their covert, and with horrid shrieks and yells, attacked them with great impetuosity. The conflict instantly became hot and sanguinary. The advantageous position occupied by the Indians enabled them to assail the whole of the whites at the same moment. The officers suffered dreadfully, and many were already killed.

The Indians gradually extended their line to turn the right of the Kentuckians and cut off their retreat. This was quickly perceived by the weight of the fire from that quarter, and the rear instantly fell back in disorder, and attempted to rush through their only opening to the river. The motion quickly communicated itself to the van, and a hurried retreat became general. The Indians instantly sprung forward in pursuit, and falling upon them with their tomahawks, made a cruel slaughter. From the battleground to the river, the spectacle was terrible. The horsemen generally escaped, but the foot, particularly the van, which had advanced farthest within the wings of the net, were almost totally destroyed. Colonel Boone, after witnessing the death of his son and many of his dearest friends, found himself almost entirely surrounded at the very commencement of the retreat.

Several hundred Indians were between him and the ford, to which the great mass of fugitives were bending their flight, and to which the attention of the savages was principally directed. Being intimately acquainted with the ground, he, together with a few friends, dashed into the ravine which the Indians had occupied, but which most of them had now left to join in the pursuit. After sustaining one or two heavy fires, and baffling one or two small parties, who pursued him for a short distance, he crossed the river below the ford, by swimming, and entering the wood at a point where there was no pursuit, returned by a circuitous route to Bryant's station. In the mean time, the great mass of the victors and vanquished crowded the bank of the ford.

The slaughter was great in the river. The ford was crowded with horsemen and foot and Indians, all mingled together. Some were compelled to seek a passage above by swimming; some, who could not swim, were overtaken and killed at the edge of the water. One of the Lexington militia, by the name of Benjamin Netherland, who had formerly been strongly suspected of cowardice, here displayed a coolness and presence of mind equally noble and unexpected. Being finely mounted, he had outstripped the great mass of fugitives, and crossed the river in safety. A dozen or twenty horsemen accompanied him, and having placed the river between them and the enemy, showed a disposition to continue their flight without regard to the safety of their friends who were on foot and still struggling with the current. Netherland instantly checked his horse, and in a loud voice, called his companions to halt, fire upon the Indians, and save those still in the stream. The party instantly obeyed, and, facing about, poured a close and fatal discharge of rifles upon the foremost of the pursuers. The enemy instantly fell back from the opposite bank, and gave time to the harassed and miserable footmen to cross in safety.* The check was, however, but momentary. The Indians were seen crossing in great numbers above and

---

*Bradford's Notes.

below, and the flight again became general. Most of the footmen left the great buffalo track, and plunging into the thickets, escaped by a circuitous route to Bryant's station. But little loss was sustained after crossing the river, although the pursuit was urged keenly for twenty miles. From the battle ground to the ford the loss was very heavy, and at that stage of the retreat, there occurred a rare and striking instance of magnanimity, which it would be criminal to omit.* Aaron Reynolds, already famous for his reply to Girty at Bryant's station, after bearing his share in the action with distinguished gallantry, was galloping with several other horsemen in order to reach the ford. The great body of fugitives had preceded them, and their situation was in the highest degree critical and dangerous. About half way between the battle-ground and the river, the party overtook Colonel Patterson, of Lexington, on foot, exhausted by the rapidity of the flight, and in consequence of former wounds received from the Indians, so infirm as to be unable to keep up with the main body of the men on foot. The Indians were close behind him, and his fate seemed inevitable. Reynolds, upon coming up with this brave officer, instantly sprung from his horse, aided Patterson to mount into the saddle, and continued his own flight on foot. Being remarkably active and vigorous, he contrived to elude his pursuers, and turning off from the main road, plunged into the river near the spot where Boone had crossed, and swam in safety to the opposite side. Unfortunately, he wore a pair of buckskin breeches, which had become so heavy and full of water as to prevent his exerting himself with his usual activity, and while sitting down for the purpose of pulling them off, he was overtaken by a party of Indians, and made prisoner.

A prisoner is rarely put to death by the Indians, unless wounded or infirm, until they return to their own country; and then his fate is decided in solemn council. Young Reynolds, therefore, was treated kindly, and compelled to accompany his captors in the pursuit. A small party of

---

*Bradford.

Kentuckians soon attracted their attention, and he was left in charge of three Indians, who, eager in pursuit, in turn committed him to the charge of one of their number, while they followed their companions. Reynolds and his guard jogged along very leisurely; the former totally unarmed; the latter, with a tomahawk and rifle in his hands. At length the Indian stopped to tie his moccasin, when Reynolds instantly sprung upon him, knocked him down with his fist, and quickly disappeared in the thicket which surrounded them. For this act of generosity, Captain Patterson afterward made him a present of two hundred acres of first rate land.

Late in the evening of the same day, most of the survivors arrived at Bryant's station; but many familiar forms were missing. Colonel John Todd, of Lexington, had fallen fighting to the last, with the blood flowing from many a wound. Colonel Stephen Trigg, Majors Silas Harlan, Edward Bulger, Captains John Gordon and William McBride, together with Isaac Boone, son of Colonel Daniel Boone, had all fallen.* Sixty men had been killed in the battle and flight, and seven had been taken prisoners,† part of whom were afterwards put to death by the Indians, as was said, to make their loss even. This account, however, appears very improbable. It is almost incredible that the Indians should have suffered an equal loss. Their superiority of numbers, their advantage of position (being in a great measure sheltered, while the Kentuckians, particularly the horsemen, were much exposed), the extreme brevity of the battle, and the acknowledged bloodiness of the pursuit, all tend to contradict the report that the Indian loss exceeded that of the Kentuckians.

At Lexington, Boone tells us, "many widows were made," and the whole station was given up to the most frantic grief. It was the same at Bryant's station, and soon the melancholy news spread throughout the country and the whole district of Kentucky was covered with mourning for many a long and dreary day. Colonel Logan, after being

---

*Bradford. †Bradford.

joined by many of the friends of the killed and missing from Lexington and Bryant's station, continued his march to the battle-ground, with the hope that success would embolden the enemy, and induce them to remain until his arrival.

On the second day after the battle, in solemn silence the whole party reached the field. The enemy were gone, but the bodies of the Kentuckians still lay unburied on the spot where they had fallen. Immense flocks of buzzards were soaring over the battle ground, and the bodies of the dead had become so much swollen and disfigured, that it was impossible to recognize the features of the most particular friends. Many corpses were floating near the shore of the northern bank, already putrid from the action of the sun, and partially eaten by fishes.* The whole were carefully collected by order of Colonel Logan, and interred as decently as the nature of the soil would permit. Being satisfied that the Indians were by this time, far beyond his reach, he then retraced his steps to Bryant's station, and dismissed his men.

The fatal battle of the Blue Licks like the massacre of Wyoming and Braddock's defeat, which it so much resembled, brought misery and slaughter when least expected, and like them, will be read of with increasing interest as time advances. The last great blow struck by the Indian for the recovery of his favorite hunting grounds, will become adorned by age, with a golden halo of romantic attractions not less bright than that which now encircles the last struggle of the chivalric old Moors for the possession of Spain.

The women of Lexington—women like the one who came to the rescue of the dying hunter at the gate of the fort—were not idle during this time of siege, and battle, and retreat. With tearful hearts, but brave words, they hastened on their husbands and brothers to the aid of Bryant's station, and with but feeble help, guarded the fort until relieved by the footmen who escaped from the savages

---

*Bradford's Notes.

who surrounded that apparently doomed place.* They tenderly dressed the wounds of the brave fugitives with many a thought of Ruddell's and Martin's station, shuddering at the sound of the distant war whoop, and praying for the defeat of the savage army. The seige was raised. Elated with success, the settlers, young and old, abandoned Lexington to join the force now wild to pursue the Indians; and again the fort was left to be garrisoned this time, almost entirely, by the brave women who were fit companions of the men who charged through twenty times their number, to aid the little band in Bryant's station. Who can picture the hours of watchfulness and solicitude, the alarms, the terror, and the heroic conduct of these true, devoted, and undaunted mothers of Lexington, while discharging their sublime duty. The pioneer women of Lexington, may we not class them with the patriotic women of the Revolution? Were the women of old colonial Lexington stouter-hearted than those of the Lexington of the savage wilderness?

> "The mothers of our forest land,
>   Their bosoms pillowed men;
> And proud were they by such to stand
>   In hammock, fort or glen,
> To load the sure old rifle,
>   To run the leaden ball,
> To watch a battling husband's place,
>   And fill it, should he fall." †

One of the most thrilling and remarkable incidents in the entire history of border life and warfare, occurred at this time.‡ A settler named James Morgan, with more daring than prudence, lived with his wife and one infant child in a cabin outside the fort at Bryant's station. When he discovered the presence of the Indians by their firing on the fort, he raised one of the slabs of the cabin floor, concealed his wife under it, strung his baby to his back, and unbarred the door to escape. As he bounded out he was attacked by several Indians. He killed two of them and

---

*Bradford.   †W. D. Gallagher.   ‡Western Monthly, 1833.

outstripped the rest, but an Indian dog pursued him with all the ferocity of a wild cat; he finally succeeded in killing him: and then looking back for the first time, saw his cabin and part of the station in flames. In agony at the impending fate of his tenderly beloved wife, but utterly unable to assist her, he watched his burning dwelling until he was on the point of being captured, when he again retreated, and finally arrived at Lexington.

When the Indians raised the seige he left his baby in the care of one of the sympathizing women in Lexington station, and hastened with a throbbing heart to the spot where his cabin had so lately stood. He found a heap of ashes, some smoldering embers, and a few poor charred bones which he reverently gathered and buried, almost insane with grief and the desire for revenge. He went to the Blue Licks, and while rushing into the midst of the conflict, he saw an Indian wearing a handkerchief which he recognized as his wife's. He raised his rifle and killed him with savage joy. During the retreat he was wounded, and after dragging himself some distance from the scene of conflict, he had laid himself down to die, when he was discovered and rescued by the wife he had mourned as dead. It turned out that the Indians who rushed into his cabin after his escape, quarreled over the little spoil in it, got to fighting, and one of them was killed. In her fright, Mrs. Morgan screamed, was discovered, and was carried a captive along with the retreating savages, but managed to escape, and at once set out to find her husband and child. The bones found and buried by Morgan, were those of the Indian who was killed by his comrades.

Clark and retribution followed the Indians after the battle of the Blue Licks, as Sullivan and extermination followed them after the massacre of Wyoming. The call of the Lion of Kentucky for troops was promptly answered by a thousand mounted riflemen, a number of whom were from Lexington, and in September, after a rapid march under their brilliant leader, they penetrated the heart of the Indian country.* Five of the Chillicothe towns, where the savages had gathered before starting to Bryant's station, were reduced to ashes, their crops were destroyed, the country for miles around made desolate, and such of the swiftly-fleeing Indians as were overtaken met with no quarter at the hands of the enraged avengers of the pioneers who were slaughtered at the Blue Licks. The Indians were disheartened. They had dealt their heaviest blow, and it had rebounded against themselves. They now despaired of ever recovering Kentucky, and no great body of them ever after invaded the state. But though they came not with an army, the rifle, tomahawk, and scalping knife of the plundering and murdering Indian was not yet entirely banished from the now truly Dark and Bloody Ground.

Lexington station gained another school-teacher this year, in the person of John Filson, the author, in 1784, of the first history ever written of Kentucky. He afterward gave to Cincinnati her first name, "Losantiville." Filson was an early adventurer with Daniel Boone, and after the discoverer of Kentucky returned to Lexington, in October, from the Chillicothe towns, Filson wrote, at his dictation, the only narrative of his life extant from the old pioneer's own lips. This narrative was indorsed at the time by James Harrod, Levi Todd, and Boone himself. Filson taught in Lexington for several years, and did no little to secure the early organization of Transylvania Seminary.† He was killed by the Indians near Cincinnati, in 1789.

In the November after the Blue Lick's massacre, Colonel Thomas Marshall, surveyor of Fayette county, opened an office in Lexington, and a calamitous scramble for land recommenced.‡ Colonel Marshall was a Virginian, had distinguished himself in the war of the Revolution, and soon became one of the leading citizens of Kentucky.

---

*Butler and Marshall. †Old Gazette. ‡Butler.

CHAPTER X.

Peace—McKinney and the Wild Cat—The Old Fort—Lot Owners and Early Settlers—Christopher Greenup, Humphrey Marshall, John Sharp, Robert Todd, John Carty, Sen., Benjamin Howard, William Dudley, William Russell.

ON the 20th of January, 1783, hostilities ceased between the armies of the United States and England, and the news was received with great joy by the settlers in Fayette county. This much desired event did not necessarily bring with it security from the Indians, but the pioneers hoped it would. At any rate Clark had demoralized the savages, so that this year was one of comparative peace. The Lexington settlers were now, for the first time, encouraged to build cabins outside the walls of the fort, and the land which they had bought with the heavy price of blood and suffering they commenced to occupy and improve. Some attention could now be paid to gardening; vegetables and other comforts of civilized life began to appear. The live stock, unmolested by the Indians, fattened and multiplied, and the settlers, free from the prison-like restraints of the fort, felt a new pleasure in life.

A log school-house, located on Cheapside, was one of the first buildings erected outside of the fort walls, and here, early one morning in June,* Mr. John McKinney, the teacher, became the hero of a now celebrated combat. He was sitting at his rude desk waiting for the appearance of his little band of pupils, when a wild cat of uncommon size made its appearance at the door, and, without seeming to notice him, suddenly leaped into the room, snapping its jaws and foaming at the mouth. On observing it, his first

---

* Western Review.

thought was, what fine sport it might afford him, if he had a good dog and the door was closed. But, to his great surprise, on casting its eyes around and seeing him, instead of precipitately retreating as he had expected, it advanced toward him in a menacing manner. He instantly reached forward to a table near him, and attempted to grasp a ruler, but before he had obtained it, the animal was upon him, and seized him by the teeth on the collar bone near his throat. With some difficulty, by striking at it upward under his jacket, he relieved himself from this grasp, but the enraged animal instantly caught him by the right side, and, with its long crooked tusks, pierced through his clothes, and penetrated between his ribs, where it held him so fast that he found it impossible to extricate himself. At the same time its sharp claws were employed with astonishing rapidity in cutting off his clothes, and tearing the flesh from his side. From its situation he was unable to strike it with any considerable force, but, in the effort, only wounded his own hand against the table. Finding he could do nothing in that way, he seized the animal with both arms, brought its hinder part between his thighs, and pressed it with all his force against the table. It struggled violently, and fearing it might escape from his grasp and again attack him with its claws, he now for the first time made an exclamation, in the hope that some one might come to his relief. The ladies, who were engaged near the place milking their cows, were most of them alarmed at the cry, and ran precipitately into the fort, exclaiming that something was killing Mr. McKinney in the school-house. Three of them, however, Mrs. Masterson, Mrs. Collins, and Miss Thompson, being less timid than the rest, ran toward the house, and after some deliberation among themselves as to who should venture to look in first, entered the door. Mr. McKinney, perceiving that they were females, and knowing Mrs. Masterson to be in a delicate state of health, was fearful of alarming them, and, notwithstanding his own dreadful situation, assumed an air of composure, and, with a smile, observed: "Don't be alarmed, it is only a cat I have caught, and I want some person to assist me in killing it." He was thus careful not to inform them, as he might have done with far greater correctness, that THE CAT HAD CAUGHT HIM. The ladies then boldly advanced toward him, and one of them, stooping down and observing the size of the animal, exclaimed, "what a monster!" ran to the door and called a gentleman who happened to be passing by. He came in, and proposed cutting off the claws of the cat, but Mr. McKinney, perceiving it to lie perfectly still, concluded he had killed it, which, on rising, he found to be the fact. They then endeavored to draw out the animal's teeth from Mr. McKinney's side, but finding them so hooked in between the ribs that they could not extricate them, the whole party left the school-house, and advanced toward the fort, to which, by this time, the alarmed and excited people were rushing in crowds, under the impression that the Indians were about to attack the place. After reaching the fort, new efforts were made to relieve Mr. McKinney from the tusks of the cat, which were at length rendered successful by placing its head in the same position as when it made the attack.

Notwithstanding his wounds, Mr. McKinney attended his school that morning, but at noon found himself so exhausted, and his pain so extreme, that he was compelled to dismiss his scholars and resort to his bed. By proper applications, however, he was soon relieved; his wounds healed rapidly and his usual health was speedily restored. McKinney afterward settled in Bourbon county, and lived to a green old age, and the account here given is an almost verbatim statement made by him in 1820.

The alarm occasioned by the wild cat's attack upon McKinney was the last one that ever brought the garrison together in arms within the fort. The block-house remained standing for several years after this, however, as the settlers never knew at what time they might need the protection of its friendly walls. At last, the only vestige of the "Old Lexington Fort" went down before the power of advancing civilization, but the memory of the trials and sufferings endured within it, recollections of Boone, Kenton, Harrod, G. Rogers Clark, Patterson, Todd, and many others it had sheltered, and remembrances of the days of grief and anguish that hung like a pall over all its inmates after the bloody ambuscade at the Blue Licks, consecrated it till death in the hearts of the pioneers of Lexington.

In this year (1783), the trustees reserved three lots "where the garrison stands," for public use, and other lots were disposed of to the following persons,* viz: Humphrey Marshall, Benjamin Netherland, Caleb Williams, Robert Todd, John Carty, Martin Dickinson, Samuel January, Christopher Greenup, Wm. Anderson, John Sharp, Thomas Marshall, Patrick Owens, Robert Parker, Valentine Dickinson, Widow McDonald, Christopher Kirtner, George Shepherd, John Mikins, Archibald Dickinson, Andrew Steele, John McDowell, William Steele, Stoffre Zunwalt, James Mitchell, Benjamin Haydon, Jane Todd, David Blanchard, Widow Kirtner, Amor Batterton, John Brooke, Matthew Patterson, William Galloway, Adam Zunwalt, Jacob Zunwalt.

The names of many of these lot owners are linked with the history of the state. Christopher Greenup, who had been a soldier in the war of the Revolution, settled in Kentucky, together with many of his comrades in arms, at the close of that struggle. When he located in Lexington, he had just been sworn in as an attorney at law in the old district court. He was elected governor of Kentucky in 1804, and died in 1818.†

Humphrey Marshall, eminent in his day as a land lawyer, represented Fayette in the Danville convention of 1787, and in the Virginia convention which ratified the constitution of the United States. His duel with Mr. Clay is well known. He subsequently removed to Franklin county, and was long one of its most distinguished citizens. After having served as United States Senator, he published a well-known and greatly esteemed, though rather partisan history of Kentucky. He died at the residence of his son, Thomas A. Marshall, in Lexington.‡

Major Ben. Netherland, named in the above list of lot-

---

*Trustees' Book.   †Collins, 332.   ‡Collins, 317.

owners, who had made himself noted by his gallant conduct at the Blue Licks battle, was born in Powhatan county, Virginia, on the 27th day of February, 1755. During the war of the Revolution he volunteered his services as a private soldier in the army of the South, under General Lincoln, and was taken a prisoner of war at the siege of Savannah, where he was kept in close confinement for ten months. At the end of this time he made his escape, but was retaken again as a prisoner of war, and confined at San Augustine, a British post in Florida. Whilst the American army was in full retreat from Savannah, he again attempted to make his escape, and was successful. He joined the army at Beaufort, in South Carolina. After he had served twelve months as a private soldier, he was promoted to a lieutenancy. He came to Kentucky in 1781, settled at Lexington station, and became a prominent actor in all the Indian wars that for so long a time deluged Kentucky in blood. He finally removed to Jessamine county, where he died, in October, 1838, and was buried with the honors of war.*

John Sharp, whose son was afterward jailer of Fayette county, was one of the Lexington militia ambuscaded at Bryant's station. He was pursued by several Indians, but managed to keep them at bay with his rifle, until he escaped in a cane thicket.

Robert Todd was senator from Fayette in the first session of the legislature; was for a long time circuit judge, and held other important positions.

John Carty, Sen., was born in 1764,† in Burlington, New Jersey, of which place his parents were old citizens. His young school-days were interrupted by the bloody struggle of the colonists for independence, and while yet a boy, at the age of seventeen, he assisted at the repulse of the British at Springfield, in his native state, and shortly after shared in the campaign which ended in the defeat and surrender of Cornwallis. At the close of the war he joined the host of westward bound emigrants, and settled perma-

---

*Old Kentucky Statesman.   †Family Record.

nently at "Lexington station," together with a number of his comrades in arms. His wife, Mary Ayers, was born near Annapolis, Maryland.

The freaks of fortune are marvelous. Shortly after his arrival, the young settler was offered a large tract of land comprising several "out-lots," then thickly covered with cane and forest trees, in exchange for his well-worn old fashioned "bull's eye" watch; but, as the ancient timepiece had been his father's, and as he had already one lot to improve, he refused to exchange it for "cheap canebrakes."* Much of the best part of Hill street now occupies the refused "canebrakes," and is valued at several hundred thousand dollars.

John Carty, Sen., was one of the organizers of the "Society of the Cincinnati," established at a very early day in Lexington, by citizens who had participated in the Revolutionary war;† and he and the elegant and amiable Waldemarde Mentelle, Sen., introduced into Kentucky the manufacture of earthenware,‡ which, in that day of slab tables, wooden spoons, and horn cups, was welcomed with gratitude by the pioneers, and soon became an important branch of trade. John Carty, Sen., was with General Anthony Wayne in his celebrated Indian campaign of 1794, and participated in the decisive victory of August 20, near the river Miami of the lakes. During that war, he was sergeant of a company of which the afterward "General" Harrison was then lieutenant. Mr. Carty lived to see an elegant and flourishing city take the place of the canebrakes and the old fort. He died at his residence in Lexington, November 25, 1845, at the green old age of eighty-one, and was buried in the family lot in the Episcopal Cemetery. He was mourned by a multitude of friends, by whom he had long been greatly beloved and respected. One of his sons, Henry Carty, died a glorious death on the bloody field of Buena Vista, and now sleeps under the shadow of the state military monument at Frankfort.

John Carty, the successful merchant and true man, who

---

*Old Inhabitants.   †Old Gazette.   ‡S. D. McCullough.

died April 8, 1867, was another son, whose rare sagacity and noble qualities will long be remembered by Lexington.

Benjamin Howard, a native of Goochland county, Virginia, was another soldier of the Revolution, who settled in Fayette about the year 1783. He received five wounds at the battle of Guilford Court-house. One of his daughters was the first wife of Robert Wickliffe, Sen., and his only son, Benjamin, was governor of Missouri. This venerable pioneer died at the extraordinary age of one hundred and three years, in Lexington, at the residence of Major Woolley (who married a grand-daughter), after having been a member of the Presbyterian Church for upward of eighty years.*

Colonel William Dudley, of Spottsylvania county, Virginia, emigrated to Kentucky when quite young, and settled at an early date in Fayette. His tragic fate is well known. He served under General Harrison in the campaign of 1813, as colonel of Kentucky militia. On the 5th of May in that year, he was sent with some raw troops to silence a British battery opposite Fort Meigs. He succeeded in spiking the guns, and then, in a moment of rash gallantry, attacked some troops in the vicinity, was surrounded by the Indians, and terribly defeated. Weak and disabled by wounds, Colonel Dudley defended himself desperately against a swarm of savages who closed in upon him. He fell at last, and his body was mutilated in a most barbarous manner.† The disastrous fate of this brave man and his command will cause "Dudley's defeat" to be long remembered by Kentuckians.

Colonel William Russell, one of the most distinguished of the settlers of Fayette county, arrived in 1783. He was a native of Culpepper county, Virginia, and was born in 1758. He served his country well in the revolutionary struggle, and bore a valiant part in the glorious and decisive victory of King's Mountain. After removing to Kentucky, he successively held posts of danger and honor under Scott, Wilkinson, and Wayne, in their expeditions against the Indians; was made colonel in the regular

---

*Collins.   †Combs and Collins.

army; was a prominent actor on the bloody field of Tippecanoe; was assigned the command of the frontier of Indiana, Illinois, and Missouri, and led several successful expeditions against the Indians. He represented Fayette repeatedly in the legislature, and was always one of her most useful and honored citizens. Russell county, in this state, was, with great propriety, named in his honor.* Colonel Russell died, July 3, 1825, at his old home in the county he had served so well.

---

*Collins.

CHAPTER XI.

The Village of Lexington—First Dry Goods Store—A Disciple of Tom Paine—The First General Election—James Wilkinson—John Coburn—First Presbyterian Church—The Rankin Schism—Pastors—Church Edifices—Incidents.

By this time (1784), Lexington had assumed the appearance of a frontier village. The few cabins which existed, were all log ones, and very much scattered; Main street was extended a short distance through and beyond the fort, in the direction of the present Lexington Cemetery, but it was sadly obstructed by roots and stumps, and in bad weather was almost impassable; the favorite paths of the settlers were "traces" made as hard as modern roads, by the wild animals which had traveled over them for centuries. There was a one-story log school-house, but no church building, and most of the present city was then occupied by groves, corn-fields, cow pastures, and patches of cane. But the coming and going of emigrants made the village look lively in spite of disadvantages, and as the emigrants frequently brought with them articles much needed by the settlers, and as game was abundant, and the soil was being successfully cultivated, the inhabitants began to live better, and they even found time for amusements. Trials of skill with the rifle, horse and foot races, and dancing were the pastimes, as most of them are yet, in modern Lexington; "house raisings" are not to be forgotten, nor "fives," nor "long bullets," a game in which the sturdy settlers vied with each other, in efforts to jerk a cannon ball to the greatest distance. Much to the delight of the inhabitants, particularly the female portion, that extraordinary and welcome novelty, a dry goods store, was opened in the village by General James Wilkinson, in the spring of 1784.* It was the second one of the kind opened in Kentucky, and the gaudy calico and other "store finery," gave immense satisfaction. The goods came from Philadelphia to Pittsburg by wagon, from thence by flat-boat to "Limestone," now Maysville, and from thence to Lexington on pack horses, which traveled slowly in single file over the narrow "trace" which connected the two settlements.

A novel trial took place in the village of Lexington, in the latter part of May, 1784, caused by the appearance of a disciple of Tom Paine, named Galloway, who propagated the doctrine of his master, that Virginia had no right to the lands of Kentucky, which ought to be taken possession of by Congress. Encouraged by Galloway, several persons actually took preliminary steps toward appropriating their neighbors lands, under an act of Congress which he assured them would soon be passed. A great hubbub was the result, and Galloway was arrested; but upon what ground could he be punished, was the perplexing question. Fortunately, after much searching, an old law of Virginia was found, which inflicted a penalty in tobacco at the discretion of the court, upon the "propagation of false news, to the disturbance of the good people of the colony." Galloway was quickly fined a thousand pounds of tobacco, but as it was impossible to get so much tobacco at that time in Kentucky, he had a fine chance to spend some time in the stocks. At last he was let off on condition that he would leave the district, which he joyfully did without loss of time.†

During the summer, at the suggestion of prominent citizens of Kentucky, the militia companies of Fayette and of the other counties of the district each elected a delegate to meet in convention, at Danville, to consider the subject of self-defense,‡ as it was believed at that time that the Indians were preparing to again invade Kentucky. The election was accordingly held, and the convention met,

---

*Marshall. †Id. ‡Id.

December 27, 1784. This convention proved to be the entering wedge to separation from Virginia.

General James Wilkinson, whom we have already mentioned as having settled in Lexington this year, was probably the most eminent of the many distinguished officers and soldiers of the Revolution, who had so much to do with the rapid advancement which Lexington made in refinement and intelligence. General Wilkinson was born in Maryland, in 1757. He went into the American army at the very commencement of the Revolution, and was appointed captain when but eighteen. He served with Arnold in Canada, was on Gates' staff as lieutenant-colonel, was brevetted brigadier-general in 1777, was at the surrender of Burgoyne, and subsequently served in the legislature of Pennsylvania. When he came to Lexington, at the close of the war, he represented a large trading company formed in Philadelphia. From this time forward, he was one of the most energetic and influential of the leaders in the early civil and military conflicts of Kentucky. In 1784, he made a speech in Lexington, urging the immediate separation of Kentucky from Virginia, headed the "country" party which favored it, strongly opposed the "court" party led by Colonel Thomas Marshall, and was twice a delegate from Fayette to Danville conventions. His appearance at this time is thus described by one with whom he was by no means a favorite :*

"A person not quite tall enough to be perfectly elegant, was compensated by its symmetry and appearance of health and strength. A countenance open, mild, capacious, and beaming with intelligence; a gait firm, manly, and facile; manners bland, accommodating, and popular; an address easy, polite, and gracious, invited approach, gave access, assured attention, cordiality, and ease. By these fair forms he conciliated; by these he captivated. The combined effect was greatly advantageous to the general on a first acquaintance, which a further intercourse contributed to modify."

During the summer of 1787, General Wilkinson origi-

*H. Marshall.

nated and opened up trade between Lexington and New Orleans. He subsequently commanded successful expeditions against the Indians, was made brigadier of regular infantry, and commanded the right wing of Wayne's army in the battle of the Maumee. In 1796, he was appointed general in chief of the northwestern army, and in 1806, governor of Louisiana Territory. It was while he occupied this last position, that he was charged with favoring Burr's designs to form a new empire, of which New Orleans was to be the capital, but an investigation demanded by himself cleared him of these allegations.* In 1816, he wrote his voluminous "Memoirs," another example of his great physical and mental energies. This enterprising man and distinguished soldier, who did so much for the material welfare of Lexington, and reflected so much honor upon his adopted home, died near the city of Mexico, December 28, 1825. General Wilkinson's residence in Lexington was on the site of the house now standing on the corner of Main and the alley next the negro Baptist church, between Broadway and Jefferson.

The prospects of Lexington as a future mercantile point gave her another accession in 1784, in the person of Judge John Coburn, who afterward became an influential democratic politician, judge of the territory of Michigan, and one of the most efficient political writers of his time in this state. He was a citizen of Lexington for ten years, during which he married Miss Mary Moss, of Fayette. He finally settled in Mason county, and died there in 1823.†

The first Christian church established in Lexington was organized in 1784, by the Presbyterians,‡ who were more numerous in the village at that time than any other religious people. They secured a lot and erected a log house of worship, on the southeastern corner of Walnut and Short streets, where city school No. 1 now stands, and called to the pastorate of the church, the Rev. Adam Rankin, of Augusta county, Virginia, who arrived early in October of the same year (1784). The church was first

---

*Am. Ency.   †Bishop and Davidson.   ‡Id.

known as "Mount Zion," but is now more generally recognized as "Mr. Rankin's Church."

Mr. Rankin's call was the signal for strife. The Presbyterian churches at that time were convulsed with disputes upon Psalmody, one party strongly claiming that the literal version of the old Psalms of David should be used, and the others as stoutly demanding the version of Dr. Watts. Mr. Rankin was a declared enemy of the Watts' version, and finding it in use in Mount Zion church on his arrival, labored earnestly for its expulsion. In course of time, two parties were formed, and the congregation was soon in the same distracted condition as many bodies of their brethren. Finally, in 1789, charges were preferred against Mr. Rankin, before the presbytery of Transylvania, one of them being, that he had "debarred from the table of the Lord, such persons as approved Watts' psalmody." Mr. Rankin made a trip to London about this time, and his case was not tried until April, 1792, when he protested against the proceedings of the presbytery, and withdrew from it, carrying with him a majority of his congregation which sustained and indorsed his action, and claimed and held the meeting-house, on the corner of Walnut and Short. In May, 1793, Mr. Rankin and adherants joined the Associate Reformed Church, and remained connected with it for twenty-five years, but at the end of that time, broke off from it and became independent. After Mr. Rankin resigned the pastorate of Mount Zion, in 1825, the church rapidly declined, and after struggling on for some years, finally became extinct.

Mr. Rankin was a native of Pennsylvania, and was born in 1755. He graduated at Liberty Hall (now Washington and Lee University), in 1780, and two years after married Margaret McPheeters, of Augusta county, Virginia. He was a talented, intolerant, eccentric, and pious man, and was greatly beloved by his congregation, which clung to him with a devoted attachment through all his fortunes. After leaving Lexington, he set out on a tour to Jerusalem, but died on the way, in Philadelphia, November 25, 1827.

The party in Mr. Rankin's church favoring Watts'

psalms, and adhering to the presbytery, gave up Mount Zion church to the seceders, and took "the new meeting-house," a half-finished frame building commenced some time before the church trouble had culminated. This edifice stood on the corner of Short and Mill streets, fronted on Mill, and the lot on which it stood, which had been "granted to the *Prisbyterians*,"* by the trustees of Lexington, extended back to the present Cheapside. The subscriptions for building this house were mostly paid in bacon, hemp, and corn.† By 1795, through the exertions of Robert Patterson, John Maxwell, James Trotter, Robert Megowan, Robert Steel, and other members of the church, the building was put in a comfortable condition, and the Rev. James Welsh, of Virginia, was called to fill its pulpit, and was ordained the succeeding year first pastor‡ of what is now called the First Presbyterian Church. Ministers of all churches were so poorly paid at that day, that most of them had to resort to other means than preaching to obtain a living. Mr. Welsh was no exception to the rule, and was obliged to practice medicine to support his family, and did so up to 1799, when he was appointed professor of languages in Transylvania University. In that year, also, the church edifice was further improved, a gallery was made, a cupola raised, and a bell hung. Mr. Welsh continued in the pastorate of the church up to 1804, after which the pulpit was temporarily filled by Dr. James Blythe, then president of Transylvania University; Rev. Robert Stuart, nearly forty years pastor at Walnut Hill, and the faithful and earnest John Lyle, all of whom served at different times until the installation of the second regular pastor, the Rev. Robert M. Cunningham, of Pennsylvania, in 1807.

Just before Mr. Cunningham came, the church leased or sold its property on Mill and Short, and commenced the erection of a brick house of worship on the southwest corner of Broadway and Second streets. This house was opened and the pews rented in the summer of 1808.‖

Mr. Cunningham remained in charge of the church until

---

*Trustees' Book. †Kentucky Gazette. ‡Davidsons.
‖Old Journal.

1822. He died in Alabama, in 1839. Mr. Cunningham's pulpit was frequently filled by Rev. William L. McCalla, then a young minister, and also by Dr. John Poage Campbell. Mr. McCalla was the son of that good man, Andrew McCalla, of Lexington, Kentucky. He was at one time chaplain to the navy of the Republic of Texas, and was noted for his powers as a debater. Dr. Campbell (whose father was one of the early settlers of Lexington) was born in Virginia in 1767, and lived to be one of the most brilliant and scholarly ministers of his church in Kentucky. Gifted as he was, he was compelled to eke out a living on a miserable salary, and at one time his family existed for six weeks on pumpkins only; but so proud and sensitive was he, that the fact did not become known until accidentally discovered by his neighbors.* He died in 1814, from disease contracted by exposure while preaching. In 1815, the Second Presbyterian Church was founded, and its history will be found under that date. In July, 1817, during the pastorate of Mr. Cunningham, while the congregation was at worship, the church was struck by lightning, and two ladies were killed.

The Rev. Nathan Hall, of Garrard county, Kentucky, succeeded Mr. Cunningham in 1823. He was the initiator of the protracted meetings which resulted in the great revival of 1828, which gave the finishing blow to infidelity, which before that had been only too prevalent in Lexington. Mr. Hall was a powerful exhorter, and on one occasion, after several vigorous efforts, admitted over a hundred persons to the church. Mr. Hall was pastor of the church for twenty-three years, during which time it greatly prospered; but, unfortunately, just a little while before he resigned his charge, a number of his congregation became dissatisfied, seceded, and united with the McChord or Second Church. Mr. Hall died in Columbus, Missouri, June 22, 1858.

Dr. Robert J. Breckinridge, long the most prominent minister of the Presbyterian Church of Kentucky, followed Mr. Hall in 1847, and continued in the pastorate until 1853,

---

*Davidson's History.

when he removed to Danville, having been appointed professor in the Theological Seminary at that place. Dr. Breckinridge was a son of Hon. John Breckinridge, and was born in Fayette county, Kentucky, March 8, 1800, graduated at Union College in 1819, commenced the practice of law in Lexington in 1823, after which he repeatedly represented Fayette county in the Kentucky legislature. In 1828 he connected himself with the Second Presbyterian Church of Lexington, retired from political life, devoted himself to the study of theology, and in October, 1832, was ordained pastor of the First Presbyterian Church of Baltimore, where he became distinguished as a minister, and noted for his anti-slavery views and for his bold and uncompromising opposition to Roman Catholicism. During his pastorate of the First Presbyterian Church of Lexington, he wrote his work on the "Internal Evidences of Christianity," and a few years after, published his "Theology, Objectively and Subjectively Considered," which are considered his most able productions. At the beginning of the late war, Dr. Breckenridge and others established the *Danville Review*, which strongly supported both the Federal Government and the General Assembly. Dr. B. died December 27, 1871, and was buried in the Lexington Cemetery.

The successor of Dr. Breckinridge was Rev. J. D. Matthews, whose ministry was so acceptable to the congregation that he was for many years retained as pastor, and much beloved and esteemed. In 1853 he succeeded Dr. Breckinridge as Superintendent of Public Instruction. In 1857, while Dr. Matthews had charge of the church, the old house of worship, which had been used for fifty years, was torn down, and the building now owned and used by the Broadway Christian Church was built, and all went on harmoniously and prosperously until the beginning of the late war. All during the war, trouble was brewing from causes too recent to require mention, and resulted, at the close of that terrible struggle in an open rupture in both the First and Second Churches, and the formation of two congregations in each church. In the First Church, Dr.

Matthews was the pastor of the Southern Assembly party, and Rev. R. Valentine pastor of that of the General Assembly. In May, 1869, the difficulty was adjusted, and the church property distributed. The pastors of the several churches resigned. The two congregations adhering to the Southern Assembly united, and the other two adhering to the General Assembly did the same, forming two churches out of four. The property of the churches was valued and divided in proportion to membership. The Broadway property fell to the Southern Assembly party, now known as the First Church, and the Market street house to the General Assembly adherents, or the present Second Church. In March, 1870, Rev. William Dinwiddie, of Virginia, the present efficient and beloved pastor of the First Church, commenced his ministerial labors in Lexington. In May of the same year, the church on the corner of Second and Broadway was sold to the Christian congregation, and a new, large, and handsome edifice was commenced on Mill street, between Church and Second, and completed in the spring of 1872.

CHAPTER XII.

Town Fork—Taverns—Streets—Elections—Bourbon County Created—Mrs. Vaughn, the First White Woman born in Kentucky.

THE state of affairs in Lexington, in the year 1785, may be inferred from a number of things. " Main Cross street," now Broadway, was opened. The trustees ordered "all cabins, cow-pens, and hog-pens to be removed from the streets."* Notice was given that all vacant lots would be reclaimed, " if not improved in one year by the erection of a good hewed log-house on the same."† Robert Parker was appointed the first surveyor of the town, and clerk of the trustees, and allowed four shillings and sixpence for every deed by him drawn."‡ Boys were prohibited from obstructing the "gangway" over Town Fork, when fishing in that stream, which was then of quite a respectable size, in fact, frequently when there was a " rise," it would cover the entire width of the present Vine and Water streets.

The first tavern of which Lexington could boast, was opened about this time. It stood on West Main street, " between Main Cross (Broadway), and the graveyard" (Baptist churchyard). A little swinging sign in front of the comfortable size log-house bore the coat of arms of Virginia, and the ambitious announcement, " Entertainment for man and beast, by James Bray."

The early taverns of Lexington were veritable old English " Inns," with quaint signs, smiling bonifaces, and everything to match. Robert Megowan's tavern, sign of the " Sheaf of Wheat," was the second one built. It was a two-

---

*Trustees' Book. †Id. ‡Id.

story log-house, stood on Main street, between Upper and Limestone, occupying the site of the building now used by Thomas Bradley. In 1792, the first State Treasurer's office was temporarily in this tavern. These taverns were succeeded by "The Buffalo," kept by John McNair, on Main street, opposite the present court-house, and Kiser's "Indian Queen," which stood on the corner of Hill and Broadway, on part of the lot now owned by Mr. John T. Miller. This "house of entertainment" was kept by the grandfather of our highly respected fellow-citizen, Mr. Ben. Kiser, now probably the oldest native resident of Lexington. Ayers' tavern, sign of the "Cross Keys," was on the corner of Spring and Main. Satterwhite's "Eagle" tavern was on Short, back of the court-house. Usher's "Don't Give up the Ship," stood on Short, near the Lusby house, and the noted old Brent tavern was on Jordan's Row, near the corner of Upper and Main. The Phœnix Hotel is the oldest house of entertainment now in existence in Lexington. It was first known about the year 1800, as "Postlethwaite's tavern," and then as "Wilson's." The famous Aaron Burr was its guest at one time during Wilson's proprietorship. His presence was first detected by a young boy,* who saw him as he entered town on horseback, followed by his white man-servant, and recognized him by a wonderfully faithful representation he had seen of him in a collection of wax works exhibited in Lexington, a short time before. The tavern was next known as "Keene's," and then as "Postlethwaite's and Brennan's," since which time it has been kept by Messrs. John Brennan, Chiles, Worley, Robinson, and others, and under the name of "Phœnix Hotel," has for many years been known far and wide.

We might mention here, that Mill street, which was not opened for some time after "Main Cross," received its name from a cow-path which led out to a wind-mill, which stood near the present work-house. Limestone street was opened still later, and was so called from the fact that it was part of the road leading to "Limestone," now Mays-

---
*Ben. Kiser.

ville. This street is now inappropriately and unfortunately called "Mulberry."

A new county was created by Virginia, in 1785, out of the immense territory of Fayette, and given the name of Bourbon. Two elections were also held in Fayette this year, to choose delegates to the second and third Danville conventions, which assembled in May and August respectively. The delegates elected to the second convention were: Robert Todd, James Trotter, Levi Todd, and Caleb Wallace. Those elected to the third one were: James Wilkinson, Levi Todd, Caleb Wallace, and Robert Patterson.

The first white woman born in the savage wilds of Kentucky lived for many years in Lexington. Here she died, and here she sleeps. Many now living still remember the venerable Mrs. Rhoda Vaughn, the first born of the wilderness. She was the daughter of that Captain John Holder, spoken of by Boone in his narrative, as the man who pursued the Indians who had attacked Hoy's station in August, 1782. Captain Holder was one of the old pioneer's earliest companions. He assisted in building and defending Boonesborough fort; and within the palisades of that noted stronghold, and about the year 1776, his daughter, afterward Mrs. Vaughn, was born. Her earliest recollections were of savages, sufferings, alarms, and bloodshed; and she passed her infant years in the midst of memorable sieges and desperate conflicts. When she grew to womanhood, and was married, her father started her in life with a home and servants, but she lost both in a few years, by her husband's mismanagement, and after his death, times with her grew worse and worse.

At a very early day, she settled in Fayette county, and subsequently made Lexington her home, and here she remained and raised her children. One of her sons was the gallant adjutant, Edward M. Vaughn, a Lexington volunteer, who fell upon the bravely contested field of Buena Vista, in 1847. His blood-soaked gauntlets were carried reverently to his mother, and they told at once, to her stricken heart, the same tragic and eloquent story that the armless and battered shield expressed to the Spartan mother in the classic days of old. Other afflictions and misfortunes followed; and destitute and desolate, the brave old lady struggled on through a life, not unfrequently made brighter by kind and sympathetic friends. Mrs. Vaughn lived for some time in the residence lately occupied by Rev. J. D. Matthews, on Winchester street, between Limestone and Walnut. She died, however, at the residence of Mrs. Susan Craig, on the south side of Short street, between Georgetown and Jefferson street, in the month of June, 1863, aged about eighty-seven years, and was buried in the Whaley lot, in the Episcopal Cemetery, where her remains still repose.

The only relic of the venerable heroine known to be in existence is a patch-work quilt which she made with her own hands, and gave to a sympathetic lady of Lexington, who was a friend to her in her days of sorrow and affliction.

That Mrs. Vaughn was the first white woman born in Kentucky, there can not be the slightest doubt; the fact is placed beyond dispute by the frequent declarations of many of the earliest settlers of this state to persons still living. Mrs. Vaughn, herself, always declared that she had never heard a statement to the contrary.

Mrs. Vaughn was a woman of excellent mind, warm heart, and sincere piety; and neither her true pride, nor the beautiful characteristics of her christian life, were abated by her poverty and misfortunes. How strange were her experiences. The fate-star of sorrow, which beamed upon her birth, seemed ever to follow her with its saddening influence. She was born when the tomahawk and the torch were busiest; the hope of her declining years died upon a field of battle, and she breathed out her own life in the midst of a terrible civil war. Her parents helped to reclaim and settle an empire; their daughter died without a foot of land that she could call her own. Will justice, even now, be done to her memory? Will the state appropriately mark the spot where rest the mortal remains of the first white woman born in the now great Commonwealth of Kentucky.

CHAPTER XIII.

Baptist Church—Pastors—Incidents—The Creath, Fishback, and Pratt Troubles—Fires.

THE Baptists were the pioneers of religion in Kentucky, and were the most numerous body of Christians in the early settlement of the state; but, as we have seen, they were not the first to found a church in Lexington. But they were not far behind, for a little band of them were meeting, from house to house, as early as 1786,* and were frequently preached to by Elder Lewis Craig, who, in 1783, had organized, in Fayette county, on South Elkhorn, the first worshiping assembly in the state.† This valiant soldier of the cross was born in Spottsylvania county, Virginia, and was several times imprisoned, in the Old Dominion, for preaching contrary to law. He was greatly gifted as an exhorter, and his constant theme was, "practical godliness and every-day christianity." He died in 1827, aged eighty-seven years, sixty of which he spent in the ministry. In 1787, Elder John Gano, of New York city, settled in Central Kentucky,‡ and, in conjunction with Elder —— Payne, aided greatly to build up the church in Lexington. In 1789, the congregation erected a log meeting-house on the same lot where the present church stands, in the "old Baptist graveyard," and Rev. John Gano became its first pastor. Mr. Gano, who was born at Hopewell, N. J., July 22, 1727, had been a chaplain in the American army during the Revolutionary war, was one of the most eminent, eccentric, and successful ministers of his day, and was *personally* known almost throughout the United States. Elder Gano, after being connected with the Lexington church for many years,

---
*Old Journal. †Taylor's History. ‡Benedict.

moved to Frankfort, and died there in 1804. He was buried at Harmony Church, Woodford county, Kentucky.

The Baptist Church in Lexington had its troubles, too, and early in its history. In 1799, Arianism crept into the flock, and created some dissention, but finally died out under the vigorous blows of Elder Gano, who, upon one occasion (while a cripple from a fall), was held up in the arms of his friends to preach against it. But the Arian trouble had hardly died out before another one came up. In 1804, the "Emancipators," who claimed that no fellowship should be extended to slaveholders, commenced to distract the church with their zealous efforts, and the mischief grew into a mountain in 1807, when the notorious difficulty about a negro trade took place between Jacob Creath, Sen., and Thomas Lewis; and great party strife and injury to the church ensued. At last peace came with the secession of the "Emancipators," who formed a separate association, long ago extinct, but the church was greatly weakened. It languished on with decreasing numbers until 1817, when prosperous times dawned upon it. In that year, on the 4th of January, a number of its best scattered members assembled and reorganized the church, with the assistance of Elders Toler, Jacob Creath, Sen., and Jeremiah Vardeman; Berry Stout being moderator, and Samuel Ayers, clerk. On the church list of members about that time, we find, among others, the names of James Trotter, R. Higgins, William C. Warfield, Walter Warfield, W. H. Richardson, William Stone, Matthew Elder, William Payne, Edward Payne, J. H. Morton, J. C. Richardson, Gabriel Tandy, Thomas Lewis, and William Poindexter.

The congregation met at this time in the chapel of Transylvania University, but immediate steps were taken to build a new house of worship. It was completed and occupied in October, 1819,* and was located on North Mill street, opposite the college lawn. It was a substantial two-story brick, provided with galleries, and is noted as being the building in which the first general Baptist Convention of

---

*Church Records.

Kentucky was organized. Immediately after the reorganization of the church, Dr. James Fishback, who had just been ordained to the Baptist ministry, was called to the pastorate, at a salary of four hundred dollars per year, a sum considered at that time quite extraordinary for a preacher's services. A quaint feature of the day was the custom, kept up for a long time in the Mill Street church, of giving out hymns line after line.

In 1826 the influence of the religious movement headed by Barton Stone and Alexander Campbell caused the introduction of a resolution into the First Baptist Church, to change its name to "the Church of Christ,"* which was advocated and opposed by the two parties which had then formed in the church. After a prolonged discussion, the party favoring the resolution " swarmed out," under the the leadership of Dr. Fishback, and organized " the Church of Christ," and worshiped in the building now known as the Statesman office, on Short street, between Upper and Limestone. This church was eventually dissolved. Many of the congregation went back to the First Baptist Church, and the remainder connected themselves with the body now called the " Christian Church."

When Dr. Fishback left the First Baptist Church, Rev. Jeremiah Vardeman was called to the pastorate. Mr. Vardeman was born in Wythe county, Virginia, July 8, 1775, and came to Kentucky in 1794. He was a faithful and laborious minister of the gospel, and in the pulpit was clear, earnest, fervid, and convincing.† He was often assisted by Elders W. C. Breck and J. B. Smith. Mr. Vardeman was pastor up to 1831.

Rev. R. T. Dillard was the next incumbent. Mr. Dillard was born in Caroline county, Virginia, November 17, 1797, served in the war of 1812, came to Kentucky, and settled at Winchester in 1818, and began the practice of law, which he abandoned in 1825, when he was licensed to preach. He came to Fayette in 1828, and was for very many years pastor of David's Fork and East Hickman Baptist Churches.

---

*Church Record. †Sprague's Annals.

In 1838 he traveled in Europe for his health. He was subsequently Superintendent of Public Instruction, has married six hundred and seventy couples, and is at present a resident of Lexington.

Rev. Silas M. Noel* succeeded Mr. Dillard, in October, 1835. Dr. Noel was born August 12, 1783, in Essex county, Virginia, and was educated for the bar. He came to Kentucky in 1806, and practiced law until 1811, when, after much study of the subject of religion, he united with the Baptist Church, and was ordained to the ministry in 1813. Being poorly paid, like all the Western preachers of that day, he accepted, in 1818, the position of circuit judge in the Fourth Indiana district, without relinquishing his superior office. Mr. Noel was the originator of the Baptist Educational Society of Kentucky. He was a man of much more than ordinary powers, and as a speaker was noted for his fluency, chasteness, and elegance. He died May 5, 1839, and was buried near Frankfort, Kentucky.

Mr. Noel's successor was Rev. W. F. Broadus, who was born in Culpepper county, Virginia, about the year 1802. He was descended from a preaching family, and was himself a laborious pastor and excellent preacher. He filled the pulpit in this city until 1845, after which he became president of a female college, in Shelbyville. He is now one of the prominent Baptist ministers of Virginia.

The church called Rev. William M. Pratt, of New York, in 1845. During his administration the congregation worked together with harmony, its efforts were attended with great success, and in 1854, the old church opposite the college lawn was sold, and a handsome new one erected on Mill, between the present new First Presbyterian house of worship and Church street. It was dedicated the 19th of November, 1855, the regular pastor, Mr. Pratt, being assisted by Rev. R. T. Dillard and Dr. S. W. Lynd, then president of the Theological Seminary at Georgetown. This house was unfortunately destroyed by fire, January 1, 1859, but in the May following the erection of another one was

---

*Sprague's Annals.

commenced in the old churchyard, on Main, the site of the pioneer Baptist Church of Lexington. While digging the foundation many relics of the old settlers and citizens were exhumed, and all not identified were buried in a vault under the church. This house was dedicated January 1, 1860. President Campbell, of Georgetown, Rev. G. C. Lorrimer, and the pastor officiating.

In 1863, after having been pastor for seventeen years, Mr. Pratt resigned, and the Rev. W. H. Felix, a native of Woodford county and graduate of Georgetown College, was called. Some months after Mr. Felix came the church was again burned, but mainly through his efforts another one was built on the same spot, and dedicated August 20, 1865, only to be visited by fire again in February, 1867. The untiring congregation set to work once more, and the present building was completed in a short time after the disaster. Even at this late date the war feeling had not entirely died out. A little while after the last fire, Mr. Pratt, W. E. Bosworth, and others asked and were given letters of dismission, and they proceeded to organize a "Second Baptist Church." The little congregation met for some time in the City Library building, but is now disbanded, most of the members having returned to the First Church. Mr. Felix resigned his charge in April, 1869, and was succeeded the June following by Rev. George Hunt, the present faithful pastor, a native of Fayette county. The Baptist Church has exhibited great energy under many misfortunes, and is now enjoying the abundant prosperity it so well deserves.

CHAPTER XIV.

Paint Lick Expedition—Delegates to Conventions—Society for Promoting Useful Knowledge—Old Kentucky Gazette—The First Western Newspaper—Lexington Racing Clubs—Kentucky Association—Founders—Incidents—Officers—Great Horses—Improvements—Turfmen—Breeders—The Great "Lexington."

THE events of the year 1787, if not of great importance, were of more than ordinary interest. The Indians continued to show great restlessness and dissatisfaction. On information given by some friendly Shawanese that a party of Cherokees, at Paint Lick, were meditating a predatory raid, Colonel Robert Todd made an expedition against them and dispersed them, killing three, and taking seven prisoners, who escaped the next day after capture.*

Fayette sent two delegates to the Virginia convention, which in this year ratified the constitution of the United States. The delegates were Humphrey Marshall and John Fowler.†

Another convention, the fifth, met at Danville, in Septemtember, 1787, and Fayette was represented by Levi Todd, Caleb Wallace, Humphrey Marshall, John Fowler, and William Ward.‡

A number of gentlemen, alive to the interests and advancement of the district, assembled in the month of December, 1787,‖ and arranged for the establishment of the "Kentucky Society for Promoting Useful Knowledge." At least half of the members of the society were citizens of Lexington, and many of them were afterward counted

---

*Marshall. †Butler. ‡Old Gazette. ‖Gazette.

among the most eminent men of the state. We give the names of all the members. They were: Christopher Greenup, Humphrey Marshall, J. Brown, Isaac Shelby, James Garrard, Charles Scott, George Muter, Samuel McDowell, Harry Jones, James Speed, Wm. McDowell, Willis Green, Thos. Todd, Thos. Speed, G. J. Johnson, Joshua Barbee, Stephen Armsby, J. Overton, Jr., John Jewett, Thos. Allen, Robert Todd, Joseph Crockett, Ebenezer Brooks, T. Hall, Caleb Wallace, Wm. Irvine, James Parker, Alex. Parker, John Fowler, John Coburn, George Gordon, A. D. Orr, Robert Barr, Horace Turpin, Robert Johnson, John Craig, David Leitch.

The first newspaper ever published west of the Alleghany mountains was established in Lexington, in 1787, by John Bradford. It was then called the Kentucke Gazette, but the final *e* of Kentucky was afterward changed to *y*, in consequence of the Virginia legislature requiring certain advertisements to be inserted in the Kentucky Gazette. This paper was born of the necessities of the times. The want of a government independent of Virginia was then universally felt, and the second convention that met in Danville, in 1785, to discuss that subject, resolved, "That to insure unanimity in the opinion of the people respecting the propriety of separating the district of Kentucky from Virginia and forming a separate state government, and to give publicity to the proceedings of the convention, it is deemed essential to the interests of the country to have a printing press." A committee was then appointed to carry out the design of the convention; but all their efforts had failed, when John Bradford called on General Wilkinson, one of the committee, and informed him that he would establish a paper if the convention would guarantee to him the public patronage. To this the convention acceded, and in 1786 Bradford sent to Philadelphia for the necessary materials. He had already received every encouragement from the citizens of Lexington, and at a meeting of the trustees in July, it was ordered "that the use of a public lot be granted to John Bradford *free*, on condition that he establish a printing press in Lexington; the lot to be free to him as long as the press is in town." Mr. Bradford's first office was in a log cabin, on the corner of Main and Broadway, now known as "Cleary's," but then known as "opposite the court-house." He subsequently used a building on Main, between Mill and Broadway, about where Scott's iron front building stands.

At last, after being months on the route, the precious printing material arrived, and on August 18, 1787, appeared the first number of the first newspaper ever published in the then western wilderness. It was a quaint little brown thing, about the size of a half sheet of common letter paper, "subscription price 18 shillings per annum, advertisements of moderate length 3 shillings." It was printed in the old style—*f* being used for *s*. The first number is without a heading, and contains one advertisement, two short original articles, and the following apology from the editor:

"My customers will excuse this, my first publication, as I am much hurried to get an impression by the time appointed. A great part of the types fell into pi in the carriage of them from Limestone (Maysville) to this office, and my partner, which is the only assistant I have, through an indisposition of the body, has been incapable of rendering the smallest assistance for ten days past.

"JOHN BRADFORD."

No wonder "the types fell into pi," for they had to be carried from "Limestone" to Lexington on pack-horses, that had swollen streams to cross, fallen trees to jump, and many a terrible "scare" from the sudden crack of Indian rifles, for there was not a half mile between the two places unstained with blood. The Gazette of 1787 is the only indicator extant of the size and importance of Lexington, at that time. We are able to surmise some things, at least, after looking over the first volumes of the Gazette. They are adorned with rude cuts and ornaments gotten up by Bradford himself. It is well known that he cut out the larger letters from dog-wood. In these volumes we find advertised, among other things, knee-buckles, hair-powder, spinning wheels, flints, buckskin for breeches, and saddle-bag locks. "Persons who subscribe to the frame meeting-house can pay in cattle or *whisky.*" In another place the editor condemns the common practice of "taming bears," and also that of "lighting fires with rifles." Proceedings of the district convention are published. No. 5, of volume 1, contains the constitution of the United States just framed by the "grand convention" then in session. Notice is given to the public not to tamper with corn or potatoes at a certain place, as they had been poisoned to trap some vegetable stealing Indians. In another number, "notice is given that a company will meet at Crab Orchard next Monday, for an early start through the wilderness; most of the delegates to the State Convention at Richmond (to adopt constitution of United States), will go with them." Chas. Bland advertises, "I will not pay a note given to Wm. Turner for three second-rate cows till he returns a rifle, blanket, and tomahawk I loaned him." Later, the names of Simon Kenton and 'Squire Boone appear. The columns of the Gazette are enriched with able and well-written articles, full of that mental vigor and natural talent for which our pioneer fathers were so justly celebrated; but "locals" are vexatiously scarce. Still the editor got up some. He often speaks of stealing, murdering, and kidnapping by Indians. At one time he speaks of a wonderful elephant on exhibition in a certain *stable*, and at another, "the people of the settlement are flocking in to see the dromedary"—quite a menagerie at that day. We must remember, if we think his " items " scarce, that at that time steamboats didn't explode, nor cars run off the track, for none of these, or a thousand other modern item-making machines, were in existence.

Still the Gazette must have been read with the most intense interest; in fact, a writer in one of its earliest numbers says: "Mr. Bradford, as I have signed the subscription for your press, and take your paper, my curiosity *eggs* me on to read everything in it." And no wonder, for all documents of public interest had up to this time been written, were often illegible, and one copy only was to be seen at each of the principal settlements. And then it was the only paper printed within five hundred miles of Lexington, and there was no post-office in the whole district. It was published, too, at a time of unusual interest in politics, and while party spirit ran high. The old national government was crumbling to give place to the new; the settlements were distracted by French and Spanish intrigues; the people were indignant and hot-blooded over the obstructed navigation of the Mississippi, and convention after convention was being held to urge on the work of separation from Virginia. What a treat the Gazette was to the pioneers! Often when the post-rider arrived with it at a settlement, the whole population would crowd around the schoolmaster or " 'squire," who, mounted in state upon a stump, would read it, advertisements and all, to the deeply interested and impatient throng.

Bradford's editorial situation, contrasted with the magnificent surroundings and princely style of a New York journalist of the present day, was quite interesting. His steamboat, railroad, telegraph, and mail carrier was a pack mule. His office was a log cabin. His rude and unwieldy hand-press was of the old-fashioned style, that for centuries had not been improved, and, in addition, it was a second-hand one. He daubed on the ink by hand with two ancient dog-skin inking balls, and probably managed to get sixty or seventy copies printed on one side in an hour. If he wrote at night, it was by the light of a rousing fire, a bear-grease lamp, or a buffalo tallow candle; an editorial desk made of a smooth slab, supported by two pairs of cross legs; a three-legged stool, ink horn, and a rifle composed the rest of the furniture of his office. The Gazette was, for some time, in its early history, printed on paper made near Lexington, at the mill of Craig, Parker & Co. This pioneer journal of the West existed for nearly three-quarters of a century. There is no greater treasure in the Lexington library than the old files of the Kentucke Gazette.

John Bradford became a citizen of Lexington in 1786. This useful man, whose name is so closely linked with the early history of our city, was born in Fauquier county, Virginia, in 1749, and married Eliza, daughter of Captain Benj. James of the same county, in 1761. He took part in the Revolutionary war, and was also in the battle with the Indians at Chillicothe. In 1785, he brought his family out from Virginia, and settled in Fayette county. He founded the Kentucke Gazette in 1787, and published the next year the Kentucke Almanac, the first pamphlet printed west of the mountains. Mr. Bradford was chairman of the Lexington Board of Trustees, which welcomed Governor Shelby, in 1792, to our city, which was then the capital of the state. He was the first state printer, and received from the legislature one hundred pounds sterling. He printed books as early as 1794, and some of them of that date are still to be seen in the Lexington library. He was at one time, chairman of the Board of Trustees of Transylvania University, and filled many places of trust and honor in Lexington. He was greatly respected, and after leading a life of much usefulness, went to his rest, sincerely mourned by all who knew him. His residence was on the corner of Mill and Second streets. It was built by Colonel Hart, and is the same one now occupied by Mrs. Ryland.

The center of "the garden spot of Kentucky," justly famous the world over for its magnificent blood stock, was devoted to the turf while Lexington was scarcely a village. As early as 1787, "the commons," as our present Water street was then called, was a favorite resort of horsemen when their charming pastime of racing through Main street was interfered with by the troublesome trustees of the rising town.* The settlers pursued pleasures under difficulties in those days, as the "red-skin varmints" had all by no means disappeared from the state. In August, 1789, the only newspaper published in Kentucky† contained the following notice, which we give verbatim, viz: "A purse-race will take place at Lexington, on 2d Thursday in Octo-

---

*Trustees' Book.   †Old Kentucke Gazette.

ber next, free for any horse, mare, or gelding; weight for age agreeable to the rules of New Market (three-mile heats), best two in three. Each subscriber to pay one guinea, and every person that enters a horse for the purse to pay two guineas, including his subscription. The horses to be entered the day before running with Mr. John Fowler, who will attend at Mr. Collins' tavern on that day. Subscriptions taken by Nicholas Lafon, Lexington." Races were pretty regularly kept up after this time. Simeon Buford and Colonel Abraham Buford owned the winning horses in 1795. In 1802, races were in full blast in Lexington, and in 1809, the Lexington Jockey Club was organized. It existed until 1823, and held its meetings near Ashland. The report made by the secretary, W. G. Wilson, of its final October meeting, is as follows :*

"The first day's purse, for the four-mile heats, was taken by Mr. Burbridge's gelding, Tiger by Tiger, 5 years old, at two heats, beating Captain Harris' b. h. Paragon, by Whip, 4 years old, and Colonel W. Buford's s. m. Carolina, by Sir Archie, 4 years old. Paragon was drawn the second heat. Time of the first heat, 8:15; of the second heat, 8:25.

"The second day's purse, three-mile heats, was won by Mr. Watson's s. h. Sea Serpent, by Shylock, beating Mr. Blackburn's Sophy Winn, by Whip, at two heats. Time of the first heat, 6:7; of the second heat, 6:10.

"The third day's purse, two-mile heats, was won by Mr. Barnett's s. h. Diamond, by Brilliant, 3 years old, at three heats, beating Mr. W. Sanders' Stifler, by Ex-Emperor, and Mr. Harlans gelding, Black Snake, by Sky Lark. The Black Snake won the first heat and was drawn the third heat. Time of the first heat, 4:2; of the second heat, 4:3; the third heat was won by Diamond with ease.

"The Handy Cap purse on Saturday, one mile heats, best three in five, was won by Captain Harris' Paragon, beating the Irishman and Virginia. Time of the first heat, 1:52; of the second heat, 1:51; of the third heat, 1:53; each heat was closely contested by the Irishman and Virginia."

---

*Lexington Paper.

The present noted Kentucky association was organized at Mrs. Keene's inn, Lexington, July 29, 1826, by about fifty of the prominent turfmen of Central Kentucky, among whom were E. Warfield, T. H. Pindell, Jas. K. Duke, Leslie Combs, J. Boswell, R. Downing, J. L. Downing, Geo. H. Bowman, John Bruce, John Tilford, B. W. Dudley, W. R. Morton, R. J. Breckinridge, Wm. Buford, John Brand, and Robt. Wickliffe.* The object of the association, to use the words of the original agreement, was "to improve the breed of horses by encouraging the sports of the turf." The first racing meeting held under the arrangement commenced October 19, 1826, on the old Williams' track, which was on what is now known as the Lee property, near the Lexington Cemetery. The first race was for a purse of $300; four started; was won by Andrew Barnett's Diomed gelding, Sheriffe, in two straight heats. For the second day's purse of $200, three started. Won by Ralph P. Tarlton's horse, Old Count. The third and last day's racing, for the purse of $100, was won by Ludwell Berkley's gelding, Sir Sidney. For this purse, five horses started. The time is not given.†

For the year 1827, the race for the first day was for a purse of $150, for two miles and repeat; the second day, a race of four miles and repeat, for a purse of $400, and the third day a race of three miles and repeat, for a purse of $250. The first was won by Willa Viley's b. m. Mariah, in 4:15. The time of second heat not given. The four mile race was won by R. B. Tarlton's s. s. Old Count, in 8:17, 8:48. The three-mile race was won by Sidney Burbridge's b. m., Limber. The heats were broken. The time as follows: 6:09, 6:07, 6:46, 6:18. A sweepstakes was opened for the following day, one mile, best three in five, which was won by Willa Viley's Mariah. Time, 1:53½, 1:52½, 1:51½, 1:51, 1:51.‡

The old Williams' track was used by the association until 1828, when the present track, at the east end of Fifth street, was bought by John Postlethwaite. In 1834,

---

*Association Records.   †Observer and Reporter.   ‡Id.

a tract of land adjoining the course, was purchased from Jeremiah Murphy, and added to the original purchase. The association now own about sixty-five acres of land, all of which is inclosed with a high plank fence. In this year (1834), it was ordered that the wieghts heretofore adopted, be changed to conform to those established by the Central Course of Maryland. It was also ordered that Wm. Buford, W. Viley, J. K. Duke, A. K. Woolley, and Leslie Combs, be appointed a committee to apply to the legislature for a charter.*

A motion was adopted instructing the secretary to have a bulletin of the races published every morning, giving a description of horses and rider's dress, which is carried out to this day.

An early frequenter† of the course says of this period (1834): "We can recollect when nothing but an old post and rail fence inclosed the track; the judges' stand stood at the cow-pens, and the grand stand was an old, rickety building, with high steps, which stood on top of the hill in the center of the course. Admittance to the course was free, to the stand twenty-five cents. John Wirt was secretary. We recollect seeing Woodpecker, the sire of Gray Eagle, run. We remember vividly the race between Dick Singleton and Collier, when the latter sulked, and John Alcock rode Collier and broke a beautiful ivory whip over the head of the obstinate beast.

"We can recollect when the judges' stand was placed where the timing stand is now, when Rodolph ran at Lexington, and subsequently defeated the great Tennessee crack Angora, at Louisville, Kentucky, in 1836. The year the course was fenced in, about 1835, we witnessed the great sixteen-mile race between Sarah Miller, Jim Allen, and Grayfoot; the great and exciting struggle between May Dacre (afterward Belle Anderson, the dam of Zenith) and Susette, three-mile heats; the brilliant promise of Gray Eagle, as a three-year old, in 1838, and his subsequent defeat by the renowned Wagner, at Louisville, in 1839.

---

*Association Records.   †See Turf, Field, and Farm, April, 1872.

These two great races between Wagner and Gray Eagle excited the highest interest throughout the country."

The year 1840 was memorable at Lexington for the great three-mile heat race, in which nine stallions started. Blacknose, by Medoc, out of Lucy, by Orphan, won the first heat in 5:40, the fastest and first time 5:40 had been made in America. Red Bill, another son of Medoc, won the second and third heats in 5:48, 5:49. The following year, 1841, was no less memorable, when Jim Bell, by Frank, ran a second heat in 1:46, the fastest mile up to that time ever run in America. This time stood for many years before it was beaten. In 1842 the great match between Zenith and Miss Foote was made. Zenith broke down in training, and Miss Foote walked over. The last of the same meeting Miss Foote beat Argentile and Alice Carneal, the honored dam of the unapproachable Lexington, four mile heats, in 7:42, 7:40, the best time ever made in Kentucky before.*

In 1843, the Great Produce Stakes for three-year olds, seventy-two subscribers, at $500 each, $100 forfeit, with a gold cup valued at $500 added, was won by Ruffin, by imp. Hedgford, dam Duchess of Marlborough, by Sir Archy. This was one of the most valuable stakes ever run for in Kentucky.

In 1836, the date previously fixed to be taken in deciding the age of horses, was changed to the 1st of January. The months of May and September were decided upon in 1844, as the times for the spring and fall meetings, and have been adhered to ever since.

The fastest time for three-quarters of a mile ever run on the association course is 1:18¼.

The fastest time for one and one-quarter miles is 2:14½.

The fastest time for one and half miles is 2:38, which was made by Exchange in the spring of 1870. This time has never been beaten on any course except by Glenelg, who ran in 2:37¾.

The fastest time for two and one-half miles is 5:22½.

---

*Turf, Field, and Farm.

The following is the number of races run on the course since its organization up to 1871, for the different distances: Three-quarters of a mile, 4 races; one mile, 213 races; one and a fourth miles, 2 races; one and a half miles, 3 races; two miles, 141 races; two miles and a half, 2 races; three miles, 49 races; four miles, 23 races; hurdle races, 2.*

The following is a list of the presidents and secretaries of the association from the date of its organization, in 1826, to the present time, viz:

Presidents.—1826, Wm. Pritchart; 1830, E. J. Winter; 1833, Thos. H. Pindell; 1845, Thos. H. Hunt; 1848, Charles Buford; 1853, Leslie Combs; 1855, John R. Viley; 1864, B. G. Bruce; 1866, John R. Viley; 1871, John R. Viley; 1872, John C. Breckinridge.

Secretaries.—1826, John Wirt; 1837, Thos. P. Hart; same year, Richard Pindell; 1845, J. R. McGowan; 1850, E. E. Eagle; 1857, Charles Wheatly; 1865, E. E. Eagle; 1869, H. Rees; 1871, T. J. Bush.

The efficiency and accomplishments of Captain Bush in his department are too well known to require comment.

The Kentucky Association is the oldest living club in America, and General Combs is believed to be the only living representative of the original fifty subscribers who formed it.

That it is the fastest course in America can easily be demonstrated.† Fadladeen and Salina each ran a mile on this course in 1:43, in 1871. Frogtown ran one and one-quarter miles in 2:09½, in 1872. Exchange ran one mile and a half in 2:38, in 1871. Frogtown ran one mile and three-quarters in 3:07, in 1872. Lyttleton ran two miles in 3:34½, in 1871.

The time here given is the fastest and best on record. It is true that Glenelg ran two miles in 2:37¾ with 100 lbs.; but Exchange, carrying 110 lbs., ran the same distance on this course in 2:38, which makes his the best time. Hegira ran two miles on the Metairie course, carrying 71½ lbs., in

---

*Observer and Reporter, 1871.   †Home Journal.

3:34¼, but Lyttleton, with 104 lbs., made it on the Kentucky Association course in 3:34½.

This old course has been the scene of the *debut* and subsequent renown of the most noted horses that have figured on the American turf for the last thirty years. Here Jim and Josh. Bell, Sarah Morton, Rocket, Motto, Grey Medoc, Ruffin, Ludu, Alaric, Darkness, Doubloon, Florin, Louis D'Or, Rube, Zampa, Star Davis, Sally Waters, Frankfort, Blonde, the renowned Lexington, Wild Irishman, Charley Ball, Dick Doty, Vandal, Balloon, Princeton, Daniel Boone, Ruric, Bonnie Lassie, Nantura, Lavender, Satellite, Mollie Jackson, Lightning, Thunder, Asteroid, Lancaster, Sherrod, Colton, Magenta, Solferino, Mammona, Bettie Ward, Goodwood, Lilla, Herzog, Versailles, Fadladeen, Littleton, Longfellow, Enquirer, and a host of others, first gave promise of their after fame and renown.

Extensive improvements were made by the association in the spring of 1872.* The track was regraded and widened to about double its former width. It is now just one mile and six inches long. The old stands have been torn down and new ones erected. The grand stand, which is built twenty-seven feet back from the track, is a model building of its kind, being one hundred and fifty by thirty feet, and about thirty-two feet high. The lower story is built of brick. Immediately in front of the grand stand, and just at the edge of the track, is the judges' stand, an octagon building, with a small room below, where the scales are placed to weigh the riders. Just across the track is the timers' stand. The old distance stand has also been removed, and a new one erected. Where the old stand was, there has been built a substantial frame building, which is intended to accommodate all those who formerly went to the field. The cooling ground has been changed from the rear to the front. There are eleven stables on the ground, in which more than seventy-five horses can be accommodated.

The association course is now one of the handsomest in

---

* Daily Press.

the United States. Captain O. P. Beard, who directed and personally superintended these improvements, was presented with a fine timing watch, ordered from England, by his friends, as a token of their appreciation of his taste and untiring energy.

Nearly a hundred horses owned near Lexington were present at the last spring meeting of the association. The stables in attendance belonged to J. A. Grinstead, B. G. Thomas, H. P. McGrath, John Clay, Zeb. Ward, J. F. Robinson, A. Buford, George Cadwallader, John Harper, Daniel Swigert, J. W. Hunt Reynolds, Warren Viley, A. K. Richards, Caleb Wallace, and others.

We may mention with propriety, in this connection, that in addition to the twenty-five or thirty regular breeding establishments in Fayette county, nearly every farmer in it is to some extent a breeder, and the whole county is one vast stock farm. Here was bred, by Dr. Elisha Warfield, the world-renowned "Lexington," and this county is the native place of the famous thorough-breds, "Grey Eagle," bred by H. T. Duncan, Sen.; "Daniel Boone," "Kentucky," and "Gilroy," bred by John M. Clay; "Herzog," bred by B. G. Thomas; "Fadladeen," bred by Mr. McFadden; and "Frogtown," bred by William Stanhope and H. A. Headley. At the head of the list of noted fast trotters that were bred in Fayette are Dunlap's "Lady Thorn," William Bradley's "John Morgan," Enoch Lewis' "Ericson," Andrew Steele's "Blackwood," and Dr. L. Herr's "Mambrino Bertie." The following is a list of the principal breeders and the names of the stallions at the head of each stud, viz:

Thoroughbreds.—John M. Clay, "Star Davis;" J. A. Grinstead, "Lightning" and "Gilroy;" H. P. McGrath, "Blarney Stone;" B. G. Thomas, ——; J. R. Viley, ——; Zeb. Ward, ——; George Cadwallader, ——.

Trotters.—Dr. L. Herr, "Mambrino Patchin;" Enoch Lewis, "Ericson;" Drs. S. and D. Price, "Sentinel;" R. Lowell, "Abdallah Pilot;" Hunt Brothers, "Darlboy;" Thomas Coons, "American Clay;" John Mardis, "Clark Chief, Jr.;" Charles Headley, "Banquo;" A. Coons, ——;

W. J. Bradley, ——; Alexander Brand, ——; R. & J. Todhunter, Jos. Bryant, Jr., ——.

The names of the professional trainers in Fayette are: Thomas Britton, C. B. Jeffreys, B. J. Tracy, R. Lowell, James Chrystal, W. R. Brasfield, A. L. Rice, H. Lusby, and W. J. Bradley.

The history of the Kentucky Association, and also of Fayette county, "the breeder's paradise," would never be considered complete without a sketch of the pride of both, viz: the famous race-horse, "Lexington," the blind old Milton of the turf, and the king of coursers. "Lexington"* was bred by Dr. Elisha Warfield, of Lexington, Kentucky, and was foaled in 1850, at his home, "The Meadows," which is about half a mile from the association grounds. "Lexington"* was by Boston, out of Alice Carneal, by Sarpedon, dam Rowena, by Sampler; great granddam Lady Gray, by Robin Gray. Boston was by Timoleon out of Robin Brown's dam, own sister to Tuckahoe and Revenge, by Florizel. Alice Carneal, Lexington's dam, was foaled in Kentucky, in 1836, and although she ran second in the first heat of a four-mile race to Miss Foote in 7:42, being distanced in the second heat, she never won a race. Lexington was first known on the turf as Darley, and under that name won his first race, a three-year old stake, at the Lexington, Kentucky, May meeting, 1853, mile heats, beating thirteen opponents. He was purchased on the evening after this race by Mr. Ten Broeck, and his name changed to Lexington. At the same meeting he won a two-mile heat race for three-year olds, and his owner soon after matched him to run a three-mile race against the four-year old filly, Sally Waters, by Glencoe, out of Maria Black, for $8,500; the backers of the filly staking $5,000 to $3,500 on Lexington. The race occurred on the Metairie course, New Orleans, December 2, 1853, and Lexington won, distancing Sally Waters in the second heat. The time was 6:23½ and 6:24½, and the track very heavy. His next engagement was in the three-year old stake, at New Orleans,

---

*Cincinnati Commercial.

January 7, 1854, two-mile heats, but being amiss, he paid forfeit to Conrad the Corsair, Argent, and Hornpipe. The following April, on the same course, he won for Kentucky the Great State Post Stake, for all ages, four-mile heats, beating Lecomte, the representative of Mississippi, second in both heats, Highlander, of Alabama, and Arrow, of Louisiana. Highlander was distanced in the second, and Arrow in the first heat; time 8:08¾, 8:04, and track heavy. The next meeting of Lexington and Lecomte was on April 8, over the same track, for the Jockey Club purse of $2,000, four-mile heats, and here Lexington sustained his only, defeat, Lecomte winning two straight heats in the fastest time ever made up to that date, viz: 7:26, 7:38¾. Lexington was second in both heats, and Reube, third on the first, was distanced in the last heat. Notwithstanding his horse's defeat, Ten Broeck offered to run him against Lecomte's best time or against Lecomte himself for $20,000, four-mile heats. Eventually, a match was made for $20,000, Lexington to run against the fastest time, at four miles, that is, Lecomte's 7:26, over the Metairie course, New Orleans. This memorable race occurred April 2, 1855, and Lexington, carrying 103 pounds—three pounds over-weight—and ridden by Gilpatrick, won in 7:19¾, which, for seventeen years, has never been equaled. The time was 1:47¼, 1:52¼, 1:51½, and 1:48¾; total, 7:19¾. Not satisfied with this, General Wells started Lecomte against Lexington for the Jockey Club purse of $1,000, with an inside stake of $2,500 a side, four-mile heats, April 24, 1855, on the Metairie course, and this time Lexington obtained a decisive victory over his old conqueror, winning the first heat in 7:23¾, and galloping over in the second heat, as Lecomte had been withdrawn.

Lexington soon after broke down, and, being withdrawn from the turf, was purchased by the late R. A. Alexander, of Woodburn, Woodford county, Kentucky. He is now blind, and has been so for some years. Mr. Alexander paid Mr. Ten Broeck $15,000 for "Lexington," and was ridiculed for giving so large an amount; but subsequent events justified his foresight. A few years later, Lexington's son, "Norfolk," won the two stakes for three-year olds at St. Louis, and was then sold for $15,000. Since then, another son, "Kentucky," sold for $40,000, and double that sum would not purchase " Harry Bassett," the greatest of his progeny.

CHAPTER XV.

First Celebration of the Fourth of July—Convention Election—Woodford County Formed—Cincinnati Settled—Free Masonry in Lexington — Native and Resident Painters: West, Jouett, Frazer, Bush, Price, and others.

THE first regular and formal celebration of Independence Day in Lexington took place in 1788. The scene then exhibited stands in striking contrast with modern usage, and the toasts and sentiments of the occasion not only show at once the native strength and clearness of the pioneer mind, but the condition and feelings of the people on the state of affairs in the then District of Kentucky.

At one P. M. on the day mentioned, a large company of ladies and gentlemen assembled at what was then known as Captain Thomas Young's tavern, where an elegant entertainment and feast of fat things had been prepared, and an hour was passed in festive enjoyment. After dinner an ode composed by a Lexington gentleman was sung to the tune of "Rule Britannia," the entire company joining in the chorus—

"Hail Kentucke, Kentucke, thou shalt be
Forever great, most blest and free."

This unique production was a poetic embodiment of the universal desire of the people for a separate state government, and was sung with the greatest spirit and enthusiasm.

The following toasts and sentiments were then drank, with a discharge of fourteen rifles at each interval:

The United States of America.

The illustrious George Washington, Esq.; may his services be remembered.

The Western World: perpetual union on principles of equality or amicable separation.

The navigation of the Mississippi at any price but that of liberty.

Harmony with Spain and a reciprocity of good offices.

May the savage enemies of America be chastised by arms, and the jobbing system of treason be exploded.

"The Convention of Virginia." May wisdom, firmness, and a sacred regard for the fundamental principles of the revolution, guide her councils.

Trial by jury, liberty of the press, and no standing army.

May the Atlantic States be just, the Western States be free, and both happy.

No paper money, no tender laws, and no legislative interference with private contracts.

The above presents a perfect picture of affairs in Kentucky at that date, and at no subsequent period in her history up to the eve of the late war has our state been so strangely situated. While Kentucky was struggling for separate state sovereignty the ruins of the old confederation were lying all around her. The Virginia Convention to deliberate on the constitution of a new union was then in session, listening to the eloquent wisdom of Henry, Mason. Pendleton, Grayson, and its other great and sagacious statesmen, and Kentucky was watching with the most eager interest for its decision. Here, in the very infancy, or rather at the very birth of the republic, we see the Yankee at work. Louisiana was then a Spanish province, and Don Gardozni, Minister from Spain, was making every exertion to effect a political union between the West and Louisiana, and Kentucky was being tempted with the free navigation of the Mississippi; and to all this may be added the ravages of the Indians and the dissensions among her own citizens. Kentucky has never celebrated a much more momentous "Fourth."

A regular old "five days election" for delegates to the Seventh Danville Convention was held in Lexington and Fayette county this year, and was an unusually spirited one. Colonel Thomas Marshall, at the head of the "Court" party, and General Wilkinson, the leader of the "Country" party, labored with unusual zeal. The "Court" won, and sent Thomas Marshall, Caleb Wallace, William Ward, and John Allen to the convention. General Wilkinson was the only one on the "Country" ticket elected.

Virginia contracted the wide borders of Fayette considerably this year, by organizing Woodford county out of part of her territory.

The city of Cincinnati was settled by a company from Lexington; two citizens of Lexington owned most of the ground on which it stands, and one of them gave it its original name, "Losantiville."* The following notice, which we give verbatim, was published in the old Kentucky Gazette, September 6, 1788:

"NOTICE.—The subscribers, being proprietors of a tract of land opposite the mouth of the Licking river, on the northwest side of the Ohio, have determined to lay off a town upon that excellent situation. The local and natural advantages speak its future prosperity, being equal, if not superior to any on the bank of the Ohio between the Miamis. The in-lots to be each half an acre, the out-lots four acres; thirty of each to be given to settlers, upon paying one dollar and fifty cents for the survey and deed of each lot. The 15th day of September is appointed for a large company to meet in Lexington, and mark a road from there to the mouth of the Licking, provided Judge Symmes arrives, being daily expected. When the town is laid off, lots will be given to such as may become residents before the first day of April next.

"MATTHIAS DENMAN,
ROBERT PATTERSON,
JOHN FILSON."

The road was marked, the present site of Cincinnati was duly visited, and a settlement was made there by Colonel Patterson's party, in December, 1788. In the following June the little village was strengthened and protected by the building of Fort Washington, by which name Cin-

---

*Cist Papers, 12.

cinnati was long known to the pioneers of the West. After effecting the settlement, Colonel Patterson returned to Lexington, where he continued to reside until 1804.

Freemasonry in Kentucky, and in all the region west of the Alleghany mountains, had its commencement in "Lodge No. 25," established in Lexington, District of Kentucky, November 17, 1788, by the Grand Lodge of Virginia. "Masons' Hall," in Lexington, was at that time a small house of primitive style, located on the same lot where the present hall stands, on the corner of Walnut and Short streets. The ground on which it stood was donated to the lodge by William Murray, the first Grand Master of the Grand Lodge of Kentucky. In 1796, the hall was improved from funds realized from a lottery gotten up for the purpose, and the membership of the lodge had so increased by 1799, that St. John's day was celebrated with considerable display.* On the 8th of September, 1800,† a convention of delegates from all the lodges in Kentucky met at "Masons' Hall," to consider the propriety of separating from the jurisdiction of the Grand Lodge of Virginia, and forming a Grand Lodge in Kentucky. James Morrison, of "No. 25," was chairman. The delegates at this convention from "Lexington Lodge, No. 25," were Thomas Bodley, Alexander McGregor, and James Russell. Separation was determined upon, and was agreed to by the Virginia Grand Lodge; and on Thursday, October 16, 1800, in Masons' Hall, in Lexington, the representatives of the lodges of Kentucky opened a Grand Lodge for the State of Kentucky, "the first on the great American roll of the nineteenth century." Nearly half the officers of the Grand Lodge were selected from "No. 25," viz: Alexander McGregor, Deputy Grand Master; James Russell, G. Secretary; John Bobbs, G. Tyler. At this first session, the seal of Lexington Lodge, No. 25, was adopted by the Grand Lodge, and used for some time. "No. 25" was also placed first in the order of subordinate lodges, in deference to its priority of age, and then became "Lexington Lodge,

---

*Kentucky Gazette. †Proceedings of G. L.

No. 1," by which title it has been known ever since that time.* Among the distinguished men who were members of Lodge No. 1 may be named Henry Clay, W. T. Barry, Joseph H. Daviess, Jesse Bledsoe, George M. Bibb, Felix Grundy, and B. W. Dudley. In 1806, Lodge No. 1 sent Daniel Bradford and John Bobb as delegates to the convention, which met in Lexington that year to frame a Grand Lodge constitution. At the meeting of the Grand Lodge, August 27, 1812, in Lexington, an imposing funeral ceremonial was performed in honor of the heroic Grand Master, Joseph H. Daviess, who fell at the battle of Tippecanoe, November 7, 1811. The pall bearers were eight Master Masons of Lodge No. 1.†

Daviess Lodge was erected this year (1812) by a number of the members of Lodge No. 1, and was duly chartered by the Grand Lodge. It was named in honor of the lamented hero, to whom funeral honors had just been paid, and formed the first instance, in Kentucky, of a lodge being named after an individual. David Castleman was first master, and John Pope, one of the first members, represented it at the next session of the Grand Lodge.‡ The sword of Colonel Daviess, incased in a casket made of the wood of the oak under which he was standing when he received his death wound, was presented to the Grand Lodge in October, 1858, by Levi L. Todd. Daviess Lodge ranks third in age among the lodges now in existence in Kentucky.

In 1813, the propriety of erecting a grand hall in Lexington was first discussed in the Grand Lodge; and in 1817, Lexington Lodge, No. 1, presented to the Grand Lodge its lot on Walnut street as a site on which to build the new temple, "No. 1" reserving to itself the privilege of meeting in said temple.§ The donation was accepted, but it was finally concluded to erect the hall on East Main street, west of Broadway, below what is now known as "Cleary's corner." The building was commenced in 1824, and was dedicated, with appropriate ceremonies, October 26, 1826. The hall was a handsome one, three stories high, and cost between $25,000 and $30,000. It was in this hall that

*Pro. G. L.   †Old Journals.   ‡Robert Morris' Hist.   §Pro. of G. L.

General Lafayette was received by the Masons of Lexington in 1825. Two Indians—one of them the celebrated Colonel Ross—were duly examined, introduced and welcomed to the Masons in this hall. They were the only full-blooded Indian Masons ever thus received in Lexington. The hall was used as a hospital during the terrible cholera season of 1833.

The question of removing the Grand Lodge from Lexington to Louisville was first agitated in 1830, and in 1833 it was located in Louisville, after having existed in Lexington thirty-three years.

The Grand Hall on Main street was destroyed by fire in 1837. This event caused the question of the location of the Grand Lodge to be again agitated. The lot of No. 1 was again tendered to the Grand Lodge on the original terms, again accepted, and with the understanding that the sessions of the Grand Lodge would be permanently held in Lexington, another hall, the present one, costing $25,000, was erected upon the site of the first building devoted to masonic purposes in Kentucky. This hall was solemnly dedicated to masonry, according to the ancient form and usage, September 1, 1841, and the next day the Grand Lodge "ordered that its annual communication should be held in the city of Lexington."

Devotion Lodge was chartered in September, 1847, Oliver Anderson being first master.

In August, 1848, Good Samaritan Lodge was chartered, Samuel D. McCullough, first master.

The Grand Lodge was again removed from Lexington to Louisville in October, 1858, and its sessions are still held in that city. Lexington was the meeting-place of the Grand Lodge, including both times of its occupation, for sixty years.

The high character of the masonic lodges of Lexington is known everywhere, and is abundantly attested by the great number of officers they have furnished to the Grand Lodge. The lodges, at present, are fully up to the old standard of merit and prosperity.

The art annals of Lexington are not to be despised.

William West, who came to this city in 1788, was the first painter that ever settled in the vast region "this side the mountains." He was the son of the then rector of St. Paul's Church, Baltimore, and had studied under the celebrated Benjamin West, in London. His family was a talented one. His brother, Edward West, who had preceded him to Lexington three years before, was the wonderful mechanical genius who invented the steamboat in this city in 1793 (see chapter of that date), and his son, William E. West, is now remembered for the portrait he painted of Lord Byron, at Leghorn. William West painted but few pictures, and they were of only moderate merit. He is best known as "the first painter who came to the West." He died in New York.

Asa Park, a Virginian, was the second painter who settled in Lexington. He was an intimate friend of William West, in whose family he lived, greatly beloved, for years. He died in the year 1827, and was buried by the West family on their lot, near the corner of Hill and Mill streets, opposite the present Letcher property. Though Mr. Park attempted portraits, his best productions were fruit and flower pieces. His pictures, like West's, owe their value mainly to the fact of his having been one of the pioneer painters of Lexington. One of the very few of Park's productions is still in existence, and in the possession of Mrs. Ranck. It is an oil portrait of her grandfather, Lewis Ellis.

Mr. Beck, erroneously mentioned in Dunlap's Arts of Design as "the first painter who penetrated beyond the Alleghanies," settled in Lexington about the year 1800. He belonged, at one time, to a company of scouts under General Anthony Wayne. He and his wife conducted a female seminary in this city for many years, in which painting was a prominent feature. Mr. and Mrs. Beck were both artists of some ability, and painted many pictures, principally landscapes. W. Mentelle, S. D. McCullough, John Tilford, Mrs. Thomas Clay, and many others own pictures by Beck. Mr. Beck died in 1814. His wife survived until 1833.

In 1818, John Neagle, afterward known as the painter of "Pat Lyon, the Blacksmith," visited Lexington with the intention of settling, but he found Jouett so far his superior that he left and settled in Philadelphia. He came to this city again in 1844, at the instance of the Whigs of Philadelphia, to paint for them a full length portrait of Henry Clay, which he did, Mr. Clay sitting for him at the Phœnix Hotel. In November of that year, he presented to Daviess Lodge, of this city, a portrait of Colonel Joseph H. Daviess, from the original by Jouett. The picture is now owned by Major S. D. McCullough.

Chester Harding, a native of Montgomery county, Kentucky, and who afterward acquired a national reputation, painted some excellent portraits here in 1819. Mrs. H. J. Bodley, Mrs. Wm. Preston, Mrs. Woodward, Mrs. A. H. Woolley, and others have pictures by him. Harding's studio was in "Higgins' Block."

Louis Morgan, a native of Pittsburg, settled in Lexington in 1830, and remained here for many years. He painted pictures which evinced a very high order of talent, and it was only the lack of energy that prevented him from becoming noted. His best effort is his well-known portrait of Simon Kenton from life. He was gifted with exquisite taste and remarkable feeling for color. He died about the year 1860. Dr. Robert Peter owns some of his pictures.

The greatest painter that Kentucky has yet produced, and one whose name has shed no little lustre upon the art annals of America, was Matthew H. Jouett. He was born near Lexington, in 1783, and educated for the bar. After participating in the war of 1812, he returned to Lexington, where he attempted to practice law, but being devoted to art, and rendered dissatisfied by the aspirations of his genius, he abandoned his profession, and in 1817 went to Boston and studied under the noted Gilbert Stuart. In less than five years from that time, he was celebrated as the best portrait painter west of the Alleghany mountains. His studio in Lexington, was first in a two-story brick building, which formerly stood on Short street, between the Northern Bank and the residence of the late D. A. Sayre.

Subsequently he used a room above the first National Bank on the same street. Among his best pictures are those of Henry Clay, Joseph H. Daviess, Dr. Holley, Major Morrison, Governor Letcher, John J. Crittenden, Isaac Shelby, and the full length portrait of the Marquis Lafayette, now owned by the State of Kentucky. Mr. Jouett died in Lexington, August 10, 1827, having just returned from a professional trip to the South. Mr. Jouett was tall and thin of form, gifted with great taste, rare humor, and splendid conversational powers, and his literary and social culture was only second to his great artistic genius. Nearly half a century has elapsed since Jouett's death, but his superior as a portrait painter has never yet arisen in the West.

Oliver Frazer, another artist-son of Lexington, was born February 4, 1808, and studied for several years under Jouett. After the death of his distinguished instructor, Mr. Frazer, in company with George P. Healy, went to Europe, where he remained for four years, studying the great works of the old masters. On his retun, he married Miss Martha, daughter of Dr. Alexander Mitchell, of Frankfort, and achieved flattering success as a portrait painter. He died, April 9, 1854, and was buried in the Lexington Cemetery. Unfortunately, his eyesight became injured some years before his death, which prevented him from being a prolific painter, but the few productions of his pencil are of rare merit. His portrait of Clay, and a family group in the possession of Mrs. Frazer, are considered among his best efforts. Mr. Clay spoke in the strongest terms of satisfaction of his portrait by Frazer, who received a number of orders for copies of it. Others of Mr. Frazer's pictures are owned by Major Lewinski, F. K. Hunt, Mrs. M. T. Scott, Wm. Warfield, Judge Robertson, Mrs. W. A. Dudley, J. S. Wilson, Mrs. A. K. Woolley, J. J. Hunter, and others, and are characterized by their delicate coloring and accurate delineation. Another has well said that Mr. Frazer was a true artist, and loved his profession for its own sake. He was honest, kind, and true, and was devoted to the retirement of his happy home. He was greatly gifted in conversation, well read in the best art and other literature, and his taste was exceedingly delicate and correct.

Another artist, Joseph H. Bush, made Lexington his home for many years. Mr. Bush was born in Frankfort, Kentucky, in 1794, and was the son of Philip and Elizabeth Bush. At the age of eighteen, he went to Philadelphia, under the care of Mr. Clay, and remained there three years, studying under the celebrated artist, Sully, after which he pursued his profession in New Orleans, Vicksburg, Louisville, and Lexington, and attained an enviable distinction. How skillfully he handled his pencil is evidenced in the reputation of his full-length picture of General Zachary Taylor, and the coloring and the beautiful effect of light and shade in his portraits of Dr. Ben. Dudley, Mrs. Fanny Bullitt, and the rest of his numerous productions. Mr. Bush died in Lexington, January 11, 1865, only a few months after the decease of his fellow-artist, Oliver Frazer.

Mr. Bush was a man of deep religious feelings, and extensive reading and culture, and was most genial and companionable with those he knew well. His studio was in an upper room over Sayre's banking house, corner of Mill and Short.

In 1867, Mr. Alexander painted some fine pictures in Lexington, one of General John C. Breckinridge, and another of Judge W. B. Kinkead, being among the number.

Since Jouett's time, a number of artists have either sojourned in Lexington temporarily, or made it their home. John Grimes, who excelled in delicate forms and colors, painted here, for several years anterior to 1832, at which time he died in Lexington, and was buried in the Episcopal Cemetery. His studio was in the building on Main street, now occupied by Mr. Thomas Bradley. Several of his productions are in the possession of his aunt, Mrs. Thos. Grant, and Mrs. Fannie Dewees and J. J. Hunter each have one.

The well-known miniature engravings of Clay and Jackson are from original portraits by Dodge, who resided for some time in Lexington.

J. H. Beard, the American Landseer, during a visit to Lexington, painted portraits of the late Robert Alexander, Colonel W. S. Price, and one or two others.

William Ver Bryck, who has since attained much celebrity, executed some very fine portraits in this city, in 1868, one of Mrs. Dr. Whitney, one each of Mr. and Mrs. John Carty, and portraits of several members of Dr. H. M. Skillman, and Mr. Isaac Scott's families. No visiting artist ever met with as much success in Lexington as Mr. Ver Bryck. His studio was in the Phœnix Hotel. He come to Lexington from the city of New York.

Mr. B. F. Rhineheart, in 1869, had a temporary studio in the present Library building, and painted in very superior style, portraits of General John C. Breckinridge, General John H. Morgan, Mrs. Basil Duke, Dr. and Mrs. Warren Frazer, Mr. Thos. Mitchell, and others. His chief excellences are fine modeling and coloring. Mr. Rhineheart is a native of Ohio.

Mr. E. Troye, who was born in England, but has long been a resident of New York, has painted a number of fine animal pictures. Some of his best efforts—pictures of blood horses—are in the possession of Messrs. J. A. Grinstead, A. K. Richards, A. Buford, M. Alexander, of Woodford, and others. As an animal painter, Mr. Troye has no superior in this country. He has, as yet, attempted but few composition pictures, the "Dead Sea" being one of them.

General W. S. Price is one of the most promising resident painters Lexington has had since Jouett. He is a son of the late Daniel B. Price, of Nicholasville, Ky., and was a pupil of the lamented Oliver Frazer. His first effort, made at the age of seventeen, was a portrait of "Old King Solomon," the unterrified grave-digger during the cholera of '33, and long one of the "institutions" of Lexington. This picture merits the celebrity it has attained. Another early picture is a fine portrait of Postmaster Ficklin. The portrait of President Fillmore, in the Phœnix Hotel dining-room, is by Price, and was painted in 1855. One of his most successful efforts is a large picture of General George

H. Thomas, which has become extensively known. Mr. Price has received letters highly complimenting his work from both Mr. Fillmore and General Thomas. A striking likeness of Judge Robertson must not be forgotten. Latterly, General Price has attempted composition pictures, and with marked success. The "Night before the Battle of Chickamauga," the "Young Artist," and "Caught Napping," indicate the latitude, as well as the superiority of his talents. He has reflected honor upon the art history of his state. His studio is in the second story of the Post-office building, on the corner of Mill and Short streets.

Mrs. Eliza Brown, widow of Professor John Brown, of Transylvania University, who died in 1855, has painted a number of beautiful landscapes, the merit of which is heightened by the fact that Mrs. Brown commenced with the pencil at a time of life when art efforts generally cease. A Rhineland scene, the "Yosemite Valley," a Canadian landscape, and an exquisite bit of Minnesota rock and water, are worthy of special mention. Mrs. Brown, who is now nearly seventy, attempted a few months ago, and for the first time, portrait painting, and with extraordinary success, considering her age. Her residence and studio is on the corner of Short and Upper streets.

Mr. Stuart, a South Carolinian, but now a resident of St. Louis, painted some excellent portraits in this city last spring; one each of Mrs. Rosa Jeffrey, Mr. Cooper, city Librarian, and R. A Buckner, Sen., deceased.

CHAPTER XVI.

Town Affairs—James Brown—The Methodist Church—Father Poythress—The Cloud—Adams and Centenary Secessions—Pastors and Incidents—The Lexington Light Infantry—Its Brilliant Record—Share in the War of 1812—Death of Hart and Searles—The Killed—Incidents—The Man who smoked out the Indians—List of Captains.

In 1789, the trustees of Lexington, with an eye to the public comfort and welfare, directed "all fences to be removed from the streets," and prohibited "the cutting and removing of timber from the public grounds." A curious phenomenon caused great anxiety among the good citizens this year. It was so dark in the afternoon of October 31, that the people had to dine by candle-light, and the darkness lasted nearly three hours.*

James Brown, who became one of the eminent public men of this county, settled in Lexington in 1789. He was born in Virginia, September 11, 1766, and was educated at William and Mary College. He commanded a company of Lexington riflemen, in Wilkinson's expedition against the Indians, in 1791. At the organization of the commonwealth in this city, the next year he became the first secretary of state of the new government, which subsequently necessitated his removal to Frankfort. Soon after the cession of Louisiana, he removed to that state, and was twice elected to the United States Senate. He was also minister to France from 1823 to 1829. He died in Philadelphia, in 1835, distinguished for his eloquence and legal ability. When Mr. Brown lived in Lexington, his residence was

---

*Old Gazette.

on the corner of Mill and Short streets, on the site of the building now owned by Mr. Wolverton.

The Methodist Church commenced its history in Lexington, in 1789, with a feeble but devout little band of Christians, who assembled at times in a dilapidated log cabin which stood on the corner of Short and Dewees streets, where the Colored Baptist church now stands. Two years before this, the first Methodist church built in Kentucky (a log one) had been erected at Masterson's station, five miles northwest of Lexington, and in 1790, the first annual conference of the church in Kentucky was held there, and had the great and good Bishop Francis Asbury as its presiding officer.* The father of the little church at Lexington was the impassioned, the self sacrificing, and the unfortunate Francis Poythress, who went from station to station, preaching and toiling and suffering in silence. At a conference in Baltimore, in 1776, Father Poythress had been admitted into the traveling connection, and in 1778 he was sent to Kentucky. As a preacher, few, in those days, excelled him. His voice was clear and musical, his knowledge of the Scriptures vast and accurate, and his sermons fell as the dews of life upon the hearts of his congregation. His mind finally gave way, from the excessive draughts made upon it, and he never preached again after the fall of 1800. He died and was buried near Nicholasville.† John Page, James O'Cull, and Thomas Allen preached at various times to the Methodists in Lexington, from 1792 to 1800, when Lewis Hunt, a Virginian, was appointed to "Lexington town," where he labored with much acceptability to his little flock. In 1803, the church at Lexington was detached from the circuit, and organized into a station.

This was the first Methodist station in Kentucky, and comprised seventy-seven members, forty-seven white and the rest black. Thomas Wilkinson was pastor at that time. He was succeeded by Nathaniel Harris and Burwell Spurlock. Dr. Caleb W. Cloud was assigned to the care

---

*Redford's History.   †Collins, 126.

of the church in 1811, at which period he was one of the most able and prominent preachers in the state. Dr. Cloud's ability and piety was only equaled by his eccentricity and independence, and his elaborate "spencer," nick-tailed horse, and imprudent language soon occasioned trouble among the members of the church, which, at that day, was noted for its great simplicity.

An incident, characteristic of the man, occurred when Postlethwaite's tavern was burned. The doctor, who was then an enthusiastic officer of a fire company, saw a man sitting on a horse amusing himself by watching the fire. He ordered him to assist at the engine; the man declined, saying that he was a "county" man, and "did n't have to help at town fires." Without more ado, the doctor, with words more plain than elegant, pulled him from his horse and *made* him "help."

The church became so dissatisfied with the doctor's "ways," that, in 1812, he withdrew from it, carrying a number of the members with him, and formed the Independent Methodist Church. After preaching for several years at his own house, he built "St. John's Chapel," on Main street, where Douglass' carriage factory now stands. The doctor officiated gratuitously, and often invited the various denominations to worship in his chapel. After preaching independently for a long series of years, he at last went back to the church he had left. He died May 14, 1850, aged sixty-nine, and was followed to his grave by the Masons, the medical profession, and a large number of other citizens.

But to return. After the withdrawal of Dr. Cloud, the church was blessed with the services of Mr. Akers, but the congregation, crippled by the secession of the independent doctor and his adherents, languished until 1820, when it began to grow under the pastorate of Edward Stevenson, and was still further enlarged by Richard Tydings. Its prosperity was such in 1822, that a new church building was erected on Church street, between Upper and Limestone, at a cost of $5,000, and was dedicated in that year by Bishop George. It was a plain, well-finished, brick edifice, measuring fifty by sixty feet. It held seventy-five pews on the ground floor, and was provided with a gallery above. T. P. Satterwhite, Stephen Chipley, Nicholas Headington, John Shrock, T. K. Layton, Thomas Gibbons, James Hamilton, J. W. Russell, Harvey Maguire, and B. W. Rhoton were members of the church at that time. In 1829, William Holman was pastor. His successor was Bishop H. H. Kavanaugh, who was born January 14, 1802, in Clarke county, Kentucky. He joined the Methodist Church at the age of fifteen, was licensed to preach in 1822, and was regular pastor of the Lexington church, both in 1830 and 1847. He was elected bishop at the general conference of the Methodist Episcopal Church South, at Columbus, Georgia, in 1854. Bishop Kavanaugh was a resident of Lexington for many years, and was greatly beloved and esteemed.

Among the ministers who succeeded him may be named George C. Light; the worthy and useful Spencer Cooper, who died in 1839, and the eccentric, widely-known, and now aged Peter Cartwright. The wonderfully eloquent Maffit conducted a revival in the church on Church street in 1834. Immense audiences were entranced by his glowing words, and many connected themselves with the church. Maffit preached in Lexington again in 1837.

The present church edifice on Hill street, between Upper and Mill, was commenced in 1841, and dedicated by the gifted bishop, Henry B. Bascom, in 1842. Bishop Bascom was born in New York, May 27, 1796. His boyhood life was a hard one, and his early manhood full of trials and discouragements, but surmounting every obstacle, he lived to gain from Henry Clay the eulogy, "He is the greatest natural orator I ever heard." He was appointed chaplain to the House of Representatives in Congress in 1841, but soon resigned, and accepted, in 1842, the presidency of Transylvania University, which position he held for seven years. In 1849, his volume of sermons was published. He died in Louisville, Kentucky, September 8, 1850.

On the division of the Methodist Church in the United

States, in 1844, the church in Lexington connected itself with the Southern Conference, and it had abundant prosperity until 1856, at which time a dispute arose, concerning the power of the officers of the church, and ended in the secession of a large number of the members, under the leadership of Samuel Adams and Nicholas Headington. The seceders bought the old medical hall lot, on the corner of Church and Market streets; built the house now known as the City Library with subscriptions raised from the general public; organized an independent church, and made Samuel Adams their pastor. The church was called "Morris Chapel," after Bishop Morris, of Ohio. A disagreement between the congregation and the officers of the new church resulted in the resignation of Mr. Adams and the calling of C. B. Parsons, who failed to give satisfaction, and at last, after existing independently for eight or nine years, most of the members returned to the "church on the hill," and deeded their property to the Church South.

The names of some of the ministers who labored for the Hill Street church before this secession are William Gunn, L. D. Huston, S. Adams, T. C. Shelman, J. H. Linn, E. P. Buckner, R. Heiner, W. C. Dandy, Mr. Spruell.

The Methodist Church, like the Baptist and Presbyterian, had its war troubles also, which grew worse and worse, until they culminated, in September, 1865, in an open rupture, when the party favoring the Northern Conference seceded, and formed what is now called the Centenary Methodist Church (see chapter on 1865). Since that time the Hill Street church has enjoyed the services of the following pastors, viz: H. P. Walker, B. M. Messick, R. K. Hargrove, S. X. Hall, H. A. M. Henderson, and W. S. Rand, the present untiring and acceptable minister. No church in Lexington has had more discouraging circumstances to contend with than the Hill Street church, but she has come out nobly from them all, and is now rapidly growing in strength and usefulness.

The Lexington Light Infantry, of glorious memory, and the oldest military company in Kentucky, and perhaps in this country, was organized in 1789.* Its formation was due to a threatened Indian invasion, and to the martial passion of General James Wilkinson, who was chosen its first captain. Its first ensign was John Fowler, afterward postmaster of Lexington. Since that time a host of stirring associations have clustered about the simple name "Old Infantry," for it has been connected with victories and defeats, conflicts and massacres, and with some of the most brilliant military achievements recorded in the annals of Kentucky. It was led by Wilkinson in successful expeditions against the Indians; shared in the disastrous defeats of Harmar and St. Clair; bore a gallant part in the victorious campaign of "old Mad Anthony" Wayne against the Sciota and other Indians,† and, in 1792, escorted Governor Shelby into Lexington, then the capital of the state, and assisted in the ceremonies of his inauguration. These were the days when the "Old Infantry" delighted in flint-lock muskets, and in tinder-boxes and steel.

In 1803, the company was called out by President Jefferson to go to Louisiana, but the purchase of that state by the government superseded the necessity. It was about this time that the well-known and historic uniform suit of the company was adopted. It consisted of a blue cloth coat, with cuffs, breast, and collar faced with red and ornamented with bell-buttons. The pantaloons were of blue cloth, the hat black, and the plume red. The favorite parade ground of the company, at this time, was a beautiful level spot back of, and belonging to the property of Mrs. John Carty, on Broadway. Subsequently, the Maxwell Spring grounds were used. A "turn-out" of the Old Infantry in early days was a grand event in Lexington, and was always witnessed by a large and admiring crowd of natives of all ages, sexes, colors, and conditions.

The Lexington Light Infantry was one of the first companies to volunteer in the war of 1812, it having organized for the campaign on the 11th of May of that year, with N. S. G. Hart as captain. The "silk-stocking boys," as

---

*Old Journals.   †Gazette, and Ob. and Rep.

the members of the company were then often called, were attached to the Fifth Regiment of Kentucky Volunteer Militia, commanded by Colonel William Lewis, and marched for the Northwestern army in August, 1812. On the march to Fort Wayne an incident occurred, which, amusing as it may appear, speaks volumes for the principles which actuated the men. A member of the company having stood manfully up under the severe fatigues of the march until the last day, at length sank on the grass of the prairie through which the company was marching, and, whilst his comrades were passing rapidly on, he shed bitter tears at his condition. An officer* approached him, in company with one or two others, to aid him to one of the few wagons that attended the march, and on inquiring the cause of his tears, he earnestly exclaimed, " *What will they say in Lexington when they hear that James Huston* GAVE OUT ?"

The glorious share which the "Old Infantry" had in the terrible battle and sickening massacre at Frenchtown, on the river Raisin, in this campaign, is told in our chapter on the year 1812. At that river of death, the heroic band lost half its members in killed, wounded, and prisoners; the brilliancy of their uniform causing the men to be readily picked off by the enemy. The gallant captain of the company, who was wounded and disabled in the battle, was barbarously murdered by the savages after having trusted himself to the protection of his pretended friend, Captain Elliott, of the British army, who infamously abandoned him to the mercy of the Indians.†

The heroic death of Charles Searles, another gallant member of the Light Infantry, wounded in the battle of the 18th, should never be forgotten.‡ On the morning of the 23d, by strong exertion, he was able to walk, and so to conceal his wound, that he was allowed to accompany his captors unmolested, until they stopped for the night. No doubt the fatigue, aided by the sufferings from his wound, at length revealed to the savages his disabled condition, and marked him out as a victim. He, with several other prison-

---

*Gen. J. M. McCalla.   †Western Annals.   ‡McCalla's Address.

ers, was seated on the ground, partaking of some food, when one of the savages rose up, and drawing his tomahawk, approached Searles from behind.

The prisoner marked the movement, and apprehending his intention, watched the descending blow, and tried to catch it in his hand, but only partially succeeded, the weapon inflicting a deep wound in the shoulder. Rising to his feet, he seized his antagonist, who was unprepared for such a bold resistance, and snatching the tomahawk from his hand, was about to inflict a deserved vengeance on his cruel assailant, when Dr. Bower, of the regiment, told him that if he struck the Indian all the prisoners would be murdered, and his death, now inevitable, would not be prevented. As soon as he found that he might endanger his comrades by resisting, he dropped the uplifted arm, let fall the weapon, and, without a murmur or a complaint, waited until the astonished savage picked up the tomahawk, and coolly and deliberately dispatched his victim.

Can Roman or Grecian annals display a more sublime instance of manly generosity and magnanimity than this?

It was at the battle of Frenchtown that a member of the "Old Infantry" company, James Higgins,* astonished even the boldest of his comrades by his daring contempt of death. Vain efforts had been made to dislodge a large number of Indians from a barn, into which they had crowded, and from which they were pouring a destructive fire into Colonel Lewis's command. The soldier we have mentioned asked permission to "smoke 'um out." It was granted. He then coolly picked up a large blazing "chunk" from a camp fire, deliberately walked up to the barn in the very face of a hail storm of bullets, and applied the "chunk." The barn was soon one mass of flames, and the brave infantryman quickly had the satisfaction of seeing all the Indians "smoked out." The most remarkable feature of the case was that the man had always been regarded at home as ridiculously timid, and had often been imposed upon, both by his neighbors and comrades in arms. But after this bold deed, the past

---

*General S. L. Williams and T. P. Dudley.

was forgotten, and it was not safe for any one to say anything in the presence of the "Old Infantry" against the man "who smoked out the Indians." James Higgins, the hero of this glorious incident, was born near Side View, Montgomery county, Kentucky, but removed to Lexington, and was one of her citizens when he enlisted in the Old Infantry. This gallant man died many years ago.

A few names of the killed of this company have been preserved, viz: N. S. G. Hart, Charles Searles, J. E. Blythe (son of President Blythe, of Transylvania University), Jesse Cock, Alexander Crawford, Samuel Elder, William Davis, Jesse Riley, Armston Stewart, George Shindlebower, Samuel Cox, and Charles Bradford.

On the 11th of September, 1839, the Light Infantry celebrated in Lexington its fiftieth anniversary. At eleven o'clock A. M., a procession, consisting of the Louisville Guards, Captain Anderson; the Volunteer Artillery, Captain Trotter; the Mechanics Infantry, Captain Forbes; and the "Old Infantry," under Captain G. L. Postlethwaite, marched to the beautiful woodlands of John Love (now J. H. Mulligan's, adjoining the Maxwell Spring grounds), where an exceedingly appropriate and interesting address was delivered by General John M. McCalla, after which came a banquet, and then the survivors of the war of 1812 reviewed their hardships and dangers, and fought their battles over again.

At the commencement of the war with Mexico, the Light Infantry again took the field, under the command of Captain Cassius M. Clay, and was known in the army by the remarkable name of the "Lexington Old Infantry Cavalry." In that war, the Kentucky cavalry used as its regimental flag the colors which the ladies of Lexington had presented to the "Old Infantry," some years before, on an anniversary of the battle of the Raisin.

In times of peace, the company amused itself with target shooting at Maxwell's spring. On one of these occasions, Captain Richard Parker, then commanding the Old Infantry, but now one of our oldest citizens, was accidentally shot in the hip, and he still suffers from the wound then received.

In 1860, the Old Infantry took its stand in the Kentucky State Guard, with the following officers, viz: Captain, Samuel D. McCullough; First Lieutenant, George W. Didlake; Second Lieutenant, S. W. Price; Third Lieutenant, J. B. Norton; Ensign, R. H. Prewett; Surgeon, Dr. G. W. McMillin; Right Guide, Charles Dobyns; Left Guide, W. W. Dowden; Third Sergeant, B. W. Blincoe; Fourth Sergeant, Charles Schultz; Fifth Sergeant, M. Hogarty.

In the memorable summer of 1861, just before Kentucky was drawn into the gigantic civil contest then waging, the Old Infantry held a reunion in the densely crowded Odd Fellows' Hall, on the corner of Main and Broadway. The company was conducted to the hall by those two noted organizations, the "Lexington Rifles" and the "Chasseurs," headed by the splendid Newport band. An opening address was delivered by Judge L. L. Todd, of Indianapolis, a former captain of the Old Infantry, after which a new flag was presented to the company by General Combs, in behalf of the donor, Mr. David A. Sayre. The old flag of the Old Infantry, which had gone through the leaden storm of Buena Vista, was then unfurled, a roll of all the captains called, and the Star Spangled Banner sung, after which the meeting adjourned.

Many of the members of the company served gallantly on either side in the terrible war between the States, and fully maintained the ancient renown of the venerable organization, which, for the credit of Lexington, should never be permanently abandoned.

From the year 1789 to the present time, the Lexington Light Infantry has been commanded by the following captains, viz: General James Wilkinson, 1789; James Hughes and Samuel Weisiger, 1791; Cornelius Beatty, 1793; John Postlethwaite, 1797; Thomas Bodley, 1803; N. S. G. Hart, 1811-12; and since the last date by Daniel Bradford, J. G. Trotter, Adam Beatty, William Logan, Levi L. Todd, Robert Megowan, Richard Parker, G. L. Postlethwaite, T.

P. Hart, Thomas Smith, R. Morrison, John M. McCalla, Lawrence Daly, James O. Harrison, T. Monks, T. W. Lowry, W. Allison, Lewis Barbee, F. G. West, Joseph Hoppy, G. L. Postlethwaite, J. B. Clay, C. M. Clay, S. D. McCullough, S. W. Price.

CHAPTER XVII.

*Town Affairs—Harmar's Defeat—John Pope—The Jail—
Fire Companies.*

WHILE the actual population of Lexington, in 1790, was not large, the town was a place of some importance as a stopping point for traders, as it was on the line of communication between the East and the West. In this year, the trustees ordered a "canal" to be dug to carry the water of the "Branch" straight through town. They also made the announcement that "the town commons shall hereafter be known as Water street." Lexington's encouragement of art in 1790 is exhibited in the eagerness of the citizens to obtain "black profile likenesses, taken by the physiognotrace."

In July of this year, the delegates from Fayette attended the eighth convention, held at Danville. At this convention, an act of separation, passed by the Virginia legislature, was finally accepted, and a ninth convention, to form a state constitution, was called for April, 1791.

Incursions and murders by the Indians had now become so frequent and unbearable that the new general government, which had just gone into operation, sent out a military force to protect the frontier. In the fall, Colonel Trotter, with some volunteers from Lexington, went to Fort Washington (Cincinnati), and joined the expedition of General Joseph Harmar against the Miami towns. The campaign ended disastrously.

That distinguished statesman, John Pope, came to Lexington in 1790, at which time he was about twenty years of age. He lived in this city for many years. Mr. Pope was born in Prince William county, Virginia, and emigrated to Kentucky while quite a boy.* He was a man of great ability and remarkable talents, and was one of the most formidable opponents Mr. Clay ever had; and, like Mr. Clay, he attained distinction by his own exertions. Mr. Pope was often a member of the Kentucky legislature, was for many years a representative in Congress, was United States Senator in 1807, and was for six years governor of the Territory of Arkansas. He died in Washington county, Kentucky, in 1842, aged seventy-two. He built and resided in the house now occupied by Joseph Wolfolk, near the junction of Rose and Hill streets. When Mr. Pope ran against Mr. Clay, in the Lexington district, it was in the vigor of their days, when each one was able to do his best. It was Wagoner and Gray Eagle against each other. Mr. Clay was the winner, but did not, we believe, distance his competitor. The race was honorable to both, and if Mr. Pope had had the same passionate determination, and the same fiery and never-relaxing ambition of Mr. Clay, there would have been two Clays in the state without room enough to hold them. An amusing incident occurred during this race.† Mr. Pope had but one arm. On the approach of the contest, Mr. Clay called upon an Irishman in Lexington, who had been his political friend heretofore, but now declared his intention to go for Pope. Mr. Clay wanted to know the reason. The answer was, "Och, Misther Clay, I have concluded to vote for the man who *has but one arm to sthrust into the sthreasury.*"

A log jail succeeded the pillory and the stocks in Lexington in 1790, and stood near the first court-house on Main, not far from the corner of Broadway.‡ In these early days, when imprisonment for debt was in vogue, the "jail bounds," or the precincts within which a debt prosoner could walk, was marked on the pavements and the houses near the jail by a broad stripe of black paint. A larger jail was erected in 1797, on the same ground where the present jail stands, was destroyed by fire in 1819, and another one was completed the next year. The building

---

*Collins.   †Correspondence Cincinnati Gazette.   ‡Old Gazette.

of the present prison commenced in 1850. The following is an incomplete list of those who have filled the office of jailer, viz: Innis B. Brent, —— Clark, —— Barker, Wm. Bobbs, Nathaniel Prentiss, Richard Sharp, Joseph R. Megowan, T. B. Megowan, —— White, Ben. Blincoe, W. H. Lusby, and Thos. B. Megowan. Including all the terms he has served, Mr. T. B. Megowan has been a jailer for nearly forty years.

Lexington's first regular fire company was organized at Brent's tavern in 1790, with John Bradford as secretary. It was styled the Union Fire Company, and used buckets only. Before this, in case of a fire, each citizen was required, when the alarm was given, to attend with a bucket filled from his own well. The Union company's "bucket-house" was a building on Main, near Scott's block. Later, it was on Water street, and was finally converted into an engine house. In 1805, the officers of the "Union" were: Captains—Dan'l Bradford, Christopher Keiser; Directors—William Macbean, George Anderson, John Jones, Alexander Frazer, Thomas Hart, Jr., John Jordan, Jr., Thomas Bodley, Alex. Parker, Charles Wilkins, Lewis Sanders, William Ross, Thomas Whitney, Maddox Fisher. The trustees passed a resolution in 1812, authorizing a committee "to procure four additional ladders, four fire-hooks, three rope-ladders, and three tubs to put under the pumps, all to be marked with the name of the company, etc., and a fine of ten dollars imposed on any person who will use them, unless in case of fire." In 1818, two little "newly-invented" engines were bought by the town authorities. They attracted great attention and admiration.

The fire department was organized in 1832, when the city was incorporated. In 1840, the city could boast of the "Kentuckian," "Lyon," and "Resolution" hand-engines, and others were added from time to time. The period included between 1850 and 1860 was the golden age of the fire companies in Lexington. Then the Fourth of July was the day of their glory, and the old Lyon, Clay, Kentuckian, and other engines, with their hose carriages, were resplendent with beautiful decorations fashioned by the ladies of the city. Three hundred firemen have been known to turn out in procession on such occasions, presenting a splendid appearance with their brilliant uniforms and gay trappings. But these are memories of an age which ended with the purchase of the first steam fire engine, in March, 1864. The "Lyon" engine house was on Limestone street, near the corner of Hill; the "Clay," on Broadway, between Short and Second, now known as Pruden's marble works; the "Union," on Short, between Upper and Limestone, is now the headquarters of the steam fire department.

CHAPTER XVIII.

*Survey of Lexington—Expeditions of Scott and Wilkinson—
St. Clair's Defeat—Delegates to the Ninth Convention.*

DURING the spring of 1791, the trustees of Lexington made war on "wooden chimneys," the use of which, for the future, was prohibited. They also ordered "all the post and rail fences across Short street to be taken down." In the latter part of March, the following survey of the town was made, the report of which we give verbatim, with the drawing which accompanied it.*

"Surveyed by order of the trustees of the town of Lexington, 204 acres of land, including the court-house of Fayette county in the center, in a circular figure of two miles in diameter. Beginning at A, one mile southeast from the said court-house, at a post on the northeast side of the road, running thence south 56¼, west 125 poles to a post crossing Tate's creek road at 85 poles; thence south 78¾, west 125 poles to a post, thence north 78¾, west 125 poles to post; thence north 56¼, west 125 poles to post crossing the Hickman road at 25 poles, thence north 33¾, west 125 poles to post crossing Craig's mill road at 45 poles; thence north 11¼, west 125 poles to a stake in Hackney's field, about 40 poles southeastwardly from his house; thence north 11¼, east 125 poles to post; thence north 33¾, east 125 poles to post 15 poles northeast of the old Leestown road, crossing the head of McConnell's mill pond at 45 poles; thence north 56¼, east 125 poles to post, passing and leaving out Eckle's and Brown's plantations; thence north 78¾, east 125 poles to post, crossing Johnston's mill road at 35 poles; thence south 78¼, east 125

---
*Trustees' Book.

poles to post, leaving out Irvine's house, 14 poles; thence south 56¼, east 125 poles to post crossing Russell's road at 75 poles; thence south 33¾, east 125 poles to post near Springle's house in the survey, and crossing Bryan's road at 25 poles; thence south 11¼, east 125 poles to post; thence south 11¼, west 125 poles to post near Captain Wilson's house, leaving him in the survey; thence south 33¾, west 125 poles to the beginning, leaving Javell 14 poles in the survey, and passing Masterson, and leaving him out."

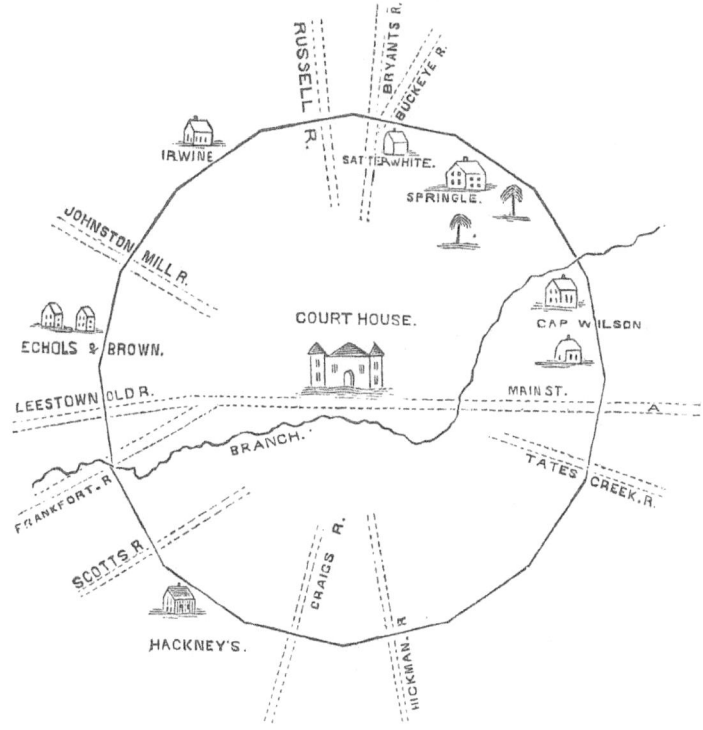

The Indians, greatly emboldened by their success over Harmar, extended their incursions, and immigrants were killed by them even in the neighborhood of Lexington. In May, General Charles Scott organized an expedition of mounted volunteers to punish the Indians on the Wabash, and General James Wilkinson, who was appointed second in command, augumented the force with a number of men from Lexington. The troops began their march from Fort Washington, May 23, 1791, and early in the following June, destroyed three Kickapoo towns, killed thirty warriors, and took fifty-eight prisoners, without the loss of a man.* By the 18th of June, all the volunteers from Lexington had returned, highly elated at their success. It is a matter of great regret that only the following few names† of soldiers from this city have been preserved, viz: Thos. Allen, Jas. M'Dowell, Jas. Brown, Wm. M'Millin, John E. King, Sam'l Patterson, Jos. Jones, Rich'd Bartlett, John Peoples, John Arnold, Benj. Gibbs.

In July, General Wilkinson was appointed by Governor St. Clair to complete the work so successfully commenced by Scott. He organized his expedition in Lexington, and engaged the celebrated Indian-hunter, Bland Ballard, as his guide. He started for the Wabash country August 1st, and on the 7th, surprised and burned the town of Kathtippecamunk, not far from the ruins of which afterward stood the celebrated Prophet's town destroyed by General Harrison in 1811, killed six braves, and took thirty-four prisoners, for all of which he was duly thanked by his country. Wilkinson's loss was two killed and one wounded. The prisoners taken justified their defeat by constantly declaring "Kentucky too much." Only the following names of the volunteers from Lexington and Fayette in this expedition are extant, viz:‡ James McDowell, Levi Todd, F. M'Murdie, Jos. Logsdon, Dav. Caldwell, W. M'Dowell, Wm. Lewis, Wm. Berry, Thos. Atkins, Rich. Bartlett, Moses Caldwell, Patrick Burk, Philip Phillips, John Arnold, Chas. Snedeger, Samuel Harrod, Wm. Clark, Thos. Bruer.

During the entire spring, and while these expeditions were in progress, preparations for the great invasion of the Indian country by General St. Clair were progressing. As early as May, St. Clair had come to Lexington in person to get the aid of the militia; but the infirm old man, with his well-known character for rigid discipline and bad luck,

---

*Old Gazette.   †Old Gazette.   ‡Kentucky Gazette.

met with very small encouragement. One company of sixty men, under William Ellis* (one of the founders of Grant's station), comprised all the volunteers from the whole of Lexington and Fayette county. The balance of the troops obtained by St. Clair from Kentucky had to be drafted, and they, without confidence in their commander's ability, and regarding the regular force which they were compelled to serve with as doomed to destruction, deserted every day.† Beset by a combination of unfavorable circumstances, St. Clair, with his disaffected troops, commenced his march from Fort Jefferson against the Miami villages, and on the 4th of November, while encamped on a tributary of the Wabash, was suddenly attacked by twelve hundred Indians, and suffered one of the most terrible and overwhelming defeats recorded in the annals of savage warfare. The news of this great disaster brought sorrow to many a household in Fayette county; but no record of her loss is known to be in existence. In an old journal,‡ mention is casually made that "Israel Hart, William Bryan, Charles Bland, William Lee, Matthew Robinson, Noble Wood, and James M'Farin had been paid for their services during St. Clair's campaign." An incident of the day was the arrival in Lexington of a band of friendly Chickasaw warriors on their way to join the army of St. Clair, who had been defeated just the day before they got to this city.

In December, 1791, Fayette elected the following delegates to the convention to form a constitution for Kentucky, viz: Hubbard Taylor, Thos. Lewis, George S. Smith, Robert Frier, and James Crawford. This was to be the last of the long series of Danville conventions, as Congress, on the 4th of the preceding February, had admitted Kentucky into the Union.

---

*St. Clair's Report.   †Collins, 44.   ‡Kentucky Gazette.

CHAPTER XIX.

Indian Depredations—First Session of the Kentucky Legislature: Proceedings, Addresses, Ceremonies, and Appointments—Removal of the Capital—List of Public Officers since 1792—Circuit Judges and Clerks—State Representatives and Senators—United States Representatives and Senators.

THE spring of 1792 had hardly come, before the Indians, exulting in St. Clair's defeat, renewed their incursions, and the danger soon became such that immigrants and settlers were compelled when traveling to go in armed bands. About the first of March, the Indians burnt two houses, and killed a man and woman on North Elkhorn, and shortly after, as if determined to aggravate their white foes by every possible means, they crept even nearer to Lexington, and stole negroes, carried them off and sold them.* The last man killed by the Indians, in the vicinity of Lexington, was shot and scalped in the spring of 1792. His body was brought to town, and was prepared for burial in a house on Hill street, between Spring and Merino. Bad as matters were, no expeditions against the Indians were attempted, as fruitless efforts were then being made by the government to effect a peace with the enraged savages.

The ninth and last convention met in Danville, April 1st of this year, and on the 19th of the month, and the seventeenth anniversary of the battle of Lexington, Massachusetts, the first constitution of Kentucky was adopted, to go into effect on the 1st of June following. In May, the governor and other officers, and the members of both houses of the legislature, were elected. On the 4th of June, 1792,† commenced in Lexington the first session of the Kentucky

---

*Old Gazette. †State Papers, and Old Gazette.

legislature, and the organization of the state government. Early in the morning of that eventful day, the infant capital of the new state presented a scene of unusual bustle and excitement. The streets were crowded with citizens and soldiers. Men, women, and children, arrayed in the gayest pioneer fashion, poured in from the country in every direction. Orderlies dashed about, drums beat, sabers clattered, and ramrods rattled, and such a cleaning of rifles, patching of buckskin suits, snapping of flints, and gathering of provisions, was wonderful to behold. The day was well worthy of the attention it received. It had been eagerly and anxiously desired by the people of Kentucky for years, and was destined to be an era in their history, for on that day Isaac Shelby was to take the oath of office as governor of a commonwealth then but three days old, and the work of setting up the political machinery of the new state was to be regularly begun.

As the morning waned, news came in that the governor, then being escorted from Danville by a detachment of the Lexington troop of horse, was approaching the town, and forthwith the "county lieutenant," the board of trustees, the members of the legislature who had arrived, and a large number of prominent gentlemen, went out to meet him. At the corner of Main and Broadway, he was received with military honors by the "Old Infantry Company," and, in the midst of enthusiastic cheers from the great crowd there assembled, was presented by the chairman of the board of trustees of Lexington with the following *written* address:

" To His Excellency, Isaac Shelby, Esq., Governor of the State of Kentucky:

" SIR: The inhabitants of the town of Lexington beg leave through us to present to your excellency their sincerest congratulations on your appointment to the office of chief magistrate of the State of Kentucky.

" Truly sensible that no other motive than a sincere desire to promote the happiness and welfare of your country could have induced you to accept an appointment that must draw you from those scenes of domestic ease and private tranquillity which you enjoy in so eminent a degree.

"Having the fullest confidence in your wisdom, virtue, and integrity, we rest satisfied that under your administration the constitution will be kept inviolate, and the laws so calculated as to promote happiness and good order in the state.

"In the name of the inhabitants of Lexington, we bid you welcome, and assure you that we, and those we represent, have the warmest attachment to your person and character.

"May your administration insure blessings to your country, and honor and happiness to yourself.

"By order of the trustees of Lexington.

"JOHN BRADFORD, *Chairman.*"

After the presentation of this address, the oath of office was administered; then the horse and infantry paraded on the public square, and, after firing alternately fifteen rounds, a general discharge of rifles was given in honor of the new governor, who was escorted to his lodgings by the largest and most picturesque procession that the western country had then known. "Store clothes" were scarce in that multitude, while tow-linen shirts, powder-horns, moccasins, buckskin pants, and coonskin caps were abundant.

Later in the day the following reply to the address of welcome was sent by Governor Shelby:

"*To Mr. John Bradford, Chairman of the Board of Trustees of Lexington:*

"SIR: I receive, with the warmest sentiments of gratitude and respect, your very polite and genteel address, which, added to the friendly treatment exhibited by you this day in conducting me to this place, commands my most cordial respect and esteem; and, although I am thoroughly sensible of my want of experience and abilities to discharge the very important duties committed to me, the warm congratulations only of my country induce me to come forward, with some hope that by a strict attention to the duties of my office, and a firm adherence to public justice (both of which, I trust, are in my power), I may in some degree merit a part of that confidence which they have placed in me.

"Unacquainted with flattery, I only use the plain language of truth to express my warm attachment to the inhabitants of this place, and assure them, through you, sir, that I shall be happy to render them any service in my power which may not be incompatible with the interests of our common country.

"I have the honor to be, with great regard and esteem, sir, your most obedient servant,

"Isaac Shelby."

This address was read to the citizens, and also the announcement of the appointments, by the governor, of James Brown as secretary of state, and George Nicholas, attorney-general.* The legislature met and organized by electing Alexander S. Bullitt, of Jefferson county, speaker of the senate; Robert Breckinridge, speaker of the house, and John Logan, of Lincoln, state treasurer, after which it adjourned, and the rest of the day was spent in rejoicing and in interchange of courtesies between the citizens and their distinguished guests.

On the 6th of June, after the general assembly had been fully organized, the members of both houses assembled in the senate chamber of the state-house, a two-story log building of the regular old pioneer type that stood nearly in the center of the east side of Main street, between Mill and Broadway. At twelve o'clock, Governor Shelby entered the hall, attended by the secretary of state, and was immediately conducted to a position on the right of the speaker of the senate, where, after respectfully addressing, first the senate and then the house, he proceeded to read the communications he had prepared. He was listened to with the deepest attention, and amid the most profound silence on the part of the mass of the legislators and citizens, who filled almost to suffocation every nook and corner of the gloomy but substantial edifice. At the close of his address,

---

*Kentucky Gazette.

the governor delivered to each speaker a copy of the manuscript, and retired as he had entered. The two houses then separated, and, after voting an address in reply to that of his excellency, adjourned.* What a scene for a painter, what a subject for a glowing pen, was that of the opening of the first session of the Kentucky legislature, where the courtly practice of the British kings and colonial governors appeared in such strange and striking contrast with the rude and simple surroundings of early western life. The pomp and state of the house of lords in a log cabin, the royal ermine, and the republican coonskin, European refinement and elegance, western simplicity and virtue. Probably just such another scene has never been enacted before or since. The example set by Governor Shelby, of addressing the legislature in person, was followed in Kentucky up to the time of Governor Scott, when it was changed to the present one, in accordance with a precedent established by President Jefferson.

The legislature was engaged during its first session in organizing the government, the judiciary and revenue requiring much of its attention. The session lasted twelve days. The first bill that secured the sanction of the governor was entitled "an act establishing an auditor's office of public accounts."† Acts were passed "establishing the town of Versailles, at Woodford court-house;" and forming the county of Clark from a part of Fayette. Bills were passed establishing the various courts, and taxes were imposed on land, carriages, cattle, billiard tables, ordinary licenses, and retail stores. Commissioners were appointed by the house of representatives to select a permanent seat of government, then a matter of great jealousy and contention between the people of the opposite sides of the Kentucky river.‡ Five gentlemen were chosen, any three of whom might fix upon a location. Their names were Robert Todd, of Fayette; John Edwards and John Allen, of Bourbon; Henry Lee, of Mason; and Thos. Kenneday, of Madison. The commissioners met soon after their appoint-

---

*Kentucky Gazette. †State Papers. ‡Butler.

ment, when it was found that two were in favor of Frankfort, and two for Lexington. The matter was decided by the vote of General Robert Todd for Frankfort. Why General Todd decided against his own town has long been a mystery to many, but it is known that he regarded his position as a delicate one, inasmuch as he owned a large amount of land in this vicinity, and feared if he gave his vote for his own place of residence, it might be attributed to motives of personal interest. Modern legislators are seldom troubled with such acute sensibilities. What a pity it is that General Todd listened to the seductive voice of old Mrs. Grundy. But he did, and Lexington lost the capital.

Some of the first appointments in the militia made by the governor were those of Benj. Harrison, Thos. Kenneday, and Robert Todd, as brigadier-generals; William Russell, James Trotter, Henry Lee, William Steele, and Levi Todd, lieutenant-colonels; James McDowell, John Morrison, and John McDowell, majors. Robert Parker was appointed surveyor of Fayette county.*

The members of the assembly received one dollar per day for their services, and as no revenue had yet been collected, the treasurer had to borrow that, and when they were at last paid they had to rest content with "cut money;" silver dollars cut into convenient "change," sometimes counted, but oftener *weighed*.† Old time wages of a dollar per day in "cut money," would not be extravagantly relished, we imagine, by our present public servants. The office of the first state treasurer, who had neither treasure, nor building to put it in if he had, was in "the big log tavern" of Robert Megowan, deceased, then *the* tavern of this place, which stood on the spot now covered by Mr. Thomas Bradley's hardware store on Main street.‡

At the time of this first session, Lexington was the largest town in the state, and contained one thousand inhabitants, the population of the entire commonwealth being about ninety thousand. The nine counties then in

---

*State Papers.   †Marshall.   ‡Old Inhabitants.

existence were Fayette, Mercer, Madison, Lincoln, Jefferson, Mason, Bourbon, Nelson, and Woodford.

As we said above, this first meeting of the Kentucky legislature was an event of great moment and heartfelt satisfaction to the people. The infant republic of the vast wilderness had seen nothing but trials, vexations, and disheartening obstacles in its way from the time it was a district of Virginia till it became an independent state. Nine conventions met and toiled before the much-desired result was obtained. The whole work was done over and over again. They were aggravated by the tardiness of Virginia to complete the work of separating the district from the mother State. The old Congress of 1788 declined emphatically to act on Kentucky's petition to be received into the Union. The distinguished John Brown, first and only member from Kentucky in the old Congress, said that "the New England states wanted no new Southern states admitted.*

Here was another delay. Kentucky had to wait till the old crumbling government had dissolved, and the new one had gone into effect. To these repulses may be added the other troubles of French, Spanish, and English intrigues, the ambitious and disturbing conduct of some of her own statesmen, and ever recurring Indian troubles. But all difficulties were overcome. The first legislature met, and the citizens of the new commonwealth rejoiced with exceeding great joy.

The magistrates composing the Fayette court of quarter sessions in 1792 were Thomas Lewis, John McDowell, and Robert Todd; and those of the county court were James Trotter, Walter Carr, Percival Butler, Edward Payne, Joseph Crockett, William Campbell, Abraham Bowman, Hubbard Taylor, and James McMillan. The other public officers who have served the town and county since the organization of the state government are as follows, viz:

---

*Gazette.

CIRCUIT COURT JUDGES.

Samuel McDowell, Buckner Thurston, John Coburn, Thomas Lewis, Robert Todd, Benjamin Howard, Henry Payne, John Monroe, John McDowell, John Parker, William Warren, Benjamin Johnson, Benjamin Mills, Jesse Bledsoe, T. M. Hickey, Daniel Mayes, A. K. Woolley, Richard A. Buckner, W. C. Goodloe, C. B. Thomas.

CIRCUIT COURT CLERKS.

Thomas Bodley, H. I. Bodley, T. S. Redd, James Wood, J. B. Norton, J. B. Rodes.

STATE REPRESENTATIVES.

First Representatives of Fayette in Legislature of Kentucky, May 1, 1792—William Russell, John Hawkins, Thomas Lewis, Hubbard Taylor, James Trotter, Joseph Crockett, James McMillan, John McDowell, Robert Patterson.

1793. David Walker, James Hughes, Edmund Bullock, Joseph Crockett, John South, Thomas January, Robert Frier, Reuben Searcy.

1794. Joseph Crockett, E. Bullock, John McDowell, J. Hughes, D. Walker, J. South.

1795. E. Bullock, J. Crockett, John Parker, J. McDowell, J. Hughes, D. Walker.

1796. Bullock, Parker, William Russell, Hughes, McDowell, Walker, Walter Carr.

1797. McDowell, Bullock, Parker, Russell, John Bradford, Thomas Caldwell, James Morrison.

1798. Bullock, C. Beatty, J. Parker, J. H. Stewart, R. Patterson, McGregor, Carr, Breckinridge, H. Harrison, McDowell, Thomas Caldwell, W. Russell.

1799. W. Russell, John Breckinridge, John Bell, John South, Hez. Harrison, W. Carr.

1800. W. Russell, John Breckinridge, John Parker, Hez. Harrison.

1801. Benjamin Graves, James Hughes, Benjamin Howard, John Bell.

1802. Benjamin Howard, Wm. Russell, James Hughes, John Bradford.
1803. Wm. Russell, Jas. Hughes, James True, Henry Clay.
1804. Henry Clay, Wm. Russell, Benj. Graves.
1805. Henry Clay, Wm. Russell, Grimm R. Tompkins.
1806. Henry Clay, Wm. Russell, John Pope.
1807. Henry Clay, Wm. Russell, John Pope.
1808. Henry Clay, John Parker, James Fishback.
1809. W. T. Barry, H. Clay, Alfred W. Grayson, Geo. Trotter (elected to fill vacancy by Clay resigning, who went to United States Senate).
1810. David Todd, John H. Morton, Joseph H. Hawkins.
1811. George Trotter, David Todd, J. H. Hawkins.
1812. J. H. Hawkins, David Todd, Jesse Bledsoe.
1813. D. Todd, J. H. Hawkins, Robert Russell.
1814. W. T. Barry, Henry Payne, T. T. Crittenden.
1815. H. Payne, James True, Levi L. Todd.
1816. Jos. C. Breckinridge, J. Parker, J. True.
1817. Jos. C. Breckinridge, J. Parker, W. T. Barry.
1818. Jos. C. Breckinridge, Thos. T. Barr, Thomas T. Crittenden.
1819. J. Parker, H. Payne, R. Wickliffe.
1820. Percival Butler, H. Payne, George Shannon.
1821. Jas E. Davis, John R. Witherspoon, Matthias Flournoy.
1822. James Trotter, Geo. Shannon, J. R. Witherspoon.
1823. Wm. Russell, R. Wickliffe, James True.
1824. H. C. Payne, R. Wickliffe, James True.
1825. R. J. Breckinridge, H. C. Payne, J. True.
1826. R. J. Breckinridge, M. Flournoy, J. True.
1827. R. J. Breckinridge, Leslie Combs, J. True, Jr.
1828. R. J. Breckinridge, Leslie Combs, J. True, Jr.
1829. Edward J. Wilson, Combs, and True.
1830. John Curd, Combs, and True.
1831. H. E. Innis, Chas. Carr, R. H. Chinn.
1832. A. K. Woolley, J. R. Dunlap, H. E. Innis.
1833. L. Combs, G. R. Tompkins, J. R. Dunlap.
1834. G. R. Tompkins, J. R. Dunlap, A. K. Woolley.
1835. Jacob Hughes, John Curd, Robt. Wickliffe, Jr.

1836. H. Daniel, W. Rodes, Robt. Wickliffe, Jr.
1837. H. Clay, Jr., W. Rodes, Robt. Wickliffe, Jr.
1838. H. Clay, Jr., W. Rodes, Larkin B. Smith.
1839. Jacob Hughes, Rich'd Pindell, J. Q. McKinney.
1840. C. M. Clay, J. Curd, Clayton Curle.
1841. Neal McCann, Robt. S. Todd.
1842. R. S. Todd, E. A. Dudley, O. D. Winn.
1843. T. S. Redd, Elisha Hogan, C. R. Thompson.
1844. Robt. S. Todd, Thos. A. Russell.
1845. L. Combs, G. W. Darnaby, J. Cunningham.
1846. L. Combs, Richard Spurr.
1847. L. Combs, D. L. Price.
1848. George Robertson, R. J. Spurr.
1849. H. C. Pindell, John C. Breckinridge
1850. R. A. Athey, C. C. Rogers.
1851. Changed to two each second year.
1853. M. C. Johnson, F. K. Hunt.
1855. R. J. Spurr, R. W. Hanson.
1857. Leslie Combs, M. C. Johnson.
1859. T. H. Clay, R. A. Buckner.
1861. R. A. Buckner.
1863. R. J. Spurr.
1865. J. C. Vanmeter.
1867. R. C. Rogers.
1869. D. L. Price.
1871. W. Cassius Goodloe.

STATE SENATORS.

1792, Robert Todd and Peyton Short; 1796, James Campbell; 1800, James Trotter; 1805, Edmund Bullock; 1809, Edmund Bullock; 1813, Edmund Bullock; 1817, W. T. Barry; 1821, Matthias Flournoy; 1825, Robert Wickliffe; 1829, Robert Wickliffe; 1833, R. H. Chinn; 1837, A. K. Woolley; 1841, William Rodes; 1845, R. S. Todd; 1849, Oliver Anderson; 1851, Elihu Hogan; 1853, J. F. Robinson; 1857, W. S. Darnaby; 1859, W. S. Darnaby; 1861, J. F. Robinson; 1865, W. A. Dudley; 1867, W. A. Dudley; 1869, A. L. McAfee.

CONGRESSIONAL REPRESENTATIVES.

1796, John Fowler; 1804, John Fowler; 1806, Benjamin Howard; 1808, Benj. Howard; 1810, W. T. Barry; 1812, Henry Clay; 1814, Henry Clay; 1816, Henry Clay; 1818, Henry Clay; 1820, S. H. Woodson; 1822, Henry Clay; 1824, Henry Clay; 1825, Herman Bowmar; 1827, James Clarke; 1829, James Clarke; 1831, James Clarke; 1833, Chilton Allen; 1835, Chilton Allen; 1837, R. Hawes; 1839, R. Hawes; 1841, Thos. F. Marshall; 1843, Garret Davis; 1845, Garret Davis; 1847, C. S. Morehead; 1849, C. S. Morehead; 1851, J. C. Breckinridge; 1853, J. C. Breckinridge; 1855, A. K. Marshall; 1857, J. B. Clay; 1859, W. E. Sims; 1861, R. A. Buckner; 1863, Brutus Clay; 1865, G. S. Shanklin; 1867, J. B. Beck; 1868, J. B. Beck; 1870, J. B. Beck.

UNITED STATES SENATORS.

The following citizens of Fayette county have served terms in the Federal Senate, viz: 1792, John Brown; 1796, Humphrey Marshall, John Brown; 1801, John Breckinridge, Buckner Thruston; 1813, Jesse Bledsoe, John Pope; 1818, Henry Clay; 1825, Henry Clay; 1836, Henry Clay; 1861, John C. Breckinridge.

XX.

Lexington Indignant—A Virginia Town—Democratic Society Founded—John Breckinridge—Inventors and Inventions—West and the First Steamboat—Barlow's Planetarium—Music of Light—Speeder Spindle—Burrowes' Mustard—Locomotive—Vaccination.

THE removal of the state capital to Frankfort, in 1793, caused great disappointment in Lexington, and no little indignation, as Lexington was at that time the most important settlement on the frontier. A few months after the removal, and while the general assembly was in session in Frankfort, the Indians drove some hunters within five miles of the town, and shortly after actually penetrated into the place.* These incidents formed a standing subject of wit and ridicule among disappointed Lexingtonians for weeks after their occurrence.

Lexington, in 1793, was a perfect type of the Virginia towns of that period. The manners, tastes, and appearance of the people, and the general characteristics of the place were Virginian, and though many of the citizens were emigrants from Maryland, North Carolina, New Jersey, and Pennsylvania, the great mass of them had come from the Old Dominion. The grand old customs and distinguishing features of the mother of states and statesmen, then impressed upon Lexington by her children, are happily not yet extinct.

Early in the summer of 1793† was founded the "Democratic Society of Lexington," John Breckinridge being president, and Thomas Bodley and Thomas Todd, clerks.

---

*Old Gazette, August 2, 1794.   †Butler.

This society was noted for its hostility to federalism, its efforts to secure the free navigation of the Mississippi river, and its passionate sympathy for the young republic of France. The members of the society, which embraced all the democrats in Lexington, wore tri-color cockades, and planted poles, surmounted with the cap of liberty, on every corner. One of these "liberty poles" remained standing for several years, on the corner of Main and Cheapside. The federalists, to show their aversion of the tri-color, wore a black cockade with an eagle button on the left side of the hat. Party spirit was high and fierce, and if the democratic society of Lexington, with little regard for the general government, encouraged the agents of the French republic in their efforts to organize a force to wrest from Spain her Louisiana territory, it is not to be wondered at when we remember that Spain stubbornly refused the western people an outlet to the ocean, and the federal government, in addition to the almost studied coldness shown to Kentucky, was remarkably slow in bringing Spain to terms.

John Breckinridge, president of the Democratic Society, had arrived in Kentucky just a few months anterior to the formation of the society. He was born in Augusta county, Virginia, December 2, 1760. His father's early death compelled him, while but a boy, to labor hard to sustain his widowed mother and her impoverished family. Under these discouraging circumstances, Mr. Breckinridge practiced law in Albemarle county, Virginia, from 1785, until his removal to Kentucky, and as a lawyer, no man of his day excelled him, and but few could compare with him. While a member of the Kentucky legislature, he inaugurated the movement against the alien and sedition laws, and was prominent and influential in the convention which framed the state constitution of 1799.

As a senator in Congress, as attorney-general of the United States under Jefferson, and as a great leader of the old democratic party, he displayed the qualities of a patriot, and made himself famous as a statesman. He resided for some time in a house which stood in the rear of the present residence of Mr. B. Gratz, fronting on Broadway, and between Second and Third. He died near Lexington, December 14, 1806. Mr. Breckinridge was the grandfather of our distinguished fellow-citizen, General John C. Breckinridge.

With the year 1793 commences the history of invention in Lexington, for at that time, in all reasonable probability, was invented the first steamboat that ever successfully plowed the waters of the world. The inventor, Edward West, was a Virginian, and moved to this city in 1785. He was the first watchmaker who settled in Lexington. His shop and residence both were near the corner of Mill and Hill streets, opposite the present residence of Mrs. Letcher. Mr. West was a hard student and close investigator. He spent all his leisure time in experimenting with steam and steam machinery of his own construction, and the little engine that so successfully propelled his little boat, was the result of years of untiring industry. He obtained a patent for his great invention, and also one for a nail-cutting machine, the first ever invented, and which cut 5,320 pounds in twelve hours, the patent for which " he sold at once for ten thousand dollars."* Models of both inventions were deposited in the patent office, but they were unfortunately destroyed when Washington was burned by the British in 1814. It is said that John Fitch, of Pennsylvania, made the initiatory step in steam navigation in 1787, but it is also known that he had no *success* till August, 1807, while West's boat was notoriously a success as early as 1793, years before Fulton had built his first boat on the Seine. In that year (1793), in the presence of a large crowd of deeply interested citizens, a trial of West's wonderful little steamboat was made on the town fork of Elkhorn, which was damned up near the Lexington and Frankfort freight depot for that purpose. The boat moved swiftly through the water. The first successful application of steam to navigation was made, and cheer after cheer arose from the excited spectators. A number of our most

---

*Michaux.

respected and venerable citizens remember witnessing this experiment when boys. In confirmation of the early date of this invention, we quote the following editorial notice from the old Kentucky Gazette, dated April 29, 1816:

"STEAMBOATS.—A steamboat owned by a company of gentlemen of this town (Lexington) was to sail for New Orleans yesterday, from near the mouth of Hickman creek. We are informed that she is worked on a plan invented by Mr. West, of this place, nearly twenty years ago, and in a manner distinct from any other steamboat now in use. On trial against the current of the Kentucky, when that river was very high, she more than answered the sanguine expectation of her owners, and left no doubt on their minds that she could stem the current of the Mississippi with rapidity and ease."

The editor settles the question of the antiquity of the invention, but speaks indefinitely. John B. West, the inventor's son, states decidedly that it was in the year 1793. The memory of Edward West should be cherished by all his countrymen; for to his genius is due one of the grandest inventions recorded in the "geographical history of man," since Jason sailed in search of the golden fleece, or the Phœnicians crept timidly along the shores of the Mediterranean, in their frail, flat-bottomed barges. The time when steam was first used as a motive power will form an era in the world's history, for the revolution it has worked has been a mighty one, and a hundred years from now, the little stream called the "Town Fork of Elkhorn" will have become classic. The identical miniature engine that West made and used in 1793 is now in the museum of the lunatic asylum in this city. Edwin West died in Lexington, August 23, 1827, aged seventy.

In 1796,* Nathan Burrowes, an ingenious citizen of Lexington, introduced the manufacture of hemp into Kentucky, and also invented a machine for cleaning hemp. Like many other inventors, he was betrayed, and derived no

---

*S. D. McCullough.

benefit from either. He afterward discovered a superior process of manufacturing mustard, and produced an article which took the premium at the World's Fair, in London, and which has no equal in quality in existence. The secret of its compounding has been sacredly transmitted unrevealed. It is now three-quarters of a century since "Burrowes' Mustard" was first made, and it is still manufactured in Lexington, and has a world-wide celebrity. Mr. Burrowes settled in Lexington in 1792, and died here in 1846.

At the beginning of the present century, John Jones, who died in Lexington in 1849, at the advanced age of ninety years, invented a speeder spindle and a machine for sawing stone, which were afterward "caught up" by eastern impostors.

Though not an invention, it may not be inappropriate here to state that vaccination had been introduced for several years in Lexington by Dr. Samuel Brown, of Transylvania University, when the first attempts at it were being made in New York and Philadelphia.* Up to 1802, he had vaccinated upward of five hundred persons in Kentucky.

In 1805, Dr. Joseph Buchanan, long known as one of the most remarkable citizens of Lexington, invented, at the age of twenty, a musical instrument,† producing its harmony from glasses of different chemical composition, and originated the grand conception of the music of light, to be executed by means of harmonific colors luminously displayed; an invention which will, if ever put in operation, produce one of the most imposing spectacles ever witnessed by the human eye.

About 1835, Mr. E. S. Noble, of Lexington, invented an important labor-saving machine, for the purpose of turning the *bead* on house-guttering.

One of the greatest mechanical geniuses, or inventors, that Lexington has produced, and one who has done honor to America, was Thomas Harris Barlow. His shop was, for a long time, located on Spring street, between Main and

---

*Michaux's Travels. †Collins, 559.

Water. He settled in Lexington in 1825, but first attracted public attention in 1827, by making a locomotive which would ascend an elevation of eighty feet to the mile, with a heavily-laden car attached.* He, at the same time, constructed a small circular railroad, over which the model locomotive and car ran successfully in the presence of many spectators, some of whom are still alive. This model is yet in existence in the Lunatic Asylum of this city. Lexington can claim, therefore, the first railroad and the first locomotive ever constructed in Western America. After this, Mr. Barlow invented a self-feeding nail and tack machine, which was a success. He sold it to some Massachusetts capitalists. In 1855, he invented and perfected a rifled percussion cannon, for the testing and experimental manufacture of which Congress appropriated $3,000.† This gun attracted the attention and admiration of the Russian minister at Washington during the Crimean war, which was then raging, and is believed to be the pattern which subsequent inventors of rifled guns have more or less followed. It weighed seven thousand pounds, the bore was five and a half inches in diameter, twisting one turn in forty feet. It was cast at Pittsburg.

His last, and greatest achievement, and one that will long cause his name to be gratefully remembered by the learned and scientific throughout the world, was the invention of the planetarium, now so celebrated, both for the wonderful ingenuity of its harmonious arrangement and working, and for the ease and accuracy with which it represents the motions and orbits of the planets. The planetarium was the result of ten years' patient study and labor, having been commenced in 1841, and finished in 1851.‡ It was finally perfected and exhibited in a room in the upper story of the building which formerly occupied the site of the present banking-house, on the corner of Main and Upper streets.|| The first planetarium Mr. Barlow made, was purchased for Transylvania University. The instrument is now used at Washington, West Point, and in most of the great ed-

---

*Obs. and Rep.   †Milton Barlow.   ‡Id. ||Wm. Swift.

ucational institutions of this country. At the late grand Exposition at Paris, in 1867, Barlow's planetarium was examined with delight and admiration by the savants of Europe, and received a premium of the first class. Mr. Barlow was born in Nicholas county, Kentucky, August 5, 1789, and died in Cincinnati in 1865.

CHAPTER XXI.

Game — Wayne's Victory—Lexington Post-office—Incidents, and List of Postmasters — The Catholic Church — Father Badin—Pastors.

GAME, once so abundant about Lexington, had greatly diminished by the year 1794. Teal and duck were still plentiful, and the deer had not left the forests, but the buffalo and the elk had disappeared, and wild turkeys were never seen. Immense numbers of quails, which before the settlement of Kentucky had been unknown, now migrated from the other side of the mountains, following up the grain scattered by emigrants.

Relief from the plundering and murdering Indians was now at hand. General Anthony Wayne, the successor of the ill-fated St. Clair, after having organized his forces with great care and deliberation, moved against the Miami savages in the summer of 1794. General Wilkinson, Robert Todd, and Thomas Lewis, and a large number of mounted volunteers from Lexington and Fayette county, constituted a part of the army, and participated in Wayne's brilliant and decisive victory over the Indians at the rapids of the Miami, August 20, 1794. A few months after the battle, peace was effected with the northwestern tribes, and, after long years of bloodshed and misery, anxiety and watching, the settlers of the Dark and Bloody Ground had rest from their savage foes, who never again ventured upon Kentucky soil.

The Lexington post-office was established about the year 1794, the inefficiency of the old confederation and the incomplete organization of the new government rendering it impossible until that late period. Before that time, all letters and papers received by the citizens were obtained through the kindness of friends and immigrants, or came by private enterprise. A lady in Lexington, at that early day, whose husband had gone to Crab Orchard, received a letter from him which he had intrusted to a party of settlers who intended to go through Lexington on their way west. In passing through the "Wilderness," the Indians attacked the party, killing the man who had the letter, and his companions carried it to the anxious wife stained with his blood.*

In 1787, Bradford's "post-rider" brought letters to the citizens, and in 1790 to still further accommodate them, he opened a letter-box in his office where all letters and papers brought to town could be deposited, and he published a list of them in the Gazette once a month.* The first postmaster, Innis B. Brent, who was also jailer, had his office in the log jail building which stood on Main street, between Graves' stable and the corner of Broadway. It was next located in "Postlethwaite's tavern" (Phœnix). In 1808, it was in a building with immense hewed log steps, which occupied the site of the new Odd Fellows Hall, on Main. Mr. Jordan was then postmaster, and our venerable fellow-citizen, Mr. Ben Kiser, was his deputy.

In the year 1812 and for some time after, the post-office was located in a little red frame-house which stood on the site of Hoagland's stable, on Main, between Limestone and Rose. Persons are still living who remember when the news came to Lexington that the war with England was over. The post-rider, with the mail bag strapped behind him, and furiously blowing his horn, dashed up to the post-office door with the word "Peace" in big letters upon the front of his hat.

At a later period the post-office was near the old Kentucky Gazette office, near Clark & Bros. grocery, on Main. In 1861, it was removed from the building now known as Rule's cigar store, on the corner of Main, to its present location, on the corner of Mill and Short streets.

---

*Cist, 129.   †Old Gazette.

Joseph Ficklin, who was appointed postmaster in 1822, is believed to have held the office longer, and through more presidential administrations than any other postmaster in this country. The names of the postmasters of Lexington, in order of their succession, are Innis B. Brent, Peter G. Voorhies, John W. Hunt, John Jordan, Jr., John Fowler, Joseph Ficklin, Thomas Redd, Squire Bassett, Jesse Woodruff, L. B. Todd, S. W. Price.

The Catholic church in Lexington owes its establishment to the self-sacrifice and untiring energy of the Rev. Stephen Theodore Badin,* who commenced, in January, 1794, to gather together the few Catholics then in the town. Father Badin was a native of France, and had been a subdeacon of the diocese of Orleans. He escaped from Bordeaux in 1792, while the furious Jacobins were murdering his fellow-priests, and sailed for the United States. He was ordained in Baltimore, by Bishop Carroll, the following year, being the first priest of his church ever ordained in this country, and shortly after set out for Kentucky. He journeyed from Limestone (Maysville) to Lexington on foot, and passed over the field of the disastrous battle of Blue Licks, and though the defeat had taken place more than eleven years before, the scene of it was still marked by the whitened bones of the massacred settlers. For a number of years after his arrival in Lexington, Father Badin, like the majority of the pioneer preachers, fared badly.

A little hut was his home; he ground his own corn with a hand-mill, and once had to go several days without bread.† Father Badin celebrated mass in private houses until the year 1800, when his congregation erected a log church in a corner of the lot on which the First Baptist Church, on Main, is now located. Here he officiated until 1812, when the wants of his flock demanded a larger house. A gothic chapel of brick was accordingly built in the old Catholic graveyard, on Winchester street, and was dedicated May 19, 1812.‡ The subscription for this new church was

---

*Spalding. †Davidson. ‡McCabe.

opened on St. Patrick's day in 1810, at which time the Rev. F. O'Flynn preached in the court-house an eloquent panegyric on Ireland's patron saint. Three hundred dollars were subscribed on the spot, and enough was raised shortly after to commence work on the chapel.

Father Badin labored in Lexington for many years, beloved by his congregation, and respected by all who had the good fortune to know him. This early and zealous missionary, whose goodness, learning, and wit would have made him an ornament in the most polished society, spent his life with hunters and hardy settlers, in doing what he believed to be the best for his fellow-men. In 1822 he went to Paris, France, and while there published a book entitled "Early Catholic Missions in Kentucky." In 1832 he labored among the Potawatomie Indians. After traversing Kentucky and other states on missionary duty a hundred times through rain and storm, and heat and cold, he went to his rest at last in 1853.

Rev. G. A. M. Elder, born in Marion county, Kentucky in 1793, succeeded Father Badin. He was a student at Emmettsburg College, Maryland; was ordained by Bishop David in 1819, and is noted as the founder and first president of St. Joseph's College at Bardstown. He was a man of strong mind and unconquerable energy. Rev. Elder died September 28, 1828, in the institution he had established, and which remains as his monument.

St. Peter's Church, on Limestone street, was built during the pastorate of Rev. Edward McMahon, a native of Ireland, and was dedicated December 3, 1837. On Sunday, August 13, 1854,* just a few moments after the congregation had retired from this building, the entire ceiling fell in with a crash that would have carried death and destruction with it if it had occurred a little while before. Fathers Butler, John Maguire, and Dismariæ succeeded each other. Father Dismariæ was an Italian, learned and scholarly, and endowed with unusual philosophical talents. He died in

---

*Observer and Reporter.

Philadelphia, a few years ago. In 1859, Rev. Peter McMahon and Rev. H. G. Allen were the resident priests.

Rev. John H. Bekkers, a Hollander, took charge of the church in 1864, and has remained its faithful and efficient pastor ever since. Under his direction, the present handsome and commodious St. Paul's Church, on Short street, between Broadway and Spring, was completed. The cornerstone of this church was laid by the Rt. Rev. G. A. Carroll, on Sunday, November 12, 1865, and was dedicated, with impressive services, October 18, 1868, by Archbishop Purcell.

CHAPTER XXII.

Brick Houses—Immigration—Infidelity—Free Navigation of the Mississippi—German Lutheran Church—Lexington Library, Founders, Incidents, Librarians.

BRICK houses began to take the place of wooden ones in Lexington in 1795. The first one erected is believed to have been the one built by Mr. January in the back part of the lot, between Mill and Broadway, on which the residence of Mr. Benjamin Gratz now stands.*

The fear of all future invasions by the Indians having been removed by the decisive campaign of General Wayne, immigrants in great numbers poured into Kentucky, and many of them settled in Lexington, whose substantial growth dates from this year. Unfortunately, some of the newcomers were admirers of Thomas Paine, and exerted themselves to spread his peculiar views through the community, and being aided by the existing partiality for French ideas, met with some success, and laid the foundation of the infidelity and lax morality which became unpleasantly prominent shortly after.

There was great rejoicing in Lexington, in the fall of 1795, over the welcome news that a treaty had been concluded with Spain, by which the United States was conceded the free navigation of the Mississippi river to the ocean, with a right of deposit at New Orleans.

About this time (1795), the organization of a German Lutheran church was effected in Lexington, mainly through the efforts of Captain John Smith, Jacob Kiser, Casper Kernsner, and Martin Castel.† Money enough was secured, by means of a lottery, to purchase the lot on Hill street, between Mill and Upper, on which the Southern Methodist

---

*McCabe.   †Old Kentucky Gazette.

Church now stands, and to erect a story and a half frame building, which was used both as a church and school-house. The pastor of the church was the Rev. Mr. Dishman, the teacher was Mr. Leary. The congregation was composed almost entirely of Germans, among whom were Henry Lanckart, Jacob Springle, John Kiser, Adam Webber, George Adams, Haggard, Edward Howe, Malcolm Myers, and Mr. Bushart. Many members of the Lutheran Church were buried in their old graveyard, which is still to be seen back of the present Hill Street Methodist Church.

About the year 1815, the little frame Lutheran church was destroyed by fire, and no other was ever erected. The congregation became scattered, and finally died out, even from the memory of many. When the old church lot was sold to the Lutheran Methodists, only one trustee of the Lutheran Church, Adam Webber, was still alive.

The Lexington Library, the oldest institution of its kind in Kentucky, if not in the West, commenced its existence in this year (1795). On New Year's day, a number of gentlemen met in the "old state-house" to consult in regard to establishing a library for the benefit of the citizens of Lexington and the students of Transylvania Seminary. It was resolved to organize such an institution, to be called "Transylvania Library," and the following citizens were appointed a committee to perfect the work, viz: Robert Barr, John Bradford, John Breckinridge, James Brown, R. W. Downing, Thomas Hart, Thomas January, James Parker, Samuel Price, Fred. Ridgely, H. Toulmin, and James Trotter.

So earnest were these gentlemen in the good work to which they had been called, that in a few days they had secured subscriptions from the public amounting to five hundred dollars. A purchasing committee was appointed, and the money forwarded for the books.* At this time, Transylvania Seminary, as the present university was then called, was a small school, with no collection worthy the name of "library," and there were no private libraries in the city, though it could boast, even at that early day, of many citi-

---

*Kentucky Gazette.

zens of culture and education, who no doubt waited with the greatest impatience for the infant library. Patience was needed, for it took nearly a year to collect and transport the books to Lexington. But they came at last (four hundred volumes) in January, 1796, and were placed for safe keeping in the seminary building.

In 1798, when the Presbyterian grammar school, "Kentucky Academy," was merged in Transylvania Seminary, forming Transylvania University, the library was increased by the addition of the little library of Kentucky Academy. By this means, the library came in possession of valuable theological works, obtained through the generous exertions of Rev. Doctor Gordon, of London,* and also books bought by subscriptions obtained by Rev. James Blythe from President Washington, Vice-President Adams, Aaron Burr, and other distinguished gentlemen. The library now numbered over six hundred volumes, and the committee, believing it could be made more useful if placed in a more central location, removed it to the drug store of the first librarian, Andrew McCalla, which was located at that time on the corner of Market and Short streets, where the Daily Press office now stands, and its name was changed to "Lexington Library." By this name it was incorporated November 29, 1800. The shareholders named in the charter are: Thomas Hart, Sen., James Morrison, John Bradford, James Trotter, John A. Seitz, Robert Patterson, John McDowell, Robert Barr, William Macbean, James Maccoun, Caleb Wallace, Fielding L. Turner, Samuel Postlethwait, and Thomas T. Barr. At a general meeting of the shareholders, held at the house of John McNair, on the first Saturday in January, 1801, a complete organization under the charter was effected by the election of a board of directors.

In 1803, the library contained seven hundred and fifty volumes, and had been removed to a room in the old statehouse on West Main street, between Mill and Broadway. The juvenile library of one thousand one hundred and

---

*Winterbotham's History, vol. iii, p. 155.

thirty-five books, which had been collected by an association of ambitious and energetic boys, was consolidated with the Lexington Library in 1810. It was further increased by donations and sales of shares, until, in 1815, it had grown to two thousand five hundred and seventy-three volumes. In 1824, the books of the Lexington Athæneum were turned over to it. Small as it was, the Lexington Library was now the largest and most prominent one in the western couutry, and it received frequent contributions of books, pamphlets, journals, and documents from various literary, scientific, and philosophical societies throughout the country, not to mention many donations of books from private citizens of Lexington and Fayette county. The library numbered over six thousand volumes in 1837, and was increased the next year through the efforts of Henry Clay, Robert Wickliffe, Jr., and A. K. Woolley, who addressed public meetings in its behalf. In 1839, Leslie Combs gave one thousand three hundred dollars in turnpike stock to the institution. At present, the number of books in the library is estimated at ten thousand, a small number when the age of the library is considered, but its smallness is due, to some extent, to the vicissitudes it has encountered during an eventful history. It has suffered from frequent removals, from fire, and from water. At one time, the books were kept in the old Odd-Fellows' hall, on Church street, between Upper and Limestone. The building was destroyed by fire, and the books sadly damaged. They were then removed to the Medical hall, which at that time occupied the site of the present library building, on the corner of Church and Market street. This hall was also destroyed by fire, and many books were lost. The library found another refuge in the new Medical Hall, erected on the corner of Broadway and Second streets, but still the fire fiend pursued it; the hall was burned, and the books, for the third time, were damaged, both by the fire itself and water from the engines. That the library was not scattered and almost entirely destroyed, Lexington may thank the watchful care of our late fellow-citizens, Leonard Wheeler, and also William A.

Leavy, Lyman W. Seeley, and John S. Wilson. The
library finally landed in the house now owned by the
library company, on Jordan's row, and at present occupied as the internal revenue office.

In 1865, the present library building was bought by
money raised from issuing bonds of the company for six
thousand dollars, and the books were forthwith removed to
it. This important occasion is the result of Mr. Thomas
Mitchell's enlightened exertions.

The following bondholders have, up to the present time,
given up their bonds, and have accepted, instead, perpetual
shares, viz: Benjamin Gratz, M. C. Johnson, Mrs. John
Carty, D. A. Sayre, Wm. Warfield, H. T. Duncan, Jr., E.
D. Sayre, J. B. Payne, J. S. Wilson, J. M. Elliott, W. W.
Bruce, M. P. Lancaster, S. S. Thompson, J. B. Morton,
M. E. Graves, C. W. Fouschee, M. G. Thompson, J. W.
Berkley, J. W. Cochrane, J. W. Cochran.

At the meeting of the Kentucky Press Association in
Lexington, in January, 1870, the editors in attendance resolved to send their various journals free to the library.
The Lexington Library is an exceedingly valuable one,
abounding as it does in rare old works, which can not now
be obtained elsewhere for any consideration, and the good
that it has done can not easily be overestimated. The
names of the librarians, in the order of their succession,
are: Andrew McCalla, Lewis H. Smith, David Logan,
Thomas M. Prentiss, James Logue, Lyman W. Seeley,
James Logue, Wellington Payne, William M. Matthews,
Henry C. Brennan, Allie G. Hunt, Joseph Wasson, William
Swift, and J. B. Cooper. The office was held longer by
James Logue than by any other librarian. He was custodian of the books for more than twenty-five years. Mr.
Swift will be remembered for his accurate and extensive
information and for his extraordinary memory. The institution has never had a librarian more devoted to its interests than the present one, Mr. Cooper.

CHAPTER XXIII:

*Episcopal Church—First Building—Rev. James Moore—
Early Members—The " St. Paul" Schism—List of Rectors
of Christ Church—Present Condition.*

THE history of the Episcopal Church in Lexington commences with the year 1796, when a feeble little band organized the present Christ Church, in a dilapidated frame house which stood on the site of the present church, on the corner of Market and Church streets. Rev. James Moore, who was the first minister of the Episcopal Church of the United States who settled permanently in Kentucky, was the first rector of Christ Church. He came from Virginia to Lexington in 1792,* and was at that time a candidate for the ministry in the Presbyterian Church, but shortly after, considering himself too rigorously treated by the Transylvania Presbytery, he connected himself with the Episcopal Church. He was a man of learning, great piety, and beautiful manners. In 1798, he was appointed acting president of Transylvania University, which office he held for several years. He died June 22, 1814, at the age of forty-nine.

A little brick house succeeded the frame one, in 1808 and was furnished by means of a lottery, of which William Morton, Walter Warfield, Daniel Sheely, and John Wyatt were managers.† Among others, who were either members of the church at that time, or were adherents of it, may be named‡ John D. Clifford, Thomas January, John Bradford, Henry Clay, John W. Hunt, Thomas B. Pinkard, Frederick Ridgely, John Jordan, Elijah Craig, Alexander Parker, John Postlethwaite, William Essex, John Brand, Matthew, Elder, Matthew Shryock, and T. King.

---

*Collins.   †Old Gazette.   ‡Church Records.

The Rev. John Ward succeeded Mr. Moore in November, 1813. Mr. Ward conducted a successful female school in Lexington for many years. He died in this city in 1860, aged eighty-two. After performing the duties of the rectorship for six years with great acceptability, he was succeeded, in September, 1819, by Rev. Lemuel Burge, who officiated as *pro tem.* pastor for five months, when he was called to the church eternal.

The zealous and talented Dr. George T. Chapman, who is still living, at a very great age, in Massachusetts, became the next regular rector, in July, 1820. His volume of "Sermons to Presbyterians of all Sects," which was published in 1828, passed through several editions.* He was rector of Christ Church for ten years.

During Dr. Chapman's ministry, the little brick chapel gave way to a larger and more church-like edifice, which was built on the same spot which had been occupied by both of its predecessors. The building was of brick, stuccoed to imitate stone, and the aisles and other parts of it were, in time, strewn with memorial slabs and tablets to those who were buried in and around the edifice. This church building was badly constructed, and it became more and more insecure every year. A knowledge of this fact made the growth of the congregation very slow as long as it was occupied.

The present bishop of the diocese, the Rev. Benjamin Bosworth Smith, was called to the rectorship of Christ Church in November, 1830. Bishop Smith was born June 13, 1794, in Bristol, R. I., was graduated at Brown University in 1816, ordained priest in 1818, and consecrated bishop in St. Paul's Church, New York city, October 31, 1832. This learned, faithful, and now aged minister, resigned the rectorship in October, 1838, since which time he has been constantly employed in a laborious oversight of the diocese. In addition to publishing several sermons and charges, Bishop Smith has contributed largely to religious journals.

Dr. Henry Caswell,† an English clergyman, was assist-

---

*Caswell. †B. B. Smith.

ant rector of Christ Church for a part of Bishop Smith's term. In 1834, he was called to the professorship of Sacred Literature in the Episcopal Theological Seminary, then just established in Lexington, which position, with that of assistant rector, he held for three years. In 1839, he published a volume entitled "America and the American Church," and, about the same period, returned to England, and was for ten years vicar of Figheldean, Diocese of Salisbury. He came back to the United States a few years ago, and subsequently died in Franklin, Pennsylvania.

In 1837, Christ Church became divided* upon some comparatively unimportant questions, and a part of the congregation organized a church, which they named "St. Paul's." They worshiped in Morrison College, but only for a short time. The trouble was soon settled, and the seceding members renewed their connection with Christ Church.

For a short time after the resignation of Bishop Smith, the amiable Rev. Edward Winthrop, a native of New Haven, Connecticut, was temporary rector. He died in New York, in 1865.

The regular successor of Bishop Smith was Rev. Edward F. Berkley, who entered upon the duties of the rectorship in January, 1839. Mr. Berkley was born in Washington City, September 20, 1813. He came to Lexington in 1835, was for three years a member of the Episcopal Theological Seminary in this city, and was ordained to the ministry in Christ Church in December, 1838. Mr. Berkley's fine qualities of head and heart so endeared him to his congregation, that he was retained in the service of the parish for nearly nineteen years. He resides at present in St. Louis, Missouri.

On the 17th of March, 1847, the corner-stone of the present tasteful and elegant church edifice was laid, with appropriate ceremonies, and a dedicatory address was delivered by the Rev. James Craik, of Louisville. The remains of those buried in and around the church were subsequently removed to the Episcopal Cemetery. The memorial tablets

---

*Church Records.

of Mr. Moore, first pastor of the church, and Mr. John D. Clifford, one of its early and generous benefactors, were preserved through the provident attention of Mr. John S. Wilson, and, in 1858, when the church was still further improved, they were set in the wall of the building, where they still remain.

Mr. Berkley resigned in November, 1857, and was succeeded, in March, 1858, by the Rev. James H. Morrison, of Pemberton, Virginia, a gentleman of superior scholarly attainments.

The present rector, the Rev. Jacob S. Shipman, took charge of Christ Church on the 14th of October, 1861. Mr. Shipman was born in Niagara, New York, November 30, 1832. In completing the Yale College course he enjoyed the special instruction of Dr. Joseph M. Clark. Mr. Shipman was ordained to the priesthood in 1858, and had been rector of two churches successively before he was called to Christ Church. Scholarly and original, possessed of a cultivated mind and a warm and generous heart, Mr. Shipman has gained the highest esteem of his congregation, which has enjoyed abundant peace and prosperity under his efficient ministry.

Christ Church has been steadily increasing in membership and influence for many years, and its present very flourishing condition is a source of great gratification to all christian people.

CHAPTER XXIV.

Lexington Immigration Society—Size of Town—Town Property—Market Houses—Theater—Henry Clay: His Character as an Orator, Statesman, and Man—Incidents.

THE year 1797 produced an association in Lexington, whose influence was so salutary that it was soon imitated in other places; and this was the "Lexington Immigration Society." Strong exertions, and successful ones, were made by it to induce industrious farmers and mechanics to remove to this region. Publications were made and circulated full of information regarding the amount of the ordinary products of the soil per acre, the common prices of marketing, the various species of mechanical labor, and productions, etc. Of this society, Thomas Hart was president; John Bradford, secretary.

The following particulars from one of these documents are extracted for the benefit of the curious:

AVERAGE PRODUCE OF ONE ACRE OF LAND.

Of wheat sown in corn-ground, 25 bushels; in fallow-ground, 35; corn, 60; rye, 25; barley, 40; oats, 40; potatoes, Irish, 250—sweet,—; hemp, 8 cwt.; tobacco, 1 ton; hay, 3 tons.

LEXINGTON MARKET PRICES.

Wheat, per bushel, $1; corn, 20 cents; rye, 66 cents; barley, 50 cents; oats, 17 cents; potatoes, Irish, 33—sweet, $1; hemp, per ton, $86.66; tobacco, per cwt., $4; hay, per ton, $6.

The establishment of this society shows that our enterprising ancestors were determined to build up their flourishing town, which consisted of sixteen hundred inhabitants, and over two hundred houses,* a few of them brick ones, many of them frame, but the most of them log ones, with chimneys built on the outside. A town lot was worth thirty dollars, and good farms in the vicinity could be bought for five dollars per acre.† The best farmers lived in log cabins, and even when they went "to town" wore hunting-shirts and leggings. The then beautiful vale through which town fork poured, was variegated with corn-fields, meadows, and trees. The means used for carrying on the town government were not as extravagant then as those of modern times, as all the town property in the hands of the trustees consisted of "two oxen, a cart, a wheelbarrow, sledge, mattock, crowbar, shovel, and a two-foot rule."‡

By this time, the ground-room of the old state-house, which had been converted into a market-house, had become entirely too small for the ambitious citizens of Lexington, and a subscription was raised, which resulted in the building of a substantial market-house on the public ground, between the present court-house and Cheapside, from which circumstance Market street derived its name.

In 1814, a market-house was built on Water street, but the Cheapside structure was not removed until 1817. The market-house now in use was built in 1844.

How Lexington supported a place of amusement in 1797, we are not prepared to say, but she certainly had one. "An exhibition-room, adjoining Coleman's tavern," was erected by George Saunders, and opened to the public Monday evening, June 5th. " Admission at sunset; performance to begin at dark; pit, 3s. 9d.; gallery, 2s. 3d."§ A theatrical performance was held in the court-house in 1798. In 1807, Melish, the traveler, was in Lexington, and visited the theater, which then stood on the corner of Water and Limestone, but his metropolitan tastes were not entirely gratified, as he said afterward, that " the performance did very well, but there was a deficiency of actresses, and one

---
*Joseph Scott's Directory.   †Brown's Gazetteer.   ‡Trustees' Book.
§Old Gazette.

of the men had to play a female part, which did not suit my taste at all."

In 1812, "Macbeth" was played at the "Hotel Theater," and on the evening of May 30th, in that year, "John Bull," a comedy, was performed before a packed audience, by Thespian amateurs belonging to the "Old Infantry" company, in honor of the Lexington volunteers for the war against England. A goodly sum was realized, and used to buy arms, clothing, and camp equipage for the soldiers.*

"Usher's Theater" was built about the year 1816.† It was located on the old Bruen property, at the corner of Spring and Vine streets, and, though it was on a small scale, it could boast of regular boxes, a pit, and a gallery. The celebrated Drake family constituted one of the first regular companies which appeared in the theater. Edwin Forest, who had before played minor parts in Philadelphia, made his *debut* as a leading actor in "Usher's Theater." He was brought out by Collins and Jones.‡ Sol. Smith, the noted comedian, who died in St. Louis in 1869, raised his first theatrical company in Lexington, and played in this theater for several weeks previous to his first tour.

In 1832, and frequently thereafter, the Masonic Hall was used for theatrical purposes. The theater was located, in 1837, on the lot now occupied by John S. Wilson's residence, on Upper street, and here the noted Mrs. Duff made her first appearance in Lexington. The remarkable Gus Adams charmed a crowded audience, in 1840, in a building neither very large nor very pretentious, which the citizens dignified with the name "Theater." It stood on Short street, between Broadway and Jefferson, opposite the residence of J. B. Wilgus.

After this time, Melodeon Hall and other rooms were used; but for the last fifteen years, the Odd Fellows' Hall, corner of Main and Broadway, has been "the theater." The followers of Thespis and Orpheus who have visited Lexington would make an army, and we can only mention, in addition to the distinguished artists already named, the

---

*Observer and Reporter.   †Benj. Kiser.   ‡Marsh.

famous elder Booth, the great pioneer actor Cooper, Julia Dean, Murdoch, Mrs. Lander, Joe Jefferson, Sontag, Patti, Parodi, Brignoli, and Ole Bull.

Henry Clay, whose greatness is crystallized in history, and whose name is the most illustrious one associated with Lexington, came to this city in November, 1797, and made it his home for the rest of his life, a period of more than half a century. Here he struggled. Here he triumphed. Here he sleeps.

On the 12th of April, 1777, in the "Slashes" neighborhood, of Hanover county, Virginia, in the midst of a great revolution, Henry Clay was born. His father, a Baptist minister, died when Henry was four years old, and left his family no legacy but poverty and toil. Fortunately, the mother of Henry was a woman of vigorous intellect and great energy, and she managed to maintain her large family in comparative comfort. Both parents were natives of Virginia. The early years of the future orator were years of much labor and little education, and it was then that he was known as "the mill-boy of the slashes,"* from the fact that he was often seen, when the meal-barrel was low, going to and fro between his mother's house and the mill, on the Pamunky river, mounted on a scrub pony, with a meal-bag for a saddle and a rope for a bridle. Up to the age of fourteen, he had received three years' "schooling," in a log house of the period, and from Peter Deacon, of whom little is known, except that he was the only teacher of Henry Clay. He was now placed by Captain Henry Watkins, whom his mother had married, in the store of Richard Denny, of Richmond. At the end of a year, Peter Tinsley, of Richmond, clerk of the high court of chancery of Virginia, gave him a situation in his office, and about the same time, namely 1792, his mother removed with his stepfather to Kentucky, and settled in Woodford county, where she died in 1827.

While engaged in the chancery court office, Henry Clay attracted the attention of Chancellor Wythe, who engaged

---

*Colton Papers, 19.

him as an amanuensis, assisted him in mental improvement, and encouraged him to study law, which he subsequently did, in the office of Robert Brook, then attorney-general of Virginia.

Mr. Clay, having obtained a license to practice law from the judges of the court of appeals of Virginia, immigrated to Lexington, Kentucky, in November, 1797. Here (to use his own words), *" I established myself, without patrons, without the favor of the great or opulent, without the means of paying my weekly board, and in the midst of a bar uncommonly distinguished by eminent members." Lexington was then the metropolis of the West, claiming sixteen hundred inhabitants, and George Nicholas, Joe Daviess, James Brown, John Breckinridge, William Murray, and James Hughes were the leading lawyers. Mr. Clay, at this time, seemed to be in bad health.† He was delicate in person and slow in his movements; but he quickly rallied. His first speech in Lexington was made in a young men's debating club. The smiles provoked by his awkward beginning were succeeded by cordial cheers and congratulations.‡ The first fee Mr. Clay received was fifteen shillings. His first public speech he made at the age of twenty-one, in the summer of 1798. The news had just arrived in Lexington that Congress had passed the infamous alien and sedition laws, and while crowds of excited and indignant men were discussing the news on Main street, a cart was drawn out, and Clay was put in it and told to "speak." He did speak; and the brilliant and crushing eloquence of his denunciations of those odious enactments, revealed his genius to the people, and laid the foundation of his fame. He rose rapidly in his profession. In 1799 he married Lucretia, daughter of Thomas Hart, one of the earliest citizens of Lexington. The marriage took place in the house on the corner of Mill and Second, now occupied by Mrs. Ryland. Mrs. Clay was born in Hagerstown, Maryland, 1781.

As we have seen, Mr. Clay united himself at an early period with the Jeffersonian or Democratic party. In

---

*Speech at Lexington, 1842.   †Collins.   ‡Colton.

1803, he was elected from the county of Fayette to the lower house of the Kentucky legislature, and was re-elected to that body every succeeding session, until 1806, when he was chosen United States senator, to fill out the unexpired term of General Adair. The rapidity with which these favors were showered upon Mr. Clay evidence how soon he had gained a strong hold upon the popular heart. After serving during the session for which he was elected, Mr. Clay resumed the practice of his profession in Lexington. He was now thirty, the leader of the bar, and overwhelmed with important cases.

In the summer of 1807, he was again sent to the state legislature, and was elected speaker of the house. He was continued in the assembly until 1809, when he was returned to the United States Senate to fill out the unexpired term of Buckner Thurston. He bore a conspicuous part in the discussion of the great national questions before the senate. His first speech of the session foreshadowed the outlines of that vast scheme of "protection," known as the "American system," of which Mr. Clay has been called the "father." His powerful efforts in favor of the "protection" of domestic manufactures, on the "line of the Rio Perdido," and in opposition to the rechartering of the United States Bank, stand pre-eminent in congressional history. Mr. Clay subsequently changed his opinion, and urged the chartering of the United States Bank, and gave his reasons for the change with characteristic force.

In 1811, Mr. Clay was elected to the lower house of Congress, and entered on the great period of his life, commencing with his election as speaker of the house of representatives, and terminating with his death, during which all his great endowments became so conspicuous through services and efforts so illustrious.* He had never before been a member of that house, which renders it still more remarkable that he should have been elected its speaker on the day he took his seat. He was re-elected speaker six times, and after occupying the chair about thirteen years,

---

*Address of Dr. R. J. Breckinridge.

left it to become secretary of state in the cabinet of the younger Adams, in 1825, which situation he held till the close of that administration in 1829. He was out of Congress during two short periods; first in 1814–15, while engaged as one of the American commissioners in negotiatating the treaty of Ghent, and again in 1820–22, when the condition of his private affairs obliged him to return to the bar. After the close of his service as secretary of state, in 1829, he remained in private life till the autumn of 1831, when he was elected to the senate of the United States for the third time, and commenced a senatorial career even more protracted and glorious than his previous career in the more popular branch of Congress. He was elected to the senate the fourth time in 1837. In March, 1842, after twelve years continuous service in the senate, covering six years of the administration of General Jackson, the whole of Mr. Van Buren's administration, and the first two years of Mr. Tyler's, he resigned his seat in the senate, and retired, as he supposed, finally to private life. In 1848, he was elected to the senate for the fifth time, and was a member of it till his death, in 1852. From his entrance into public life, just fifty years had expired at his death; and of these more than forty years had been passed in the most laborious public service. From his entrance into the house of representatives, in 1811, he had served thirteen years as a speaker of that house, about sixteen years as a senator, and four years as secretary of state, thus occupying far the greater part of the last forty years of his life in a career unsurpassed by any statesman of his era.

That career of forty years was as diversified as it was brilliant.* During the war of 1812 he was "the master spirit, around whom all the boldness and chivalry of the nation rallied. He was the life and soul of the war party in Congress." In 1815, we find him one of a commission concluding a treaty of peace with England, in the ancient city of Ghent, and shortly after enjoying the society of the most noted characters in Europe. Then comes his review of the

---

*Niles' Register and Congressional Globe.

Seminole war; his triumphant efforts in behalf of internal improvements, and for the recognition of the South American republics; his Herculean labors to avert the convulsion which threatened the nation in 1821, on the application of Missouri for admission into the Union; his eloquent appeals in behalf of Greece; his achievements in the protection battles of 1832–33; opposition to the sub-treasury system in 1836; thrilling farewell scene in the senate in 1842; retirement to Ashland; practice of his profession; recall to the senate in 1848; and the mighty efforts of "the old man eloquent" during the perilous slavery excitement in Congress in 1850–52.

Mr. Clay was thrice a candidate for the presidency; first, in 1825, when his opponents were Andrew Jackson, John Quincy Adams, and W. H. Crawford. The people failed to make a choice. The election was thrown into the house of representatives, where Mr. Clay gave his vote and influence for Mr. Adams, who thus became President. Upon the inauguration of the new President, Mr. Clay was made secretary of state. The course pursued by Mr. Clay on this occasion subjected him to the bitterest denunciations and abuse. It was charged that he had bought his seat in the cabinet, and the cry of "bargain and corruption" was repeated over and over again, to the end of his life, and defeated him in every subsequent race for the presidency. Where now is the man who may hope to keep his greatness and purity undefiled from the ever accumulating filth of the political arena? Slander is the soul-scorching price of political eminence. In a speech delivered at Lexington, Kentucky, September 9, 1842, Mr. Clay said: "My error in accepting the office tendered me arose out of my underrating the power of detraction and the force of ignorance, and abiding with too sure a confidence in the conscious integrity and uprightness of my own motives." It is enough to say that the life-long friends of Mr. Clay, those who knew, indeed, the integrity and clearness of his inner life, have always scouted this charge with scorn and contempt.

In 1832, Mr. Clay, who had disconnected himself from the Jeffersonian Democrats, was again nominated for the presidency by the "National Republicans," or Whigs (as they were beginning to be called), a new party, mainly created by himself. His great antagonist was General Jackson, the candidate of the "Democratic" party. This contest was one of the fiercest and most stubborn that had yet been waged in America, and never did the energy and genius of Mr. Clay shine out more resplendent. Mr. Clay's triumph was complete in his own state, but the indomitable old hero of New Orleans was re-elected President. The Whig party, of which Mr. Clay was the idol, passionately desired to lift him to the chief magistracy of the nation, and again nominated him in 1844. He was opposed by James K. Polk, the Democratic candidate. Mr. Clay was powerfully and almost successfully supported by his party. The contest, which was remarkably close and long, seemed doubtful, and was decided by the vote of New York, and the prize fell to Mr. Polk, while apparently within the very reach of Mr. Clay.

On the slavery question, Mr. Clay was conservative. While deprecating the evils of African slavery, and favoring its gradual abolishment, he invariably denounced the wild and violent sentiments of radical abolitionists.

Mr. Clay was engaged in two duels. The first was with Humphrey Marshall, author of the History of Kentucky. Mr. Clay was wounded in this duel. The second was with John Randolph.

The voice of the world has pronounced Mr. Clay a great man—great as a statesmen, and pre-eminently great as a lawyer; but it is as an orator that he will live longest in the memory of men. The accompaniments of his great intellect were a finely-formed, graceful, and commanding person, fascinating manners, a piercing eye, and a voice of wonderful melody and power. Upon great occasions, he was all earnestness, all feeling, body and soul seemed merged in one spiritual essence, and from his lips flowed a stream of irresistible eloquence, which has given him a place in history as one of the grandest orators the world has ever produced.

Mr. Clay's personal appearance in 1845 is thus described :*
"He is six feet and one inch in height; not stout, but the opposite; has long arms and a small hand; always erect in carriage, but particularly so in debate; has a well-shaped head and a dauntless profile; an uncommonly large mouth; upper lip commanding, nose prominent, spare visage, and blue eyes, electrical when kindled; forehead high, hair naturally light, and slow to put on the frosts of age; a well-formed person, and an imposing aspect." Taken as a whole, his appearance and bearing were singularly impressive. His presence was always felt.

Mr. Clay was accurate in business, and exceedingly careful to attend to the little things of life.† If he casually borrowed even a dime, he returned it punctually and scrupulously. He met all his obligations, and expected every one else to do the same. He was always neat in his dress. He sent for a barber on the morning of his death, and was cleanly shaved at his own expressed desire. He always showed great respect for religion. He was born with an appreciation of the courtesies due on all occasions. He was a hard worker. He prepared himself for all public occasions. His speeches were the result of study and forethought. While he was ready at all times to defend his honor at the pistol's mouth, he was magnanimous and generous, and if, in the heat of the moment, he gave unmerited offense, he was quick to apologize and ask forgiveness. He was great everywhere. He towered when among the most distinguished. One of Mr. Clay's most remarkable traits was his power over men. He was born to command. On one occasion, after the burning of the old court-house, and while court was being temporarily held in the "old Rankin Meeting-house," which stood on the site of the present city school-house, on the corner of Walnut and Short streets, Mr. Clay was called upon to defend a prisoner. Mr. Clay demanded the warrant, looked at it, found it defective and illegal, and turning at once to the prisoner, said to him, "Go home, sir!" The man hesitated. "Go

---

*Colton. †James O. Harrison, executor of Mr. Clay.

home!" thundered Mr. Clay. The man jumped up at once and "put out," without an effort on the part of the astounded sheriff or judge to stop him. No one thought of resisting that imperial personal power.

On the 25th of June, 1847, Mr. Clay united with the Episcopal Church in Lexington.

The tremendous exertions made by Mr. Clay in 1849–50, in behalf of the compromise measures, which employed his whole heart and brain, night and day, sapped his vital powers. The excitement while it lasted kept him alive, but bodily decay soon followed. The last summer Mr. Clay spent with his family and friends in Lexington was in 1850. His health was quite delicate. He looked like a victim of consumption.* Returning to Washington city, "broken with the storms of state," and scathed with many a fiery conflict, Henry Clay gradually descended toward the tomb. After the month of March, 1852, he wasted rapidly away, and for weeks lay patiently awaiting the stroke of death. For some days before his death, he was not allowed to walk, even with the support of others. His physician, the eminent Dr. Jackson, of Philadelphia, told him on one occasion not to attempt to walk, that if he stood erect he would faint, and that if he should faint he would breathe no more. "Why is this?" asked Mr. Clay. "Because there is not enough of vitality in the heart to give circulation to the blood." "Has it then come to this," said Mr. Clay, and for a moment sorrowfully. And seeing the necessity, he suffered himself to be borne like a child to and from his bed.

On the morning of June 28, the great change commenced, and found him ready. The dying statesman whispered to his friend, the Rev. Dr. Butler, "I have an abiding trust in the merits and mediation of our Savior." At night he was calm, but his mind wandered. In a low and distinct voice he named his wife and son and other relatives in a disconnected manner. On the morning of the 29th, he continued perfectly tranquil, though exceedingly feeble, and manifesting a disposition to slumber. About ten

---

*Journals.

o'clock he asked for some cool water, which he was in the habit of taking through a silver tube; upon removing the tube from his mouth, he appeared to have more difficulty in swallowing than previously. He turned to his son and said, "Do n't leave me." Soon after he motioned to have his shirt collar opened, and then added, "I am going soon." Serenely he breathed his last, at eleven o'clock A. M., in the presence of his son Thomas, Governor Jones, of Tennessee, and his favorite servant, Charles. His last moments were calm and quiet, and he seemed in full possession of all his faculties, and apparently suffering but little. His countenance to the last indicated a full knowledge of his condition.

He had long since made every preparation for his death, giving his son full instructions as to the disposition of his body and the settlement of his worldly affairs.

The sad news was at once flashed to Lexington, when every place of business was immediately closed, and the solemn tolling of the bells announced the great grief that had fallen upon the home of Clay. After every tribute of respect and love had been rendered the illustrious dead in Washington, solemn and impressive funeral honors and services were conducted in the senate chamber at twelve M. of June 31, in the presence of the President and his cabinet, both houses of Congress, the diplomatic corps, and a host of distinguished men from all parts of the country. After laying in state in the capitol building until four o'clock P. M., the body was placed upon a train for Baltimore, but did not reach Lexington until the whole nation, by the most extensive and beautiful demonstrations, had evinced its love and sorrow for the departed sage.

On the morning of Saturday, July 10, his funeral took place at his home, Lexington. (See chapter on 1852.) In the presence of a mighty concourse of the sorrowing, at the sound of the dirge, the minute guns, and the tolling bells, a great procession of his mourning fellow-citizens carried him tenderly, and with every token of love and respect, from the old house at Ashland to Christ Church, and from thence to the Lexington Cemetery. Mr. Clay's body was first deposited in the public vault, afterward it was interred by the side of his mother, and lastly, in 1857, it was incased in a beautiful marble sarcophagus, and placed permanently in the chamber of the Clay monument, then completed. On one of the last days of his life, he said to Judge Underwood, his colleague in the senate, "There may be some question where my remains shall be buried. Some persons may designate Frankfort. I wish to repose in the cemetery at Lexington, where many of my friends and connections are buried."* And so it is this day. Upon the marble sarcophagus, in enduring letters, can be seen these memorable words, uttered by Mr. Clay:

"I can, with unshaken confidence, appeal to the Divine Arbiter for the truth of the declaration that I have been influenced by no impure purpose, no personal motive, have sought no personal aggrandizement, but that, in all my public acts, I have had a sole and single eye, and a warm, devoted heart, directed and dedicated to what, in my best judgment, I believed to be the true interests of my country."

Another marble sarcophagus rests near that of Mr. Clay. It contains the remains of his wife and life-long companion, Mrs. Lucretia Clay, who died in April, 1864, aged seventy-three.

Mr. and Mrs. Clay had eleven children—six daughters and five sons. Two daughters died in infancy. Lucretia died at Ashland, aged fourteen. Eliza died at the same age, while *en route* for Washington city. Mrs. Duralde only lived to be twenty. Mrs. Irwine died in 1835. Henry, Jr., was killed at Buena Vista, in 1847. James B. died in Canada, in 1864, aged forty seven. Theodore died in 1871, at the age of sixty-nine. Thomas H., born in 1803, died in 1872. John M. Clay, born in 1821, is the only surviving child of the Cicero of the West. All of the deceased members of the household sleep in the family lot in the Lexington Cemetery, where also repose the remains of Elizabeth Watkins, the mother of the great Clay.

Ashland, for nearly half a century the home of Mr. Clay, is situated about a mile and a half from the Lexington

---

*Judge Underwood.

court-house, on the southwest side of the turnpike leading to Richmond. The grounds are beautiful, and the forest trees magnificent. The land, which is not surpassed for richness in the famous "Blue Grass Region," cost Mr. Clay about ten dollars an acre, in 1805 or 1806. The "old house" which Mr. Clay occupied, stood on the site of the present beautiful residence, which was erected by James B. Clay, in 1857. The "old house" was a spacious and comfortable brick mansion, devoid of architectural adornment. Here Mr. and Mrs. Clay entertained, with simple elegance, Daniel Webster, Lafayette, President Monroe, Mr. Lowndes, Martin Van Buren, Mr. Politica (the Russian minister), General Bertrand, Lord Morpeth, and a host of other distinguished men of this and foreign countries.

Mr. Clay's law office* was, for a long time, in the house now occupied by Dr. Bruce, on Mill, between Church and Second streets. He, and his son James, also used the office now occupied by Judge Carr, on Short, between Upper and Limestone streets. Some of Mr. Clay's grandest oratorical efforts were made in the present court-house, and in the yard surrounding it. Before Mr. Clay purchased Ashland, he lived in a house erected on the site of the Hunter residence, on Mill street, and opposite his old law office.

---

*Jas. O Harrison and Wm. Swift.

CHAPTER XXX.

Resolutions of "'98"—St. Andrew's Society: List of Members—Caledonian Club—Jesse Bledsoe.

NOWHERE in the United States was the administration of President John Adams more odious than in Lexington, and when, on the 9th of November, 1798,* the Kentucky legislature passed the resolutions introduced by John Breckinridge, of Fayette, protesting against the notorious alien and sedition laws, the gratification and excitement of the citizens was intense. Liberty poles and tri-color cockades were more numerous then in Lexington than in any other place in the whole country.

The Scotchmen of Lexington organized an association on the 17th of November, 1798,† which they entitled the "St. Andrew's Society of Lexington, in the State of Kentucky." John Maxwell was the chairman of the meeting of organization, and George Muter, afterward one of the judges of the supreme court of the state, was elected the first president. The objects of the society, as stated verbatim in the preamble to its constitution, were: "To promote philanthropy amongst those of the natives of Scotland who have chosen as their residence different parts of the State of Kentucky, and to promote a friendly union and intercourse with the descendants of parents who came originally from that country; desirous, also, to extend the benevolent hand of relief to such of this description, whether presently residing in said state, or who may hereafter arrive therein."

The first anniversary meeting was held in Megowan's tavern, on Friday, November 30, 1798, when a dinner was

---
*Butler. †Society Records.

given, which was enjoyed by the members of the society, and a number of invited guests. The original members of the society were Alexander McGregor, John Cameron, William McBean, John Maxwell, David Reid, Richard Lake, John Arthur, William Todd, Thomas Reid, George Muter, Miles McCoun, James Russell, Alexander Springle, and James Bain. Up to 1806, the following additional names had been added to the roll of the society, viz: Robert Campbell, Allan B. McGruder, John Bradford, Daniel McBean, John Brand, John Ferrier, Thomas Bodley, E. Sharpe, William Miller, George Anderson, John Jackson, and Joseph McClear. The St. Andrew's Society has been succeeded by the present "Caledonian Club," which regularly celebrates the birthday of Robert Burns.

About the year 1798, Jesse Bledsoe commenced the study of law in Lexington.* Judge Bledsoe was born in Culpepper county, Virginia, April 6, 1776, and was the son of Joseph Bledsoe, a Baptist preacher, and Elizabeth Miller, his wife. Judge Bledsoe was brought by an elder brother to the neighborhood of Lexington when a boy, and was sent to Transylvania Seminary, where he soon made himself conspicuous by his talents, industry, and scholarly attainments. After completing his collegiate course, he studied law, and commenced its practice with success and reputation. About this time, he married the eldest daughter of Colonel Nathaniel Gist.

He early attracted popular attention and favor, and was frequently elected to the Kentucky legislature. He was at one time state senator from Bourbon county, after which his superior abilities caused him to receive the appointment of secretary of state under Governor Charles Scott. In 1812, while a member of the legislature, he was elected to the United States Senate, the distinguished John Pope being his colleague. He was appointed circuit judge in the Lexington district, by Governor Adair, in 1822, whereupon he removed to, and settled permanently in Lexington; where, before, he had only resided at times. Simul-

---

*Collins.

taneous with his appointment as judge, he was made professor of law in Transylvania University, and after ably filling both places for a number of years, he resigned, and resumed the practice of law.

Subsequently, he abandoned his profession for a short time for that of the ministry; and in 1831,* he preached the dedication sermon on the opening of the Christian Church, on the corner of Mill and Hill streets. In 1833, Judge Bledsoe removed to Mississippi, and from thence, in 1835,† to Texas, and was gathering materials for a history of that new Republic, when he was taken sick and died, June 25, 1836, at Nacogdoches. Judge Bledsoe was a man of powerful intellect, no little eccentricity, and remarkable eloquence. His speeches were noted for strength, wit, originality, and fire, and rarely failed to carry conviction with them. In his best days, but few men were considered the mental equals of Judge Bledsoe. Amos Kendall, who knew him in his palmiest day, said of him:‡ " Mr. Bledsoe was a man *sui generis*. He was endowed with splendid talents, and with the exception of Henry Clay, was the most eloquent man in Kentucky. His manner was slow and deliberate, his language beautiful, his gestures graceful, and his thoughts communicated with the utmost clearness." Judge Bledsoe's residence in Lexington was, at one time, on the place now occupied by Mr. A. M. Barnes, fronting on Fourth street, and at the head of Walnut. At another time, he lived on Short, between Walnut and Dewees streets, and in the house now occupied by Mr. Armstrong.

---

*Observer and Reporter.   †Collins.   ‡Kendall's Biography.

CHAPTER XXVI.

Street Improvement—Second Constitutional Convention—Kentucky Vineyard Association.

THE first improvement of the streets of Lexington commenced in 1799, in which year a part of Main street was paved. Up to this time, the citizens had contented themselves with narrow "log-walks," with here and there a broad, flat stone. Macadamized roads were unknown, and mud-holes were so deep and numerous on Main street and the "public square," that the trustees had a "bridge" extended from the court-house to what is now called Carty's corner.* The "Branch," or as it was then frequently called, the "Canal," rose so high in 1799, that it overflowed the bridge which extended across it on Upper street.

It did not take the people of Kentucky many years to discover that they wanted a more democratic constitution than that of 1792, and a convention to revise it was accordingly called by the legislature. In May, 1799, the following delegates were elected in Fayette to the convention, which met the succeeding June, viz: John McDowell, Buckner Thurston, John Breckinridge, W. Carr, and John Bell. The convention framed the second constitution of Kentucky, which went into effect in June, 1800.

The Kentucky Vineyard Association was formed in Lexington in 1799, and seven hundred and fifty acres of land, "lying in the big bend of the Kentucky river, near the mouth of Hickman creek," were purchased. The association assured the public that, "in less than four years, wine may be drank on the banks of the Kentucky, produced from European stock." This was, probably, the first regular attempt to cultivate a vineyard in America.

---
*Trustees' Book.

CHAPTER XXVII.

Population of Lexington—Death of Washington—The Great Revival.

IN the year 1800, Lexington was the rising town of the West. Her population amounted to two thousand four hundred, while the adjacent village of Cincinnati, which bought much of its merchandise in Lexington, could only claim a population of seven hundred and fifty.

The news of the death of Washington, which occurred December 14, 1799, was a long time in creeping "out West;" but as soon as it was known in Lexington, due respect was paid to the memory of the Father of his Country. On the 22d of January, 1800,* the town council unanimously "Resolved, That the trustees of Lexington will join the procession on Saturday next from respect to the memory of George Washington, as commander-in-chief of the Revolutionary army of the United States, who led his country to independence, and then resumed his station as a private citizen in 1783." The "procession" formed at Masons' Hall, at twelve o'clock M., on Saturday, January 25, 1800, and was composed of military with arms reversed, musicians, trustees, president, professors and students of Transylvania University, Masons in regalia, clerk of the town and board of trustees, clergy, justices of the peace, and private citizens. To the measure of a solemn dirge, the procession slowly moved to the frame Presbyterian church on Cheapside, when an appropriate address was delivered by Professor James Brown, of Transylvania University.†

The remarkable religious excitement which had commenced in the Green river country some time before, reached

---

*Town Records.   †Old Gazette.

Lexington and Fayette county in 1800. It was confined to Methodists, Presbyterians, and Baptists, and before the "great revival," as it is called, had ended, the most astonishing events transpired. At Lexington and Walnut Hill, meetings were commenced which frequently extended through entire days and nights. The people attended in vast crowds from all the surrounding country, on foot, on horseback, and in every imaginable vehicle, bringing with them tents, provisions, and cooking utensils for a protracted visit, and often a camp-meeting concourse would number from ten to twenty thousand persons. The wildest excitement, and the most ridiculous extravagances, characterized these meetings. A hymn or an exhortation was the signal to the living mass of humanity to shout and groan and laugh and scream until the noise was almost equal to the ocean in a storm. Visions and trances were of frequent occurrence. In Lexington,* a woman swooned, and when she awoke, said she had been walking on the tree tops. One fainted and had a vision of heaven, and another had a view of hell. These epileptic evidences of piety were succeeded by growling and barking, kissing and hugging, dancing, jerking, falling, rolling, and tumbling. The influence of the imagination on the nervous system has never been more strikingly illustrated than during the "great revival" of 1800.

---

*Lyle, 7.

CHAPTER XXVIII.

The First Kentucky Bank—Nail Factory.

THE first bank chartered in Kentucky was the Lexington Insurance Company, which was incorporated by the legislature in 1801,* and inadvertently with banking privileges. The clause giving it such powers was not perceived or understood by the members, and they voted for the bill, while they were bitterly hostile to all banks. The officers of "the bank," as the institution was always called in early days, were: President, William Morton; directors, John Jordon, Stephen Waute, Thos. Hart, and Thomas Wallace; cashier, John Bradford; clerk, Wm. McBean. The bank was located on Main, between Mill and Broadway, about where the Scott bakery now stands, and issued bills of various denominations. The bank was subsequently located on the site of Thompson and Boyd's saddlery store, on Main, between Upper and Limestone. The institution exploded in 1818.

A cut-nail manufactory, the first one in Kentucky, was established in Lexington, by George Norton, in 1801. Tenpenny nails were sold at one shilling fourpence per pound, and six pennies at one shilling sixpence. Cincinnati bought all her nails in Lexington, and purchasers often came from points two hundred miles distant for Lexington nails, and carried them home in saddle-bags on horseback. In fact, Lexington was then the metropolis of a great territory, and was noted among other things for† her stores, manufactories, newspaper, taverns, paper and powder mills, tanyards, and her two rope-walks, which supplied the shipping on the Ohio.

---

*Acts Legislature.   †Michaux.

CHAPTER XXIX.

Medical Society—Members—Musical Society—Lorenzo Dow—Miscellaneous—G. M. Bibb—Dr. Joseph Buchanan.

THE "Lexington Medical Society" was in active operation in 1802, and numbered among its members Drs. B. W. Dudley, Samuel Brown, Frederick Ridgely, Walter Warfield, J. L. Armstrong, and others.*

Thomas Paine's writings afforded Lexington subjects for long and animated discussions in 1803. In this year, a musical society was formed. The excitement in regard to the acquisition of Louisiana was such that "volunteers for New Orleans" paraded on the streets.†

The citizens of Lexington celebrated the annexation of Louisiana, in the spring of 1804, by a grand barbecue, at Maxwell Spring, at which patriotic toasts were given, and salutes were fired by four military companies. In June, twelve splendid looking Indian chiefs of the Osage nation, passed through the city on their way to Washington, to try to effect a treaty with the United States. The noted and eccentric Lorenzo Dow arrived in Lexington, on foot, October 3d, and preached a characteristic sermon.

In 1804, and for several years after, the late distinguished George M. Bibb was a member of the Lexington bar. He was a native of Virginia, and a graduate of Princeton. He died April 14, 1859, aged eighty, after having been successively senator in Congress, chief justice of Kentucky court of appeals, and secretary of the treasury under Tyler. Hon. John J. Crittenden studied law in Lexington, under Mr. Bibb, in 1805.

---

*Old Kentucky Gazette. †Id.

Dr. Joseph Buchanan* settled in Lexington in 1804, and soon became noted as one of her most extraordinary citizens. He was born in Washington county, Virginia, August 24, 1785, but spent his boyhood in Tennessee, where he attended a grammar school, and astonished every one by his remarkable progress. In the course of nine months, in 1803, he mastered the Latin language. He was so fond of originality in all his essays, that he would not even condescend to write on any subject on which he had ever read anything.

He entered Transylvania University at the age of nineteen,† and was so delicate and diffident that he passed for a simpleton, until he detected and offered to demonstate an error in his mathematical text-book (Ferguson on Optics), which brought him into direct collision with the professor of mathematics. During the vacation of the college, he published a mathematical pamphlet of twenty pages, in which he demonstrated the sufficiency of gravitation for all the celestial motions, and showed the inaccuracy of some of the hypotheses of the very distinguished Sir Isaac Newton.

In 1805, he commenced the study of medicine with Dr. Samuel Brown. Removing to Port Gibson, Mississippi Territory [then], in 1807, in order that he might, by medical practice, obtain means to complete his medical education in Philadelphia, Dr. Buchanan then wrote a volume on fevers, which, while it defeated his first object, that of earning money, was his favorable introduction to the distinguished professors of the University of Pennsylvania, and especially to Professors Barton and Rush. But his means being insufficient for the completion of his medical studies there, as well as for the publication of his book, he *walked* back to Lexington, in 1808, in twenty-seven days, where the degree of A. B. having been conferred on him, at the instance of President Blythe, he was, in 1809, appointed to the chair of the Institutes of Medicine in the university.

In 1812, he published an able volume on the "Philosophy

---

*University Records. †Collins.

of Human Nature," and almost immediately abandoned the medical profession, to visit the East to learn the new Pestalozzian system of education, and to introduce it into Kentucky. Subsequently, he invented a "capillary" steam engine, with spiral tubes for boilers; and in 1825, he made a steam land carriage which attracted general attention in Louisville, through the streets of which city it was run; and, we are told, discovered a new *motive principle*, described as being derived from combustion, without the aid of water or of steam.

This remarkable philosophical, mathematical, and inventive genius died in Louisville, in 1829, "little known, except as a writer, to more than a small circle of friends."

In the language of his biographer, "the life of Dr. Buchanan affords an instructive moral," to young men, we add, showing that for success in this world, talents of the highest order, industry the most untiring, or self-denial the most strict, are not alone sufficient, unless combined with steadiness of purpose and unvarying concentration of effort in the right direction.

CHAPTER XXX.

Burr's Visit—Trustee Chronicles—William T. Barry.

AARON BURR, one of the most extraordinary men of his age, made his first visit to Kentucky in 1805, arriving in Lexington, August 19th, and attracting universal attention. After a stay of several days, he went south, but returned again, and remained a considerable time in Lexington. It was at this time that Colonel Burr commenced, it is believed, to lay his unsuccessful plans for the erection of a magnificent Southern empire. He was met in Lexington by the studious and accomplished Blannerhasset and his gifted wife, around whose lives fate wove so strange and sad a web.

The trustees of Lexington distinguished themselves, in 1805, by prohibiting the citizens from keeping "pet panthers;" by encouraging the introduction of "chimney sweeps," and by indorsing the "Bachelors' Society for the Promotion of Matrimony," which met weekly at Wilson's tavern. For the sum of five dollars, they "allowed Thomas Ardon to shew his lyon," which constituted the first menagerie that ever visited Lexington.

William Taylor Barry commenced the practice of law in Lexington in 1805. This illustrious orator and statesman was born in Lunenburg county, Virginia, February 15, 1784.* His parents, who were respectable, energetic, and poor, emigrated to Kentucky in 1796, and settled first in Fayette, and then in Jessamine county; and conscious that they could not give their son wealth, resolved to educate him. Young Barry was sent to the Kentucky Academy in Woodford, and finishing his collegiate course at Transylvania

---

*Observer and Reporter.

University, after the union of the Kentucky and Transylvania Academies.

After he left the university, he commenced the study of law with the Hon. James Brown, minister to France, and finished his law studies at William and Mary College in Virginia. Then, like his great competitor of after years, Henry Clay, he commenced life in Lexington at the age of twenty-one—young and poor, with neither family nor influence to bring him into notice, and with nothing to recommend him but his virtues and attainments. Shortly after, he commenced business he married the daughter of Waller Overton, of Fayette county. His first wife dying in 1809, in 1812, he married again, in Virginia, a daughter of General S. T. Mason.

From the year of his arrival in Lexington to the time of his death in a foreign land, the life of the gifted Barry was a brilliant panorama of success. Soon after he came to the bar, he was appointed attorney for the commonwealth, which office he filled for several years, and in 1807 he was for the first time, elected a representative from Fayette county, and was re-elected for several years in succession almost without opposition. He rose rapidly in his profession; soon took the first rank as a great lawyer and an eloquent advocate, and in a little while was the recognized peer of Rowan Bledsoe, Haggin, and "Harry of the West." In 1810, Mr. Barry was elected a representative to Congress from the Ashland district, and distinguished himself by his eloquent denunciations of the aggressive insults then being offered to the United States by England. After the declaration of war in 1812, he not only strongly advocated its vigorous prosecution, but took the field as an aid to Governor Shelby, and served during the severe and glorious campaign, which resulted in the capture of the British army, the death of Tecumseh, and the conquest of a large part of Upper Canada.*

In 1814, Mr. Barry was again sent to the state legislature by an almost unanimous vote; was made speaker of the

---

*Collins.

house, and shortly after elected to the United States Senate, where he remained for two sessions. Here occurred one of the most remarkable events of his life. He resigned his seat in the senate, to accept the position of circuit judge with a meager salary. Public men rarely abandon national honors, position, and pay so easily at this day. It was during Mr. Barry's judgeship that a tipsy mountaineer stalked into the presence of the court shouting: "I am a horse!" "Sheriff," said Judge Barry, "take that horse to the stable."

In 1817, he was forced by the people to become a member of the state senate. While in the legislature, Mr. Barry, who was ever alive to home interests, was actively engaged in promoting the success of Transylvania University, and was persevering in his efforts to have it endowed, and to bring it under the patronage of the state.* He succeeded in his undertakings, for his struggles and his eloquence principally induced the legislature to give the institution about $20,000, and the name of Wm. T. Barry gave it free passport among the people. The law department of this institution, with which, by his profession, he was more particularly connected, also commanded his attention. He was instrumental in giving it funds sufficient to purchase a good library. In this department he was the first regular professor and law lecturer after the reform in the university. Under his management it prospered beyond expectation, and surpassed the most sanguine anticipation of its friends.

In 1820, he became a candidate for the office of lieutenant-governor. The people recollected his services and his struggles in their cause, and gave him an overwhelming vote. At this period he decidedly stood foremost in the affections of the people of Kentucky. Subsequently, he was made secretary of state during the administration of Governor Desha, and after the appellate court of the state was reorganized, he was appointed chief justice. In the change of parties in Kentucky in 1825, produced by Mr.

---

*Observer and Reporter.

Clay's adherence to Mr. Adams,* Major Barry became the leader of the Democratic party in the state, and was devoted to its principles to the day of his untimely death.

In 1828, Mr. Barry was the Democratic candidate for the office of governor, while Mr. Clay was the champion of the opposing party, and it was during that bitter and hotly contested struggle that Barry exhibited so powerfully the wonderful resources of his great intellect, and achieved his greatest triumph, for though he was defeated by a small majority for governor, it was mainly through his almost superhuman exertions in that campaign that the vote of Kentucky was given to General Jackson in the presidential election which followed. Mr. Barry's astonishing oratorical powers were all brought out in this campaign. As a speaker† he was full of energy, action, and fire, and on the stump, filled as he always was, on such occasions, with eloquence and majesty, he seemed every inch a towering tribune of the old Roman commonwealth. The rare peculiarity of Mr. Barry's style was, that, instead of commencing a speech with deliberation and coolness, and gradually warming up with his subject, he launched out at once with words as bold and eloquent as those which invariably attended his blazing perorations. One of Judge Barry's finest efforts was made in 1828, when standing upon a table placed against the rear wall of the present court-house, he defended himself, before an immense crowd, against some partisan charges made by his political opponents.

Mr. Barry was called to Washington in 1829, as postmaster-general, which office he held until unable, from physical disability, to discharge its onerous duties. Ardently hoping that a milder climate would restore the now shattered health of this ornament of his cabinet, President Jackson appointed him minister to Spain, for which country Mr. Barry sailed in 1835. He was destined to never reach Madrid. His health rapidly declined, and Barry, the great orator, the favorite of fortune, the idol of the people, died a few days after reaching Liverpool.

---

*Collins. †James O. Harrison.

It has been truly said that "no man who has figured so largely in the well-contested arena of western politics ever left it with fewer enemies or a larger number of devoted friends than William T. Barry." His great abilities and lofty virtues made him the hero of his party, and his political opponents loved him as they felt the singular charm of his mild and conciliating disposition, and the influence of his generous and exalted soul.

In our court-house yard stands an unpretending, weather-beaten monument of granite, surrounded by a plain iron railing. It has been there so long, and has such an old-fashioned look, that hundreds pass it daily without once giving it so much as a glance, and without the thought once occurring to them that it stands there to remind them of one of the loftiest spirits that ever did honor to Lexington and our commonwealth. The rains and snows of many winters have descended upon it, but the angel of immortality has shielded that old shaft with her protecting wings, and it still tells its proud story.

On one side is the inscription:

"To the memory of William Taylor Barry this monument is erected by his friends in Kentucky (the site being granted by the county court of Fayette), as a testimony of their respect and admiration for his virtues."

On another side is carved this beautiful sentence:

"His fame lives in the history of his country, and is as immortal as America's liberty and glory."

Mr. Barry lived in the house now owned by Joseph Wolfolk, near the corner of Hill and Rose streets.

The remains of Barry, after reposing nearly nineteen years in a foreign land, were brought back to Kentucky, by act of the legislature, and reinterred in the State cemetery at Frankfort, with many honors and great respect, November 8, 1854. The eloquent Theodore O'Hara, who was the orator of the occasion, concluded his eulogy upon Barry in these burning words:

"Let the marble minstrel rise to sing to the future generations of the commonwealth the inspiring lay of his high genius and lofty deeds. Let the autumn wind harp on the dropping leaves her softest requiem over him; let the winter's purest snow rest spotless on his grave; let spring entwine her brightest garland for his tomb, and summer gild it with her mildest sunshine, and let him sleep embalmed in glory till the last trumph shall reveal him to us all radiant with the halo of his life."

CHAPTER XXXI.

Currency—Stray Pen—Felix Grundy.

THE currency used in trade in Lexington, in 1806, was miscellaneous in its character. Raccoon and other skins were given in exchange for goods, but Spanish dollars, cut into halves, quarters, and eighths, were mostly used, while very small change was effected by means of papers of needles and pins. In this year a Lexington merchant carried one hundred pounds of "cut silver" with him to Philadelphia.

The Lexington "stray pen" was located about this time, on Market street, near the present Press office.

Felix Grundy, long eminent as a Democratic leader and statesman, was a resident of Lexington and a trustee of Transylvania University in 1806, and for some time anterior to that date. He was born in Berkley county, Virginia, September 11, 1777, came to Kentucky when a boy, studied law, and soon acquired a high reputation as an advocate in criminal cases. Before his removal to Nashville in 1808, he had served in the Kentucky legislature, and as chief justice of the court of appeals. He died December 19, 1840, after filling the positions of representative and senator in Congress, and attorney general of the United States.

CHAPTER XXXII.

*The Observer and Reporter—Editors—Biographical Notices—
Incidents.*

THE Observer and Reporter, now the oldest newspaper in existence in Kentucky, if not in the West, was founded in 1807,* by William W. Worsley and Samuel R. Overton, and was first called the "Kentucky Reporter." Their first office, as the early copies of the paper state, was opposite Mr. Sanders' store," and therefore occupied the site now filled by Clark & Bro.'s warehouse, on East Main street, and was between the first capitol building of the infant commonwealth of Kentucky, and the Free and Easy tavern, so notorious in the early history of Lexington. Near it was a rakish-looking craft of a building, nine feet wide and forty feet long, then commonly called the "Old Gun-boat." This was the first silver-plater's shop used in this city by the late David A. Sayre, and there the ring of his busy hammer was often heard far into the night.

Mr. Worsley came to this place from Virginia at an early day, and married a sister of Thomas Smith, at that time editor of the Kentucky Gazette, and afterward editor of the Observer. Aside from his capacity as a writer and publisher, Mr. Worsley was noted for his strict integrity and remarkable amiability. Mr. Overton, who was connected with the Observer only a few months, and in a business way, was a son of Waller Overton, of this county.

The Observer commenced its career as a strong Jeffersonian Democratic organ, or rather "Republican," as the party was then called. Its first prospectus contains this

---
*Ob. and Rep. in Lex. Lib.

language :* " The character of the Reporter with relation to politics shall be strictly republican. Highly approving of the principles of the revolution, as contained in the federal constitution, and duly appreciating the enlightened policy pursued by the present administration, it shall be the undeviating object of the editors, as far it may come within the sphere of their influence, to contribute to the promotion and preservation of the former, and embrace every opportunity of testifying to the virtue and faithfulness of the latter. Whenever we may discover ourselves deviating from the principles held sacred by the people, we shall invariably be disposed to retrace our steps and make such assertions as may clearly and satisfactorily present themselves. We shall also rely with confidence on the vigilance of the people to point out those errors to which we may be subject and in which their interests may be involved." The public is also informed that " for the more speedy conveyance of the Reporter, the editor has established at great expense some private posts."

Mr. Overton retired from the paper, and left Mr. Worsley sole proprietor until February, 1816, when he took into partnership his brother-in-law, Mr. Thomas Smith. Mr. Smith married Miss Nannette Price, a niece of Mrs. Henry Clay. He was at one time president of the Frankfort and Lexington railroad. Smith bought out Worsley's interest in 1819, and conducted the paper alone until April, 1828, when he took in James W. Palmer as a partner. Mr. Palmer was an Englishman, whose beautiful disposition and engaging manners made him exceedingly popular. He wrote elegantly, but not strongly. He was a devoted Episcopalian, and for years, as was then the custom here, made the responses at public worship in behalf of the congregation. He was well known as the calculator of the almanacs for Kentucky. Mr. Palmer was connected with the Reporter about a year, after which Mr. Smith had entire charge again, until March, 1832, when the paper passed into the hands of Edwin Bryant and N. L. Finnell, who united

---

*See files Observer and Reporter.

with it the "Lexington Observer, the consolidated papers being called "The Kentucky Reporter and Lexington Observer."* Mr. Smith removed to Pewee Valley, where he died only a few months ago. On his retirement from the paper the gentlemen of Lexington gave him a public reception.

Mr. Finnell came to this place from Georgetown, and had published a paper in Winchester. He was the father of General J. W. Finnell, of Covington, and a practical printer, and often stood at the case and "set up" his own editorials. He was a sprightly writer, and a man of great energy. When his connection with this paper ceased, he, with considerable enterprise, established and labored hard to keep up "The Lexington Atlas," a daily paper, but without success. His subscription list became quite extensive, but the expenses of the establishment were so great that he was compelled to give up the attempt, after several months of disastrous experience. He died near Frankfort, in 1853.

Judge Edwin Bryant came from the old Berkshire hills of Massachusetts, to this city, when but a boy, and was soon a Kentuckian, both in sentiment and by adoption. He was an editor of signal ability, courtesy, and success. After the Observer, he assumed the management of the "Louisville Dime," in connection with Mr. W. N. Haldeman, of the present Courier-Journal.

In 1847, failing health induced him to take an overland mule-back journey to the Pacific, and he joined Fremont in one of his famous expeditions. He assisted in the capture of California, and was the first American alcalde (judge) who ever administered justice on that then far distant coast.

Returning home, Judge Bryant published a volume entitled, "What I saw in California," which had a very extraordinary sale.

He resided in Pewee Valley, Kentucky, until the time of his death, which took place in December, 1869.

Robert Nelson Wickliffe, brother of D. C. Wickliffe, succeeded Bryant in 1833. He graduated with distinguished

---

*Observer and Reporter.

honors at Transylvania University, was admitted to the bar, and in all subsequent oratorial efforts evinced a rare fertility and resource of scholarship and literary knowledge. As an editor, he was fully equal to Prentice, and as an orator, was considered by many to be the peer of Clay.

Mr. Wickliffe represented his county in the legislature, was a delegate to the convention which framed the present state constitution, and in 1851 was Democratic candidate for lieutenant-governor,* but he never attained the position his extraordinary powers entitled him to, as he lacked ambition, and was totally indifferent to political and professional honors. For years after his official connection with the Observer had ceased, Mr. Wickliffe contributed to the editorial department. He died at the age of fifty, February 26, 1855.

In September, 1838, Hon. D. C. Wickliffe became sole editor and proprietor of the Observer and Reporter.†

Daniel Carmichael Wickliffe was born in Lexington, Kentucky, on the 15th of March, 1810. He was educated at Transylvania University, and graduated with much honor at the very early age of seventeen. He adopted the law as his profession.

On the 25th of November, 1844, Mr. Wickliffe married Miss Virginia Cooper, a daughter of the Rev. Spencer Cooper, widely-known local Methodist minister of this city.

Anterior to his marriage, and in September, 1838, Mr. Wickliffe succeeded Mr. N. L. Finnell as editor and proprietor of the Observer and Reporter, and he gave all the rest of his active life to the profession of journalism, not even excepting the period when he was secretary of state of Kentucky, during Governor Robinson's executive term He was editor of this paper for nearly twenty-seven years, and in very many respects was the ablest one that ever wielded a pen in the whole commonwealth of Kentucky. He gave Mr. Clay no weak support.

Mr. Wickliffe, to his great honor be it said, was almost en-

---
*Old Kentucky Statesman.   †Observer and Reporter,

tirely a self-made man. In June, 1865, Mr. Wickliffe severed his connection with the press. He died May 3, 1870.

John T. Hogan became associated with Mr. Wickliffe in the editorial department in 1855, and filled the position for four years.

In September, 1862, the Observer office was used by General John Morgan as his headquarters, and in 1864 it was occupied by federal troops.

The establishment was purchased by a number of gentlemen in 1865, and the concern was styled the "Observer and Reporter Printing Company," with William A. Dudley as editor. Mr. Dudley resigned the editorial chair for a seat in the senate of Kentucky. He died March 19, 1870, at the age of forty-six, after an exertion of energy in connection with, first, the Lexington and Frankfort, and then the Short Line railroad, that made him most widely known.

W. C. P. Breckinridge succeeded Mr. Dudley, having been elected by the company in July, 1866. The author of this volume succeeded Colonel Breckinridge in July, 1868, and became sole editor and proprietor of the Observer and Reporter. In April, 1871, he disposed of the establishment, which is at present owned and managed by a company. Dr. Thomas Pickett, of Maysville, Kentucky, succeeded the writer as editor, and he in turn was succeeded by the present editor, Mr. J. S. Smith.

CHAPTER XXXIII.

Miscellaneous—Sheep Excitement—Dr. Ben. W. Dudley.

IN 1808, and long after, it was the custom in Lexington to call the hours from twelve o'clock at night until daylight.

All Lexington and Fayette county was excited in the summer of 1808 over a "living elephant," the first one ever seen in the community. One of the newspapers of the town urged every one to go and see it, as "perhaps the present generation may never have the opportunity of seeing a living elephant again."

A long list of "school-books manufactured in this place," was advertised in a Lexington newspaper in 1809.

At an early period, probably at this time (1809), a great excitement was created about Merino sheep, which suddenly acquired an enormous value, and the few in the country were sought after with the most ridiculous avidity. The extent of the speculation may be inferred from the tradition that a master mechanic actually received three merino sheep from Mr. Samuel Trotter as payment for building for him the residence now owned by Judge Robertson, and situated at the corner of Hill and Mill streets.*

Dr. Benjamin W. Dudley, who afterward became so famous as a surgeon, commenced his public career in 1809, in which year he was appointed to the chair of anatomy and surgery in Transylvania University.

Dr. Benjamin Winslow Dudley† was born in Spottsylvania county, Virginia, on the 12th day of April, 1785; was brought by his parents to Kentucky county, where they landed six miles east of Lexington, on the 3d day of May,

---

*Benjamin Kiser.   †Observer and Reporter.

1786. His earlier education was obtained at country schools, and finished in Transylvania University. He came to Lexington in 1797, and for a time worked in the store of Samuel and George Trotter. He studied medicine with the late Drs. Ridgely and Fishback, after which he attended medical lectures in the old school of Philadelphia, graduated in 1806, and returned to Lexington, where he continued the practice of medicine, and acted as professor in the medical college until 1810, when he visited Europe, and spent four years, profiting by the instructions of the most distinguished medical and scientific teachers. During his stay in London, he was made a member of the Royal College of Surgeons.

Returning to Lexington, he soon stood in the front rank of the profession. In 1818, on the reorganization of the medical college of Transylvania University, he was recalled to the chair of surgery and anatomy, and remained in that connection for forty years, during which time the college acknowledged no superior on this continent. Its great success was largely due to Dr. Dudley, whose professional fame spread throughout the civilized world. He attended a laborious practice for about fifty years, when he contracted poison in performing a surgical operation, from which he suffered greatly, and never recovered. He died suddenly, after about two hours of illness, at a quarter to one o'clock, on Thursday morning, January 20, 1870, of apoplexy.

Dr. Dudley's achievements in the operation of lithotomy alone are so great as to be actually incredible to the most distinguished surgeons of Europe, and are sufficient of themselves to hand his name down to a distant posterity. He operated for stone in the bladder about two hundred and sixty times, losing only two or three patients. He operated upon the eye in numerous cases, and frequently perforated the cranium for the relief of epilepsy. In spite of the fact that he left no production of his pen behind, his scientific triumphs will long cause him to be remembered as the great surgeon of Kentucky. Dr. Dudley's office was on the corner of Mill and Church streets, and occupied the site of the present residence of E. Sayre.

CHAPTER XXXIV.

Great Prosperity of Lexington in 1810—Center of the Western Trade—Manufacturers and Business—Decline—Lexington Bible Society—Freshets.

LEXINGTON was at the zenith of her commercial prosperity in 1810. Situated on the great line of communication between the older settlements of the East and the fertile West, she was benefited by every great wave of immigration that swept into the wilderness. Since 1800, her growth had been so rapid that her population had tripled itself, and was now eight thousand, while that of Fayette county was twenty-one thousand three hundred and seventy. By this time, almost the entire trade of the West centered in Lexington, which had also become the grand depot of supplies for emigrants, and the great manufacturing point of an immense region. It is said that in 1810 the sales of the most extensive business house in Lexington amounted to one hundred thousand dollars per month. A careful eye witness of the prosperity of Lexington at this time said :* " Main street presents to the eye as much wealth and more beauty than can be found in most Atlantic cities. A prodigious quantity of European goods are displayed and retailed to the crowds of customers who resort here from the neighboring settlements."

A tolerably correct estimate of the business and manufacturing importance of Lexington in 1810 is extant.† Its enumeration is as follows, viz: four paper mills, two tobacco factories, three nail factories, one mustard factory, four cabinet shops, six powder mills, five wool-carding

---

*Brown's Emigrant Directory.   †Cumming, 160.

machines run by horse power, one sail-duck factory, one brush factory, one reed factory, one umbrella factory, one white lead factory, four chair factories, one oil-mill, thirteen rope-walks, seven brick-yards, five hat factories, ten blacksmith shops, seven saddlery shops, ten tailor shops, fifteen boot and shoe shops, three blue dyers, two copper and tin shops, two printing establishments where books were made, one bindery, seven distilleries, four billiard tables, five paint shops, one looking-glass factory, one Venetian blind factory, two foundries, three cotton mills, five bagging factories, and five coarse linen factories. One steam flour mill, the first in Kentucky, had just been erected by Stevens & Winslow. Twenty-five large stores are mentioned. Negroes from fourteen to thirty years of age quoted at from three hundred and fifty to four hundred dollars. "Vauxhall" is described as "a public garden, kept by Mr. Terasse, from St. Bartholomew, with summer-houses, and arbors illuminated every Wednesday evening with variegated lamps, a fashionable resort for music, dancing, and feasting." In Lexington and Fayette there were one thousand looms, which wove two hundred and seven thousand yards of hemp, flax, and cotton cloth. "Lexington," says a traveler,* "is expected to become the largest inland town of the United States. Perhaps there is no manufactory in this country which is not known here."

The trade and population of Lexington, after 1810, declined, and did not begin to grow again until about the year 1820. The cause of this decline is easily accounted for. It commenced with the successful opening of steam navigation upon the Ohio river, an event which revolutionized the trade and trade channels of the western country. The same cause which produced this decline in Lexington, made Cincinnati, with its favorable location, an important city. In 1810, when Lexington had eight thousand inhabitants, Cincinnati had but two thousand five hundred; but the steamboat came, and, in 1820, Cincinnati had grown to four times the size of Lexington. The prosperity of Lex-

---

*Cumming.

ington in the future will largely depend upon the use she makes of the same great agent which has operated against her. Steam, upon artificial highways, can bring back to her much of what it carried away upon the natural channels of trade.

A "Bible Society" was formed in Lexington in 1810,* of which Robert M. Cunningham was president. It grew and prospered, and, in 1820, its corresponding secretary, James Blythe, supplied many persons with Bibles printed in Lexington. Its successor was the "Lexington and Vicinity Bible Society," which was formed November 24, 1836,† and its officers were: President, L. P. Yandell; Vice-presidents, J. M. Hewitt, J. C. Stiles, Walter Bullock, D. M. Winston, George Robertson, R. T. Dillard, and Mr. Harris; Executive Committee, James Fishback, Edward Stevenson, T. K. Layton, M. T. Scott; W. A. Leavy, Corresponding Secretary; Edward Winthrop, Recording Secretary; William Richardson, Treasurer. The object of this society, as set forth in its constitution, is, "to aid in the circulation of the Holy Scriptures, without note or comment. It interferes with no man's views of truth and duty; requires no sacrifice of principle; aims to establish no peculiar creed; but wants all to meet on common ground, to give the Bible to their fellow creatures." The society is still in existence, and doing a great work of usefulness and good.

Alarming freshets were not unfrequent at this period. The miserable "canal" then in existence could not accommodate the water which ran from all the streets and high lots, and collected in the "Town Fork of Elkhorn creek," and sometimes, after a rain, the water extended from the present Phœnix Hotel far beyond Water and Vine streets.‡ A lead factory and a paper mill were on Water street at that time, near where the present Louisville freight depot stands, and the mill-races were fed from the then flourishing Town Fork, now so insignificant.

---

*Old Kentucky Gazette.   †Society Records.   ‡McCullough.

CHAPTER XXXV.

Earthquake—Battle of Tippecanoe—Joseph H. Daviess, His Career and Gallant Death—St. Tammany Society.

ON the morning of December 16, 1811, the citizens of Lexington were startled and alarmed by several successive shocks of an earthquake,* accompanied by a sound like that of distant thunder. Fortunately no other damage was done than the breaking of window glass and the disturbance of a few bricks from chimneys.

In 1811, the Indians of the Northwest, incited by Tecumseh and the Prophet, who were encouraged by the British, gave such marked evidences of hostility that General Harrison marched to the Wabash, where, shortly after, he was joined by Colonel J. H. Daviess and a number of volunteers from Lexington. On the 7th of November, the memorable battle of Tippecanoe took place, and Colonel Daviess was numbered among the slain.

Colonel Joseph Hamilton Daviess was born in Bedford county, Virginia, March 4, 1774.† His parents, Joseph and Jean Daviess, emigrated to Kentucky when their son was five years old, and settled near Danville. Young Daviess received his education from his mother and superior teachers of country schools, and became a proficient in the Latin and Greek languages, and evinced a remarkable talent for public speaking. In 1792, he volunteered under Major Adair, and served against the Indians, and distinguished himself by his daring conduct. After this, he studied law under the celebrated George Nicholas, in a class with Jesse Bledsoe, John Pope, Felix Grundy, and others, who afterward became noted, and studied with the

---

*Observer and Reporter. †Collins.

most untiring energy and perseverance. He was admitted to the bar in 1795, and in his first case triumphed over his learned old teacher. In 1801, he went to Washington City, and was the first western lawyer who ever appeared in the supreme court of the United States. There he gained another legal victory, which placed him at once in the foremost rank of his profession. He was married to Miss Annie Marshall, sister of the United States chief justice, in 1803, and in 1806, occurred his celebrated prosecution of Aaron Burr, during which he confronted Henry Clay and John Allin.

He removed to Lexington in 1809, and resided there up to the time of his death. During that period, there was hardly an important cause litigated in the courts where he practiced that he was not engaged in. Colonel Daviess was a federalist, but when the Indian war of 1811, which was aggravated by England, broke out, he was one of the first to enlist.* He was appointed major of cavalry, but when he was killed in the battle of Tippecanoe, he was fighting on foot in a charge made at his own solicitation. He fell wounded in three places, and met death with great calmness. General Harrison said of him :† " Major Daviess joined me as a private volunteer, and on the recommendation of the officers of that corps, was appointed to command the third troop of dragoons. His conduct in that capacity justified their choice; never was there an officer possessed of more ardor and zeal to discharge his duties with propriety, and never one who would have encountered greater danger to purchase military fame." Colonel Daviess was a man of remarkably fine personal appearance and impressive bearing. As a lawyer he was one of the ablest in the land, and as an orator he had few equals and no superiors. His death caused a profound sensation, and in Lexington imposing funeral ceremonies were performed, and a Masonic lodge was formed and named in his honor. Colonel Daviess lived in the house now occupied by Mr. William Fishback, opposite the Chris-

---

*Davidson.   †Harrison's Report, Battle Tippecanoe.

tian Church, and between Walnut and Limestone, on Main.

A St. Tammany Society was instituted in Lexington about this time (1811), and continued to exist up to 1820. The "Wigwam" was in the second story of "Connell's ale shop," which stood on the site of the Cleary building, on the corner of Main and Broadway. The sons of St. Tammany often paraded through the streets disguised as Indians, and magnificent in red paint, feathers, bows, tomahawks, and war clubs. It was one of the most noted Democratic organizations in the West. Thomas T. Barr, Richard Chinn, and others successively filled the office of "Sachem." We give verbatim one of the society's orders,* viz:

"ST. TAMMANY'S DAY.—The Sons of St. Tammany, or Brethren of the Columbian Order, will assemble at the council fire of their great wigwam, on Tuesday, the 12th of the month of flowers, at the rising of the sun, to celebrate the anniversary of their patron saint.

"A dinner will be provided at brother John Fowler's garden, to which the brethren will march in procession, where a *long talk* will be delivered by one of the order.

"An adjourned meeting of the society will be held on to-morrow evening, at the going down of the sun. By order of the grand sachem,

"N. S. POTTER, *Sec.*

"8th of the Month of Flowers, Year of Discovery, 326."

---

*Kentucky Gazette.

CHAPTER XXXVI.

War with England—Rolls of Lexington and Fayette Volunteers—The Meeting and Parting at Lexington—The Review and the March—Russell's Expedition—Trotter's Fight with the Indians—The Barracks.

THE commencement of the year 1812 found Lexington full of excitement. The frequent and long-continued outrages of England on American rights and property on the ocean were denounced in the strongest terms by the Democrats, and palliated by the Federalists. While the parties hurled at each other the epithets of "Jacobin" and "Tory," a war with England was openly threatened, and on May 2d, General James Winchester, an old officer of the Revolution, established a recruiting office in Lexington. Early in June, an immense war-meeting was held in the court-house yard, and deafening shouts of applause greeted one of the sentiments proposed: "May the legs of every Tory be made into drumsticks with which to beat Jefferson's march."*

War was declared by the United States on the 18th of June, and Lexington greeted the news with a brilliant illumination and great rejoicing, and as soon as it was known that a requisition had been made upon Kentucky for troops, and even before the governor's orders reached Lexington, a company of volunteers had been formed, and its services tendered to the state.† Six companies in all were quickly raised in the city and county, and it is a matter of the greatest regret that complete rolls of them are not to be had, either in the state military office or in the war department at Washington. Of one company, Captain Arnold's riflemen, we could obtain no list whatever, and

---

*Old Gazette. †Observer and Reporter.

the following rolls, with the exception of that of Captain Hart's company, are meager, confused, and unsatisfactory. The subjoined fragments are all that could be gathered, viz:

HART'S COMPANY.

Officers.—Captain, N. S. G. Hart; Lieutenant, L. Comstock; Second Lieutenant, Geo. G. Ross; Ensign, J. L. Herron; Sergeants, Levi L. Todd, John Whitney, Chas. F. Allen, Thos. Smith, Fielding Gosney, Thos. Chamberlain; Corporals, William O. Butler, Chas. Bradford, Isaac L. Baker, Jacob Schwing, Alex. Crawford.

Privates.—Andrew Allison, F. J. Allen, Francis Allen, Hugh Allen, Thomas Anderson, T. J. Anderson, Daniel Adams, Wm. Adams, James E. Blythe, Henry Beard, I. L. Baker, Wm. C. Bell, John Beckley, Robt. Campbell, R. T. Campbell, Lewis Charless, Hiram Clines, Elisha Collins, R. H. Chinn, Samuel Cox, Jesse Cock, Lawrence Daily, William Davis, Phillip Dunn, Benj. Davis, Samuel Elder, Edward Elder, Thos. Fant, A. Ferguson, E. Francis, K. M. Goodloe, R. W. Gilpin, James Huston, Jas. L. Hickman, Bennet Hines, Samuel Holding, James Higgins, James Johnston, Robert Kelley, Thomas King, S. Kalker, J. E. Kelley, John Kay, Charles Lewis, John Linginfelter, Adam Lake, D. Lingenfelter, John Maxwell, Jr., Thomas Monks, Jno. A. Moon, Peter Messmore, J. W. McChesney, Robt. Mather, James Maxwell, James Neale, Chas. Neil, Jas. P. Parker, W. Pritchard, James Reiley, Robert Rolling, George Rogers, Geo. Rolls, Charles Searls, Armstrong Stewart, Stephen Smith, Thomas Smith, Valentine Shally, Geo. Shindlebower, B. Stephens, V. Shawley, Daniel Talbott, J. Templeman, Sam'l B. Todd, R. S. Todd, — Townsend, Joseph Vance, Derrick Vanpelt, T. Verden, Zephaniah Williams, John Whitney.

MEGOWAN'S COMPANY.

Officers.—Captain, Stewart W. Megowan; Lieutenant, Martin Wymore; Ensign, Levi Todd; Sergeants, Richard Roach, Barnet Harvey; Corporals, T. H. Blackburn, John McMakin.

Privates.—Alexander Alsop, John Brown, Ezra Bowyer, James Cummins, John Eaves, James Fear, Bernard Giltner, T. R. Gatewood, — Griffin, John P. Hogan, John M. Hogan, Hiram Jeter, Bernard Jeter, Richie Jerrett, John P. Kinkead, Solomon Kolker, Zach. Kirby, Joseph Lankhart, John Litterell, John Moon, John P. Miller, Wm. Mitchell, Richard Masterson, Jr., S. McMakin, James Napper, Tom Petty, Lewis Pilcher, Beverly Pilcher, Geo. W. Shivery, Green Spyers, John Shivel, James Schooley, David Weigert, Hiram Worthen, Simon Waters.

M'DOWELL'S CAVALRY.

Captain, James McDowell; First Lieutenant, Michael Fishel; Second Lieutenant, J. G. Trotter.

Privates.—W. W. Ater, Patterson Bain, W. P. Bryant, T. M. Bryant, George Bowman, John Dishman, John Gist, George Hooker, William Long, Joseph Lemmon, William Montgomery, James McConnell, William McConnell, F. McConnell, Samuel McDowell, Salem Piatt, Alexander Pogue, Henry Riddle, William Royal, Thomas Royal, Byrd Smith, David Steel, William Tanner.

EDMONSON'S COMPANY—ALLEN'S REGIMENT.

Captain, John Edmonson.

Privates.—Richard Bledsoe, Walter Carr, Jr., R. P. Kinney, Robinson Prewitt, W. D. Parrish, Dudley Shipp.

HAMILTON'S COMPANY.

Captain, John Hamilton; Lieutenant, William Moore; Sergeants, Tobias Pennington, R. McCullough; Corporals, Ira Barbee, Thomas Parker, Thomas Hamilton.

Privates.—Willis Calvert, Geo. Corman, Nathan Chinn, Alfred Chinn, William Doyle, Luke Field, Michael Goodnight, James Gregg, Samuel Hicks, Philip Jones, Hartwell Long, Wm. Musgrove, Andrew Mefford, Jonathan McLain, W. D. Patterson, Wm. Patterson, Thomas A. Russell, Jas. Sanderson, William Sanderson, George Sanderson, Anderson Simpson, Andrew Simson, Nelson Tapp, Linton Tandy,

Willis Tandy, Thomas Venard, Absalom Venard, John Wilhoite.

In addition to these participants in the war, the following persons also went from Lexington or Fayette, viz: William O. Butler, afterward general; Major Ben. Graves, on the staff of Colonel Lewis; James Overton, aid to General Winchester; Chas. Carr, paymaster of Dudley's regiment; Charles S. Todd, then a young lawyer in Lexington, but subsequently minister to Russia; Thomas Bodley, deputy quartermaster-general, who died June 11, 1833, aged sixty-one; and Adjutant, afterward General, John M. McCalla, who was reported by his commander as "distinguished" in the actions of the 18th and 22d of January, 1813. General McCalla, now a venerable and highly esteemed citizen of Washington, D. C., is a native of Lexington, and a graduate of Transylvania University. He practiced law in this city for many years prior to his removal to his present residence, and was well known for his bold and skillful support of the Democratic party. He was a clear, astute, and efficient political debater, and is well remembered for his earnestness, energy, and integrity. General McCalla erected and lived in the house now owned by Mr. Benjamin Gratz, and situated on Mill street, opposite the college lawn.

The Kentucky quota was rapidly organized for the field, and the Fifth regiment, commanded by Col. William Lewis, and composed of the companies of Capts. Hart, Hamilton, and Megowan, from Fayette; Capts. Gray and Price, from Jessamine; Capt. Williams, from Montgomery, and Capts. Martin and Brassfield, of Clark, in obedience to orders, assembled in Lexington on the 14th of August, to march to the general rendezvous at Georgetown, at which place it was to join the other regiments, and be put in motion with them for the frontier.* It was a soul-stirring occasion, and thousands of citizens assembled from all quarters to witness the novel sight of a band of citizen soldiers marching to the battle-field. Gray-haired veterans of the Revo-

---

*General J. M. McCalla.

lution, and their matron companions, came to behold again what they often saw in former days; the youth of both sexes, the generation which had grown up since the storm of the Revolution had passed away, were eager to behold the unwonted spectacle, and all classes came to bid an agitated adieu to friends, to sons, to brothers, to lovers, to those whom they might never again behold. Many doubted whether the youth and effeminacy of some of the troops were not unequal to the fatigues of the campaign; all felt for them the deepest interest, the keenest anxiety. As the regiment took up the line of march from "the common" (Water street), where it was formed, and wheeled into Main street, at Postlethwaite's corner, such a spectacle was there exhibited as Lexington had never seen before, and probably may never behold again. The moving mass of people filling the street; the windows, doors, and even roofs of houses crowded; weeping females waving their parting adieus from the windows; an occasional shout from the crowd below; the nodding plumes and inspiring music; the proud military step and glancing eye of the marching soldier as he caught the last view of the girl he left behind him, or looked his last farewell to his tender mother or affectionate sister—neither language nor painting can portray the scene.

The troops marched a few miles that evening and encamped, and the next day reached Georgetown, where, with Scott's and Allen's regiments, they were formed into a brigade under General Payne. On the following Sunday they were reviewed by Governor Scott and Generals Payne and Winchester, accompanied by all the field officers. The field was covered with the friends and relatives of our brave soldiers who went to take their parting farewell. The spectators, it is supposed by some, amounted to twenty thousand persons.*

After the review was finished, the army and spectators formed a compact body and listened to an eloquent address from Henry Clay, and an animated sermon from President

---

*Old Gazette.

Blythe, of Transylvania University. Mr. Clay adverted to the causes of the war, the orders in council, the previous aggressions on American commerce, the impressment of seamen, and the incitement of the savages to hostilities. He concluded with a stirring appeal to the troops to remember that much was expected of them from abroad, that Kentucky was famed for her brave men, and that they had the double character of Americans and Kentuckians to support.

A few days after the review, the brigade was ordered to Cincinnati to receive arms, ammunition, and camp-equipage. Hardships commenced at once, for heavy rains continued from the time the troops left Georgetown until they reached Cincinnati. That was, however, but a trifle to the labors which were awaiting them, when, having crossed the Ohio under the gloom of Hull's surrender, and pressed forward to Saint Mary's, they were ordered to leave their heavy baggage, take six days' provision, and a supply of ammunition, and by forced marches, to push on to relieve Fort Wayne, then besieged by an allied Indian and British force. Here *en route*, we leave them for the present.

On the 29th of September, General W. H. Harrison, who had been appointed commander-in-chief of the Western army, left Lexington for the seat of war.

Little was done by the American forces during the year 1812, after Hull's surrender; but what was done, was largely participated in by the volunteers from Lexington. In October,* Colonel William Russell, with four hundred men, marched rapidly up the Illinois river until he got within a mile of one of the Peoria towns. A brisk charge was made upon the town defended by about one hundred and fifty Indian warriors, who were put to flight, with the loss of twenty-five found dead, besides a number carried off. The women and children fled to a swamp at the first approach of the men, and the warriors soon took shelter under the same cover. Colonel Russell had only three men wounded. Four prisoners were taken, and about sixty horses prepared to remove the women and children, with

---

*Observer and Reporter.

all their plunder, fell into his hands. The Indians of the neighboring towns had heard of General Hopkins crossing the Wabash, and seven hundred warriors marched to meet him, leaving one hundred and fifty in charge of the women and children, who were preparing to move off when Colonel Russell arrived. He destroyed everything in the town which he could not bring away, and left it on the same evening.

Captain George Trotter's company (McDowell Cavalry) was in Campbell's expedition* against the Mississinawa towns at the head of the Wabash, and was in the heat of the action of the 18th of December, in which the Indians were defeated. Two members of the company, viz: Corporal Henry Riddle and Salem Piatt were killed, and Captain Trotter, Sergeant Byrd Smith, and David Steel were wounded. When this company returned to Lexington after the expiration of its term of enlistment, it was given a public dinner.

Recruiting for the regular army was kept up in Lexington during the entire war. A rope-walk which was on the "Woodlands'" property, and which ran parallel with the Richmond turnpike, was converted into a barracks,† and used by the regular soldiers until the close of the struggle. At this place, a deserter was shot and buried.

---

*Observer and Reporter.   †T. B. Megowan.

CHAPTER XXXVII.

Battle of Frenchtown—The Raisin Massacre—Fate of Lexington Volunteers: Hart, Graves, Edmonson, and others—The Pall of Grief—" Kentucky Squaw"—New Companies—Incomplete Rolls—Dudley's Defeat—Thrilling Incidents—Battle of the Thames—Great Rejoicing—Close of the Campaign in the Northwest.

The year 1813 constitutes a tragic era in the history of Lexington, that will long be reverted to with mournful interest.

In the former chapter, we left the Kentucky troops on their weary march toward the seat of war. After undergoing every kind of hardship, they finally reached the rapids of the Maumee where, broken down and disheartened, they camped by the frozen river in snow two feet deep. But soon the call of the suffering citizens of Frenchtown (now Monroe), on the river Raisin, Michigan, roused the feelings of the troops into zeal and ardor, and a detachment of six hundred men, under Colonel Lewis, was sent to relieve them. Two marches brought the detachment in view of Raisin, and at last they were gratified with the object of their desire, the sight of an enemy in battle array. The skill of Colonel Lewis, and the bravery of the troops, brought to a successful termination the battle of the 18th January, 1813; and after contending with the enemy until the darkness of the night separated the combatants, the troops collected their wounded, and took up their position on the spot from which the enemy had been driven.

On the evening of the 20th, General Winchester arrived with two hundred regulars, and assumed command, but took none of the precautions which military foresight would have dictated, and at daylight, on the morning of the 22d, while in an exposed position, the little army was suddenly attacked by two thousand British and Indians. The scenes that followed, we describe, in the language of an eye witness and participant:* "Upon the firing of the first gun, Major Graves immediately left his quarters, and ordered his men to stand to their arms. Very many bombs were discharged by the enemy, doing, however, very little execution, most of them bursting in the air, and the fighting became general along the line, the artillery of the enemy being directed mainly to the right of our lines, where Wells' command had no protection but a common rail fence, four or five rails high. Several of the Americans on that part of the line were killed, and their fence knocked down by the cannon balls, when General Winchester ordered the right to fall back a few steps, and reform on the bank of the river, where they would have been protected from the enemy's guns. Unfortunately, however, that part of the line commenced retreating, and reaching Hull's old trace along the lane, on either side of which the grass was so high as to conceal the Indians. At this time, Colonel Lewis and Allen, with a view of rallying the retreating party, took one hundred men from the stockade, and endeavored to arrest their flight. Very many were killed and wounded, and others made prisoners; among the former, Colonel Allen, Captains Simpson, Price, Edmonson, Mead, Dr. Irwin, Montgomery, Davis, McIlvain, and Patrick; and of the latter, General Winchester, Colonel Lewis, Major Overton, etc. The firing was still kept up by the enemy on those within the pickets, and returned with deadly effect. The Indians, after the retreat of the right wing, got around in the rear of the picketing, under the bank, and on the same side of the river, where the battle was raging, and killed and wounded several of our men.

"It is believed that the entire number of killed and wounded within the pickets did not exceed one dozen, and the writer doubts very much whether, if the reinforcements had not come, those who fought the first battle, although their

---

*Rev. T. P. Dudley.

number had been depleted by sixty-five, would not have held their ground, at least until reinforcements could have come to their relief. Indeed, it was very evident the British very much feared a reinforcement, from their hurry in removing the prisoners they had taken, from the south to the west of the battle ground, and in the direction of Fort Malden, from which they sent a flag, accompanied by Dr. Overton, aid to General Winchester, demanding the surrender of the detachment, informing them they had Generals Winchester and Lewis, and in the event of refusal to surrender, would not restrain their Indians. Major Graves being wounded, Major Madison was now left in command, who, when the summons to surrender came, repaired to the room in which Major Graves and several other wounded officers were, to consult with them as to the propriety of surrendering. It is proper here to state that our ammunition was nearly exhausted. It was finally determined to surrender, requiring of the enemy a solemn pledge for the security of the wounded. If this was not unhesitatingly given, they determined to fight it out. But O, the scene which now took place! The mortification at the thought of surrendering the Spartan band who had fought like heroes, the tears shed, the wringing of hands, the swelling of hearts—indeed, the scene beggars description. Life seemed valueless. Our Madison replied to the summons, in substance, 'We will not surrender without a guaranty for the safety of the wounded, and the return of side-arms to the officers.' (We did not intend to be dishonored.) The British officer haughtily responded: 'Do you, sir, claim the right to dictate what terms I am to offer?' Major Madison replied: 'No, but I intend to be understood as regards the only terms on which we will agree to surrender.' Captain William Elliott, who had charge of the Indians, it was agreed, should be left with some men, whom, it was said, would afford ample protection until carryalls could be brought from Malden to transport the prisoners there, but the sequel proved they were a faithless, cowardly set. The British were in quite a hurry, as were their Indian allies, to leave after the surrender. Pretty soon Captain Elliott came into the room where Major Graves, Captain Hickman, Captain Hart, and the writer of this (all wounded) were quartered. He recognized Captain Hart, with whom he had been a *room-mate*, at Hart's father's, in Lexington, Kentucky. Hart introduced him to the other officers, and, after a short conversation, in which he (Elliott) seemed quite restless and a good deal agitated, (he, I apprehend, could have readily told why,) as he could not have forgotten the humiliation he had contracted in deceiving Hart's family pecuniarily. He proposed borrowing a horse, saddle, and bridle, for the purpose of going immediately to Malden, and hurrying on sleighs to remove the wounded. Thence assuring Captain Hart especially of the hospitality of his house, and begging us not to feel uneasy; that we were in no danger; that he would leave three interpreters, who would be an ample protection to us, he obtained Major Graves' horse, saddle, and bridle, and left, which was the last we saw of Captain Elliott. We shall presently see how Elliott's pledges were fulfilled. On the next morning, the morning of the massacre, between daybreak and sunrise, the Indians were seen approaching the houses sheltering the wounded. The house in which Major Graves, Captains Hart and Hickman and the writer were, had been occupied as a tavern. The Indians went into the cellar and rolled out many barrels, forced in their heads, and began drinking and yelling. Pretty soon they came crowding into the room where we were, and in which there was a bureau, two beds, a chair or two and perhaps a small table. They forced the drawers of the bureau, which were filled with towels, table cloths, shirts, pillow-slips, etc. About this time Major Graves and Captain Hart left the room. The Indians took the bed-clothing, ripped open the bed-tick, threw out the feathers, and apportioned the ticks to themselves. They took the overcoat, close-bodied coat, hat, and shoes from the writer. When they turned to leave the room, just as he turned, the Indians tomahawked Captain Hickman in less than six feet from me. I went out on to a porch, next the street, when I heard voices in a room at a short distance; went into the room where Captain Hart was engaged in conversation with the interpreter. He asked: 'What do the Indians intend to do with us?' The reply was: 'They intend to kill you.' Hart rejoined: 'Ask liberty of them for me to make a speech to them before they kill us.' The interpreters replied: 'They can't understand.' 'But,' said Hart, 'you can interpret for me.' The interpreters replied: 'If we undertook to interpret for you, they will as soon kill us as you.' It was said, and I suppose truly, that Captain Hart subsequently contracted with an Indian warrior to take him to Amherstburg, giving him six hundred dollars. The *brave* placed him on a horse and started. After going a short distance, they met another company of Indians, when the one having charge of Hart spoke of his receiving the six hundred dollars to take Hart to Malden. The other Indians insisted on sharing the money, which was refused, when some altercation took place, resulting in the shooting of Hart off the horse by the Indian who received the money. A few minutes after leaving the room where I had met Hart and the interpreters, and while standing in the snow eighteen inches deep, the Indians brought Captain Hickman out on the porch, stripped of clothing, except a flannel shirt, and tossed him out on the snow within a few feet of him, after which he breathed once or twice and expired. While still standing in the yard, without coat, hat, or shoes, Major Graves approached me in charge of an Indian, and asked if I had been taken. I answered, no. He proposed that I should go along with the Indian who had taken him. I replied: 'No; if you are safe, I am satisfied.' He passed on, and I never saw him afterward."

The author of the above narrative was finally ransomed by a generous British officer, who gave his Indian captor an old pack-horse and a keg of whisky to release him.

Another witness[*] of the cowardly massacre at Raisin gives the following experience, which particularly concerns the volunteers directly from Lexington. He says:

"On the morning of the 23d, shortly after light, six or

---

[*] G. M. Bower, American State Papers—12.

eight Indians came to the house of Jean Baptiste Jereaume, where I was in company with Major Graves, Captains Hart and Hickman, Dr. Todd, and fifteen or twenty volunteers. They did not molest anything, or person, on their first approach, but kept sauntering about until there was a large number collected, at which time they commenced plundering the houses of the inhabitants, and killing the wounded prisoners. The Indian who claimed me as his property, commanded me to hold his horse, which was about twenty paces from the house. Shortly after going to the house, I saw them knock down Captain Hickman at the door, together with several others. Supposing a general massacre had commenced, I made an effort to get to a house about a hundred yards distant, which contained a number of wounded; but on my reaching the house, to my great mortification, found it surrounded by Indians, which precluded the possibility of my giving notice to the unfortunate victims of savage barbarity. An Indian chief, of the Tawa tribe, of the name of McCarty, gave me possession of his horse and blanket, telling me, by signs, to lead the horse to the house which I had just before left. The Indian that first took me by this time came up and manifested a hostile disposition toward me, by raising his tomahawk as if to give me the fatal blow, which was prevented by my very good friend McCarty. On my reaching the house which I had first started from, I saw the Indians take off several prisoners, which I afterward saw in the road, in a most mangled condition, and entirely stripped of their clothing.

"Messrs. Charles Bradford, Charles Searls, Turner, and Ebenezer Blythe, of Hart's company, were collected around a carryall, which contained articles taken by the Indians from the citizens. We had all been placed there by our respective captors, except Blythe, who came where we were entreating an Indian to convey him to Malden, promising to give him forty or fifty dollars, and whilst in the act of pleading for mercy, an Indian, more savage than the other, stepped up behind, tomahawked, stripped, and scalped him. The next that attracted my attention was the houses on fire that contained several wounded, whom I knew were not able to get out. After the houses were nearly consumed, we received marching orders, and, after arriving at Sandy creek, the Indians called a halt, and commenced cooking. After preparing and eating a little sweetened gruel, Messrs. Bradford, Searls, Turner, and myself received some, and were eating, when an Indian came up, and proposed exchanging his moccasins for Mr. Searls' shoes, which he readily complied with. They then exchanged hats, after which the Indian inquired how many men Harrison had with him, and, at the same time, calling Searls a Washington or Madison, then raised his tomahawk and struck him on the shoulder, which cut into the cavity of the body. Searls then caught hold of the tomahawk, and appeared to resist, and upon my telling him his fate was inevitable, he closed his eyes and received the savage blow, which terminated his existence. I was near enough to him to receive the brains and blood, after the fatal blow, on my blanket. A short time after the death of Searls, I saw three others share a similar fate. We then set out for Brownstown, which place we reached about twelve or one o'clock at night. After being exposed to several hours incessant rain in reaching that place, we were put into the council-house, the floor of which was partly covered with water, at which place we remained until next morning, when we again received marching orders for their village on the river Rouge, which place we made that day, where I was kept six days, then taken to Detroit and sold."

The grief in Lexington and Fayette county, occasioned by the Frenchtown defeat, and the cold-blooded massacre after it, was as intense as it was widely spread. The emblems of sorrow and affliction were soon seen on every hand. The churches and newspapers were clothed in mourning, and, amid the tolling of bells, the relatives and friends of the murdered soldiers walked sadly in a funeral procession to church, when the sorrow of a whole community was poured out, and prayers were offered for strength to bear the great affliction.

Captain John Edmonson, who fell in the battle of Frenchtown, was a native of Washington county, Virginia,* but had settled early in Fayette county, Kentucky, where he had resided for many years before his death. His company of riflemen was connected with Colonel Allen's regiment. Edmonson county, Kentucky, was named in his honor.

Major Benjamin Graves, one of the victims of the "massacre," after the battle of Frenchtown, was also a Virginian, but had emigrated to Fayette county, Kentucky, when quite young.† He was an amiable, shrewd, and intelligent man, and represented the county several years in the legislature. He was one of the first to volunteer in 1812, and was appointed major in Colonel Lewis' regiment, and proved himself a cool, vigilant, and gallant officer. Graves county, Kentucky, bears his name.

Captain Nathaniel G. T. Hart, whose tragic fate we have recorded, and in whose honor Hart county, Kentucky, was named, was born in Hagerstown, Maryland, but was brought to Lexington, Kentucky, when a little child.‡ He studied law, and practiced in Lexington, but abandoned the profession for mercantile pursuits. In 1812, at the age of twenty-seven, he was commanding the celebrated "Lexington Light Infantry" company, and he and the company enlisted as soon as war was declared. Henry Clay and James Brown both married sisters of Captain Hart.

An amusing incident,‖ too good to be lost, occurred during this tragic period. An adventurous and exceedingly useful female, born in Fayette, went out with one of the Lexington companies in the capacity of a washerwoman, shared the captivity at Raisin, and marched with the prisoners to Malden, which was crowded with Indians, among whom were a number of squaws. The appearance of the washerwoman at once caught their attention, especially as she bore on her back a large blanket, well filled with her baggage. One of the squaws came up to her, and demanded the bundle, which she very promptly refused to give up, but the squaw seized it, and a struggle for its possession at once drew a crowd of warriors around them, who formed a circle

---

*Collins.   †Id.   ‡Id.   ‖Gen. J. A. McCalla.

to see fair play, and enjoy the sport. The pulling operation not being sufficient, the female soldier determined to show her Kentucky play, and attacked her with her fists, and, pulled her hair with vigor, until at last her antagonist gave up the attempt, and left her in possession of her bundle. With laughter and huzzas for the "Kentucky squaw," the warriors declared she should not be disturbed again, and she marched off in triumph to join her fellow prisoners. The "Kentucky squaw" remained at Malden about six months, making money by her skill and industry, and then marched back to Lexington in regular infantry style, on foot, and lived for many years to enjoy the fame of her brilliant victory over her rash and badly taken-in foe.

The following names, in addition to those already given, of soldiers killed and wounded, have fortunately been preserved. They belonged to Captain Hart's company. Killed—Alex. Crawford, Wm. Davis, Sam'l Elder, Thos. King, Wm. Lewis, Peter Mesner, Jas. Riley, Stephen Smith, Geo. Shindlebower, B. Stephens, Armstrong Stewart, Thos. Fant. Wounded—Chas. Bradford, Thos. Chamberlain, John Beckly, Edward Elder, James Higgins, S. B. Todd.

The butchery at Raisin excited a storm of the intensest indignation and excitement throughout Kentucky, which was the greatest sufferer by it. There was a general rush to avenge the slaughter of the gallant men who had fallen, and the tender of troops was largely in excess of the demand. Lexington resounded with the notes of the bugle and the beating of drums. Five companies of volunteers were rapidly organized in the city and county, and campfires blazed on every hand. The companies formed were commanded by Captains Archie Morrison, John C. Morrison, David Todd, Stewart W. Megowan, and M. Flournoy, and belonged to the regiment of Colonels Dudley and Boswell. The following is a fragment of the roll of Captain Archie Morrison's company, viz: Thomas Christian, A. F. Eastin, George Eave, Elijah Smith, Larkin Webster, John Webster, and Thomas Webster.

We also append an incomplete list of unclassified soldiers,

who served in the war, but in what years and in whose companies is not known. The list embraces:

Ashton Garrett, Thos. H. Barlow, Allen Baker, Thos. Barr, Robert Burns, Daniel Brink, Enoch Bryan, Landen Carter, Wm. Clark, Horace Coleman, William Chinn, Lewis Castleman, W. R. Combs, Enoch Ducker, J. R. Dunlap, A. S. Drake, John Darnaby, Joseph Edger, Peter Ealeman, Asa Farra, John Figg, John Figg, Jr., John Graves, Thos. C. Graves, J. G. Goodin, John Gess, William Gray, Abram Hicks, Jabez Jones, John Keiser, Jeremiah Kirtley, Adam Lake, William Lewis, Jacob Markley, Robert Masterson, James Masterson, Peter Metcalf, James Megowan, C. C. Moore, C. S. Moore, S. Moore, T. R. Moore, Thos. McIlvaine, Charles Postlethwaite, Hugh Paine, Francis Ratcliffe, Fielding Roach, James Sheely, Samuel Smith, George Simpson, George Stipp, John Stere, John Todd, Jacob Varble, Abram Ware, Joshua Webb, Benjamin Wood, George Wheeler, George Yeiser, George Yates.

The Kentucky volunteers were hurried to the relief of Harrison, and succeeded in cutting their way through the British and Indians to Fort Meigs. But the soldiers of Lexington and Fayette seemed ever destined to reach victory only after repeated baptisms of blood. Another disaster awaited them.

On the 5th of May, General Harrison sent Captain Hamilton with an order to Colonel Dudley to land eight hundred men on the northern shore of the Maumee, opposite Fort Meigs, destroy the British batteries there, and then immediately return.

Dudley succeeded perfectly in capturing the batteries, but instead of instantly returning to his boats, suffered his men to waste their time, and skirmished with the Indians until Proctor was enabled to cut them off from their only chance of retreat. They were surrounded, taken by surprise, defeated, and then came another repetition of the Raisin massacre, in which Colonel Dudley, as already related in a former chapter, was barbarously mangled and murdered, and only one hundred and fifty of his men escaped captivity or death. We insert for preservation the following comprehensive account of the disaster by one who was engaged in it:*

"When Colonel Dudley attacked the batteries of the enemy, opposite Fort Meigs, on the 5th of May, 1813, he advanced in three columns. The right, led by himself, carried them without the loss of a man. The middle was the reserve. The left, headed by Major Shelby, formed at right angles on the river, to protect from below. This arrangement was scarcely made before the spies under my command (about thirty in number, including seven friendly Indians), who flanked at some hundred yards distance in the woods, were attacked by part of the Indian force of the enemy. Unacquainted with the views of Colonel Dudley, they knew not but that it was their duty to fight. For near fifteen minutes, with the loss of several killed and wounded, they maintained an unequal conflict. In this time, Colonel Dudley having effected *his* object, and fearing their fate, had advanced to their relief with the right column. The enemy retreated. Our troops, impelled more by *incautious valor* and a desire for military distinguishment than prudence, pursued. He *then* stood firm for a short time on *his right*, and gave way on his left, which threw our lines with its back toward the river, so that every step we advanced carried us farther from under the protection of our fort. Whenever we halted, so did the Indians, and renewed their fire—we charged on them. They again retreated. *In this way*, with the loss of from thirty to fifty killed on our side, and a number wounded, was the battle fought for upward of three hours. How much the enemy suffered during this time, 't was impossible to ascertain from the circumstance of their bearing off their dead. Soon after the *commencement* of the engagement, *we* were forced to bring our whole force into action. The enemy was, during this time, receiving large reinforcements from the other side of the river, which enabled him *now* nearly to *surround us*. Our troops were generally

---

*Capt. Leslie Combs' Report to Gen. Green Clay.

much exhausted, owing to the swampiness of the ground over which they had fought, and many of them with their guns wet, or without ammunition. In this situation, the enemy in much force, fresh to the battle, pressed with a most destructive cross-fire on *our* left. It gave way. Conscious of his advantage, with a desperate effort he advanced on the remainder. *These*, disheartened and confused, were ordered to retreat to the batteries. Unfortunately, this retreat soon turned to flight, which all the efforts of the officers could neither prevent nor stop.

"The best disciplined troops in the world are sometimes panic struck—then can it be surprising that militia, *under these circumstances,* and who had seen scarce *thirty days* service, should become so? In small parties, by tens and by twenties, they arrived at the *batteries*, thereby falling an easy prey to the regular force of the enemy, who, early in the action, had retaken *them* from the right column. Thus, upward of eight hundred men, who had set out with the most flattering prospect of success, led on by imprudence, were overwhelmed by numbers, cut up, and defeated. About one hundred and seventy only having *made good* their retreat before the close of the battle, escaped across the river in our boats.

"Immediately after the surrender, we were marched off toward Fort Maumee, one and a half miles below, near the British encampment. We had gone but a short distance before we met the head of the left line of Indians who had been inclosing us. Having surrendered to Englishmen *entirely*, I expected we should be treated with that tenderness and humanity indicative of a noble mind, and always due the *unfortunate*. What was, then, my astonishment when, so soon as we met the Indians, they began, *in face of the English guard, of General Proctor, Colonel Elliot, and other officers who were riding up the line,* to rob us of our clothing, money, watches, etc. Almost all lost in this way their hats and coats, some even their shirts, and some their pantaloons also. He who did not instantaneously give up his clothes, frequently paid his life for it. No difference was made between well and wounded in this as well as what followed.

It would be almost impossible to relate all the acts of individual outrage that took place. I shall never forget the demoniac look of the villain who stripped me, nor shall I soon forget those who encouraged, since, notwithstanding my request, they did not hinder him from doing it. I showed him my wound. 'T was vain; before I could unfasten the bandage, regardless of my pain, *he tore* my coat off from my shoulders. I had gone but little farther before I saw ten or twelve men, lying dead, *stripped naked, and scalped.* Near them were two lines of Indians formed from the entrance of a triangular ditch in front to the old gate of Fort Maumee, a distance, I think, of forty or fifty feet. The idea immediately struck me that all the prisoners ahead of me had been massacred. I determined, if such was the case, to go no further. Upon inquiring, a soldier told me they were in the fort, and showed me the way, which was between those two lines of Indians. During this moment's delay, a man who was walking behind, stepped before me; just as we entered the defile, an Indian put a pistol to his back, and fired—he fell. I ran through without being touched. My feelings were somewhat relieved at finding about two-thirds of the prisoners already within. How many were killed afterward I am unable to say. We heard frequent guns at the place during the whole time the remaining prisoners were coming in. Some, although not killed, were wounded severely with war clubs, tomahawks, etc. The number who fell *after the surrender* was supposed by all to be nearly *equal to the killed in battle.* We now hoped, however, that we were secure from further insult or injury—but no sooner had all the prisoners got in than the whole body of Indians, regardless of the opposition of our little guard, rushed into the fort. There *seemed to be* almost twice our number. Their blood-thirsty souls were not yet satiated with carnage. *One Indian alone* shot *three,* tomahawked a *fourth,* and stripped and scalped them in our presence. It seems to me, even to this day, whenever I think of this circumstance, that I again see the struggles of the dying prisoner and hear him cry, in vain, for mercy. The whole then raised the war-whoop and commenced loading their guns. What were our feelings at this moment, he, who has never realized, can not imagine. A description is impossible. Without any means of defense or possibility of escape, death in all the horror of savage cruelty, seemed to stare us in the face. Rendered desperate *by this idea,* and the perfect disregard which the British evinced for that duty, held sacred by all civilized nations (the protection of prisoners), much did we wish for our arms, and had we *then* had them, they would have been surrendered but with our lives. Or, had this been carried much farther, the prisoners would, *at any risk,* have sold their lives as dearly as possible. Tecumseh, however, more humane than his ally and employer, generously interfered and prevented farther massacre. Colonel Elliot then rode *slowly in,* spoke to the Indians, waved his sword, and all but a few retired *immediately.* After a short consultation with those who remained, they came and took from among us a number of young men, of whom the British said they wanted to make sons, but *we feared* they took them as hostages for the lives of those Indians who were wounded. Just at dusk, boats came up and carried us to the fleet, eight miles below. Notwithstanding the naked condition of the prisoners, and the disagreeableness of the weather (which was rainy and excessively cold for the season), many of them were obliged to remain all night in the open boats in ankle-deep mud and water. The wounded were put into the holds of the different vessels, where their only bed (and a good many had not even this), was the wet sand thrown in for ballast, without blankets or any other kind of covering. Provision was issued to them the next day about twelve. Their treatment afterward was nearly as good, I am induced to believe, as the British could afford, being themselves scant of provisions. I feel myself particularly indebted to some of the officers for their politeness and attention.

"I can not conclude without testifying to the bravery and carelessness of danger displayed by the troops throughout the engagement. The only contest seemed to be, while any hope of victory remained, who should first oust the enemy from his hiding places. And I am convinced, when the retreat commenced, by far the greater part had no idea of surrender, but exhausted, confused, and overcome, were forced to it on their arrival at the batteries."

But an end came to defeats and massacres at last. On the 10th of September occurred the splendid and decisive victory of Perry over the British fleet, on Lake Erie. A thrill of joy went through Kentucky; Lexington in particular was given up to rejoicing. The city was illuminated, bonfires were lighted, and all the bells rung out their merriest peals. The Federalists of that day were most cordially detested by a vast majority of Kentuckians, and a chronicler* does not fail to state that, " while the joy bells of Lexington were ringing for Perry's victory, the bells of Massachusetts were tolling in disappointment at the defeat of the British."

Perry's success was the death knell of British power in the Northwest, where hostilities ceased entirely after the battle of the Thames. This glorious and eminently decisive victory occurred on the 5th of October, and in it the volunteers from Lexington and Fayette played a most gallant and distinguished part, and sustained heavy losses. The Forty-second regiment commanded by a Lexingtonian, Colonel George Trotter, who served in this campaign as a brigadier-general, was presented with a drum† taken at the battle of the Thames. The drum was ornamented with the British coat of arms, and the inscription, "41st Reg." Before being presented, the following was added to the inscription: " Presented by General Harrison and Governor Shelby to Colonel George Trotter, for the Forty-second regiment, Kentucky militia, as a testimony of its patriotism and good conduct, and for having furnished more volunteers than any other regiment."

The success of General Harrison on the Thames gave Lexington another occasion for rejoicing. The news was announced to the citizens by the mail carrier, who galloped into town with " victory," in big letters, exhibited on the

---

*Observer and Reporter. †McCabe.

front of his hat, and thereupon all the schools were dismissed, business was suspended, and there was a grand procession, speeches, and general rejoicing. The term of service of the volunteers expired about this time, and their return was the signal for balls, parties, and displays, in their honor.

With the battle of the Thames, which closed the war in the Northwest, Lexington and Fayette had no farther direct share in the struggle, which became mainly confined to the eastern and southern borders of the country. It was time that Kentucky was allowed a little rest, for she may be said to have almost fought through the two first years of the war by herself. Virginia gave the Northwest to the nation, and her daughter, Kentucky, saved it from conquest by savage and foreign foes at the cost of her noblest blood.

CHAPTER XXXVIII.

Spotted Fever—The Hero of Fort Stephenson—Joy over Jackson's Victory—Drafted Men—Amos Kendall commences Life in Lexington—Agricultural Societies—The Kentucky and Mechanical Association, Officers—W. B. Kinkead—Present Society—William Preston—Leading Agriculturists.

LEXINGTON was visited with spotted fever during the month of March, 1814, and to such an extent did it rage that from eight to a dozen persons died daily.*

On the 4th of September of this year, Major George Croghan, whose heroic defense of Fort Stephenson, in August, 1813, forms one of the most brilliant chapters in American history, was given a complimentary party in Lexington, and was honored by the citizens as he deserved. Congress, with her usual tardy justice, voted him a gold medal twenty-two years after his wonderful repulse of the British and Indians.

The patriotic citizens of Lexington indulged in an illumination on the night of October 1st, in their joy at the news just received of Jackson's victory over the British at Mobile.† The "barracks" were resplendent with candles, which were placed on the tops of the buildings, and other lights were placed in the boughs and on the tops of the trees surrounding the "barracks," making a most romantic effect. Rows of candles lined the windows of the houses in the town, and a procession, with a thousand candles, and headed by a drum and fife, paraded the streets. The battle had taken place on the 15th of September, and it was two weeks before Lexington got the news. In 1814, the transit of the ordinary mail from Washington to Lexington occupied twelve or thirteen days.

---

*Kendall's Journal. †Id.

Two companies of drafted men, under Captains James Dudley and A. S. Drake, were raised in the fall of this year, but peace was declared before they reached the seat of war. The whole number of companies raised in Lexington and Fayette, for the common defense, during the war of 1812, was thirteen. This fact is, of itself, the highest tribute that can be paid to their gallant patriotism.

Amos Kendall, who afterward became postmaster-general of the United States, and the devoted friend and right-hand man of that just and unflinching old hero, General Jackson, may be said to have commenced life in Lexington, where he arrived, a young man, in the spring of 1814.* He came poor and unknown, and at the instance of Judge Bledsoe, whom he had met in Washington City when that powerful orator was a member of the United States Senate. Mr. Kendall walked from Maysville to Lexington. He started as a teacher in the family of Mr. Clay, who was then working at the peace negotiations at Ghent. At the same time, he studied law, and subsequently took the prescribed oath, and was qualified as an attorney in our present old court-house. Mr. Kendall died November 12, 1869, in Washington City, at the age of eighty, after attaining a position before the nation befitting the high order of his mind and talents. The teacher of the children of the great and eloquent leader of the Whig party became one of the most renowned Democrats of the old *regime*. The poor tutor in Mr. Clay's family became one of the most honored and respected members of the cabinet of his most formidable antagonist, "Old Hickory." Who will say that truth is not romantic? Mr. Kendall was a native of Dunstable, Massachusetts.

The unsurpassed natural advantages of the now famous "Blue Grass Region" for stock raising were quickly appreciated by its settlers, who, at a very early day, turned their attention to the raising and improvement of live stock of various kinds. Horse and cattle "shows" were regularly held at Lexington, even before the commencement of the

---

*Kendall's Biography.

present century. But it was not until 1814 that the city could claim to have a regular society for the improvement of live stock and the promotion of kindred interests. In the year named, the "Kentucky Agricultural Society"* was organized in Lexington, and for many years held annual exhibitions at "Fowler's Garden," on the Maysville turnpike, the same property in which "Scott's Pond" is now included, and which was then the favorite place of public resort. The following programme of the society† will convey an idea of the character of primitive Lexington fairs:

"NOTICE.—A meeting of the members of the Kentucky Society for promoting Agriculture will take place at Fowler's Garden, adjoining Lexington, on the last Thursday in next September, and continue for three days, at which time and place the society will award twenty-three silver cups—one to each of the articles named below. Members are requested to be punctual in their attendance.

" To the best gelding, a silver cup.
"   "   suckling colt, a silver cup.
"   "   imported or country raised bull, a silver cup.
"   "   "   "   "   cow, a silver cup.
"   "   stall-fed bullock, silver cup.
"   "   country bred bull, silver cup.
"   "   "   "   between three and four years old, silver cup.
"   "   country bred bull, between two and three years old, silver cup.
"   "   country bred bull, between one and two years old, silver cup.
"   "   bull calf, not exceeding twelve months old, silver cup.
"   "   country bred cow, silver cup.
"   "   heifer, between three and four years old, silver cup.

---

*Kentucky Gazette.   †Id.

"To the best heifer, between two and three years old, silver cup.
" " heifer, between one and two years old, silver cup.
" " heifer, not exceeding twelve months old, silver cup.
" " carpeting manufactured in private families, silver cup.
" " hemp or flax linen manufactured in private families, silver cup.
" " table linen manufactured in private families, silver cup.
" " cloth manufactured in private families, silver cup.
" " cassinett or jeans manufactured in private families, silver cup.
" " whisky, not less than one hundred gallons, of this year's make, silver cup.
" " cheese of the present year's make, silver cup.
" " wheat, quality, quantity, and excellence of crop will be considered, silver cup.

"It is confidently believed that much fine stock will be exhibited, and much bought and sold within the three days of the fair; therefore, those who either wish to sell or purchase will do well to attend. H. TAYLOR,
JAS. SHELBY,
ROBT. WICKLIFFE,
ROBT. CROCKETT,
E. WARFIELD.
"*Committee.*"

In 1832, a fair was organized by the Kentucky Racing Association,* and in September, 1833, the first of a series of annual exhibitions on the Association Course was given under the management of a committee, consisting of Benjamin Warfield, James Shelby, Thomas Smith, John Brand,

---

*Association Record.

and Walter Dunn. Referring to this fair, a Lexington newspaper says:

"On this occasion will be assembled for exhibition, competition, or sale, specimens of the most approved and celebrated breeds of English cattle, and we learn that breeders and others will be thus enabled, by actual comparison, to judge of the relative qualities of the cattle imported by Sanders, Smith, and Tegarden, in 1817, and the short-horns imported by Colonel Powell, of Philadelphia. Garcia, Lucilla, and Pontiac, of the Powell stock, will be exhibited for premiums, and some calves by Pontiac and Sultan, of the Powell stock."

We append the list of awards for the 12th and 13th of September, 1834, viz:

FRIDAY.

To President, a bull, by Cornplanter, he by imported Tecumseh, and out of Lady Monday, and she by San Martin, and out of Mrs. Motte (imported), is awarded the first premium. The property of J. C. Talbott.

To Melville, a bull, by Haggin's full-blooded Teeswater bull, his dam by San Martin, is awarded the second premium. The property of E. Warfield.

To Pioneer, a two-year old bull, by Exchange, his dam Beauty, is awarded the first premium. Bred by B. Warfield. The property of J. Scott.

To Slider, by Duroc, dam Lady Monday, is awarded the second premium. Bred by and the property of James Garrard.

To Clay, one-year old bull, by Accommodation, dam Beauty, is awarded the first premium. Bred by and the property of B. Warfield.

To Mordecai, by Sultan, dam ———, second premium. Bred by and the property of Lewis Sanders.

To bull calf Accident, by Pioneer, dam Helen Eyre, is awarded the first premium. Bred by B. Warfield. The property of James N. Brown.

To bull calf ———, by Oliver, dam a Patton cow by Marauder, second premium. Bred by H. Clay. The property of L. P. Yandell.

To Lady Caroline, a cow of the Holderness breed, imported, is awarded the first premium. The property of Walter Dun.

To Lucilla, got by Memnon, imported, dam Virginia (begotten in England), by General, second premium. The property of George N. Sanders.

To Cleopatra, a two-year old cow, by Accommodation, dam Nancy Dawson, is awarded the first premium. Bred by and the property of S. Smith.

To Silvia, by Contention, dam young Pink, second premium. Bred by and the property of Dan. Boyce.

To Helen Eyre, a one-year old heifer, by Accommodation, dam Pink, is awarded the first premium. Bred by B. Warfield. The property of James N. Brown.

To Pocahontas, by Exchange, dam Nancy Dawson, second premium. Bred by and the property of S. Smith.

To Anna Fisk, a cow calf, by Oliver, dam Beauty, is awarded the first premium. Bred by and the property of B. Warfield.

To Mary Tilford, by Symmetry, dam Holderness cow, second premium. Bred by and the property of Walter Dunn.

To Mr. Boyce is awarded the premium for oxen.

To James N. Brown is awarded the first premium for fat bullocks.

To John King, the second.

We, the subscribers, appointed judges to award prizes to cattle, on the 12th of September, 1834, have adjudged the preceding.

H. CLAY,
JAMES RENNICK,
JACOB HUGHES,
ISAAC VANMETER,
WILL. P. HUME.

September 12, 1834.

SATURDAY.

Award on Horses.

To Lance, a stallion, the property of E. Blackburn, is awarded the first premium.

To Woodpecker, a stallion, the property of R. B. Tarlton, is awarded the second premium.

To Sir Walter, a two-year old stallion, the property of A. Stanhope, is awarded the first premium.

To Red Rover, a two-year old stallion, the property of E. W. Hockaday, is awarded the second premium.

To Henry Duncan's yearling stud colt is awarded the first premium.

To Jas. Erwin's yearling stud colt is awarded the second premium.

To Jas. Erwin's sorrel sucking colt is awarded the first premium.

To Chas. Carr's young collier colt is awarded the second premium.

To Susan Hicks, a mare, the property of E. Warfield, is awarded the first premium.

To Letitia, a mare, the property of Jas. Erwin, is awarded the second premium.

To Jas. Erwin's filly, out of Letitia, the first premium.
To G. N. Sanders' filly, ———, the second premium.
To Wm. H. Eanes' gelding, ———, the first premium.
To Jos. L. Downing's gelding, ———, the second premium.

To Jas. Erwin's carriage horses is awarded the first premium.

To Jos. L. Downing's young carriage horses is awarded the second premium.

We, the judges on horses, unanimously agreed to the above award.
C. CARR,
G. D. HUNT,
JOHN W. MOORE,
J. S. BERRYMAN,
JOHN HUDSON.

Awards on Jacks, etc.

Best jack—Warrior, exhibited by P. B. Hockaday, first premium.

Hector, exhibited by Robt. C. Boggs, second premium.

Best jenny—Miss Palafox, exhibited by A. McClure, first premium.

Calypso, exhibited by Henry Clay, second premium.

For best pair of mules—Brown mules exhibited by Isaac Shelby, first premium.

For best two-year old mules—A. Brown, exhibited by Isaac Shelby, premium.

For best year old mule—Awarded to Thos. H. Shelby's brown mare mule.

For best sucking mule—Awarded to Isaac Shelby.

We, the undersigned, appointed a committee to award the premiums on the above stock unanimously agree in awarding the above. DAVID McMURTRY,
LEWIS DEDMAN,
JAMES SHELBY.

James Shelby agrees to the above, with the exception of the mule colts, upon which he declines acting.

On Sheep and Swine.

To Henry Clay's Saxon ram is awarded the first premium.
To Bird Smith's boar is awarded the premium for boars.
We, the judges, unanimously agree to the above award.
JOHN HART,
ROBERT C. BOGGS.

In 1850, the Maxwell Springs Company was organized and incorporated,* and secured the grounds fronting on Bolivar street, and including "Maxwell's Spring," and now being converted by the city into a park. These grounds are noted for their fine springs of water, as the time-honored gathering-place to celebrate the Fourth of July, and as the spot where the "Old Infantry" and other volunteer

---

* Acts Legislature.

companies that suffered at Raisin met and bade their friends and relatives adieu, on starting to join Harrison. Here, also, on public occasions, Clay, Barry, Scott, and a host of other prominent men have addressed immense crowds.

The Kentucky Agricultural and Mechanical Association was incorporated December 7, 1850,* and bought grounds adjoining those of the Maxwell Springs Company, and in July, 1853, the two societies entered into an arrangement by which the Kentucky Agricultural and Mechanical Association obtained provisional use of the Maxwell Springs Company's land, on which to hold annual exhibitions. The entire grounds were then greatly improved, a handsome and capacious amphitheater, and all other needed buildings, were erected, trees and shrubs were planted, and the place soon became noted far and wide for its extraordinary beauty and convenience. The first officers of the Kentucky Agricultural and Mechanical Association were elected April 13, 1850, as follows:

Benjamin Gratz, president; Henry C. Payne, vice-president; Jas. A. Harper, secretary; David A. Sayre, treasurer. Dr. R. J. Breckinridge, Abram Vanmeter, Henry T. Duncan, Edward Oldham, Joseph Wasson, Charles W. Innes, James Kinnaird, Richard Allen, of Jessamine, James O. Harrison, and Isaac Shelby, were elected directors.

On the night of December 18, 1861, the splendid buildings of the association were destroyed by fire while being used by federal troops. Ever since that calamity the annual fairs have been held on the grounds of the Kentucky Racing Association.

In 1868, W. T. Hughes was president of the association, R. J. Spurr, vice-president, and Ernest Brennan, secretary and treasurer.

The agricultural associations of Fayette county have had no more energetic and valuable friend than Benjamin Gratz, whose efforts contributed greatly to their success. (See chapter on Transylvania University.)

Another public-spirited and most efficient president was

---

* Acts Legislature.

Judge W. B. Kinkead, well known both as a lawyer and an agriculturist. He was born in Woodford county, Ky., and was appointed a circuit judge by Governor Letcher. He has been a resident of Lexington for many years.

In the spring of 1872, the Maxwell Springs Company and the Kentucky Agricultural and Mechanical Association were dissolved to give place to a more effectual organization — The Kentucky Agricultural and Mechanical Society, of which Gen. Wm. Preston was made president. General Preston was born in Louisville, but has long made Lexington his home. He served in the Mexican war, has represented his state in Congress, was United States minister to Spain, and was a major-general in the service of the late Confederate States. General Preston is a fine lawyer and a good speaker. He is a man of very superior abilities, and his highly-cultivated mind is stored with information.

The last exhibition of the society was held in the beautiful grove at Ashland. Its future fairs are expected to be held in an extensive amphitheater, to be erected on the old historic grounds at Maxwell's Spring, which were so long in use before the late war.

Among the agriculturists of Fayette — in addition to those already named — who have encouraged and sustained her associations, and have been awarded premiums, may be mentioned those short-horn breeders, Messrs. Wm. Warfield, Jesse H. Talbott, W. H. Richardson, W. B. Kinkead, J. G. Kinnaird, Hart Boswell, C. W. Innis, John P. Innis, and John Burgess. Among the association's other active friends, representing various agricultural interests, are I. C. Vanmeter, R. J. Spurr, W. H. Smith, T. H. Shelby, Jr., J. R. Viley, W. R. Estill, D. S. Coleman, H. A. Headley, William Bryan, N. P. Berry, Gran Weathers, E. C. Bryan, J. W. Berry, and David Prewitt.

CHAPTER XXXIX.

Battle of New Orleans—Captain S. W. Megowan—General George Trotter—Lexington Female Benevolent Society—Second Presbyterian Church—James McChord—Pastors—Church Buildings—Division—Peace.

No regularly organized troops from Lexington participated in the war with England, after the battle of the Thames, but this did not prevent her citizens from feeling the liveliest interest in the struggle. When the great Jackson achieved his glorious and extraordinary victory over the disciplined British regulars, who had fought against the first Napoleon, Lexington was beside herself with delight. The 22d of February was observed as a day of general thanksgiving for the brilliant ending of the war; salutes were fired, addresses delivered, and at night the whole city was illuminated. Licensed by the general joy, crowds of boys marched through the streets, singing, at the very top of their voices, this stanza, composed by a Lexington wit, and considered remarkably fine:

> "In his last hopes on Orleans strand,
> John Bull was quite mistaken;
> With all his skill in Packen-hams,
> He could not save his bacon."

The only man from Lexington known to have been in the battle of New Orleans was Capt. Stewart W. Megowan.[*] In 1812 he raised and commanded a company of volunteers from this city, and, under Colonel Lewis, joined General Harrison. In 1813 he raised another company, and called them the "Lexington Rifles." He again joined Gen. Harrison, under Governor Shelby, from whom he had obtained

---
[*] Old Statesman.

his commission of captaincy. Captain Megowan was in the battle of the Thames, when Tecumseh was slain; and was present when Proctor's troops surrendered. After serving out that campaign, Capt. Megowan again returned to Lexington, and hearing New Orleans was about being attacked by British troops, he endeavored to raise a third company, but finding he would not have time to do so, he started down the Mississippi river alone, to join General Jackson. After reaching New Orleans, he and a flat-boat captain, by the name of Twiggs, beat up for volunteers in the streets of that city, and raised a company composed of sailors and Kentucky flat-boatmen.

Twiggs was elected captain, and Megowan first lieutenant. General Jackson gave the custom-house into their charge, and on the evening before the battle of New Orleans, Megowan obtained leave to take as many men as would go with him, and join General Jackson. Five Dutch sailors volunteered to accompany him, and although they neither understood the English language, nor were versed in military discipline, they followed him into the fight, and shared in the victory. Capt. Megowan died at the age of 79 years.

General George Trotter, a well-known native and citizen of Lexington, died October 13, 1815, aged thirty-seven. He was several times a member of the legislature from Fayette, and was noted for his gallant conduct in the war of 1812. He served with Colonel Campbell in the Mississinewa campaign, and was acting brigadier-general in the famous battle of the Thames. His residence was at "Woodlands," and is now used by the Agricultural College.

The "Lexington Female Benevolent Society," now preeminent for its judicious charity, great usefulness, and blessed influence, was organized in 1815, and has been in active operation ever since. The following named ladies constituted one of its early board of officers: Mrs. John Norton, President; Mrs. Morrison, Mrs. Ross, Vice-Presidents; Miss Ridgely, Secretary; Mrs. Ward, Treasurer. Managers, Mrs. Palmer, Mrs. Robert, Mrs. Bell, Mrs. Hanson, Miss Clifford, Mrs. Elliott, Miss Montgomery, Mrs. Beckley, Mrs. Stevens. The institution was not incorporated until February, 1851. The charter members were: Mrs. John Norton, Mrs. John H. Brown, Mrs. James O. Harrison, Mrs. Wyett R. Higgins, and Mrs. Isaac W. Scott. Among other members of the society, who have greatly assisted in forwarding its noble objects, may be named Mrs. Thomas Skillman, who was connected with it for very many years, Mrs. A. V. Sayre, Mrs. Eliza Blythe, Mrs. Eliza Ross, Mrs. Thos. C. Orear, Mrs. M. P. Lancaster, Mrs. John Carty, Mrs. E. McCalister, Mrs. George Brand, Mrs. H. M. Skillman, Mrs. Montmollin, and many others.

The Second Presbyterian Church of Lexington was founded in 1815, and was first known as the "Market Street Church." It was built by the united efforts of a number of non-professing admirers of the Rev. James McChord, together with a few regular members of Presbyterian churches. The building committee was composed of John Tilford, T. H. Pindell, John McKinley, Alexander Parker, David Castleman, and Joseph C. Breckinridge. These, together with the following, were the signers of the church constitution, viz: C. Wilkins, Samuel Trotter, L. McCullough, J. H. Hervey, M. T. Scott, Benj. Merrill, F. Dewees, Matt. Kenneday, W. H. Richardson, Thos. January, Thos. T. Skillman, Wm. Pritchart, C. Logan, N. Burrowes, A. M. January, T. P. Hart, J. B. Boswell, R. S. Todd, B. Chambers, T. B. Prentice, W. W. Blair, E. Sharpe, —— Butler, J. Bruen, John McChord, W. B. Logan, James Trotter, R. H. Bishop. Only one of these signers (A. M. January) is now living.

The edifice was built after the peculiar and substantial style of the day, and occupied the site of the present church building, on Market, between Church and Second streets. The walls were two and a half feet thick, the pulpit was in the middle of the front end of the house, and the seats were arranged in ascending tiers, facing the doors, so that persons entering found themselves confronted by an army of gazers. The church called the Rev. James McChord to be its first pastor, and he preached the dedicatory sermon, July 30, 1815, at which time the church was opened for worship.

James McChord was born in Baltimore,* in 1785, and removed with his parents to Lexington, in 1790. After receiving a liberal education at Transylvania University, he studied law with Henry Clay, but after mature thought, abandoned that profession for the ministry, and entered a theological seminary in New York, where he held the foremost rank. In 1809, he was licensed, and in 1811, ordained. He published a treatise in 1814, on the nature of the church, which was condemned by the Associate Reformed Presbytery, whereupon he sent in a declinature of their authority, and connected himself with the West Lexington Presbytery. He was pastor of the Market Street Church only four years, but in that short time he became famous. To his great intellect was added not only brilliant scholarly attainments, but the most powerful and thrilling eloquence, which carried all before it as the sweeping of a mighty wind. Some of his congregation, who had come only to enjoy and admire, were converted. Others who desired nothing more serious than entertaining preaching, and who, unfortunately controlled the financial affairs of the church, took the alarm, and the gifted pastor was soon made so uncomfortable† that he resigned, and for a year managed to subsist by teaching a school. His highly sensitive nature never recovered from the blow, and sad and brokenhearted, he died far too young, May 26, 1820. Love and attention revived with his death. His admirers changed the name of his late charge to "McChord Church;" his remains were interred beneath the pulpit, and a marble tablet bearing his name, the date of his birth and death, and the inscription, "the resurrection of the just shall unfold his character," was set in the wall. The memory of this good man is still reverently cherished in Lexington. McChord's sermons, including his "last appeal to the Market Street Church," have received great attention both in this country and in England.

Mr. McChord's residence was on Limestone, between Fourth and Fifth streets—the same afterward occupied by

---

*Davidson's History. †Id

Mr. Armant. During the time which intervened between the resignation of Mr. McChord and the accession of the next regular pastor, the Rev. John Breckinridge, the pulpit was supplied by the accomplished Rev. William Wallace and Father R. H. Bishop, who was for some time professor in Transylvania University, and afterward became the founder and president of Oxford College, Ohio.

Rev. John Breckinridge, who succeeded Mr. McChord in 1823,* was a son of Attorney-General John Breckinridge, and was born near Lexington, Kentucky, July 4, 1794. Like McChord, he turned from the law to the ministry, and, like him, captivated the hearts of his hearers by his charming eloquence. After serving the Second Church three years, he accepted the chair of pastoral theology at Princeton, which he held a short time. He was an advocate of colonization. At the time of his death, which occurred August 4, 1841, he was president-elect of Oglethorpe University, of Georgia.

In 1828, the Rev. John C. Young, D. D., became pastor of the church. Dr. Young was born in Pennsylvania, August 12, 1803, and, after graduating, was licensed to preach in 1827. In 1830, he resigned the pastorate of the Second Church, and accepted the presidency of Centre College, which prospered under his ripe scholarship and efficient administration. Dr. Young died in Danville, Kentucky, June 23, 1857.

The Rev. Robert Davidson, son of President Davidson, of Dickinson College, succeeded Dr. Young in 1832. Mr. Davidson was born in Carlisle, Pennsylvania, February 23, 1808, and graduated at Princeton. He is extensively known as the author of an exceedingly interesting "History of the Presbyterian Church in Kentucky." He was pastor of the church until 1840, when he was elected president of Transylvania University. He was afterward tendered the position of superintendent of public instruction, but declined it. In 1869, he was one of the delegation to the general assembly of the Free Church of

---

*Davidson.

Scotland. He lives, at present, in Philadelphia, where he is greatly esteemed. Dr. Davidson has been a laborious and useful writer.

In 1841, Rev. John D. Matthews (see chapter on First Church) was called to the pulpit, which he filled for several years.

The Rev. John H. Brown, D. D., succeeded Mr. Matthews in 1844, and was pastor until 1853, when he resigned, and settled in Chicago, Illinois, where he died, February 23, 1872, afier a successful ministry in that city.

The present elegant and tasteful church edifice was built on the site of the old building in 1847. After the erection of the church, the remains of the gifted McChord were again deposited beneath the pulpit, where they now rest. Rev. Robert G. Brank, a native of Greenville, Kentucky, a graduate of Centre College, and an exceedingly graceful and effective speaker, succeeded Mr. Brown in 1854, and remained pastor of the church for fourteen years, during which time he made himself greatly beloved by his faithful and efficient ministry.

At the close of the late war, the Second Church, like its sister churches, was filled with dissension between the two parties then formed in it—the Southern Assembly party, with Mr. Brank as pastor, and the General Assembly party, with Rev. E. H. Camp as pastor.

In May, 1869, both of these ministers resigned, and the church troubles were adjusted (see chapter on First Presbyterian Church). The Rev. Nathaniel West filled the pulpit of the church during the winter of 1869–70, after which the present regular pastor, Rev. Mr. Burch, took charge of the church, which continues to prosper under his earnest and efficient ministry.

CHAPTER XL.

Luxurious Lexington—Eastern Lunatic Asylum—List of Contributors — Superintendents — Improvements — Present Condition.

LEXINGTON, in 1816, was known as the most elegant and fashionable city in the West. Great attention was given to music, dancing, and all the lighter accomplishments; pleasure gardens and other places of amusement were liberally patronized, and social entertainments were the order of the day. A visitor, at that time, says:* "Lexington is as large as Cincinnati. The inhabitants are as polished, and, I regret to add, as luxurious as those of Boston, New York, or Baltimore, and their assemblies and parties are conducted with as much ease and grace as in the oldest towns of the Union. A summer view of Lexington is inexpressibly rich, novel, and picturesque, and the scenery around it almost equals that of the Elysium of the Ancients."

The Eastern Lunatic Asylum, founded in 1816,† under the name of the "Fayette Hospital," was the first institution of the kind established in the western country, and the second state asylum opened in the United States. The projector of this now magnificent public charity was Andrew McCalla,‡ one of the early settlers of Lexington, and a man noted for his kind heart and benevolent deeds. He was assisted by many other citizens of like character, and all of them were incorporated early in 1816, under the name of "The Contributors to the Fayette Hospital."

The names of these contributors, as far as known, are: Alex. Parker, Trotter, Scott & Co., John W. Hunt, Geo. Trotter, Jr., Thomas January, Lewis Sanders, J. & D. Mac-

---
*Brown's Gazette.   †Old Kentucky Gazette.   ‡Collins.

coun, Andrew McCalla, T. D. Owings, Sam. Trotter, F. Ridgely, John Bradford, R. Higgins & J. D. Young, David Williamson, Mrs. Eleanor Hart, Benjamin Stout, William Morton, Thos. H. Pindell, William Leavy, John Pope, E. Warfield, Daniel Bradford, Patterson Bain, Michael Fishel, Adam Rankin, Robert Miller, L. M'Cullough, Tandy & Castleman, Robert Frazer, Robert H. M'Nair, J. Postlethwait, John H. Morton, John Hart, Jas. B. January, Sam'l Ayres, Asa Farrow, Thomas Tibbats, E. W. Craig, Robert Holmes, Sanford Keen, J. & B. Boswell, Maddox Fisher, E. Yeiser, David & J. Todd, Fisher & Layton, C. Coyle, James Wier.

On the 1st of March, the contributors organized under the charter, and shortly after purchased the "Sinking Spring" property, on which the present buildings are located. The site selected owed its name to a peculiar spring, still used, which has its origin in an immense subterranean volume of water, from which, it is said, the "Big Spring" at Georgetown flows. There is a tradition* that a quantity of chaff, emptied into the "Sinking Spring," came out, some hours after, at the "Big Spring."

On Monday, June 30, 1817, on the occasion of the laying of the corner-stone of the "Fayette Hospital" building, a procession marched from the court-house to the Sinking Spring, in the following order, viz:

Two Civil Officers of the County, Judge of the Circuit Court, Justices of the Peace and Bar.
Clergy.
Trustees and Professors of Transylvania University.
Students of Transylvania University.
Trustees of the Town.
Physicians.
Students of Medicine.
Music.
Architects of the Building.
Orator of the Day.
Hospital Committee.
Contributors.
Citizens.

---

*Dillard, R. T.

In the presence of a large concourse of spectators, after an appropriate prayer by Rev. Robert M. Cunningham, the corner-stone was laid, and in it were deposited the newspapers of Lexington for that week, some silver and copper coins of the United States, two publications in favor of the institution, and a brass plate bearing the name of the engraver and the following inscription:

State of Kentucky,
LEXINGTON,
June 30th, A. D. 1817.
Deposited in the Corner-stone of the
FAYETTE HOSPITAL.
The first erected west of the
Apalachian Mountains.
Built by Contribution, under the Direction of
AND'W M'CALLA,
THOS. JANUARY,
STEPHEN CHIPLEY, } *Building Committee of the Contributors.*
STERLING ALLEN,
RICH'D HIGGINS,

Also, the 5th verse of the 11th chapter of Matthew, in the original.

The ceremony was concluded by a powerful and eloquent oration by Henry Clay.

By the time the hospital was roofed in, a financial crisis defeated the plans of the building committee, and in 1822, it was found best to tender the property to the state, which purchased it the following year, gave it the name of the "Kentucky Eastern Lunatic Asylum," and appropriated $10,000 for its benefit. The asylum was formally opened May 1, 1824, and the first patient admitted was "Charity,"* a negro woman from Woodford county. For twenty years after its opening, the attending physicians were Dr. S. Theobolds, Dr. Louis Decognets, and others, assisted by the medical faculty of Transylvania University. In 1833, and at several different times after, the cholera raged with fatal effect in the asylum, and several times it has been visited by destructive fires, in one of which a number of

---

*Superintendent's Report.

patients were consumed. In 1844, the custodial management of the institution was changed for an enlightened one.* Dr. J. R. Allen was made the first superintendent under the new order of things. Chains and jailers rapidly disappeared, and the institution soon wore a civilized appearance. Dr. Allen held his office for ten years, giving great satisfaction to all concerned, and gaining for himself an enviable reputation.

In 1850, a liberal bequest was made to the asylum by James S. Megowan, "for the purpose of adding to the comfort and amusement of the patients."

Dr. W. S. Chipley, who for many years made mental diseases his special study, succeeded Dr. Allen in 1855, and continued as superintendent for fourteen years. Under his very efficient management, improvements were made in almost every respect, and the institution attained a position of usefulness second to none in this country.

The capacity of the asylum was greatly increased in 1867, by an appropriation of $150,000 by the legislature. The new buildings erected, gave the institution two hundred and fifty additional rooms.

In 1869, Dr. Chipley resigned, and Dr. John W. Whitney became superintendent, a position which he still holds. The institution has never been more prosperous, or its affairs more efficiently managed, than since the induction of the present able and skillful superintendent. His assistants are Drs. Dudley, Layton, and Rogers.

Since 1822, the state appropriations to the asylum have amounted to nearly a million of dollars. The little patch of ground it then owned has been increased to three hundred acres; nearly three thousand five hundred patients have been admitted to the institution, of whom largely over a thousand have recovered, besides very many who were so much improved as to justify their restoration to society. The asylum is supplied with every convenience, comfort, and medical and scientific arrangement calculated to benefit its inmates; and stands in the first rank among like institutions in the United States.

---

*Report.

CHAPTER XLI.

Carriages—Negroes—Branch United States Bank.

LEXINGTON was noted, as early as 1817, for her number of carriages, which was twice that of any other town of its size in the United States.* This peculiarity has distinguished her ever since, and so much so in late years, as to gain for her, from a pungent writer, the name of "the city that goes on wheels."

The prices of negroes rose in 1817, young men being worth from $500 to $700.

A branch of the United States Bank went into operation in Lexington, January 27, 1817. The directors were James Morrison, William Morton, John W. Hunt, Alexander Parker, John Tilford, A. S. Bartow, Cuthburt Bullitt, John H. Hanna, James Taylor, W. T. Barry, John T. Mason, and John H. Morton.

---

*Palmer.

CHAPTER XLII.

Relics of the Olden Time—Leslie Combs.

THE quaint and beautiful costumes of the old colonial days were not quite extinct, even in 1818. At entertainments, and on full dress occasions in Lexington, at that date, old gentlemen were frequently seen arrayed in all the magnificence of square coats, ruffled shirt-bosom, court vest, lace cuffs, short breeches, knee-buckles, and white stockings; and elderly ladies looked grand in wonderfully long-waisted dresses, with immense ruffles about the elbows, and with their powdered hair towering aloft on cushions.

General Leslie Combs settled in Lexington in 1818, and has made it his home ever since that time. General Combs was born in Clark county, Kentucky, November 28, 1793. His father was a Virginian, and his mother a Marylander. During the war of 1812, General Combs, at the age of nineteen, distinguished himself by his courage and gallantry. In the campaign which ended at Raisin, he was sent with a dispatch from General Winchester to General Harrison, and in the execution of his trust, traversed the pathless wilderness through snow and water for a hundred miles, and endured privations which nearly cost him his life.* In April, 1813, he was commissioned Captain of scouts, and was attached to the force under General Green Clay, which had been ordered to the relief of Fort Meigs. Captain Combs volunteered, with the assistance of an Indian guide and four men, to carry the news of Clay's approach to Harrison. He succeeded in threading his perilous way through swarms of hostile savages, and had arrived in sight of the closely invested fort, when he was attacked

---

*Lossing.

by Indians, one of his men killed, another wounded, and he and the rest of his little band, after intense suffering, escaped, in a starving condition, back to Fort Defiance.

Subsequently, he took a gallant part in the disastrous defeat of Colonel William Dudley, on the 5th of May, was wounded, taken prisoner, and compelled to run the gauntlet at Fort Miami.

After the war, General Combs settled in Lexington, where he practiced law for nearly half a century. In 1836, General Combs raised a regiment for the southwestern frontier, at the time of the Texas revolution. As a lawyer, trustee of Transylvania University, member of the legislature, railroad pioneer, state auditor, and a brilliant and sparkling speaker, General Combs has stood in high repute among his fellow-citizens. After a long and eventful life, the "boy-captain of 1812" is still among us. He resides on Main, between Limestone and Rose, and adjoining the First Christian Church.

CHAPTER XLIII.

Monetary Troubles—Parody—Visit of Monroe, Jackson, and Shelby—Dr. Charles Caldwell.

THE year 1819 found Lexington suffering from the financial derangement and demoralization which extended over the whole country. The multitude of newly created banks which had been thickly planted throughout Kentucky, had been so badly managed as to excite universal contempt. The following quaint effusion, printed in the Reporter of 1819, indicates the state of feeling at that time in regard to the banks:

" *To the Editors of the Reporter:* I have ventured to send you another *squib* at the banks. Nothing, I conceive, can be more injurious to the country than the *toleration* of swindling and bankrupt moneyed institutions.

" It is high time our *non-paying* money shops were closed—their credit is irretrievably lost.

" PARODY.

(Oh! blame not the Bard, if he fly to the bower, etc.)

"Alas! for the banks, their fame is gone by—
  And that credit is *broken*, which used but to *bend;*
O'er their fall, each director in secret must sigh,
  For 't is interest to love them, but *shame* to defend.
Unprized are their notes, or at ten per cent. selling,
  Unhonor'd at home, unredeem'd on demand;
But still they've a merit—I joy in the telling—
  They're taken for pork, though rejected for land.

" But their glory is gone!—ev'ry dog has his day—
  Yet their fame (such as 't is) shall abide in my songs;
Not e'en in the hour when my heart is most gay,
  Will I cease to remember their *notes* and their wrongs.

> The stranger in passing each village shall say,
> (As he eyes the sad spot with his hand on his breast,)
> THERE ONCE STOOD A BANK!—but, unable to pay,
> It *suspended itself*, and, thank G—d, is at rest!!"

President Monroe and General Jackson, accompanied by Governor Shelby, visited Lexington, Friday, July 3, 1819,* and were escorted to Keen's tavern by the old infantry, several rifle and artillery companies, and a large and enthusiastic crowd of citizens. Salutes were fired, both when they entered town, and when they arrived at the tavern. They visited the university, and were addressed by Dr. Holly and some of the students, after which they went to Jouett's studio. The next day they "attended the Fourth of July festival at Dunlap's." Sunday, they attended church. Monday, they were given a public dinner at Keen's tavern by the citizens, who addressed the President through Colonel Morrison. The distinguished guests left town the next day.

Dr. Charles Caldwell, well known in medical circles in both America and Europe, settled in Lexington in 1819. He was born in Caswell county, North Carolina, in 1772. At the age of fourteen, he had mastered Latin and Greek, after which he opened a grammar school, taught three years, then studied medicine, and graduated under Rush in Philadelphia.

In 1795, he commenced his career of authorship, which has since made him so distinguished. He labored with prodigious energy, and his literary and scientific writings and translations are estimated at ten thousand pages.

Dr. Caldwell was the first prominent champion of phrenology in the United States, and was one of the few distinguished men who openly espoused the mesmeric theory in the face of public ridicule. He bought, in Europe, the first medical library of Transylvania University. Many of the books he gathered in Paris from dealers to whom they had been sold by once eminent and wealthy physicians, who had been ruined by the French Revolution. By this means

---

*Gazette.

he obtained many rare and valuable works, which made the Transylvania Medical Library superior to any other at that time in this country. The books were brought from Maysville to Lexington on pack-horses.

Dr. Caldwell was a resident of Lexington and professor in the Medical College for sixteen years, at the end of which time (after making himself very unpopular, by favoring the removal of the college to Louisville,) he resigned, and was largely instrumental in establishing the Louisville Medical Institute. He died some years ago, leaving behind him a wide-spread reputation as a clear writer, an able teacher of philosophical medicine, and a man of enlightened liberality in advance of his age.

CHAPTER XLIV.

Recuperation—John D. Clifford—Russell's Cave—Mrs. Lincoln's Birthplace.

In 1820, Lexington, which for several years had been decreasing in population, commenced to grow again, and business slowly but steadily increased.

John D. Clifford died in Lexington, May 8, 1820, aged forty-two. Mr. Clifford was noted for his love and knowledge of the natural sciences; for being a public-spirited friend of every learned and charitable institution, and for the liberal support he extended to the Episcopal Church. He was the president of the Lexington Athenæum, in a room of which institution he opened a museum of natural and antiquarian history, and just before his death he assisted Professor Rafinesque to survey the ancient remains near Lexington. Mr. Clifford married Mary S., daughter of William Morton.

Russell's spring and cave, in this county, were explored by Professor Rafinesque, in 1820, and were thus described by him :*

"Russell's spring is a natural curiosity. It is a subterranean stream of water issuing from a cave. Both have been traced and followed for three-quarters of a mile, and it is moreover connected with the sinks west of Russell's, since something thrown into them has been seen to come out at the spring. The cave is crooked, narrow, and rather shallow. As the stream often fills it from side to side, one must often wade to explore it, and even swim in some places. Fishes are often found in it, such as suckers and catfish. In freshets, the water fills the cavity. At the

---
* Western Review, 1820.

mouth the stream is usually one foot deep, and discharges itself into the Elkhorn, about one hundred steps below. The mouth of the cave is below a chain of rocky limestone cliffs, where some organic fossils are imbedded. A large and spacious hall lies next to it in the rock, forming another cave, which is filled by rubbish at a short distance, but communicates by narrow chasms with the other cave."

In 1820, Robert S. Todd, who died in 1849, lived on Short street, in the house adjoining and belonging to St. Paul's Church (Catholic), and at present occupied by Father Bekkers. Colonel Todd's daughter, Miss Mary Todd, afterward the wife of President Lincoln, was born in this house. Mrs. Lincoln was married November 4, 1842.

CHAPTER XLV.

Financial Crisis—Relief and Anti-Relief—Prevailing Prices —Elder T. P. Dudley.

In 1821, Lexington, like the whole state of Kentucky, was suffering from the financial distress which had been growing worse and worse ever since the close of the war of 1812. The community was flooded with all sorts and sizes of depreciated "shinplasters," as they were contemptuously called; business was ruined, everybody was in debt, and every one was suing or being sued. During this terrible depression and stagnation of commercial interests, all the old political interests were lost sight of, and the crisis brought into existence the now famous "Relief" and "Anti-Relief" parties, the first demanding a stay-law on executions from the legislature, the last opposing it. The contest was hot and protracted, and resulted in the still more famous "Old Court" and "New Court" parties.

At this dark period all the farmer had to sell went at ruinously low prices, and all he bought he got at the most exorbitant rates.* Corn sold at twelve and a half cents per bushel; wheat, thirty-seven cents; flour at two dollars and fifty cents per barrel; net pork at one dollar and twenty-five cents per hundred pounds; butter at six cents per pound, and eggs at three cents per dozen; cottons, forty and sixty cents, and prints, which would not be worn, at seventy-five cents per yard. Tea retailed at three dollars per pound, coffee at seventy-four cents, and Muscovado sugar at thirty-seven cents per pound; and, as an instance of the perverted taste of that day, it was the usual custom to exchange two pounds of tree sugar for one of the Mus-

---

* Kentucky Letter in Cincinnati Gazette.

covado. Whisky—old copper-distilled Bourbon whisky—sold at twenty-five to thirty cents per gallon. Milch cows rated from seven dollars to ten dollars per head, and good horses were often bought at twenty-five to forty dollars.

The venerable Elder Thomas P. Dudley, of Lexington, entered the ministry of the Particular Baptist Church in 1821. He was born in Kentucky county, Virginia, May 3, 1792, and in a few days after was under the government of the infant commonwealth of Kentucky. He enlisted for the campaign of 1812 in Trotter's cavalry, but left the troop at Fort Defiance to act as assistant commissary to the left wing of the northwest army. He was in the battle and massacre at the river Raisin, where he was captured. After his release from captivity, he served as quartermaster-general of the Kentucky troops sent to the aid of Jackson at New Orleans, and was in the celebrated victory of the 8th of January, 1815. After serving faithfully in the ministry for more than half a century, Elder Dudley still survives, and is one of the oldest and best known citizens of Lexington. Mr. Dudley has been the pastor of the church at Bryant's Station for many years. This church, which was organized in 1786, has had but two pastors from that time to the present, viz: Ambrose Dudley, and his son, Thomas P. Dudley, the subject of this notice.

CHAPTER XLVI.

Gambling Suppressed—Female Bible Society.

LEXINGTON was so grievously infested with gamblers in the fall of 1822, that the citizens combined to crush them out, and after an indignation meeting, a general attack was made on the sporting characters, and many of them were lodged in jail. A newspaper of the time,* "hoped that persons at a distance would understand that the society of Lexington does not tolerate any species of gaming."

In 1822, the Lexington Female Bible Society was organized. Mrs. Elizabeth Skillman, whose lovely character will long be remembered by our citizens, was one of the members of the first board of managers, and was president of the institution for nearly forty years. She died February 18, 1872, in the eighty-sixth year of her age.

---

*Observer and Reporter.

CHAPTER XLVII.

Thomas T. Skillman—D. A. Sayre & Co.—" Old Court" and " New Court" Parties—The Contest in Lexington—Incidents—Jos. C. Breckinridge.

THE " Western Luminary," the first religious newspaper published in the southwest, was established in Lexington, by Thomas T. Skillman, in 1823, to aid in counteracting the strong infidel tendency then manifested in the city. Mr. Skillman was one of the best and most useful citizens of his day. He died June 9, 1833, a victim of the terrible cholera season of that year, and the loss which his church and the community sustained, was felt to be such that it deepened still more the sadness and gloom that pervaded the suffering city.

The banking house of D. A. Sayre & Co., was founded in 1823.

In 1823, the court of appeals of Kentucky made its celebrated decision that the "relief" statutes passed at prior sessions of the legislature, retrospectively extending replevins, were unconstitutional. This decision created an immense sensation. The " Reliefs " now became known as the " New Court" party, whose sole aim was to remove the offending judges of the court of appeals, and substitute new ones who would bend to the popular will. The "Anti-Reliefs," or as they were soon called, the "Old Court" party, formed the opposition. The struggle which ensued, and which extended through three years, was the most violent and bitter one in the annals of the state, excepting the one at the eve of the late war.

In no place in the state was the combat more fierce than in Lexington, the home of several of the ablest leaders of both the parties. Every weapon of political warfare was called into play; argument, and invective, and sarcasm, and satire, and pasquinade, and ribaldry, were all exhausted in the strife of words.

It was during this exciting period, that the famous brickbat war broke out on the streets of Lexington.* The combatants in about equal numbers, were ranged on each side of the street, and while pick and crowbar were kept busy in tearing up pavements, the fighting men in the opposing ranks were equally busy for a full hour, by "Shrewsbury clock," hurling missiles at each other. Broken heads and bloody noses was the order of the day. When the fight was raging most furiously, and all were expecting a resort to firearms, R. J. Breckinridge and Charlton Hunt, opposing candidates, both of them brilliant, rising young lawyers, appeared on the street, with arm locked in arm, each waving a white handkerchief, and walking boldly between the combatants. They thus ended the fray.

Another incident characteristic of the day and the people deserves to be recorded. It was then the custom for successful candidates at the close of the polls, to give a "big treat" to their constituents. On one of these occasions, Robert Wickliffe, Sr., "treated" to punch, a barrel of which was set in the middle of Limestone street, opposite the place now known as the Sayre Institute. A strong partisan on the other side, a somewhat notorious character, who was always after called "Dr." Napper, secretly dropped some tartar emetic in the punch. Such a scene as ensued beggars all description, and could hardly be limned with the pencil of a Hogarth. The retching and heaving, the sputtering, and spewing, and spouting, with

"The two and seventy stenches,
All well defined, and several stinks,"

Which assailed the olfactories of the passers-by was due notice to give the participators in the debauch a wide berth. That was the last general political treat given in the interior of the state.

---

*Kentucky letter to Cincinnati Gazette.

Joseph C. Breckinridge, oldest son of Hon. John Breckinridge, and father of Hon. John C. Breckinridge, was for many years a citizen of Lexington. He died in Frankfort, September 1, 1823, aged thirty-five. Mr. Breckinridge was born in Virginia, graduated at Princeton, served in the war of 1812, studied law and practiced in Lexington. At an early age he was elected to the legislature from Fayette county, and at the time of his death, was secretary of state under Governor Adair.

CHAPTER XLVIII.

The "Athens of the West"—Lexington Lyceum—Botanical Garden—Jefferson Davis.

THE literary culture and educational advantages of Lexington had become such by 1824, that the city was spoken of far and wide as the "Athens of the West."* Her claims to the title were by no means insignificant. The society of Lexington was noted for its intelligence, appreciation of literature, its good taste and elegance. The pulpits of the city were adorned by able and eloquent men, the newspapers were the leaders of the state press, and the bar was probably the strongest one at that time in the United States. Transylvania University, under the distinguished Dr. Holly, had attained even a European celebrity, and the city was crowded with her learned professors, and medical, academical, and law students. Lectures were frequent and well sustained and the weekly discussions of the Lexington Lyceum, which was composed of the best men of all professions, were listened to by crowded audiences. The city library was the largest in the west, and has never been more liberally patronized. A botanical garden had just been established; the pencil of Jouett had made him famous and was now constantly engaged; and scholars and distinguished men from all parts of the country, visited Lexington to enjoy the society in the noted seat and center of learning and intellectual culture in the west.

The Lexington Lyceum mentioned above was the successor of the "Lexington Junto,"† the debating society in which Henry Clay distinguished himself by the first speech he made in Lexington, in the year 1798. The Lyceum

---

*Flint's Travels. †Old Kentucky Gazette.

met at one time in Satterwhite's tavern, and afterward in the court-house. It existed for very many years and did great good by means of lectures and public debates. The Lyceum now in existence was chartered March 9, 1868.* Its incorporators were: J. S. Phelps, J. R. Morton, H. M. Buford, J. H. Webster, G. W. Darnall, F. W. Woolley, and G. W. Ranck.

The botanical garden established in 1824 was projected by the learned Prof. C. S. Rafinesque of Transylvania University, who became its first director and manager, assisted by John W. McCalla, Thos. Smith, Joseph Ficklin, and J. M. Pike.† The garden, which was, properly speaking, a botanical, medical, and agricultural institution founded to promote the natural sciences and a knowledge of husbandry, was situated about where Judge S. S. Goodloe now lives on the Richmond turnpike. It existed but a few years, but is noted as having been the first institution of the kind projected in the west, if not the first in the United States.

Hon. Jefferson Davis, late President of the Confederate States, and who will always occupy a prominent and illustrious place in the world's history, resided in Lexington in 1824, and was a member of the senior class in Transylvania University. He is remembered as a slender, fair-haired young man, quiet, unassuming, and of very studious habits.‡ He boarded with Postmaster Ficklin, in the brick house, still standing, on the southwest corner of Hill and Limestone streets. The historic interest now attached to this spot will deepen and increase with advancing time.

---

*Acts Legislature.   †B. G. Records.   ‡Letter to the Author.

CHAPTER XLIX.

Lafayette's Visit to Lexington—Reception—Ceremonies and Incidents—The Christian Church—First Meeting Places—"Union of the Disciples and Christians"—Early Ministers—Dr. Jas. Fishback—Regular Pastors—Dissensions about Ordination—The Campbell and Rice Debate—"Excommunication"—Present Condition of the Main Street Church.

PROBABLY the grandest gathering ever seen in Lexington was on the occasion of the reception of General Lafayette, May 16, 1825. In no place in this country did the old hero recive a more cordial welcome than in the seat of the county which was named in his honor. An immense concourse of people from all parts of Kentucky and from several other states, companies of infantry, artillery, and cavalry, Revolutionary soldiers, distinguished strangers, members of all professions, went out to meet him, wearing " Lafayette badges."

The announcement that the marquis and suite were in sight was the signal for round after round of deafening cheers, volleys of musketry, and thunders of artillery, which only ceased long enough to give the following committee time to formally receive and welcome him to Lexington, viz: John Bradford, William Morton, Dr. Richard Pindell, Dr. Walter Warfield, John Fowler, Alexander Parker, Andrew McCalla, William Leavy, James Lemmon, Charles Norwood, Col. James Trotter, and Gen. Thomas Bodley.* The welcome address in behalf of Lexington was delivered by John Bradford, and that in behalf of the county by Leslie Combs. Formal replies were made by Gen. Lafayette, after which, amid renewed cheers and salutes, a

---
*Observer and Reporter.

grand procession moved through the principal streets of the town to Mrs. Keen's tavern, where rooms were prepared for the distinguished guests.

The procession marched in the following order:
First assistant marshal and staff, Col. McConnell.
Division of cavalry and mounted riflemen.
Marshal of the day and staff, Gen. McCalla.
Committee of Revolutionary officers and soldiers.
Sub-county committee.
State committee, with Colonel Wash from Missouri.
General Lafayette, with Col. Bowman, of the Eighth Virginia regiment in the Revolutionary army, in a barouche drawn by four bay horses.
Col. G. W. Lafayette, Col. Le Vasseur, and Count De Syon, in a barouche also drawn by four bays.
Governors Desha and Carrol, with their suites, Colonels Hickey and Rowan, and Colonels Shelby and Erwin.
Revolutionary officers and soldiers.
Trustees of the town.
Judges of the Federal and State courts, and members of Congress and of the State legislature.
Officers of the army and navy.
Officers of the militia.
Second assistant marshal and staff, Col. Payne.
First division of the military escort on foot.
Third assistant marshal and staff, Col. Beard.
Second division of the military escort on foot.
Fourth assistant marshal and staff, Col. Dunlap.
President, Professors, and Trustees of Transylvania University, and the clergy.
Union Philosophical and Whig Societies of the University.
Students of the University according to classes.
Fifth assistant marshal and staff, Col. Prewitt.
Citizens on foot.
Sixth assistant marshal and staff, Lieut. Col. Dudley.
Citizens on horseback.

Division of cavalry and mounted riflemen.

Seventh assistant marshal and staff, Lieut. Col. Combs.

Rest and then a sumptuous dinner followed the arrival at the tavern, after which the afternoon was spent by the marquis in a cordial reception of the enthusiastic multitude which crowded in upon him. At night a grand complimentary ball was given him in the then new Masonic Hall, on Main, between Broadway and Spring streets, which was beautifully decorated for the occasion. The managers of the ball were: E. Warfield, J. H. Morton, J. W. Hunt, J. W. Palmer, C. Wilkins, W. W. Worsley, B. Gratz, J. Postlethwait, L. Combs, T. Smith, T. S. Caldwell, W. Brand. General Lafayette was welcomed to the hall by the Rev. John Ward in behalf of his Masonic brethren.

Before his departure, Lafayette reviewed the old soldiers of the Revolution, visited Mrs. Clay and the widow of Governor Scott, and spent some time with Jouett, who afterward completed the life-size portrait of Lafayette, now owned by the State of Kentucky. One of the most prominent features of the entertainment of Lafayette in Lexington was a literary reception at Transylvania University. A classic address was made by President Holly, and eulogistic orations and poems were delivered in French, Latin, and English by the students.

In 1825,* two feeble little religious bodies, which occasionally attracted attention on account of their "new notions," struggled for existence in Lexington. The members of one met at the residence of Mrs. Bell (mother of Dr. T. S. Bell, of Louisville), who lived on Main street, between Walnut and Rose, and nearly opposite Mr. S. S. Thompson's planing mill. They called themselves "Christians," and their pastor was that learned, liberal, and great man, Barton W. Stone, who had long been at the head of a flourishing classical school in Lexington. The other little flock met in a house on Spring street, between Main and Water, which afterward became the machine shop of Thomas H. Barlow, one of the greatest inventors America

---

* Old Inhabitants.

has ever produced. They called themselves "Disciples," and held the peculiar views advanced by Alexander Campbell, who, two years before (1823), upon the occasion of his first visit to Lexington, had created a great sensation by his startling and powerful sermons. The "Disciples" were occasionally addressed by that intrepid, original, and able man of God, Elder John ("Raccoon") Smith, who now sleeps in the Lexington cemetery. Elders Wm. Poindexter and Thomas Smith also labored for this church.

The "Christians" and "Disciples" agreed in most of their religious opinions. They kept up separate organizations, however, for a number of years. The "Christians," or "Stoneites," as they were then often called, were particularly careful not to make immersion a test* of religion, and it was their practice to receive unimmersed christians of all denominations to their communion and fellowship. It was this which prevented for some time the union of the two bodies.

By the year 1831, the Christians had gathered strength sufficient to erect a house of worship, which they built on Hill street, near the corner of Mill, and opposite the present residence of Judge Robertson. The church was a very plain brick one, with an interior gallery, which, after the old style, ran around two sides and the end of the building. It was formally opened for worship on Sunday, October 16, 1831,† and the dedication sermon was delivered by the eccentric and eloquent elder, Jesse Bledsoe, who, but a short time before, had abandoned the bar for the pulpit. The "Disciples," at this time, were meeting in a building which stood near the present residence of Dr. H. M. Skillman, on Broadway.

On Saturday, January 1, 1832, the Christians and Disciples, between whom there existed a most fraternal feeling, assembled, by agreement, in the Hill Street meeting-house, to consider the probabilities of the union of the two bodies. Candid and generous addresses were delivered by Elders Barton Stone and John Smith; the members of both

---

*Christian Messenger, vol. v, p. 19.   †Observer and Reporter.

churches conferred together, harmony was arrived at, and the hoped-for union was effected upon the broad ground that the Bible was the only rule of faith and practice; that all should enjoy the right of private judgment, and that the opinions of ecclesiastical leaders should not be allowed to disturb the peace of the church. The united congregations adopted the name Christian for the church, and the Hill Street house became the sole meeting-place.

Until the services of a regular pastor were obtained, Elders Jacob Creath, Curtis Smith, Thomas M. Allen, and others preached at different times for the church.

One of the earliest and ablest of Bishop Campbell's indorsers in Lexington was Dr. James Fishback,* who subsequently became a member of the Christian ministry. He was the son of Jacob Fishback, who came to Kentucky from Culpepper county, Virginia, in 1783. Dr. Fishback was educated for the medical profession, and as early as 1805 filled the chair of "Theory and Practice" in Transylvania University. In 1816, becoming dissatisfied with the stricter views of the Presbyterian Church, of which he was a member, he connected himself with the Baptists, and became one of their regularly ordained preachers.

In 1823, when Bishop Alexander Campbell visited Lexington for the first time, Dr. Fishback paid the closest attention to the opinions and arguments he advanced, and the impressions he then received influenced the balance of his religious life. In 1827,† while pastor of the Baptist Church on Mill street, he strongly advocated a change in the name of the church from what it then was to that of "Church of Christ." Many members of the church favored it, and many denounced it as an "unnecessary change suggested by the spirit of the New Light heresy." The dissension which ensued resulted in the exclusion of Dr. Fishback, John M. Hewitt, Purnell Bishop, Alex. Gibney, E. Chinn, A. Graham, and thirty others, "for contumacy and disorderly conduct." In April, the excluded members,

---

*Davidson's History.   †Baptist Church Records.

who claimed the ownership of the church building, met in it, organized "the Church of Christ on Mill street," and in turn excluded their excluders from the church. Dr. Fishback was elected pastor of the new church, the congregation of which met for some time alternately with the other Baptists in the Mill Street church, but subsequently left that place and worshiped in the building now known as the Statesman office, on Short street. Most of this congregation finally went back to the First Baptist Church, but Dr. Fishback and others, after wavering for some time, joined the Christian Church. Dr. Fishback was a prominent preacher of this last-named body for a number of years, and died connected with it in the summer of 1845.

Dr. Fishback was a preacher of superior talents, boldness, and culture, a man of great information and fine personal appearance. He was a strong and able writer, as evidenced by his "Philosophy of the Human Mind," published in 1813, and his religious "Essays and Dialogues," of 1834. He was married twice. His first wife was a niece of Patrick Henry, and his last, a daughter of Governor Shelby.

The first minister regularly employed by the United congregations on Hill street was Elder James Challen. He was born in Hackensack, New Jersey, in 1802, came to Kentucky at an early age, entered Transylvania University, united with the Baptist Church in 1823, but a few years after changed his opinion and entered the ministry of the Christian Church. He became pastor of the Hill Street congregation in 1834. He did much to perfect a thorough organization of the church, and endeared himself greatly to his brethren by his graces and virtues. This now aged soldier of the cross is living at present in Davenport, Iowa.

Dr. B. F. Hall, a native of Fleming county, Kentucky, but who has long made Texas his home, succeeded Mr. Challen. Dr. Hall was a speaker of moderate ability. During his pastorate the church became divided on the subject of ordination, the parties in the contention being Dr. Hall, Dr. J. G. Chinn, and others, on one side, and

Poindexter and a few followers on the other. The breach was finally closed.

In 1841, Dr. L. L. Pinkerton succeeded Dr. Hall as pastor, and under his energetic ministry the church prospered, and shortly after he commenced his labors (1842), the present large church edifice on Main street was completed. Dr. Pinkerton was born in Baltimore county, Maryland, January 28, 1812, and was trained in the Presbyterian faith, but in 1830 was baptized under the personal ministry of Bishop Campbell. Before he began to preach, he practiced medicine, having graduated in the Transylvania Medical College. Dr. Pinkerton was pastor of the Main Street Church for nearly three years, after which he was very largely instrumental in forming the Orphan School at Midway, Kentucky. He was for five years professor of belles-lettres in Kentucky University. Dr. Pinkerton is gifted with generosity, independence, and liberality. His discourses are characterized by elegance, vigor, and originality, over which is cast the charm of a tender melancholy. A more uniformly interesting speaker has never filled the pulpit of the Main Street Church.

In November, 1843, the celebrated debate between those distinguished champions, Bishop Alexander Campbell and the Rev. N. L. Rice took place before densely packed audiences in the Main Street Church. The moderators on that occasion were Hon. Henry Clay, Judge George Robertson, and Colonel Speed Smith.

After Dr. Pinkerton, Elders Newton Short, William Clark, A. W. Robbins, and John I. Rogers became pastors of the church. In 1860, W. H. Hopson, a native of Christian county, Ky., was elected to the pastorate, which he filled up to the year 1862, when J. W. McGarvey succeeded, and he in turn was succeeded in 1867 by Elder Robert Graham, who was born in Liverpool, England, and graduated at Bethany College. L. B. Wilkes, a native of Maury county, Tennessee, became pastor in 1869.

During the ministry of Mr. Wilkes, a part of the congregation, by the advice of its officers, commenced to meet for worship in the Odd Fellows' Hall, on the corner of Main and Broadway, where service was held, for the first time, on Sunday, January 2, 1870, and continued regularly until May 1st of the same year, when the First Presbyterian building was bought by the Main Street church, and devoted to the use of its members meeting in the hall. The government of two congregations under one eldership created dissatisfaction among some members of the church, and was publicly condemned by one of them (Mr. Elly) as unscriptural, despotic, and dangerous. It was continued nevertheless, and, unfortunately, a spirit of illiberality at the same time rapidly manifested itself among some of the preachers and leaders of the church. Forced, by these combined causes, and desiring peace and freedom of conscience, a number of the members of the church, acting in accordance with the long-recognized rights and usage of the Christian body, quietly established, in the spring of 1871, the "Second Church of Christ," or, as it was kindly and very suggestively called by the public at that time, the "Little Church around the Corner."

In the summer of 1871, the members of the Main Street Church meeting on Broadway were organized into an independent church, after having been nearly eighteen months under the rule of the Main Street officers.

On the 22d of October, 1871, the Main Street portion of the original double body, assumed to exclude from it (the Main Street Church) such members of the Second Church of Christ as had formerly belonged to both the Main Street and the Broadway congregations. The ladies and gentlemen supposed to be excluded, were charged with "disorder and schism in withdrawing and setting up a new organization without the consent of the church."

M. E. Lard, the present pastor, who took charge of the Main Street Church late in 1871, is a native of Bedford county, Tennessee.

The Main Street congregation has been rapidly increasing in numbers for several years past, and is now very large and prosperous. The church has lately been considerably improved in appearance.

CHAPTER L.

Funeral Honors to Jefferson, Adams, and Shelby.

THE citizens of Lexington testified their sincere regret for the loss of the patriots, Jefferson, Adams, and Shelby, by extensive and impressive funeral ceremonies on Wednesday, August 15, 1826.

At eleven o'clock A. M., a procession formed at the Grand Masonic Hall, under the direction of Thomas Bodley, chief marshal; Messrs. John M. McCalla, Jas. M. Pike, Leslie Combs, C. W. Cloud, and Joseph Robb, assistant marshals; and proceeded in the following order to the Episcopal Church:

Fayette Hussars, Captain Pindell.
Light Artillery Cadets, Lieutenant Commandant, W. B. Collins.
Lexington Light Infantry, Captain West.
Fayette Rifle Corps, Captain Dailey.
Other uniform companies of Fayette county.
Committee of Arrangements.
Officiating Chaplain and Orator of the day.
Reverend Clergy.

BIER OF ADAMS,

supported by eight bearers, with white bands and sashes, and followed by a led horse, suitably and appropriately accoutered.

BIER OF JEFFERSON,

supported and followed in the same manner.
The two biers of the ex-Presidents, followed by twenty-four misses dressed in white, with white veils and suitable badges, representing the twenty-four states of the Union.

BIER OF SHELBY,
supported by four bearers, and followed by a led horse appropriately accoutered, and a female representing Kentucky, clothed in white, with an appropriate badge.
Surviving officers and soldiers of the Revolution.
Major-general and his staff.
Trustees of the town, Treasurer and Clerk.
Militia Officers, General, Regimental, and Staff.
Members of Congress.
Members of the State Legislature.
Fayette Circuit Judge, Attorney, and Clerk.
Magistrates of the county, preceded by the High Sheriff.
President, Trustees, and Professors of Transylvania University.
Principal, Visitors, and Teachers of the Lafayette Female Academy.
Union Philosophical Society, ⎫
Whig Society, ⎬ with badges.
Franklin Society, ⎭
Teachers of the several Schools in Lexington and Fayette county.
Citizens and strangers, four abreast.

After arriving at the church, which was crowded to excess, a soft and beautiful dirge was played, and then, after a touching prayer by the Rev. George T. Chapman, an eloquent and impressive funeral oration was delivered by William T. Barry. The ceremonies concluded with an anthem by the choir and a benediction.

CHAPTER LI.

A Great Rain.

AN extraordinary fall of rain occurred in Lexington, on Sunday, July 25, 1827.* It commenced with a heavy thunder shower in the afternoon, and continued all night, and by morning so great had been the volume of water that had fallen, that citizens going to their places of business, were obliged to wade through the torrents of water which poured through the streets. The cellars in the level parts of the town were completely filled with water, causing great losses to grocers and merchants. The damage done was estimated at twenty thousand dollars. Several lives were endangered by the sudden rise of the water. In one case a black woman was very nigh drowned. She was sleeping in a cellar kitchen. The water had arisen in the street till it reached the cellar windows, when it rushed in so rapidly that she either had not time or presence of mind to make her escape, but catching hold of something above her, cried for help. In a few minutes the cellar was filled, and she must inevitably have been drowned had not some person ventured in and brought her out.

---

*Western Luminary.

CHAPTER LII.

National Republicans and Democratic Republicans.

By the time the year 1828 rolled 'round, old state and local issues were forgotten in Lexington. The Old Court party was now known as the "National Republican" party, and the New Court as "Democratic Republican" party. Lexington blazed with political excitement all through this year, and it was at its highest pitch at the November election, which resulted in Jackson carrying the state by a majority of eight thousand over Adams.

CHAPTER LIII.

First Road Macadamized.

THE macadamizing of the streets and roads of Lexington was agitated in 1829, and urged in particular by Henry Clay. On the 30th of October, a large public meeting was held, at which the McAdam plan was indorsed, and steps were taken to organize a company to construct a road "connecting Lexington with the Ohio river." The following committee was appointed to advance the interests of the road, viz: Henry Clay, Charleton Hunt, Benjamin Gratz, Richard Higgins, E. J. Winter, John Brand, Benjamin Taylor, Richard Chinn, David Megowan, George Boswell, and D. Sayre. Work was commenced shortly after, on Limestone and Broadway streets, and on the road from Lexington to Maysville, which is believed to have been the first road macadamized in Kentucky.

CHAPTER LIV.

The First Western Railroad—Corporators—Officers—Incidents—First American Locomotive—Charles Humphreys.

LEXINGTON claims the honor of having constructed the first railroad in the West, and the second one in America. It was originally known as the "Lexington and Ohio Railroad," and was chartered by the Kentucky legislature, January 27, 1830; and the corporators were* Messrs. John W. Hunt, John Brand, Richard Higgins, Benjamin Gratz, Luther Stevens, Robert Wickliffe, Leslie Combs, Elisha Warfield, Robert Frazer, James Weir, Michael Fishell, Thomas E. Boswell, George Boswell, Benjamin Taylor, Elisha J. Winter, Joseph Boswell, David Megowan, John Norton, Madison C. Johnson, and Henry C. Payne. Elisha J. Winter was elected first president of the company. The second president was Benjamin Gratz, of Lexington, Kentucky.

Engineers, at that period, were not so lavish in their estimates of the cost of constructing railroads, as they have become in modern times, as it is a matter of history that the original estimate of the cost of the contemplated Lexington and Ohio road, from Lexington to Portland, was one million of dollars. Of this sum, about seven hundred thousand dollars was promptly subscribed by citizens of Lexington.†

The "corner-stone" of the road was laid on Water street, near the corner of Mill, with great display, on the 21st of October, 1831. Governor Metcalfe drove the first spike, and an address was delivered to the assembled concourse by Professor Charles Caldwell. Work on this pioneer road was then commenced.

---

*Acts Legislature.   †Louisville Courier.

The road-bed was as unique as it was substantial, and consisted of strap-iron rails spiked down to stone-sills. The cars were, for a long time, drawn by horses. The first steam locomotive made in the United States ran over this road. It had been invented by Thomas Barlow, of Lexington, as early as 1827 or 1828, and was constructed by Joseph Bruen, an ingenious mechanic, also a resident of Lexington.* The original model of this locomotive is in the museum of the Eastern Lunatic Asylum of this city. On the night of December 21, 1834, a grand ball and supper was given at Brennan's tavern, in Lexington, to celebrate the opening of the road, and the rejoicing and festivity was great.

An immense and excited crowd assembled at Lexington, on Saturday, January 24, 1835, to witness the starting of the first train for the "Villa." In the following December, the first through train arrived at Frankfort from Lexington.†

During the session of the general assembly of 1847, the Louisville and Frankfort Railroad Company was organized and chartered, and at once became the purchasers of that portion of the road lying between Louisville and Frankfort. In 1848, the Lexington and Frankfort Railroad Company was organized, and in turn purchased from the state that portion of the road between Lexington and Frankfort.

Regular trains were first run through from Louisville to Lexington in 1851.

In 1857, the management of the Louisville and Frankfort and Lexington and Frankfort railroads was consolidated. The road is now known as the Louisville, Lexington and Cincinnati Railroad.

Charles Humphreys died October 1, 1830, in the fifty-fifth year of his age. He was a self-taught scholar; was long a law professor in Transylvania University, and was an able and accomplished advocate and jurist. It is said that he was not known to have had a single enemy.

---

*Observer and Reporter, 1833.   †Observer and Reporter.

CHAPTER LV.

Whigs and Democrats—Physicians.

IN 1831, Henry Clay was nominated for the presidency against Andrew Jackson, and the Whig and Democratic parties in Lexington labored for their favorites with a passionate energy and fiery zeal never since surpassed. The newspapers flamed with phillipics and denunciations. Caucuses, speeches, clubs, barbecues, pole-raisings, and mass meetings kept up a tempest of political excitement in which all ages, sexes, and conditions took a part. Detraction and bitter animosity accompanied the heated opposition of the parties, and when the contest ended with the election of Jackson for the second time, the deep mortification of one side was only equaled by the wild and triumphant rejoicing of the other.

Among the prominent physicians of Lexington about this time (1831) were Drs. Best, Holland, William Pawling, T. P. Satterwhite, and Richard Pindell, the last-named gentleman was a native of Maryland, and had been a surgeon in the Revolutionary army. He died March 16, 1833.

CHAPTER LVI.

Lexington a City—First Officers—Poor and Work-House—Trustees' Rooms and Council Chamber—List of Mayors—Appearance of Lexington in 1832—General Jackson's Visit.

LEXINGTON became an incorporated city in 1832, and on the 12th of January of that year, the first mayor and the first board of councilmen were inducted into office.* The brief ceremonies took place at the court-house. The oath was administered to the mayor, Charleton Hunt, by Judge T. M. Hickey, after which the mayor administered it to the following gentlemen, who composed the council, viz: William A. Leavy, Richard Higgins, Stephen Chipley, Robert S. Todd, David Megowan, Richard Ashton, Thomas P. Hart, Luther Stephens, Thomas M. Hickey, Leslie Combs, John Brand, and Benjamin Gratz. The city was at once divided into four wards, a municipal seal was adopted, a work-house established, and the general machinery of the new government set in motion.

The first mayor of Lexington, Charleton Hunt, was the oldest son of John Wesley Hunt, and was born December 3, 1801. After graduating at Transylvania University, he studied law, and held a prominent position in his profession at the time of his death, which occurred December 27, 1836. He died just as a future full of promise was opening to him. Few men have been more beloved in Lexington, and his death produced a general sensation of regret and sorrow.

The first work-house was located on Limestone street, adjoining the jail, and its first keeper was T. B. McGowen.† In 1835 a poor-house was combined with the work-house, and the buildings of the joint establishment were erected

---

*City Records. †Id.

on Bolivar street. The institutions were connected about thirty-five years. The poor-house is now located in the country. The work-house remains on Bolivar street, and has lately been improved.

The trustees of the *town* of Lexington held their meetings first in the fort, then in the first court-house, afterward in a room in the old state-house, and then again in the court-house.

The city council occupied the old Odd Fellows Hall, on Church street, until it was destroyed by fire in 1854. The Medical Hall, corner of Church and Market (now replaced by the library building), was used for a long time. In 1865, the council took possession of its present hall, in Hunt's row.

The following is a list of the mayors of the city, from 1832 to the present time, viz: 1832-4, Charleton Hunt; 1835-6, James E. Davis; 1837-8, J. G. McKinney; 1839-40, C. H. Wickliffe; 1841, Daniel Bradford; 1842-5, James Logue; 1846, Thomas Ross; 1847, John Henry; 1848, George P. Jouett; 1849-50, O. F. Payne; 1851-3, E. W. Dowden; 1854, T. H. Pindell; 1855-8, William Swift; 1859, T. B. Monroe; 1860-1, Benjamin F. Graves; 1862, C. T. Worley; 1863-5, Joseph Wingate; 1866, D. W. Standiford; 1867, J. T. Frazer; 1868, J. G. Chinn; 1869-72, J. T. Frazer.

The appearance of Lexington at the time it was incorporated as a city is thus described by an admiring visitor :*

" The town buildings in general are handsome, and some are magnificent. Few towns in the West, or elsewhere, are more delightfully situated. Its environs have a singular softness and amenity of landscape, and the town wears an air of neatness, opulence, and repose, indicating leisure and studiousness, rather than the bustle of business and commerce. It is situated in the center of a proverbially rich and beautiful country. The frequency of handsome villas and ornamented rural mansions impart the impression of vicinity to an opulent metropolis. A beautiful branch of

---

*Flint's Mississippi Valley.

the Elkhorn runs through the city, and supplies it with water. The main street is a mile and a quarter in length, and eighty feet wide, well paved, and the principal roads leading from it to the country are macadamized for some distance. In the center of the town is the public square, surrounded by handsome buildings. In this square is the market-house, which is amply supplied with all the products of the state. The inhabitants are cheerful, intelligent, conversable, and noted for their hospitality to strangers. The professional men are distinguished for their attainments in their several walks, and many distinguished and eminent men have had their origin here. The university, with its professors and students, and the numerous distinguished strangers that are visiting here during the summer months, add to the attractions of the city. The people are addicted to giving parties, and the tone of society is fashionable and pleasant. Strangers, in general, are much pleased with a temporary sojourn in this city, which conveys high ideas of the refinement and taste of the country. There are now much larger towns in the West, but none presenting more beauty and intelligence. The stranger, on finding himself in the midst of its polished and interesting society, can not but be carried back, by the strong contrast, to the time when the patriarchial hunters of Kentucky, reclining on their buffalo robes around their evening fires, canopied by the lofty trees and the stars, gave it the name it bears, by patriotic acclamation."

General Andrew Jackson visited Lexington the second time on Saturday, September 29, 1832,* at which time a grand barbecue in his honor was given by the Democrats at "Fowler's Garden." General Jackson was then a candidate for re-election to the presidency, and Mr. Clay, selected by the "Nationals," was his competitor. "Old Hickory" was escorted into the city by an immense procession, composed of military companies, various orders and societies, several bands of music, and a concourse of horsemen and footmen bearing banners, appropriately inscribed, and sur-

---

*Gazette.

mounted by game cocks, which crowed lustily as they went through the streets. General John M. McCalla, Benjamin Taylor, and Abram Morton were marshals of the day. Jackson rode in an open carriage with Governor Breathitt, who had just been elected by the Democrats. The windows and streets were crowded with people, to whom the President continually bowed as they waved their handkerchiefs and hickory branches, and gave him cheer after cheer. The concourse, from the barbecue, attended the President's levee, which was held that night at Postlethwaite's tavern. On Sunday morning, Jackson attended the First Presbyterian Church, corner of Broadway and Second street, and listened to a sermon from the Rev. Nathan Hall. The house was crowded almost to suffocation, and hundreds were unable to enter. The curiosity to see the determined old hero was intense, and he never walked the streets unaccompanied by a crowd. On his way to church he passed the branch of the United States Bank (now the Northern Bank building), which had just been completed, and was then considered a very fine edifice. An amusing tradition, told with great gusto by old-time Democrats long after the reputed occurrence of the incident, declares that Jackson no sooner saw the bank than he gave it one of his most withering glances, muttering, " By the eternal!" and brought his cane down upon the pavement with a most emphatic rap. The effect was, of course, fatal. Three years from that time the bank ceased to exist. The story indicates the intensity of party feeling at that period. Jackson and his suite left Lexington on horseback the Monday succeeding his arrival, after having been given one of the most enthusiastic receptions ever accorded to a distinguished visitor in Lexington.

CHAPTER LVII.

Cholera—Its Terrible Effects—Incidents—The Lexington Orphan Asylum—First Managers.

THE terrible ravages of the cholera in 1833 will ever keep that fatal year memorable in the annals of Lexington. The devoted city had confidently expected to escape the scourge on account of its elevated position and freedom from large collections of water, but an inscrutable Providence ruled it otherwise. About the 1st of June the cholera made its appearance, and in less than ten days fifteen hundred persons were prostrated and dying at the rate of fifty a day.* An indescribable panic seized the citizens, half of whom fled from the city, and those who remained were almost paralyzed with fear. Intercourse between the town and country was suspended for six weeks; farmers had to abandon their grain to the stock for want of laborers; the market-houses in the city were empty and desolate, and famine would have been added to pestilence but for the great activity of the authorities.

The streets were silent and deserted by everything but horses and dead-carts, and to complete the desperate condition of things three physicians died, three more were absent, and of the rest scarcely one escaped an attack of the disease.† The clergy, active as they were, could not meet one-third of the demands made upon them. Business houses were closed, factories stopped, and men passed their most intimate friends in silence and afar off, staring like lunatics, for the fear of contagion was upon them. The dead could not be buried fast enough, nor could coffins be had to meet half the demand. Many of the victims were consigned to trunks and boxes, or wrapped in the bed-

---

*Davidson's History. †Id.

clothes upon which they had just expired, placed in carts, and hurried off for burial without a prayer being said and no attendant but the driver. The grave-yards were choked. Coffined and uncoffined dead were laid at the gates in confused heaps to wait their turn to be deposited in the long, shallow trenches, which were hastily dug for the necessities of the occasion. Out of one family of nineteen persons, seventeen died.

The hitherto festival day, the Fourth of July, came and found the fearful pestilence abating, and was observed in the churches with mingled tears, thanksgiving, prayers, and supplications. The fell destroyer had swept over five hundred persons out of existence,* and the whole city was in mourning. The terrors and sufferings in Lexington during the fearful cholera season of "'33" no pen can describe.

The Lexington Orphan Asylum originated from the calamities occasioned by the cholera, which left children destitute and unprotected. A public meeting was held at the court-house on Wednesday, July 17, 1833,† to raise funds to establish an asylum for these children. It was largely attended, and $4,400 were collected for the purpose. A house and lot, formerly the property of Dr. James Fishback, and located on Third street, between Broadway and Jefferson, where the asylum has ever since remained, was purchased, and on Wednesday, August 14th, the institution was organized with the following managers, viz: Mrs. Wickliffe, Mrs. Sayre, Mrs. Tilford, Mrs. Gratz, Mrs. Erwin, Mrs. Bruen, Mrs. W. Richardson, Mrs. Putnam, Mrs. Chipley, Mrs. J. Norton, Mrs. Graves, Mrs. Dewees, Mrs. Ward, Mrs. L. Stephens, Mrs. J. W. Hunt, Mrs. Peers, Mrs. Leavy, Mrs. Macalester, Mrs. Ross, Mrs. Geohegan, Miss Edmiston, Miss Barry, Miss M. Merrill, and Mrs. Short. The managers furnished the house, procured a matron and an assistant, and gathered and sheltered all the destitute orphans in the city who had been deprived of both parents.

The institution has no permanent fund, and is supported

---

*City Records.   †Observer and Reporter.

by subscriptions and donations from any who are disposed to aid in the support of orphans.

The citizens of Lexington have never allowed it to languish for want of support, but the most liberal and substantial aid it has received since its establishment, was in 1866, when, by means of public liberality, its buildings were greatly enlarged and improved.

CHAPTER LVIII.

Great Revival—Branch Bank of Kentucky—St. Catharine's Academy—City Schools—James O. Harrison's Administration.

THE fearful cholera experience of Lexington was not without its beneficial effects. Saddened and chastened, the city turned to religion for consolation, and in 1834, a great revival was the result. Meetings were held for nearly a month, and four hundred additions were made to the various churches.*

A branch of the Bank of Kentucky was established in Lexington in 1834, its first board being Benjamin Gratz, Norman Porter, James Hamilton, Stephen Swift, Joseph Bruen, W. H. Rainey, J. G. McKinney, David Heran. After a successful existence of thirty-one years, the institution discontinued business March 13, 1865. The last officers of the bank were Henry Bell, president; H. B. Hill, cashier; H. B. Hill, Jr., teller; E. S. Duncanson, book-keeper; John Carty, D. M. Craig, George Brand, M. P. Lancaster, John G. Allen, directors.

St. Catharine's Academy, on Limestone street, between Winchester and Constitution, was transferred to Lexington in 1834,† from Scott county, Kentucky, where it had been founded four years before. St. Catharine's is a branch of the Roman Catholic Academy of Nazareth, near Bardstown, in this state, and is conducted by sisters of charity. The first superioress of St. Catharine's was Annie Spalding, a relative of the late Archbishop Spalding, and a gifted and accomplished woman. She was poisoned, in 1852, by a negro woman owned by the institution, and who she had

---
*Davidson's History.   †Academy Records.

unwittingly offended. She was buried in the old Catholic Cemetery on Winchester street. The academy has been blessed with success and prosperity since its removal to Lexington, and its buildings have been greatly enlarged and improved. St. John's Academy, located on the same lot, was partially built from the brick that once composed the walls of the old Catholic Chapel in which the celebrated Father Baden officiated for so many years.

The first city school established in Lexington was organized in 1834, and, like the Orphan Asylum, resulted from the devastations of the cholera, which left many children unprovided with means of education. The old Rankin Church, on the corner of Short and Walnut streets, was obtained by the city, and the school was opened on the 1st day of March, 1834, with one hundred and seven pupils in attendance. Joseph Gayle was principal, assisted by his daughter. The school committee appointed by the council consisted of James O. Harrison, William A. Leavy, and Thomas P. Hart. The establishment of this school was largely due to the exertions of Charleton Hunt, then mayor of Lexington. In 1836, William Morton, an old and greatly respected citizen, left a legacy of $10,000 to advance the interests of this school, which is now known as "Morton School (No. 1)." The old school-house was replaced by the present one in 1849. Harrison School (No. 2), named in honor of James O. Harrison, was organized in 1849, and Dudley School (No. 3), so called in honor of Dr. B. W. Dudley, in 1851.

In 1853, the public schools had attained a prosperity, character, and efficiency greater than they ever enjoyed before or since. The number of pupils at that time was one thousand three hundred and seventy-eight,* and so great was the public confidence in the schools, that not a single private school for the education of boys was in existence in the city.† Everybody, without regard to either social or financial distinctions, sent their children to the city schools, and the processions, speeches, festivities, and

---

*City Records. †Id.

crowds which attended the closing exercises of the schools, indicated the interest and pride that were taken in them by the citizens. These gratifying results were mainly due to the energy and enlightened management of James O. Harrison, who was for a long time chairman of the school committee, and who devoted a number of the best years of his life to the upbuilding of the schools. At the present time, the city schools, owing to various causes, are neither as well attended nor as useful as they were twenty years ago.

CHAPTER LIX.

Northern Bank—Joel T. Hart—James Haggin—George Robertson—John Boyle.

THE Northern Bank of Kentucky was founded in June, 1835, at which time it purchased from the United States Bank its branch house in Lexington, its debt and specie, and became the agent to wind up the business of the concern. The first directors of the Northern Bank were B. W. Dudley, D. M. Craig, John Tilford, W. A. Leavy, P. Bain, W. Dunn, B. Gratz, H. Johnson, and W. Barr.

The officers of the bank at the present time are M. C. Johnson, president; A. F. Hawkins, cashier; E. Bacon, teller; J. T. Davidson and C. Y. Bean, book-keepers.

The Northern Bank, ever since its establishment, has used the old United States Branch Bank building, on the corner of Short and Market streets.

The now justly famous Joel T. Hart dates his career from 1835, in which year he settled in Lexington. This great self-made man, who has reflected so much honor upon our city, was born, poor and almost friendless, in Clark county, Kentucky, in 1810. After going to school for a short time, he was compelled, by necessity and the unconscious promptings of his genius, to labor with the stone-mason's hammer, and lived, up to the time of his arrival in Lexington, by building stone fences and chimneys. He was already twenty-five years old when he came to this city, and obtained work in a marble yard, on the corner of Upper and Second streets, where he cut his first letters on a tombstone. His guardian angel, who had thus pushed him one step in advance, placed him full in the path of his great destiny two years after, when he met

Clevenger, a young sculptor from Cincinnati, who discovered in him a fellow artist, and kindly instructed him in his high calling. In a short time, Hart was freed from the weight that held him down. The rough stone-mason had become what he was born to be—a sculptor.

Hart's first studio was in a building connected with, and in the rear of the present residence of Mr. Thomas Bradley, on Second street, and his first effort, as an artist in marble, was a bust of Cassius M. Clay. He soon attracted great attention, and in a short time had made himself famous by superbly executed busts of John J. Crittenden, Andrew Jackson, and Henry Clay. In 1849, Mr. Hart was engaged by the ladies of Richmond, Virginia, to execute the marble statue of Mr. Clay, which now adorns the capitol grounds of that city. He went to Italy, and settled in Florence, where he modeled the statue, and, at the same time, invented two valuable instruments to be used in his art. By means of one of these, the workmen are enabled to transfer the compositions of the sculptor from the plaster to the marble, with a degree of precision utterly impossible by the ordinary method of calipers. By means of the other invention, the form of the living subject may be transferred to the desired material, with an absolute exactitude. As a consequence, therefore, any of the great antique statues may be perfectly reproduced.

He went to London to obtain a patent for his invention, and while struggling to effect his object, suffered the direst extremes of poverty, until he fortunately attracted the attention of some discerning and cultivated gentlemen, who engaged him to make a bust of the noted Dr. Southwood Smith. His success was such as to obtain for him the patronage of the nobility of the realm, and give him a European reputation. Shortly after this, he shipped to America the marble statue of Clay, and also a bronze statue of the same statesman which he had modeled for the city of New Orleans.

Mr. Hart returned from Italy in 1860, and was received by the city of Lexington with every demonstration of respect and honor. At Frankfort, also, he met with distin guished consideration, and the legislature, then in session, appropriated $10,000 to complete the Clay monument in this city, by surmounting it with a statue of Mr. Clay, to be executed by his gifted fellow-townsman, Mr. Hart. A compliment more just or deserved was never more gracefully paid by a state to its greatest artist. But unfortunately the Monumental Association found it necessary to use six thousand dollars of the sum appropriated, to pay expenses already incurred, and the remainder was paid to a stranger for "the statue" which surmounts the Clay monument.

In the fall of 1860, Mr. Hart returned to Florence, Italy, where he still resides. He has never married. He is now known, not only as a sculptor, but also as a philosopher, a poet, a scientist. His poems, many of which have been published anonymously in England and America, are characterized by versatility, and considerable beauty and elegance of style.

Mr. Hart is at present still working upon an ideal group, the "Triumph of Chastity,"* which has engaged his genius for several years, and which, in the opinion of noted foreign and American critics, will be the most perfect achievement of modern art. The conception is entirely original. Cupid, fully armed and equipped, is ignominiously defeated in an attack upon a virgin just arrived at perfect womanhood. The figures are nude. An artist who has seen the group says: "It is scarcely too much to say that, as a carefully studied composition, evincing a thorough knowledge of anatomy and of the subtle laws of form and curvature, there is no modern work which may challenge comparison with the 'Triumph of Chastity.'"

Lexington may well be proud of her great genius, Hart. He is famous throughout the old world and the new. The splendid productions of his chisel drew from his gifted fellow-artist, Hiram Powers, the lofty and generous eulogy, "Hart is the best sculptor in the world."

Judge James Haggin, for many years a distinguished member of the Lexington bar, died of bilious fever, August

---

*Cor. Evening Post.

21, 1835. Judge Haggin was born in 1789, and removed from Mercer county, Kentucky, to Lexington, in 1810. His wife was a Miss McBrayer. Although Judge Haggin never filled any prominent public station but that of judge of the court of appeals with Barry, in 1824, he was none the less known, and his influence during some of the most stirring periods in the political history of the commonwealth was commensurate with his talents, which were of the first order. As a land lawyer, he had no superior in Kentucky, and he was long considered one of the ablest jurists in the western country. Judge Haggin's residence was on the site of the present Hocker school building, on Broadway, between Third and Fourth streets.

Judge George Robertson settled in Lexington on the 4th of July, 1835. His parents were Virginians of Irish descent, and were both endowed with sterling qualities of head and heart. They emigrated to the wilderness of Kentucky, and settled at Gordon's station, in 1779.

Judge Robertson was born in 1790, in that part of the then county of Mercer which is now known as Garrard county. After obtaining a good English education at "neighborhood schools," he spent a year at Transylvania University, and then continued his classical studies under Rev. Samuel Finley, at Lancaster, after which he assisted that gentleman in teaching.

In 1808, he commenced the study of law at Lancaster, under Martin D. Hardin, and in 1809, Judges Boyle and Wallace of the court of appeals granted him license to practice.

At the age of nineteen, he married Miss Eleanor, aged sixteen, a daughter of Dr. Bainbridge, of Lancaster. The young couple commenced life under difficulties. Poor and inexperienced, they suffered and struggled for a time, but the young lawyer was energetic, and in two or three years had a good practice. He worked on, and in 1816, was elected a representative to Congress against strong opposition, and was subsequently twice re-elected without opposition.

While in Congress, he took an active part in the legislation of the nation. He drew and introduced the bill to establish a territorial government in Arkansas. On that bill the question of interdicting slavery was introduced, and elaborately discussed. The restriction was carried by one vote. A reconsideration was had and the bill finally passed, divested of the restriction, by the casting vote of the speaker, Mr. Clay.

He was the author of the present system of selling public lands in lieu of the old system and two dollars minimum; his object being to redeem the West from debt, and promote its settlement and independence. Upon considerations of expediency, the bill was first carried through the senate.

After his retirement from Congress, Governor Adair tendered him the appointment of attorney-general of the state, but he declined it to pursue his profession and secure a competence for his family. In 1822, he was elected a representative to the legislature by the people of Garrard, in view of the all-absorbing and all-exciting relief questions. He was made speaker of the house in 1823, and was re-elected every session afterward while he remained in the legislature, except the revolutionary session of 1824. He remained in the general assembly until the relief contest was settled in 1826–7, and during that memorable period several of his speeches were extensively published. He wrote the celebrated protest of 1824, signed by the anti-relief party in the legislature, and was also the author of the manifesto signed by the majority in 1825–6.

Appointments to the office of governor of Arkansas, and subsequently as minister to Bogota, were tendered him by President Monroe, and the mission to Peru by President Adams, but all were declined. He accepted the office of secretary of state under Governor Metcalfe, and for many years was professor of constitutional law in Transylvania University.

After the rejection of the nominations of Judges Mills and Owsley to the bench of the court of appeals, he was confirmed as a judge of that court, and subsequently commissioned chief justice, which elevated position he held until April, 1843, when he resigned it to return to the bar.

He was called again to the appellate bench in 1854, and there remained for seventeen years, being chief justice most of that time. In the summer of 1872, after more than half a century of public life, Judge Robertson was stricken with paralysis, and on the 5th of September of that year, in the city of Frankfort, he resigned his elevated position under most affecting circumstances, and now in the eighty-second of his age, suffering, but in full possession of all his great mental faculties, he lingers yet a little while on this side the Jordan, in the sunshine of an honored life. He is the last survivor of the stormy and momentous congressional session, which ended in 1821. All of his contemporaries and colleagues of that eventful period—president, cabinet members, senators, and representatives—have gone before him to the mystic land.

Judge Robertson has been a laborious and persistent student, a clear, skillful, and strong speaker, noted for his wonderful command of language, his extensive information, and the power and grasp of his intellect. But it is as a lawyer that he is most distinguished. He studied law as a philosophical system; he mastered it as a science; he investigated, reasoned, and became one of the greatest jurists of this country. In dealing with constitutional questions of magnitude and difficulty, he was at home in the lists with Webster, Clay, and the other giant associates of his life. As a judge, his decisions are consulted and quoted, not only in the United States, but in Europe. This venerable and distinguished citizen of Lexington still lives in the residence he has occupied for many years, on the corner of Mill and Hill streets.

John Boyle, at one time sole professor of law* in Transylvania University, and for sixteen years chief justice of Kentucky, died in 1835, aged sixty-one years. He was born of humble parentage, in Virginia, but married, commenced the practice of law, and began life in Garrard county. He was three times elected to Congress on the Jeffersonian Democratic ticket, was appointed governor of Illinois by President Madison, and commenced his connection with the Kentucky court of appeals in 1809. His great abilities as a jurist may be inferred from the fact that the appointment of associate justice of the Supreme Court of the United States was twice within his grasp, but was declined. At the time of his death he was district judge of Kentucky.

*University Records.

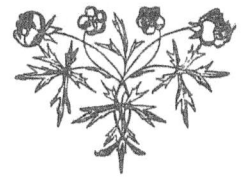

CHAPTER LX.

Hunt's Row—Runaway Negroes and Negro Jails—Thomas A. Marshall.

"Hunt's Row" was built in 1836, and was named by the city council in honor of Charleton Hunt, the first mayor of Lexington. In the summer of this year the "Lexington Ladies' Legion," composed of volunteer emigrants, left for Texas, after having been presented with a stand of colors.

It was not uncommon at this period, and for many years after, for advertisements like the following to appear in the Lexington newspapers. A cut of a negro running, and with his bundle tied to a stick and thrown over his shoulder, always adorned the advertisement:

"Three Hundred Dollars Reward.—Ran away from the subscriber, living near the city of Lexington, on the night of the 4th inst., two negroes, one a bright mulatto boy, named Isaac, about six feet high, about twenty-five years of age, very bushy hair, and very likely; the other, his wife, Celia, about twenty-one years of age, very dark complexion, very likely, and pretty stout built. The man had on a broad-brim black hat, with a beaver cloth overcoat; his other clothing not recollected. The woman's clothing is not known.

"I will give a reward of $10 for each, if taken in this county; $20 each, if taken in any of the surrounding counties; $100 each, if taken in any county bordering on the Ohio river, and $150 each, if taken out of the state, and delivered to me in Lexington, or secured in jail so that I get them, and all reasonable expenses paid."

There were several negro jails, or pens, in Lexington.

where negro slaves were kept, bought, and sold. The old theater on Short street, opposite the residence of J. B. Wilgus, was converted into one. The building now used as the Statesman office, on Short, near Limestone street, was another, as was also the house on Main, between Limestone and Rose streets, now used as a barracks for federal soldiers.

Thomas A. Marshall, son of Humphrey Marshall, the author of a history of Kentucky, settled in Lexington in 1836, and was for a long series of years professor of law in Transylvania University. Judge Marshall was born in Woodford county, Ky., January 15, 1794.* After graduating at Yale he studied law, married a niece of Mrs. Clay in 1816, and moved to Paris in 1819, where he practiced his profession until elected to Congress, in 1831. Judge Marshall was four years in Congress, and the same length of time in the Kentucky legislature. He adhered to the "Old Court" party, and was influential as a Whig leader. In 1835, he was made a judge of the court of appeals, and served in that capacity for twenty-two years, all his terms included. During his judgeship he ignored politics altogether. He removed from Lexington in 1857, and finally settled in Louisville, where he died, April 15, 1871.

Judge Marshall was more eminent as a jurist than in any other respect. Pure, logical, just, and honest, he was peculiarly fitted by nature for high legal station. His decisions are the best monument of his calm greatness. No other man in Kentucky did more to shape the character of our state laws. While residing in Lexington, Judge Marshall lived at the head of Sixth street, on the place lately owned by Mr. John Burch.

---

*Louisville Courier-Journal.

CHAPTER LXI.

Independent Order of Odd Fellows—Friendship, Covenant, and Merrick Lodges — Incorporators — Halls — Lexington Athenæum—Railroad Festival.

THE history of Odd Fellowship, in Lexington, commences with the founding of Friendship Lodge, No. 5, May 6, 1837, just eighteen years after the establishment of the order in the United States. The charter members of this lodge were John Candy, T. J. Harrison, Gabriel Beach, William Wilson, N. P. Long, Abram Spolen, and A. Maydwell.* The lodge was organized in the room in the rear, and on the second floor of the building now known as Whitney & Co.'s drug store, on the corner of Mill and Main streets, and there its meetings were regularly held for several years.

The growth and prosperity of the order was such that, on the 4th of October, 1845, Covenant Lodge, No. 22, was established, its incorporators being R. T. Timberlake, C. C. Norton, Jesse Woodruff, George Stoll, Sen., C. G. Young, W. S. Simpson, Josephus Happy, and W. H. Newberry. The first meeting of this lodge was held in the hall on the corner of Church and Market streets, where the library building now stands.

The corporators of the third and last lodge established, Merrick, No. 31, March 3, 1856, were Daniel W. Young, W. S. Chipley, Edgar A. Brown, Joseph Lanckart, and A. H. Calvin. The organization of this lodge was effected, and its meetings were held in the same building first used by Covenant Lodge.

The meeting places of the Odd Fellows have, at different

---
*I. O. O. F. Records.

times, been in Hunt's row, on Water street, in the old Methodist Church, on Church street, between Upper and Limestone, which was converted into a hall, and in the Medical Hall, where the library now stands. In 1856, the large hall, on the corner of Main and Broadway, was completed. No better indication of the rapid progress of the order in Lexington is seen than the Grand Hall on Main street, between Upper and Limestone, now used by all the lodges in the city. This handsome and commodious edifice was dedicated with impressive ceremonies, in the presence of a large concourse, February 3, 1870, opening prayer by the G. C., John W. Venable, dedication charge by the R. W. G. M., Speed S. Fry, and the oration by P. G. M., M. J. Durham. There is probably no city in the United States where Odd Fellowship is in a more flourishing condition than in Lexington.

The "Lexington Athenæum," a literary association, was established in Lexington, in April, 1838, and used a room in a building in Jordan's row.

On Wednesday, August 29, a festival, in honor of the president and directors of the Cincinnati and Charleston Railroad Company, was given by the citizens of Lexington, at which an address was delivered by General Robert T. Hayne, president of the company.

CHAPTER LXII.

Richard H. Mennifee.

RICHARD H. MENNIFEE, one of the most wonderful men that Kentucky has ever produced, settled in Lexington in 1839. He was born in Bath county, Kentucky, December 4, 1809, and was left an orphan when but four years old, to struggle with poverty and obstacles of the most discouraging kind. Endowed with an ambition second only to his great gifts, he struggled on through a wretched boyhood. He longed for an education, and had succeeded at twelve years of age in entering a school, but was compelled, after a few months, to leave it and act as bar-keeper in a tavern in Owingsville. At fourteen, he obtained some "winter schooling," and, when but a boy of fifteen, he taught a school to get means to prosecute his studies; and thus he struggled and thus he studied until he succeeded in entering Transylvania University, where he made the most astonishing progress. Subsequently, after obtaining some assistance, he studied law with Judge Trimble, and his intense energy and great ability soon gained for him the smiles of fortune.

In the spring of 1832, he was appointed commonwealth's attorney, and, in the fall of the same year, he married the eldest daughter of the distinguished artist, Jouett. He was elected to the Kentucky legislature in 1836, and there exhibited talents of so high an order that he was sent as representative to Congress the next year. He entered Congress an obscure young lawyer; he left it famous, and acknowledged as one of the great men of America. He burst upon his countrymen like a meteor long in darkness, and at once took his own place. His genius and his marvelous eloquence were upon every tongue. At the height of his sudden and deserved fame, he removed to Lexington, and measured his strength at the bar with the greatest legal minds of the state. Business rushed to him; wealth was at his door, and the future seemed ready to repay him for the bitter past. In the fall of 1840 he was engaged in a case of great magnitude, in which Clay and Wickliffe were both employed against him. He exerted himself to the utmost and accomplished wonders; but his mind and body, powerfully overtaxed, never recovered their natural tone. He sank from that time, and died, "with all his blushing honors thick upon him," at the early age of thirty-two. Mr. Mennifee's residence was on the Harrodsburg turnpike, the same now occupied by John B. Huston, and formerly by John C. Breckinridge.

CHAPTER LXIII.

Prosperity of Lexington—Trade and Manufactures—Capital Invested—Captain John Fowler.

By the year 1840, Lexington had almost recovered from the effects of the adverse circumstances that had caused her decline, and was again prosperous. The Lexington and Ohio Railroad was in active operation. Seven turnpikes ended in the city, and there were six lines of stages running, severally, to Cincinnati, Louisville, Nashville, Maysville, Richmond, and Owingsville. Six newspapers were published, viz: Kentucky Gazette, Observer and Reporter, Intelligencer, Independent Press, Christian Preacher, and Transylvania Journal of Medicine.* Seven associations of skilled mechanics were in existence, and were entitled the Lexington Typographical Society, Union Society of Journeymen Saddlers and Trunk-makers, United Society of Cabinet-makers, Hatters' Society, Tailors and Cordwainers' Society, and Master Carpenters' Association. There were in the city eighteen rope and bagging factories, with a capital of $1,300,000, and employing nearly a thousand men;† three wholesale dry-goods and china houses; fourteen retail dry-goods establishments; nine wholesale and retail groceries; five saddler shops; twelve blacksmith shops; one insurance office; twelve restaurateurs; one portrait painter; three dentists; one *native* sculptor; ten tailor shops; one bookbinding establishment; four printing offices; ten taverns; eight barber shops; two renovating establishments; three coach repositories; thirteen doctor shops; nine livery stables; two carriage-making establishments; two bookstores, two gunsmith shops; six silversmiths; one silver

---

*Observer and Reporter. †Directory.

plater; three clothing establishments; four tin and coppersmith shops; eight mantua-making houses; two exchange offices; three cigar factories; three confectioneries; two commission stores; nine boot and shoe stores; three leather stores; two comb factories; three upholstering and mattress makers; one morocco factory; one truss maker; one lottery office; two auction stores; four drug stores; one machine shop; a large number of carpenters; one looking-glass manufactory; one Bible depository; nine law offices; two bath houses; one brush factory; one wheelwright; five woolen factories—four driven by steam; two steam cotton mills; one steam flouring mill; one extensive iron and brass foundry; one large wholesale iron warehouse; three tanyards; one marble yard; six brickyards, manufacturing about five million bricks annually; five hatteries, one of them employing forty or fifty hands, and carried on by steam; and one large brewery, producing about fifteen hundred barrels of malt liquor per year.

The capital invested in the city was: In wholesale dry goods, $200,000; in retail dry goods, $1,200,000; in wholesale groceries, $450,000; in retail groceries, $150,000; in manufacturing establishments, banks, etc., $12,000,000. Total, $14,000,000.

Captain John Fowler, a greatly beloved and respected citizen of Lexington, died August 22, 1840,* at the advanced age of eighty-five. Captain Fowler commanded a company in the Revolutionary war; was the first member of Congress elected from this district, and was for many years postmaster in Lexington. He was one of the best types of the true old Virginia gentleman, and was noted for his mental culture, generosity, refinement, and gentleness. A large procession of military, firemen, benevolent orders, and citizens, followed him to his last resting-place in the old Episcopal Cemetery.

---

*Old Gazette.

CHAPTER LXIV.

John W. Hunt—Thomas M. Hickey—Grand Jury sent to Jail—Financial Distress—Thomas F. Marshall—His Career and Character—The Clay and Polk Contest—Grand Demonstrations—Daniel Mayes—Removal of the "True American"—C. M. Clay.

JOHN W. HUNT, father of F. K. Hunt, died in Lexington, August 21, 1841, aged sixty-eight years. Mr. Hunt was born in Trenton, New Jersey. He came to Lexington at an early day and engaged in the manufacture of hemp, at which he accumulated a fortune. He married Miss Catharine Grosh. Mr. Hunt was for a long time the president of the old Insurance Company, the first bank chartered in Kentucky, and was a liberal patron of the Orphan Asylum. He was a man of rare business capacity, sterling integrity, and decision of character. He died greatly esteemed and respected by his fellow-citizens.

On the 27th of December, 1842, Thomas M. Hickey, another prominent citizen, departed this life. Judge Hickey was born in Lexington of Irish parentage, in October, 1797, and rose to position and usefulness by his own energy and ability. He was educated at Transylvania University, studied law with Judge Haggin and was his partner in practice for some time. In 1828, he was appointed judge of the circuit court by Governor Desha, which position he held for about ten years. He was twice married. His first wife was a daughter of Oliver Keene, and his second the widow of William T. Barry. His mind was specially adapted to close legal investigations, and as a judge he was remarkable for his clear head and fine reasoning powers. An amusing incident is connected with the judge. On one occasion, while the grand jury, of which Mr. Benjamin Gratz was foreman, was making examinations in regard to the existence of gambling-houses in Lexington, two of the witnesses refused to testify. The jury informed the judge of the fact and refused to proceed in the matter unless the witnesses were compelled to answer questions put to them. The judge construed the action of the grand jury as contempt of court and sent them all to jail, where they were kept for a day or two, much to the amusement of the citizens, who nevertheless justified them in their course.

In 1843, Lexington felt the full force of the financial troubles which had been growing in intensity for many years. Bankruptcies multiplied, all improvements were suspended, the court dockets were cowded with lawsuits, and heavy sacrifices of property were incurred by forced sales under execution. It was only after much suffering that business again became settled and prosperous.

That great and brilliant orator and erratic wonder, Thomas F. Marshall, was long identified with the bar and city of Lexington. In 1843, his law office was on the first floor of the Press building, on the corner of Short and Market streets.

Thomas F. Marshall, son of Dr. Lewis Marshall, was born in Frankfort, Ky., June 7, 1801,* though his father's home place was in Woodford county, Ky. His early education was conducted by his mother, after which he was trained by some of the best classical scholars, including his father. He was never sent to college. His intense application to books and study prostrated his health, and it was not until he was twenty-five that he was able to commence his favorite pursuit—the law. After studying for two years under Hon. John J. Crittenden, he was licensed to practice, and settled down in Versailles, the county seat of Woodford; and, in 1832, as the friend of Henry Clay, was sent for the first time to the legislature, where he at once exhibited his astonishing gifts. Impelled by a restlessness which never left him, he removed to Louisville in 1833, intending to devote himself to his profession; for he was,

---

*Barre.

to use his own expression, "steeped in poverty to the very
lips." But he was soon again in political life, and twice
represented the city in the legislature.

In 1837, he ran for Congress against Mr. Graves, the
regular Whig nominee, and was, of course, beaten by an
immense majority. He returned at once to Woodford, was
elected the next year to the legislature, was rejected as
ineligible for want of a full year's residence, but was elected
again without opposition, and the next year also. During
all this time he was the staunch advocate in debate and
with his pen of the slave law of 1832.* He was elected to
Congress from the Ashland district without opposition in
1841. He spoke often in Congress, though but two of his
speeches were fully reported. Disgusted with the manner
in which his first speech was reported, with characteristic
irritability he insulted the reporters, and ordered them "not
to attempt again to pass upon the public their infernal gib-
berish for his English." The reporters revenged themselves by ignoring his speeches and squibbing him in their
letters from Washington. At this session, Mr. Marshall
would not support the Whigs in several important measures, and both voted and argued against Mr. Clay's bank bill.
He contended that the party had departed from its principles, and ridiculed the Tyler administration on the floor, saying that when the history of the country was written, that
administration might be put in a parenthesis and defined
from Lindley Murray, "a parenthesis to be the clause of a
sentence inclosed between black lines or brackets, which
should be pronounced in a low tone of voice, and might be
left out altogether without injuring the sense."

In 1843, he publicly announced his resolution not to support Mr. Clay for the presidency,† and from that time he
either acted with the Democratic party or in some other
connection opposed to the Whigs. In 1845, he ran for
Congress, but was beaten in the Whig stronghold by Hon.
Garrett Davis. Subsequently he raised a troop of cavalry
and served in the Mexican war. He edited the "Old

---
*Barre. †Id.

Guard" in 1850, in opposition to the present constitution; opposed the American party in 1855, and removed to Chicago in 1856, but returned the same year; sojourned in Lexington, and canvassed so energetically for Mr. Buchanan as to again almost destroy his health.

Mr. Marshall spent the most of his time in Lexington during the late war, and from its commencement warmly advocated the cause of the South. So strenuously in fact, that he was, at one time, under arrest in Lexington. The excitements of the war and his own imprudences told rapidly on his shattered constitution, and Mr. Marshall died of disease of the heart and lungs, at his old home in Woodford, on Thursday, September 22, 1864.

In person, Mr. Marshall was tall, very erect, and well proportioned. In the latter part of his life, the hair upon his expansive forehead was thin, his beard heavy, and his fine eyes as full of lustre and of fire as of old.

"Tom" Marshall fought more duels, and said more good things than any great man of his day. Had he been temperate, had he been true and just to himself, and to the high and noble faculties vouchsafed to him by God, he would have fulfilled all the loftiest expectations entertained of him. He would have been one of the master spirits of this country. He was a fine scholar, and his knowledge of the languages in particular, he always kept up. He was thoroughly grounded in the principles of law, and was a very giant at the bar. He was as great a writer as he was a speaker, as the pages of the "Old Guard" will show. His information was immense, and his knowledge of the world's history and of the political history of the United States was simply wonderful. Contrary to a popular fallacy in regard to both himself and Mr. Clay, his speeches were the result of hard study and labor, and not of extempore inspiration.

His eloquence was full of glowing and tropical magnificence and luxuriance, and he painted word pictures upon the minds of men, as Raphael painted upon canvas. While he rarely moved the deepest feelings of the heart, he never failed to excite almost idolatrous admiration. He was sometimes low when he should have been lofty, and often grotesquely humorous, when he should have been great. He was a wild, wayward, and wonderful man of talent and genius. Prentice, his great contemporary, who knew him so well and who resembled him in so many particulars, sums up the character of Thomas F. Marshall in these few, but eloquent words: "The people seemed to think, and so did he, that his greatest powers were wit, humor, fancy, poetry, and eloquence. He had all these, but his chief power was none of these. It was argument, logic—stern, inexorable cast-steel logic. His other powers, great as they were, served but as adornments of the limbs of his giant logic. No orator had greater resources in debate. They were inexhaustible, and rendered him unconquerable. Men think of him and muse upon him as he appeared to them in the long past, and they fancy themselves gazing upon a bright star seen through a golden haze."

The political events of the summer of 1844, in Lexington, will long be remembered by all who participated in the desperate struggle between Clay and Polk, in that memorable presidential campaign. Whigs and Democrats labored faithfully night and day for their standard-bearers, and barbecues, torch-light processions, pole-raisings, and mass-meetings seemed destined to never end. The grandest political demonstrations ever witnessed in Lexington took place in July, of this year. On Saturday, the 20th, an immense procession of Democrats, with music, banners, polk-stalks, military companies, and game "roosters," erected a lofty hickory pole, after which the assembled concourse was addressed by those distinguished orators, John Pope and Thomas F. Marshall.

The Whigs were not to be thus outdone. The Clay clubs of Fayette organized a grand tableaux procession, which marched the next Saturday, with flags flying, drums beating, and men screaming, "Hurrah for Clay!" In this brilliant display, every branch of industry in the county of Fayette and city of Lexington was appropriately represented in wagons decked for the occasion. The chief feature of the day was the presentation of banners to the Clay clubs by the Whig ladies of the community.

Daniel Mayes, long a citizen of Lexington, judge of the circuit court, and professor of law in Transylvania University, died in Jackson, Mississippi, in 1844. He married the widow of Charles Humphreys. In pure law arguments and clear analysis, Judge Mayes had no superior at the Lexington bar of his day.

On the 18th of August, 1845, at a great meeting, in Lexington, of the best citizens of Central Kentucky, irrespective of party, it was resolved that the press and materials of the " True American," an anti-slavery newspaper conducted in Lexington by Mr. Cassius M. Clay, should be sent beyond the confines of the state. A committee was accordingly appointed, which proceeded immediately to safely box up the articles, and ship them to Cincinnati, after which, Mr. Clay was notified of the address of the house to which they had been sent subject to his order, with all charges and expenses paid. Mr. Clay subsequently obtained a judgment for $2,500 against two of the committee, which amount was paid by citizens of Fayette and adjoining counties. The office of the " True American " was located on Mill street, in the rear part of the building now known as Whitney's drug store.

Cassius Marcellus Clay is a son of General Green Clay, and was born in Madison county, Kentucky, October 19, 1810. He was a student at Transylvania University, but graduated at Yale College, in 1832. He has represented Madison and Fayette each in the legislature. In 1839 he removed to Lexington, and on June 3, 1845, issued the first copy of the " True American," devoted to the overthrow of slavery in Kentucky. He commanded the " Old Infantry " in the Mexican War, was captured at Encarnacion, and was a prisoner for some time. On his return home, he was presented with a sword. Subsequently, Mr. Clay was minister to Russia. Mr. Clay is dauntless and unfaltering in whatever he believes is right. He resides at present in Madison county, Kentucky.

CHAPTER LXV.

*War with Mexico—Rolls of Beard's and Clay's Companies—
Incidents—W. Mentelle.*

THE trouble between the United States and Mexico, growing out of the annexation of Texas, resulted in a declaration of war by the Federal Congress, May 11, 1846, and a call for fifty thousand volunteers. Hardly a week after these exciting events, a great war-meeting was held in Lexington, and the organization of a number of companies was commenced. Only two companies, however, were perfected, and these were only accepted on condition of going as mounted infantry. The following are complete lists of the officers and men belonging to the companies, which were commanded respectively by Captains Oliver H. P. Beard and Cassius M. Clay, and were attached to Colonel Humphrey Marshall's regiment:

CAPTAIN BEARD'S COMPANY.—Oliver H. P. Beard, captain; John H. Morgan, first lieutenant; Lowry J. Beard, second lieutenant; T. L. Campbell, first sergeant; A. S. Jouett, second sergeant; N. B. Scott, third sergeant; Edmund Protzman, fourth sergeant; C. F. Coppage, first corporal; Richard Adams, second corporal; Isaac Smith, third corporal; S. O. Berry, fourth corporal; James W. Forsee, first musician, Thomas Bryan, second musician; Isaac Sheppard, blacksmith; James F. Megowan, Calvin C. Morgan, William Weigart, John M. Lowe, James M. Taylor, Edward McCarty, Lawrence Daly, R. P. Whitney, Henry Bitterman, Henry Parrott, Abner Hudgins, James B. Harris, Edward Long, Samuel P. Bascom, George Hampton, A. B. Weigart, Henry Carty, G. W. Carter, Hervey Cummings, H. I. McIntyre, John Dishman, W. W. Bayles, M. W. McCracken, James Mahoney, William Bowman, Ezekiel Twaits, Henry Fox, R. H. Jeter, James Wait,

C. Jackson, M. Barrone, C. Jones, William Rainey, B. Castleman, S. R. Patterson, John Gallegher, A. G. Morgan, J. J. Levasy, J. W. Levasy, Robert Anderson, James Moore, Christopher Tempy, William Thomas, G. W. Runyan, S. E. Roberts, George M. Gorham, James G. Martin, William Fitzpatrick, David Sheppard, James Leonard, John Wise Carver, Sylvester Conover, Samuel Byles, Joseph J. Patterson, Thomas O'Haver, Thomas T. Hawkins, G. W. M. Delph, William Twaits, Samuel Pigg, Eli Estill, John Shelton, G. B. Williams, J. B. Callaghan, James G. Burch.

CAPTAIN CLAY'S COMPANY.—C. M. Clay, captain; Jesse Woodruff, first lieutenant; Geo. M. Brown, second lieutenant; James B. Woodruff, first sergeant; Enoch Bryan, second sergeant; Robert C. Richardson, third sergeant; Samuel F. Wilmott, fourth sergeant; S. Lanckhart, first corporal; J. M. Friday, second corporal; W. H. Mullay, third corporal; James Schooley, fourth corporal; W. D. Radcliffe, farrier; Geo. Mason, musician. Privates—Alfred Argabright, Wm. Beaver, Ambrose Burton, John W. Bell, Henry C. Beaver, David Barry, A. G. Bryan, A. C. Bryan, James Bailey, Geo. W. Benjamin, S. L. Barkley, Hubbard Buckner, Dempsey Carroll, David Curtis, Nathaniel Crouch, B. A. Chapman, J. C. Currie, W. Duke, Charles C. Ellis, Richard L. Ellis, John C. Faulkner, John J. Finch, Henry M. Gaylord, R. M. Gaines, Jr., John Gallagher, Wm. Glass, Henry H. Hillox, Wesley Holley, Harrison Igo, James S. Jackson, Henry C. Jackson, David C. Jones, G. Lanckhart, John W. Letcher, John McMain, James McGuire, James H. Miller, Thomas Maupin, C. E. Mooney, J. L. Merchant, Lewis H. Nicholson, W. S. Prentiss, Thomas Powell, James Poindexter, J. J. Phillips, Sam. E. Rogers, Wm. Ragin, John Richardson, Lewis H. Redman, Wm. Smith, Alexander Sumk, Geo. W. Snyder, Henry Seesill, Wm. Shaw, John Stafford, Geo. Step, John H. Simpson, Charles Taylor, Jos. Thornton, Jackson Taylor, James M. Taylor, Thomas Weigart, Thomas White, Jackson Yarbour, Alfred Young.

On the 4th of June, the volunteers started for Louisville, having accomplished their organization and equipment in less than two weeks. On the day the soldiers bade adieu to Lexington, to which many of them were destined never to return alive, they gathered at Morrison College and were addressed by Professor McCown, and each man was presented with a Bible. The reply to the address was made by the adjutant of the regiment, E. M. Vaughn, who afterward fell so heroically at Buena Vista. The solemn and affecting farewell ceremonies concluded with prayer by the Rev. J. H. Brown, of the Second Presbyterian Church.

On the 9th of June, at Louisville, the companies were mustered into service by the celebrated Colonel George Croghan, and on the 4th of July following, they embarked on the steamer "Bunker Hill" for Memphis, from which place they went overland to Little Rock, and through Texas to Camargo, on the Rio Grande, when they entered Mexico. There we leave them to rejoin them again in our next chapter.

Waldemarde Mentelle, an early resident and greatly respected citizen of Lexington, died June 26, 1846. He was born in Paris, France, in 1769; his father was a member of the French National (scientific) Institute, and was the author of a geography. His family adhered to the cause of their unfortunate sovereigns, Louis XVI and his brave and beautiful queen. Mr. Mentelle and his accomplished wife fled from France at the commencement of the Reign of Terror to escape the savage mob then in power, and, coming to America, settled in Lexington, where they lived until the day of their death. Mr. Mentelle was for many years connected both with the old United States Bank and Northern Bank, and is still well remembered as one of the most amiable, polite, and cultivated gentlemen of the old school. He preserved, to his latest days, all the virtues and manners of the ante-revolution Frenchman.

CHAPTER XLVI.

Battle of Buena Vista—Incidents—The Charge on Marshall's Regiment—Lexington's Dead—Return of the Volunteers—Welcome Home—Honors to the Slain.

THE volunteers from Lexington did not reach Mexico until after the battle of Monterey, owing to unavoidable delays incident to army organization and the error of going by land. No incident worthy of special mention occurred before the battle of Buena Vista, except the capture by the Mexicans of Captain C. M. Clay and ten of his men, at Encarnacion. Lieutenant Jesse Woodruff then took the captain's place and commanded the company from that time until its return home. The Encarnacion prisoners were only released after a long and dreary confinement.

Both of the Lexington companies had a large and glorious share in the bloody and gallantly contested battle of Buena Vista, which occurred on the 22d and 23d of February, 1847, and to their share in the fight we confine ourself. Marshall's regiment occupied the post of honor on the extreme left of the line, on a plateau which had a ravine both in the front and rear of the command. The men dismounted and fought as infantry. It was in this position that Marshall's regiment was charged upon by an overwhelming force of Mexican lancers and hussars. We give Captain Beard's account* of the scene which ensued:

"The enemy came rushing down the hill like so many devils, cursing us, and crying *no quarter!* As soon as we reached our horses we made for the plain, and when we turned the foot of the mountain, we discovered about four thousand lancers at full speed trying to cut us off. It beg-

---
*Letter in Observer and Reporter.

gars all description to relate what followed. We had a deep ravine to cross, with rugged banks to climb, and only one could pass at a time. In ascending, my horse reared back and threw me within fifty yards of the enemy. I succeeded in reaching the opposite bank, however, but was compelled to witness the murdering of six of my best men, without being able to render them any assistance, viz: A. G. Morgan, Clement Jones, Nathaniel Ramey, William Thwaits, Henry Carty, and William Bayles, all of whom died with their faces to the enemy. They fought with desperation, until, overpowered by superior numbers, they were run through with the enemy's lances." In this terrible charge, Adjutant E. M. Vaughn, of Lexington, and private Thomas Weigert, of Captain Clay's company, were killed. Two other gallant sons of Lexington died upon this sanguinary field. The brave Colonel William R. McKee fell badly wounded, but struggled heroically until overpowered by the enemy, who stabbed him to death with their bayonets as he lay upon the ground. Lieutenant-colonel Henry Clay, or "Young Henry," as he was commonly called, having been wounded, was being borne from the field by a detachment of his men—by whom he was greatly beloved—when a discharge of grape-shot from the enemy's batteries killed three of the men, and inflicted another and mortal wound upon him. He commanded his men to leave him and save themselves. They did so. A moment more, and a Mexican lance pierced his bosom, and his heart's blood sealed his devotion to his country.

One of the thousand incidents of the battle has a home interest. The Lexington boys had nothing to eat and but little to drink for two days; but Lieutenant John H. Morgan, afterward the famous cavalry leader of the South, had succeeded in procuring a canteen of water. An officer of an Indiana regiment saw the precious fluid, and, parched with the thirst which then tormented all the army, eagerly offered him "twenty-five dollars for a drink." Morgan shared it with him, remarking that "a Kentuckian never accepted money for water."

After the battle, the Lexington companies sadly gathered

their dead heroes, whose bodies were found covered thick with wounds from Mexican lances. No timber grew near the battle-ground, so the brave volunteers were wrapped in their soldier-blankets and buried in coffins made from the sides and bottoms of army-wagons, and the same material furnished the simple head-boards which bore their names and marked their honored graves. They were buried near the little blood-baptized village of Buena Vista, which then became doubly fraught with mournful interest to Lexington.

The news of the battle was received in Lexington while the circuit court was in session. It was immediately adjourned in respect to the Kentucky slain, and the citizens offered every token of sympathy and regard to the families of the soldiers who had so gloriously fallen.

On the 12th of April, 1847,* a great public meeting was held, at which the following committee on resolutions was appointed, viz: John C. Breckinridge, M. C. Johnson, R. A. Buckner, R. Wickliffe, Sen., Edward Oldham, Waller Bullock, Geo. R. Trotter, J. O. Harrison, Robt. N. Wickliffe, Edward A. Dudley, Jas. L. Hickman, and George B. Kinkead. The committee reported as follows:

"The gallant deeds of our brave sons who shed their blood on the glorious battle-field of Buena Vista, have added additional lustre to the Kentucky character for courage and patriotism, and it is just and proper that their dead bodies should not remain in a foreign country and on an enemy's soil, but that they should be removed to their native land, and rest under the protection of their kindred and friends.

"*Resolved, therefore,* That while the citizens of Lexington and Fayette county rejoice with those who survived that memorable conflict of arms, and congratulate them on its great result, they mourn and sympathize with the friends and families of those who fell in battle, and will take immediate measures to remove their bodies for interment in Kentucky.

"*Resolved,* That Capt. George P. Jouett and Nelson Dud-

---

*City Papers.

ley, Esq., be requested and appointed to proceed to the battle-ground of Buena Vista in Mexico, and bring home the bodies of Col. Wm. R. McKee, Lieut. Col. Henry Clay, Jr., Adjutant Edward M. Vaughn, and Messrs. A. G. Morgan, Wm. W. Bayles, Clement Jones, Nathaniel Ramey, Henry Carty, Wm. Thwaits, and Thomas Weigert."

About the middle of June, 1847, the volunteers returned to Lexington, Captain Clay's company being under the command of Lieutenant Jesse Woodruff. Captain Beard's company went out with seventy-eight men and returned with forty-three. Captain Clay's, which had numbered seventy-five, had fifty-four left. The soldiers were welcomed home by an enthusiastic crowd of citizens and military, and were addressed by Judge George R. Trotter, and soon after their return a grand barbecue was given in their honor. Captain Clay, after a painful and protracted imprisonment, returned in December and was warmly greeted and congratulated.

The bodies of the heroes who had fallen, were tenderly conveyed from their distant resting places to a glory bed prepared for them in the Frankfort cemetery by the commonwealth, whose honor they had so nobly defended.

There, on Tuesday, July 20, 1847, an immense concourse assembled at the spot where now rises the stately and beautiful monument erected to the Kentucky soldiers who fell in the war with Mexico. After appropriate and impressive ceremonies, an oration was delivered by General John C. Breckinridge and an address by Rev. John H. Brown. The remains of the lamented dead were then borne to the graves by the pall-bearers, and after a military salute of three guns by the whole line of infantry and rifles, the ceremonies were concluded by the Masonic fraternity. The bodies were then lowered into the graves, and the most impressive scene of the day transpired. By an apparently impulsive movement, the large body of returned volunteers, headed by Colonel Humphrey Marshall, formed in line, marched around the graves uncovered, and in that way left the grounds with slow and solemn tread, and with sincere sorrow depicted in every countenance. It was a silent, but impressive manifestation of their feelings, which was communicated to all around. Three rounds of blank cartridges were then fired from the whole line, and the burial was completed. It was this solemn and beautiful occasion which inspired the gifted Theodore O'Hara to pen that unequaled martial requiem, the "Bivouac of the Dead," commencing with that sublime stanza:

> "The muffled drum's sad roll has beat
> The soldier's last tattoo;
> No more on life's parade shall meet
> That brave and daring few.
> On Fame's eternal camping ground
> Their silent tents are spread,
> And Glory guards with solemn round
> The bivouac of the dead."

CHAPTER LXVII.

Telegraph—Kentucky Statesman—Cholera—Lexington Cemetery—A. K. Woolley.

In 1848, a telegraph line was established between Lexington and Louisville, and the first message was flashed over the wires on the 6th of March of that year.

The Kentucky Statesman, a Democratic newspaper, was established by a company in Lexington, and B. B. Taylor became its first editor. The first number of the paper appeared October 6, 1849. The Statesman existed about thirteen years.

The cholera appeared in Lexington again in 1849, and a number of deaths resulted from it.

A revision of the State constitution was demanded by the people in 1849, and a convention was accordingly ordered for that purpose. The delegates elected from Fayette county were James Dudley and Robert Nelson Wickliffe. The convention assembled in Frankfort, and after three months' discussion and consultation, a new form of government was produced and the convention adjourned temporarily until the people pronounced upon it.

Though an act was passed by the legislature in February, 1848, incorporating the Lexington Cemetery, it was really not established until the year following. At an accidental meeting of Messrs. M. T. Scott, Benjamin Gratz, M. C. Johnson, and Richard Higgins, on the 23d of January, 1849, it was resolved that each one use every exertion to obtain a sufficient sum by subscription for the purpose of purchasing a suitable site for a cemetery and for the inclosing and laying out of the same. Their efforts were successful, and on February 12, 1849, the original charter was amended with the following gentlemen as incorporators, viz:

Benj. Gratz, M. T. Scott, M. C. Johnson, Richard Higgins, S. Swift, Joel Higgins, David A. Sayre, John Tilford, A. T. Skillman, E. K. Sayre, Robert Wickliffe, T. Hemingway, John W. Tilford, John Lutz, D. M. Craig, A. F. Hawkins, Benjamin Warfield, Robert J. Breckinridge, E. Warfield, G. W. Sutton, John Brand, H. T. Duncan, and Edward Macalister.

Shortly after the passage of this act, the beautiful woodland of Thomas E. Boswell, containing forty acres, and included in the present cemetery property, was purchased for $7,000.

The grounds were rapidly improved, and, on the 25th of June, 1850, the cemetery was solemnly dedicated. The business houses of the city were closed, and an immense procession, composed of the Masonic bodies, Odd Fellows, Sons of Temperance, societies of Transylvania University, and citizens in carriages and on foot, proceeded to the cemetery. An opening prayer, by the Rev. Dr. Miller, of the Methodist Church, was followed by an ode, composed for the occasion by Professor P. S. Ruter, of Transylvania University, and concluding with this stanza:

> "O thou God! our Friend and Father!
> May the names these grave-stones bear,
> When we all shall rise together,
> In thy Book of Life appear."

The dedication sermon was by R. J. Breckinridge, pastor of the First Presbyterian Church, and the closing prayer was delivered by Rev. E. F. Berkley, of the Episcopal Church.

Under the management of Superintendent Bell, the Lexington Cemetery has grown more and more lovely each succeeding year, until now, in point of beauty, it has no superior in the United States. There many brave Confederate and Federal soldiers sleep their last sleep, and there repose a host of Kentucky's greatest and best children.

Judge Aaron K. Woolley was one of the victims of the cholera of 1849. He was born in New Jersey, and, after completing his education at West Point, settled in Lexington, and married a daughter of Robert Wickliffe, Sen. He represented Fayette in the legislature in 1834; was for some time judge of the circuit court, and also professor in the law college of Transylvania University. He was a good lawyer and a fine speaker, possessed of a strong, clear intellect, and gifted with fine conversational powers. He died aged about fifty years.

CHAPTER LXVIII.

Population—New Constitution—County Court—B. F. Graves —R. Wickliffe, Jr.

The population of Lexington in 1850 was seven thousand nine hundred and twenty.

The constitution framed by the convention of 1849, was approved by the people of Kentucky at the May election of 1850, and, in June following, the convention reassembled, and proclaimed the present constitution to be the fundamental law of the state. The population of Fayette county at this time was twenty-two thousand seven hundred and thirty-five. In 1850, Benjamin F. Graves became county judge, being the first judge elected in Fayette under the present constitution of Kentucky.

Judge Graves was born in Fayette county, Kentucky, February 16, 1802. His father, John C. Graves, a Virginian, was one of the earliest settlers of this county, having immigrated to it in 1781. In early life, Judge Graves was engaged in the hat, fur, and tobacco trade. He was frequently elected a member of the city council. While serving in this capacity, a subscription was asked of the city for Transylvania University, and by him was made the proposition that the University should give the city fifty-five scholarships. The proposition was carried, and there are to-day numbers of young men in this and adjoining states, who, through his instrumentality, were enabled to fit themselves for the positions of honor and trust they now occupy.*

The best index to his character is the fact that he commenced the study of law at the age of forty, per-

---

*Sketch.

severed under many discouragements, and in due time was admitted to the bar. In 1859, he was elected mayor of Lexington. He has been four times elected judge of the county court, and if he completes his present term, will have been judge for sixteen years. Judge Graves is a man of no ordinary ability and character. Fayette county will never have a more faithful judge.

Judges County Court.—1850, B. F. Graves; 1854, B. F. Graves; 1858, C. D. Carr; 1862, C. D. Carr; 1866, B. F. Graves; 1870, B. F. Graves.

Robert Wickliffe—son of Robert Wickliffe, Sen., the able pioneer land lawyer—died August 29, 1850, at the early age of thirty-five. R. Wickliffe, Jr., graduated at Transylvania University, studied law, represented Fayette in the legislature, and was *charge d' affaires* to Sardinia from the United States. He worked hard at his profession, and became a good lawyer and an effective speaker, but excelled as a scholar, being specially accomplished in the ancient and modern languages. Mr. Wickliffe was a man of unusually fine personal appearance. He was summoned to the great beyond in his early manhood, when his life seemed most full of promise.

CHAPTER LXIX.

Railroads—Lexington and Danville—Maysville and Lexington—Lexington and Covington.

THE railroad subject interested Lexington and Fayette county in 1851. On the 22d of March, $200,000 was voted to the Lexington and Danville Railroad, and the same amount to the Maysville and Lexington road. The first directors of the last-named road were Henry Waller, J. W. Cochran, F. T. Hord, A. J. January, W. S. Allen, and Christopher Shultz. The first train, from Lexington to Paris, went over this road December 22, 1853. For years no work was done on the Lexington and Maysville road, and the only part of the road completed, viz: from Lexington to Paris, was leased and finally purchased by the Kentucky Central Company.

The sum of $200,000 was voted by Lexington and Fayette to the Lexington and Covington Railroad, September 6, 1851. The road was completed from Cincinnati to Paris by the fall of 1854, when the first through train from Cincinnati arrived in Lexington. This road was advocated as far back as 1841.

CHAPTER LXX.

Visit of Scott and Wool—Lexington and Big Sandy Railroad—Failure and Revival of the Road—John C. Breckinridge—Funeral of Henry Clay.

GENERALS WINFIELD SCOTT and Wool arrived in Lexington September 29, 1852, and during their brief stay addressed a large crowd of citizens. This was during the political campaign which resulted in the election of Pierce for president, General Scott being the Whig candidate.

In January, 1852, the Lexington and Big Sandy Railroad Company was incorporated by the Kentucky legislature, and the following persons were appointed to receive subscriptions to the capital stock: Robert Wickliffe, Thomas B. Megowan, D. C. Payne, Jacob Hughes, and Thomas Hughes, of Fayette county; Joseph H. Richard, A. Trumbo, John W. Barnes, M. R. Conner, and John W. Richards, of Bath county; B. J. Peters, W. H. Smith, Peter Everett, Joseph Bondurant, and Burwell S. Tipton, of Montgomery county; George W. Crawford, R. G. Carter, Jackson B. Ward, John N. Hord, and D. K. Wies, of Carter county; William Hampton, John Culver, William T. Nicholls, William Geiger, and Hugh Means, of Greenup county.

The company was organized with R. A. Apperson as president, and on the 18th of September, 1852, the city of Lexington subscribed $150,000 to it. Ground was broken at Cattlesburg, Saturday, November 19, 1853, and the work was proceeded with. In the summer of 1854, application was made by the company for the issuing of the bonds of the city of Lexington for $100,000, which was refused, on the ground that the railroad company had not complied with the conditions of its contract. The company instituted proceedings in the circuit court, which ordered the issuing of the bonds, which was done July 6, 1854, under protest by the city authorities. Subsequently the company failed, the whole amount was lost, work ceased on the road, and in 1860 it was sold to a few gentlemen for $60,000.

For many years the whole project was substantially abandoned, but was finally revived under the charter of the present Elizabethtown, Lexington and Big Sandy Railroad Company, and on the 2d of August, 1869, Fayette county and the city of Lexington each subscribed $250,000 to its stock, the property and rights of the western division of the old company were merged in the new one, work was again commenced on the road in 1871, and on March 2, 1872, twenty years after the chartering of the original company, the first rail was laid on Water street, in Lexington. The road is now completed to Mt. Sterling, and its affairs and prospects are most satisfactory.

General John C. Breckinridge, the vice-president of the Elizabethtown, Lexington and Big Sandy Railroad Company, was born near Lexington, January 21, 1821. He was educated at Centre College, graduated at the Transylvania law school, commenced the practice of his profession in Lexington, and married Miss Birch, of Georgetown, Kentucky. He served as major in the Mexican war, has been a member of the legislature, representative and senator in congress, vice-president of the United States, and major-general and secretary of war of the late Confederate States. The brilliant career of this distinguished Lexingtonian, in the forum, in the field, and in the councils of the nation, indicate the rare gifts and great endowments of the man.

Henry Clay died in Washington City, Tuesday, June 2, 1852. The sad news was at once dispatched to Lexington, and immediately upon its reception the bells were tolled, the business houses were closed, badges of mourning appeared on every side, and all ceased from their usual avocations.* The mayor immediately issued a proclamation for a public meeting of the citizens, which was accordingly held in the court-house the next day, for the purpose

---

*Observer and Reporter.

of giving expression to their feelings of sorrow for the loss of their distinguished fellow-citizen, to make arrangements for the reception of his earthly remains, and to perform such other acts as were deemed worthy of the occasion.

The meeting was called to order by Mayor E. W. Dowden, and on his motion, Dr. Benjamin W. Dudley was appointed chairman, and Benjamin Gratz, secretary.

The meeting was opened with an appropriate prayer by the Rev. William M. Pratt, of the Baptist Church. Judge George Robertson then rose and offered some eminently appropriate resolutions, which he accompanied with a brief but eloquent speech, in reference to the great loss which had been sustained in the death of Mr. Clay. The question was then taken, and the resolutions were unanimously adopted.

During the meeting, initiatory steps were taken toward the erection of a monument to Mr. Clay in the Lexington Cemetery, and the following committee was appointed to effect that object, viz: H. T. Duncan, M. T. Scott, Dr. E. Warfield, Leslie Combs, H. B. Hill, John McMurtry, G. B. Kinkead, Richard A. Buckner, J. R. Desha, Willa Viley, John C. Breckinridge.

The committee appointed to repair to Washington and accompany the body home was composed of George Robertson, H. T. Duncan, E. P. Johnson, R. Pindell, D. C. Wickliffe, Henry Bell, James A. Grinstead, H. C. Payne, Thomas S. Redd, Charles B. Thomas, C. C. Rogers, A. Throckmorton, W. W. Worsley, and A. G. Hodges.

Messrs. B. Gratz, M. C. Johnson, E. W. Dowden, H. C. Pindell, J. B. Tilford, J. O. Harrison, W. S. Chipley, S. D. McCullough, William A. Dudley, Thomas G. Randall, F. K. Hunt, E. Oldham, and John R. Dunlap were appointed a committee of arrangements for the reception and interment of the remains.

A resolution, offered by Major S. D. McCullough, requesting the ministers of the various religious congregations in Lexington and Fayette county to deliver appropriate addresses on the death of Mr. Clay, at their several places of worship, on the following Sunday, was unanimously adopted, as was also a motion by Dr. S. M. Letcher to transmit the proceedings of the meeting to Mrs. Clay. The meeting then adjourned.

The body of the illustrious orator was detained in all the larger cities through which it passed, *en route* to Lexington, that the highest honors might be paid it, and it was not until the evening of Friday, the 9th of July, that it arrived in Lexington, accompanied by the senatorial committee, consisting of Messrs. Underwood, Jones, of Tennessee, Cass, Fish, Houston, and Stockton.

Mr. Underwood, the chairman of the committee, after a brief address, which was replied to by Chief Justice Robertson, delivered the body into the care of the Lexington committee. A procession was then formed, headed by a cavalcade of horsemen, preceding the hearse to Ashland. The old home was reached, and the silent mourners moved through the grounds, guided by torches, and they laid him reverently under the roof of the dwelling whose name he had made a household word. The Clay Guard, of Cincinnati, watched all the night through beside his remains.

Long before daylight on the memorable funeral day, Saturday, July 10, 1852, crowds of people poured into Lexington by every avenue to the city. All the roads were opened free to the public, and every hospitality was extended to strangers. Soon the largest crowd of people ever assembled in Lexington was gathered together—so immense, in fact, that it was estimated at one hundred thousand souls.*

At nine o'clock A. M., the funeral escort, composed of the committee of arrangements, committee of the senate of the United States, committees from other states accompanying the body, committee of the city of Lexington sent to receive the body, the Masonic fraternity, and pall-bearers, formed on Main street, opposite the court-house, under the direction of Marshals John R. Allen, George W. Brand, R. J. Spurr, and E. L. Dudley, and from thence proceeded to Ashland, where a large crowd had already

---

*Louisville Journal.

gathered. On the porch, in front of the door of the statesman's old residence, and resting on a bier cushioned with fragrant and beautiful flowers, was the coffin inclosing his mortal remains, and all around it, and upon it, were the floral and evergreen offerings of every place on the route, from the capital of the nation to Lexington. The Rev. Edward F. Berkley, then rector of Christ's Church (Episcopal), in Lexington, delivered the funeral oration. He was equal to the occasion, and the effort was a splendid one. He commenced his discourse with the following beautiful words : "A nation's griefs are bursting forth at the fall of one of her noblest sons. A mighty man in wisdom, in intellect, in truth, lies in our presence to-day, inanimate and cold, and the voice which was ever raised in behalf of truth and liberty is silenced forever." After the sermon, an address from the young men of Cincinnati was then delivered by the chairman of the committee to Governor Underwood, to be handed to Mrs. Clay.

The concourse was then dismissed with a benediction, and the body was placed in a hearse beautifully decorated with black cloth and crape, surmounted with a silver urn and eagle, and drawn by six white horses. The funeral escort was formed under the direction of the chief marshal, General Peter Dudley, and it, together with the relatives of Mr. Clay, the officiating clergyman, and the assembled multitude, returned to the city, and took their places in the grand funeral procession, which was formed on Main street by the chief marshal, assisted by his aids, H. C. Pindell and W. J. Talbot, and moved to the Lexington Cemetery in the following order, viz :*

Marshals J. R. Dunlap and O. P. Beard.
Military in sections of six, in advance of the procession, with reversed arms, muffled drums, colors furled, and draped in mourning.
Officers of the Army and Navy of the United States.
Chief Marshal and Aids.

---

*Observer and Reporter.

Committee of Arrangements.
Marshal Postlethwaite.
Committee of the Senate of the United States.
Committees from other States accompanying the body.
Committee of the city of Lexington sent to receive the body.
Marshal C. W. Kennedy.
Masonic Fraternity.
CORPSE AND PALL-BEARERS.
Pall-bearers.

B. W. Dudley,	Benjamin Gratz,
M. T. Scott,	D. Vertner,
George Robertson,	Chilton Allan,
E. Warfield,	R. Hawes,
Charles Carr,	Garrett Davis,
Roger Quarles,	C. S. Morehead.

Family of Deceased, and officiating Clergyman.
Reverend Clergy of all denominations.
Marshal C. W. Dudley.
Governor and Heads of Departments of the State of Kentucky.
Committee of cities, towns, and counties of the State of Kentucky.
Marshal S. D. Bruce.
Mayor and Council of the city of Lexington.
President and Directors of Lexington Cemetery Company.
Trustees and Faculty of Transylvania University.
Marshal C. D. Carr.
Judges, Members of the Bar, and Officers of the Fayette Circuit Court.
Judges of the Superior and Interior Courts of Kentucky and Officers.
Judges of the United States Courts and Officers.
Members and ex-Members of the Congress of the United States.
Marshal Silas Kenney.
Independent Order of Odd-Fellows, in sections of six.
Sons of Temperance, in sections of six.
Marshals R. W. Bush and M. B. Gratz.

Fire Companies, in sections of six.
Members of the Senate and House of Representatives of
the State of Kentucky.
Teachers of Schools.
Marshal Isaac Shelby.
Citizens on foot, in sections of six.
Marshals Clifton Weir and R. Todhunter.
Citizens and Strangers in carriages, two abreast.
Marshals Robert Bullock and J. Shropshire.
Citizens and Strangers on horseback, in sections of four.

The procession was one of extraordinary proportions and impressiveness. Every drum, flag, banner, and emblem was draped in mourning. The marshals wore white scarfs and a black rosette, and a streamer of crape floated from each hat. The sables of woe were exhibited everywhere, but the decorations were particularly elaborate and beautiful upon Cheapside and Main streets. Every business house was closed, festooned and garlanded with black. Across Main street, at the intersection of Mill, an immense golden eagle, tastefully draped, was swung high in the air, and mourning banners and garlands floated down almost to the heads of passers-by, and waved gently and sadly in the breeze. The streets, windows, house-tops, and every available place of observation were densely packed with spectators, but good order and a decorous silence prevailed while the honors were being paid to the illustrious dead. The firing of minute guns and the tolling of bells signaled that the procession was put in motion. It moved slowly through the silent street to the sound of beautiful but mournful music; sable plumes nodded, a myriad of bayonets and ornaments glittered in the sunlight, and thus, with tens of thousands of his sorrowing friends about him, was Henry Clay borne to his rest. On the arrival of the procession at the Lexington Cemetery, the exquisite and impressive burial service of the Episcopal Church, of which the great orator was a member, was read, after which the Masonic fraternity took charge of the body, and deposited it in the public vault, in accordance with the ancient forms and touching ceremonies of their order. During all of these last solemn rites, the tears of family and friends and mourning multitudes were falling, and the soft tolling of bells, and the sad booming of minute guns, sounded in the distance. When the mortal remains of the Sage of Ashland were hidden from sight, the procession returned to the shrouded city in its original order, and after reaching the court-house, each committee and company filed off, and quietly dispersed. Thirty-one guns, fired at the setting of the sun, completed the obsequies.

CHAPTER LXXI.

City Lighted with Gas — Sayre Institute — "Old King Solomon" — "Know Nothings."

AFTER several years discussion, gas works were at last established in Lexington, and, in 1853, the city took $10,000 worth of stock in the company. The city was lighted with gas, for the first time, on the night of Wednesday, July 27, 1853, and lard-oil lamps went out of use, greatly to the joy of the citizens, in general, and the policemen, in particular.

The Sayre Female Institute, on Limestone street, established by David A. Sayre, was organized November 1, 1854, under Rev. H. V. D. Nevius. Subsequently, that accomplished educator, the beloved and lamented Prof. S. R. Williams, became principal, and retained the position, with increasing reputation, for many years. It is at present in charge of Prof. H. B. McClellan, a scholar well fitted for the position.

"Old King Solomon," one of the kindliest souls, and one of the quaintest and most noted of Lexington institutions, died November 27, 1854, and not a few were saddened when they heard that he was gone. William Solomon, to call him by his proper name, was born in Virginia, in 1775, and always boasted that he and "Henry," as he familiarly called the Sage of Ashland, had been boys together. He admitted, though, that "Henry" had risen somewhat higher than he—the "King" was a cellar-digger. Nobody knew when "King Solomon" came to Lexington—he seemed to have always been here; and no one ever saw him with new clothes—his "rig," as he called his clothes, appeared to have been old from the start. His same old hat always had the same old mashed look, and his pants were about as close-fitting as the hide on a rhinoceros. He was never known to catch cold from washing his face; his hair managed itself, and the button and button-hole of his shirt collar never met long enough to make the slightest acquaintance. "Old King Solomon" was never so happy as when, half-seas over, and provided with the stump of a cigar (he never had a whole one), he was allowed to smoke in peace upon a comfortable rock-pile. But with all these eccentricities of genius, "Old Solomon" was none the less honest, upright, and industrious; and he had a stout and pitying heart withal, for many a grave he dug during the awful cholera days of 1833, when many a more boastful and better-dressed man had fled in terror from the city.

A more everlasting, incorruptible, and Jackson-defying Whig than "Old King Solomon" never lived; he clung to "Henry" through thick and thin, and no one ever mourned him more sincerely. He was one of the most independent voters in Fayette. A candidate, on one occasion, gave him some money and advised him to go and vote. Old Solomon pocketed the money, and straightway did vote, but voted against his benefactor, who was not of his party and principles.

At one time—how it happened, we know not—"King Solomon" was very strangely and unfortunately mistaken for a vagrant, and was arrested and sold to an old negro woman for eighteen cents. He proved to be a good investment, for he brought her in seventy-five cents per day.

How Solomon got to be a "King," happened in this wise: One day, when he was not as sober as a judge, he was employed to trim a tree in the court-house yard. He got astride of a big limb, and, while in a meditative mood, he trimmed it so closely and so deeply between himself and the trunk of the tree, that it snapped off, and landed him suddenly and short of breath on the ground. The rare wisdom he displayed as a trimmer gained for him at once the title of "King Solomon," after the wisest man that ever lived.

When the quaint old soul went to his rest, he was tenderly interred in the Lexington Cemetery. Fortunately, while he was in the heyday of his attractions, an admirable picture of him was painted by Colonel Price. He was induced to sit for it by being provided with the wherewith to make himself comfortable on his favorite seat—a rock-pile.

During the years 1855 and 1856, popular attention was largely directed to the "Know Nothing," or American party, which came into existence in 1853. The rise and fall of the "Know Nothings" was attended with great excitement, during which such party names as "Say Nichts," "Dark Lanternites," and "Blood Tubs" prevailed.

CHAPTER LXXII.

Lexington Rifles--Rosa's Poems--Ceremonies Incident to Laying the Corner-stone of the Clay Monument—Description of the Monument.

THE "Lexington Rifles," organized in 1857, was the first military company in Kentucky to report to the governor as a part of the state guard in 1860. The armory of the "Rifles" was in an upper story of the building lately replaced by the bank, on the corner of Main and Upper. The first officers of the company were: John H. Morgan, captain; Chas. H. Brutton, first lieutenant; J. H. Shropshire, second lieutenant; Joseph R. Gross, third lieutenant; Richard Cox, ensign; C. W. Kennedy, first sergeant; R. C. Morgan, second sergeant; Hiram Reece, third sergeant; Harry Browne, fourth sergeant; Wm. M. Yates, first corporal; Jas. Dudley, second corporal; C. H. Dobyns, third corporal; H. A. Saxton, fourth corporal; Thos. Wilson, quartermaster.

A volume of poems of much beauty, tenderness, and power was published, in 1857, by Mrs. Rosa V. Jeffrey. In 1870, her "Daisy Dare," appeared. Mrs. Jeffrey was born at Natchez, Miss., but has spent the most of her life in Lexington.

On the 4th of July, 1857, the corner-stone of the Clay monument, in the Lexington Cemetery, was laid with imposing ceremonies under the auspices of the Monumental Association, which consisted of James O. Harrison, H. T. Duncan, Henry Bell, Benjamin Gratz, and H. B. Hill. The day was beautiful, business was suspended, the city was crowded with spectators, and the houses leading to the cemetery were adorned with flowers, evergreens, flags, streamers, and banners.

The procession moved from headquarters, opposite the Phœnix Hotel, amid the thunder of artillery and the enlivening music of four splendid bands.* The Masonic fraternity, to whom the ceremonies were intrusted, and the Odd Fellows were out in full dress regalia. The Union and Lafayette fire companies of Louisville, together with all the Lexington companies, were present. The military organizations in the procession were the Guthrie Grays and Continentals, of Cincinnati; an artillery company from Frankfort; the Falls City Guards, of Louisville; National Guards, of St. Louis; Independent National Guards, of Indianapolis; City Guards, of Baltimore, and the Madison Guards, of Richmond, Ky.

The family carriage, presented to Mr. Clay, in 1833, by the citizens of Newark, N. J., which was the only one admitted into the cemetery grounds, was ornamented with white funeral plumes and wreaths of flowers and evergreens. It was occupied by Aaron Dupuy, an old negro servant of Mr. Clay, who had been in his service for many years. In the back seat was a bust of Mr. Clay and an engraving of his leave-taking in the senate.

Long before the procession arrived at the cemetery, a large concourse had assembled to witness the interesting ceremonies.

Upon the platform, near the foundation of the monument, were the members of Mr. Clay's family, consisting of Thos. H. Clay and James B. Clay and their families, Isaac Shelby and family, and others.

The following distinguished gentlemen were observed on and in the vicinity of the platform: John C. Breckinridge, Vice-President of the United States; Governor Morehead, Senator Crittenden, Hon. James Guthrie, Hon. Garrett Davis; Ex-Gov. Trimble, of Ohio; Chief Justices Geo. Robertson and T. A. Marshall; J. B. Huston, Speaker of the House of Representatives of Kentucky; Hon. James Harlan, Attorney-General; Hon. Richard Hawes; Dr. Green, of the Normal School; President Bartlett, of the American

---

*Association Pamphlet.

Council of the United; States Hon. Oscar F. Moore, of Ohio; Roger W. Hanson, Esq.; Zophar Mills, Esq., of New York, and the president and directors of the Clay Monument Association.

The Masonic fraternity occupied the inclosure where the ceremonies were performed, while the military, firemen, and the rest of the procession, selected such positions in different portions of the grounds as they preferred.

The president of the association assigned to the M. W. Grand Master of the Grand Lodge of Kentucky, Mr. T. N. Wise, the duty of laying the corner-stone.

In the stone was placed a box hermetically sealed; in a glass jar, a history of the occasion, with the names of the president and vice-president of the United States, the governor of Kentucky, the names of the officers of the Grand Lodge of Kentucky, and of the president and directors of the Clay Monumental Association; a copy of each of the papers of the city of Lexington; a picture of Cincinnati in 1802, published in the Cincinnati Gazette; also a parchment prepared by the Cincinnati Guthrie Grays, in testimony of their appreciation of the man who preferred to be right rather than to be president of the United States; a medallion in copper, struck from the die of the Clay gold medal, presented by the Clay Festival Association of New York, with a copy of all the festive songs and odes sung and read before that association for the last twelve years, and giving a history of that association; also a beautiful medallion likeness of Mr. Clay, by C. Younglove Haynes, Esq., of Philadelphia, together with copies of Philadelphia papers from the same gentleman, with coins of the present day (American), in gold, silver, and copper; a Bible, and other articles.

The stone was laid to its place, and pronounced by the grand master well formed, true, and trusty, when corn, wine, and oil were poured upon it, and the ceremonies concluded by prayer. During and preceding the ceremonies, the Newport United States band discoursed the sweetest music, and salutes were fired.

After laying the corner-stone, the procession was reformed and proceeded to the fair grounds, whose vast amphitheater was soon filled to repletion with the gathered beauty, intellect, and worth of Kentucky.

After prayer by Rev. E. F. Berkley, of the Episcopal Church, Dr. R. J. Breckinridge, orator of the day, delivered an address in every way worthy its great subject and the occasion. Dinners and picnics in the beautiful groves followed, and at four o'clock there was a grand review of the military by Governor Morehead, the Newport band discoursing beautiful music, and the regular proceedings of the day closed.

The Clay monument,* some 120 feet in height, is built of the magnesian limestone of this state, which resembles very much the famed Caen stone of Normandy, and is a column modeled after the Corinthian style of architecture, consisting of a stereobate, pedestal base, shaft and capital, the whole surmounted by a statue of the statesman.

The stereobate, or subbase, some 20 feet in height, and 40 feet square, is in the Egyptian style, plain and massive, and has its appropriate cornice of very simple character throughout its whole circuit, broken on each side around a projecting facade in the same style, but of more elaborate finish. In the center of the southern face is an entrance to a vaulted chamber, of the dimensions 12 by 24 feet, and 16 feet high in the center, lighted from above by heavy plate glass fixed in bronze frames in such manner as to be unseen from without. The chamber is of polished marble of Kentucky, appropriately finished as a receptacle for sarcophagi, and, if desirable, a life-size statue. The opening is closed by a screen of bronze. The remaining space within the subbase is a closed vault, access to which is had by means of a doorway, ordinarily closed with masonry.

Above the stereobate or subbase is the pedestal of the column, divided horizontally into two members, each with its base and cornice. The lower one is $8\frac{1}{2}$ feet in height, and the upper 14 feet in height. The faces of both mem-

---

*Description from Association Pamphlet.

bers of the pedestal are in sunk panel, to be filled ultimately with bas reliefs in bronze, if desirable.

Above the pedestal rises the shaft, which, with the base and capital, is 69 feet in height; the lower diameter being 6 feet 8 inches, and the upper 5 feet 10 inches, built solid. The shaft, instead of the ordinary 24 flutes, with their intermediate fillets, is composed of a cluster of thirteen spears (one for each of the "Old Thirteen"), the heads of which, of bronze, interlaced and grouped with corn leaves and appropriate national emblems, form the capital of the column, conformable, in outline and proportion, to the best examples of the order. On the abacus of the capital rests an acroter of bronze, of a parabolic contour, and formed of ash and ivy leaves, serving as a pedestal to the statue.

CHAPTER LXXIII.

Sons of Malta—M. T. Scott—Change in City Government—Robert Wickliffe, Sen.

HELMET LODGE, No. 1, Sons of Malta, was organized in Lexington, April 3, 1858, and held its meetings in an upper story of the building, on the corner of Main and Mill streets, known as Whitney & Co.'s drug store.

Matthew T. Scott, who filled for many years the position of president of the Northern Bank of Kentucky, died in Lexington, in the seventy-second year of his age, August 21, 1858. He was a man of rare financial sagacity and of irreproachable integrity, and had been identified with the banking interests of Kentucky for more than forty years.

In 1859, the Democrats obtained control of the city government of Lexington, after it had been in the hands of their variously-named opponents for nearly a quarter of a century.

Robert Wickliffe, Sen., died at his residence in Lexington, September 1, 1859, in the sixty-sixth year of his age. Mr. Wickliffe came from Virginia at an early day, and by his energy, persistent labor, and ability, gained a conspicuous position at the bar. He repeatedly represented Fayette in the legislature, was chairman of the board of trustees of Transylvania University, filled other important public offices, and was for half a century one of the leading spirits in state politics. Mr. Wickliffe was one of the shrewdest and ablest land lawyers in Kentucky, and as such made himself rich. He was twice married. His first wife was Margaretta Howard, and his last, Mary O. Russell. He was buried at "Howard's Grove," Fayette county, Kentucky. Mr. Wickliffe resided on the corner of Second and Jefferson streets, where General William Preston now lives.

CHAPTER LXXIV.

Population—Parties—St. John's Academy—Lexington Chasseurs—List of Officers and Privates.

THE population of Lexington, in 1860, was nine thousand five hundred and twenty-one, and that of Fayette county, twenty-two thousand five hundred and ninety-nine.

The political parties which acted so prominent a part on the eve of the great struggle between the North and the South, were the Douglas Democrats, Breckinridge Democrats, the Bell and Everett, or Union party, and the Republican or Abolition party.

St. John's Academy, a Catholic parochial school connected with St. Catharine's Academy, on Limestone street, was established in 1860, mainly through the efforts of Father McGuire.

The Lexington Chasseurs, one of the most noted of the military companies ever raised in Lexington, was organized May 9, 1860, in the grand jury room of the present court-house, and in a very short time was fully equipped. On the 4th of July, 1860, in the presence of the largest crowd ever assembled on the old fair grounds (now the city park), Miss Abby Stewart, in behalf of the ladies of Lexington, presented the Chasseurs with a beautiful flag. The reply to the presentation address was made by Mr. O. L. Bradley, in behalf of the company. The reading of the declaration of independence by D. C. Wickliffe, an oration by R. W. Cooper, and a handsome barbecue given by the Chasseurs and their many friends concluded the exercises of the day.

The brilliant uniform and splendid evolutions of the Chasseurs now constitute one of the most charming memoirs of the days "just before the war." The Chasseurs were the favorites of everybody, and the company rarely had a parade that it was not invited to partake of the hospitalities of some private residence. In 1861, a silver canteen was presented to the company, to be the prize of that member of the Chasseurs who should prove himself the best rifle shot, and to be retained by him until won by another. On one side is the inscription:

Lexington Chasseurs,
Organized
May 9, 1860.
Non nobis sed patriæ.

The other side bears the name of the giver, and also those of the winners of the prize, viz:

Presented February 22, 1861, by John G. Kiser, Esq.
Private R. T. Anderson.
Corporal L. P. Milward, July 26, 1861.
Private David Prewett, June 16, 1868.

The hiatus from 1861 to 1868 represents a period too well and too sadly remembered to need explanation.

The Chasseurs were not simply peace soldiers. At the beginning of the late terrible war, a large majority of this favorite company volunteered and served gallantly in one or the other of the contending armies. The members of the old Chasseurs fought bravely on many a bloody field; not a few attained an enviable distinction, while others "sleep their last sleep" from wounds inflicted or diseases contracted in that desperate struggle.

The following is a list of the first officers elected by the Chasseurs, and the names of all the privates who have ever belonged to the company:

Captain, S. D. Bruce; first lieutenant, J. C. Cochran; second lieutenant, W. F. Matheny; third lieutenant, C. H. Harney; first sergeant, James Dudley; second sergeant, L. W. Ealier; third sergeant, T. D. Carr; fourth sergeant, Charles Swift; fifth sergeant, T. J. Nicholas; first corporal, John B. Castleman; second corporal, J. M. Yates; third corporal, L. P. Milward; fourth corporal, T. J. Bush; surgeon, Dudley Bush; clerk, G. R. Letcher; bugler, C. H.

Brutton; color bearer, J. Munos. Privates—R. T. Anderson, J. W. Alexander, O. L. Bradley, E. Brennan, B. W. Blincoe, H. C. Brennan, F. W. Brodie, John Bryan, L. Brechus, J. Bright, L. C. Bruce, G. R. Bell, W. Bright, D. M. Craig, J. Cochran, A. B. Chinn, C. Coleman, A. Clark, R. W. Cooper, B. T. Castleman, J. Clark, E. Cropper, G. Castleman, H. G. Craig, J. Cooper, H. Castleman, S. Dudley, E. S. Duncanson, H. C. Dunlap, J. G. Dudley, G. A. Doll, J. Dillon, J. Dill, G. Dozier, H. T. Duncan, Jr., J. W. Dillard, T. P. Dudley, Jr., C. Ely, W. Ferguson, R. Ferguson, N. Ferguson, R. Foley, W. F. Fulton, J. L. Gilmore, S. C. Graves, W. D. Gilmore, C. Goodloe, F. Gilmore, D. S. Goodloe, Jr., Z. Gibbons, H. B. Hill, Jr., J. O. Hill, F. X. Hollerger, D. M. Hawkins, F. A. Hanson, P. B. Hunt, P. C. Hartnell, J. Hayes, T. Hawkins, L. Harris, S. Hawkins, J. A. Harper, M. Hebrati, C. C. Johnson, Jas. Johnson, John Johnson, B. H. Johnson, E. Keene, T. J. Kelly, D. Kastle, J. Keene, G. Kinnear, J. G. Keiser, B. Letcher, S. Letcher, H. Luther, J. W. Lee, S. Lawless, J. P. Lawless, Linzen, E. Lewis, G. L. Lancaster, P. Lampher, W. Lockhart, R. McCann, J. Munos, W. M. Matthews, R. Maguire, H. McManus, C. Milward, T. W. McCann, H. McCann, B. J. McCabe, T. D. Mitchell, T. McCaw, J. McNeal, W. McCracken, Monks, W. Montmollin, N. H. McClelland, G. McMurtry, F. Matthews, J. C. Morris, J. Montmollin, H. McKee, W. Maglone, J. R. Morton, S. Mahone, W. B. McIntire, L. C. Nicholas, J. C. Newcomb, J. Nemelly, M. Offutt, H. Oots, G. L. Postlethwaite, W. Postlethwaite, E. Payne, A. B. Pullum, W. Perkins, J. R. Price, J. C. Pierce, M. Reed, J. Reed, T. A. Russell, R. C. Scott, E. Swift, S. Swift, G. Sprague, J. P. Shaw, W. Spencer, J. Sellier, C. H. Swift, J. B. Steves, W. T. Scott, D. Scott, T. Scott, O. Saxton, L. Spurr, H. C. Stewart, C. Spillman, J. Shaw, J. Sepp, J. F. Thompson, B. F. Thompson, A. W. Trabien, R. Underwood, W. H. Varty, J. A. Vaughn, R. J. West, P. Wilging, D. V. Woolley, L. Warfield, C. Warfield, E. Warfield, N. Williams, L. N. Walton, W. Wood.

CHAPTER LXXV.

Fair Amphitheater Burnt—Pruden's Statue of Clay—Ethelbert Dudley—S. D. McCullough.

ON the night of December 18, 1861, the handsome amphitheater on the magnificent fair grounds of the Kentucky Agricultural and Mechanical Association, near Maxwell's spring, in Lexington, was destroyed by fire, a calamity still deeply regretted.

In 1861, Mr. M. Pruden, whose talents as a sculptor are well known, executed a fine statue of Henry Clay, which is still in his possession. Several years before this, his excellent busts of Mr. Clay and Judge Robertson were made. Mr. Pruden is a native of Pennsylvania, but has spent the most of his life in Lexington.

Dr. Ethelbert L. Dudley, son of Ambrose Dudley, died at the age of forty-five, of typhoid fever, at Columbia, Kentucky, February 20, 1862. At the time of his death, he was Colonel of the Twenty-first Kentucky (Federal) Infantry. Dr. Dudley was born near Lexington; was educated at Harvard University, and graduated at the Transylvania Medical College, in which he was afterward professor of the principles and practice of surgery. He was a physician by nature, talents, and education, and before the commencement of the late war, he had attained a prominence consistent with his rare abilities and skill. He seemed destined to take the first place in his profession in Kentucky. Dr. Dudley was not more admired as a physician than he was beloved as a man. To the strength of his mind and character, there seemed added every knightly attribute and grace. He was brave and generous, quick to resent, and quick to forgive. He was big-hearted, kind, sympathetic, and gentle. Littleness and meanness he despised unutterably, while his soul warmed instinctively to every high and noble action. His heart went out to his friends, and his multitude of friends clung to him with a devotion that is as rare as it was beautiful. No citizen of Lexington was ever more deeply and universally beloved than Dr. Dudley—perhaps none as much so.

The funeral services took place on Monday, the 24th of February, in the Odd Fellows Hall,* on the corner of Main and Broadway, which had been draped in mourning, and throughout the entire sad exercises could be heard the sobs of hundreds in the dense and sorrowing crowd. The remains of the greatly beloved physician were borne to the Lexington Cemetery, where they now sleep, followed by the "Old Infantry," the Chasseurs, the various orders and professions, and a multitude of other mourners of every rank and condition of life.

The handsome form, the eagle eye, and generous heart of Dr. Ethelbert Dudley will long be remembered in Lexington.

Samuel D. McCullough, now one of the oldest natives of Lexington, was born June 26, 1803. His father, a native of Maryland, was one of the early settlers of Lexington. Major McCullough was graduated A. B., at Transylvania University, in 1824, and a few years after received the degree of A. M. In 1829, he married Miss Harriet Wallis, a great grand-daughter of Rev. Samuel Daviess, of Princeton College. After conducting a female academy for fourteen years, Major McCullough inherited the secret, and for many years conducted the manufacture of Burrowes' world-renowned Lexington mustard. His love for painting, local history, and antiquities is well-known, but his particular forte is astronomy. "McCullough's Almanacs," Map of the Heavens, and Text-book on Astronomy have more than a local reputation. The major has been one of the "lights" of the Masonic fraternity since 1824. He is a quaint relic

---

*Observer and Reporter.

of the olden time of Lexington, and his warm heart and well-stored head, and his praiseworthy desire and efforts to save from destruction the monuments and memoirs of the past, justly entitled him to the name of "Old Mortality."

CHAPTER LXXVI.

Banking House of Grinstead & Bradley—Wm. C. Goodloe.

THE banking house of Grinstead & Bradley, located on Upper, between Maine and Short streets, was established in 1863.

Judge William C. Goodloe removed to Lexington in 1863. He was born in Madison county, Ky., October 7, 1805;* graduated at the Transylvania Law School in 1824; commenced the practice of his profession in Richmond, and was soon after appointed commonwealth attorney by Governor Metcalf. In 1826, he married Miss Almira, daughter of Governor William Owsley. He was appointed circuit judge in 1846, and served under the appointment until the adoption of the state constitution of 1850, when he was elected to the same office by the people. After that he was twice re-elected and continued in office until 1868, having been upon the bench for twenty-two consecutive years. At the time of his death, which occurred in Lexington, Aug. 14, 1870, he was a professor in the Law College of Kentucky University. Judge Goodloe was a fine lawyer, and possessed very extensive legal information. As a judge he was quick to comprehend cases and arrive at conclusions, and was exceedingly prompt and able in the dispatch and transaction of the duties of his office.

*Kentucky Statesman.

CHAPTER LXXVII.

Jewish Church—James B. Clay—John H. Morgan.

THE Jews, the most ancient people of the Most High, are few in Lexington, and have no regular and established organization, but the requirements of their faith are not entirely ignored. In the year 1864, in their month of Tishri, they assembled at the residence of one of their brethren, and observed their Sabbath of Sabbaths, the great Day of Atonement, with fasting, humiliation, and prayer. From that time to the present, this, the most solemn day of the whole Jewish year, has been annually commemorated by the Israelites of Lexington.

James B. Clay, son of Henry Clay, died in February, 1864, in Canada, aged forty-seven. Mr. Clay was born in Lexington, and was educated for the bar, where, in time, he made a good reputation. Mr. Clay was the only member of the family that seemed to inherit any of the father's oratorical talent—he was a fine stump speaker. After filling the position of *charge* to Portugal, Mr. Clay ably represented his district in Congress. In the late war, he warmly espoused the cause of the Confederate States, and was on his way to join the Southern army, when he was arrested and exiled to Canada, where he died of consumption at the time stated above. His remains are buried in the Lexington Cemetery. His residence was Ashland, which he purchased after his father's death.

General John H. Morgan, the Marion of Kentucky, and the most brilliant partisan leader of the late war, was killed by treachery at Greenville, East Tennessee, September 4, 1864. He was born at Huntsville, Alabama, June 1, 1825, and was a son of Calvin C. Morgan, and his wife, a daughter of John W. Hunt, of Lexington, Kentucky. General

Morgan's parents removed to Lexington when he was a small child, and nothing of special interest occurred in his life until he arrived at the age of nineteen, when he enlisted in the Mexican war. On his return, he married Miss Bruce, and engaged regularly in business in Lexington.

At the beginning of the late war, he was captain of the noted "Lexington Rifles," and, espousing the cause of the South, escaped, by stratagem, with a number of that company, on the 20th of September, 1861, and arrived safely at Green river. Shortly after, at Bowling Green, he was elected captain of a cavalry company, which was duly enrolled in the Confederate service. From that time until the day of his death, he figured in great events, which made his name famous. As captain, colonel, and then brigadier-general, he led his rangers on rapid and astounding "raids," through the carnage of Shiloh, at the capture of Cynthiana, and in many a desperate contest. After the death of his wife, Morgan married again. His second wife was Miss Ready, of Tennessee. His daring raid through Ohio, his capture, imprisonment, and romantic escape, are too fresh in the public mind to need recapitulation.

This gallant leader and his famous band swept through Kentucky, in 1864, for the last time, and on the 10th of June were in possession of Lexington. In less than three months from that time, his knightly career was ended. His remains were buried first at Abingdon, Virginia, but in a short time were deposited in a vault at Hollywood Cemetery, Richmond, where they remained until 1868. On the 17th of April of that year, his old comrades and soldiers, in the presence of a host of mourners, laid him to rest in the Lexington Cemetery, and gentle women of the South wreathed, with flowers and evergreens, the grave of one of the greatest partisan leaders named in the history of the world. Up to the time of his first marriage, General Morgan lived at his mother's residence, on the corner of Mill and Second streets. Just before the late war, he lived on the corner opposite his old home, in the house now occupied by Mrs. Ryland.

CHAPTER LXXVIII.

First National and City National Banks—Centenary Methodist Church.

THE First National Bank of Lexington was organized in the spring of 1865, and commenced business in an office on Jordan's Row. Its first directors were Jacob Hughes, W. R. Estill, William Warfield, S. F. Tebbs, and B. F. Buckner; Jacob Hughes, president, and Thos. Mitchell, cashier. The office of the bank is now on Short street, between Upper and Market.

In the same year (1865), the City National Bank was established. W. C. Goodloe, president; A. M. Barnes, cashier; directors, G. W. Norton, W. S. Downey, Persicles Scott, J. B. Wilgus, and D. F. Wolf. Banking office located on corner of Main and Cheapside.

The Centenary Methodist Church of Lexington was organized, in the fall of 1865, by a number of persons who seceded from the Southern Methodist Church on Hill street, for reasons intimated in the chapter on the latter named church. Members of the families of Persicles Scott, Hiram Shaw, L. P. and W. R. Milward, J. Gunn, J. W. Cannon, Dr. Bright, and others, combined to organize the new church, which met for a short time in the present city library building, with Rev. H. P. Henderson, of Ohio, as pastor.

On the 4th of January, 1866, the congregation engaged the city council room in Hunt's Row, and conducted worship there for several years, under the ministry of Rev. Duke Slavin and his successor, Rev. J. R. Eads. Ably assisted by their next pastor, the Rev. Daniel Stevenson, formerly superintendent of public instruction for Kentucky, and a scholarly gentleman, the congregation, with great zeal, set to work to build a church, and on Sunday, July 24, 1870, the present elegant edifice on the corner of Broadway and Church streets was dedicated. The dedicatory exercises were conducted by the Rev. C. H. Fowler, assisted by the pastor, Mr. Stevenson. The Rev. George Strowbridge, the present pastor, who is an exceedingly entertaining speaker, succeeded Mr. Stevenson. The affairs of the Centenary Church have been conducted with great energy and zeal; it has met with encouraging success, and is now in a most prosperous condition.

CHAPTER LXXIX.

Kentucky Gazette—Red Men—Aaron Dupee—Kentucky Statesman—Farmers' Home Journal—Poems by the Misses Wilson—Good Templars—Fayette Farmers' Club—John Carty.

THE first number of the present Kentucky Gazette, H. H. Gratz, editor, appeared June 23, 1866.

Oceola Tribe, No. 8, Improved Order of Red Men, was constituted in Lexington, August 29, 1866, with the following officers, viz: James Chrystal, Sachem; T. A. Hornsey, S. S.; B. P. Watkins, J. S.; D. A. King, P.; A. W. Trabein, C. R.; V. N. Gardner, K. W. The tribe was organized in the third story of Viley & Co.'s drug store, on the corner of Mill and Short streets. It now uses the hall in Kastle's block, on Main street.

Aaron Dupee, well-known as the faithful negro servant of Henry Clay, died in February, 1866, at the age of eighty. He was buried in the Presbyterian Cemetery, and a neat headstone, with an inscription embodying these facts, marks his grave.

The first number of the present Kentucky Statesman appeared January 1, 1867, William Cassius Goodloe and W. Owsley Goodloe being editors and proprietors; office on Short street, near the corner of Limestone, where it still remains. Subsequently, W. O. Goodloe became sole editor and proprietor. In January, 1871, he sold to Messrs. W. C. Goodloe and L. P. Tarleton. At the present time, the establishment is owned by a company, and the paper is ably edited by Mr. Samuel R. Smith. The Statesman is Republican, or Radical, in politics.

The Farmers' Home Journal was established in May, 1867, by J. J. Miller and J. R. Marrs, on Market street, near the Episcopal Church. It is now owned by Messrs. H. T. Duncan, Jr., and Hart Gibson; and Mr. J. A. Reynolds, who has been so long and so favorably connected with the Kentucky press, is its editor.

Miss Susie Wilson and Miss Belle Wilson, sisters, and both natives of Lexington, published in the newspapers, about this time (1867), as they have frequently since, poems of great sweetness, tender eloquence, and acknowledged merit.

The order of Good Templars originated in Lexington, with the organization of Arlington Lodge, November 22, 1867, in the building used by City School No. 2. Ashland Lodge of Good Templars was organized December 8, 1868. Both lodges now use the hall in Kastle's building, on Main, between Mill and Broadway.

On Saturday, the 19th of January, 1867, a meeting of farmers was held in the wareroom of J. M. Tipton, on Short street, between Limestone and Upper, to take steps toward organizing a Farmers' Club. General William Bryan was called to the chair, and E. C. Bryan was made secretary. A number of speeches were made, strongly in favor of the project, and the following committee was appointed to draft a constitution and by-laws for the proposed club, viz: W. B. Kinkead, J. J. Hayden, D. S. Coleman, S. Chew, and E. Allen. At a meeting held at the same place the succeeding Saturday, January 26, the constitution and by-laws reported by the committee were adopted, the organization named "The Farmers' Club," and the following officers were elected: President, W. R. Estill; vice-president, J. J. Hayden; corresponding secretary, William Warfield; treasurer, D. S. Coleman; recording secretary, J. M. Tipton. Those who subscribed to the constitution, at this meeting, were William Bryan, Samuel H. Chew, W. B. Kinkead, J. J. Hayden, W. R. Estill, W. Halley Smith, Edward Allen, D. S. Coleman, C. C. Gibson, Joseph S. Frazer, William Warfield, David Prewitt, James W. Berry, Granville Smith, S. P. Kennedy, R. J. Spurr, William Cassius Goodloe, E. C. Bryan, Elisha Smith, John Clark, William D. Sutherland,

J. M. Tipton, John L. Cassell, A. K. Marshall, S. M. Hibler, David Harp, and W. G. Anderson.

The club was established to advance the general interests of agriculture in this portion of Kentucky; to spread intelligence of the markets for stocks and other products throughout the farming community, and by mutual consultation protect their interests against undue advantage being taken of them; to bring together experience as to the best method of cultivating the various crops; of breeding and raising stock of the various descriptions; of the best farming implements, and embracing also the interests of horticulture, fruit raising, the dairies, etc.

The club has been in successful operation ever since its establishment. Its weekly discussions and proceedings, which have been exceedingly useful and interesting, have been given to the public in a clear, graceful, and able manner, by Mr. J. A. Reynolds, editor of the Farmers' Home Journal, and the authorized reporter of the club. In justice to itself and to the interests of agriculture in Kentucky, the club should, by all means, gather and preserve these reports in a durable volume.

John Carty, one of the most remarkable and successful merchants that Lexington has ever produced, died at his residence on Broadway, Monday, April 8, 1867, aged sixty-one. His father, John Carty, a soldier in the Revolution and in subsequent Indian wars, was one of the pioneer settlers of Lexington. His grandfather, John Carty, was a native of Burlington, New Jersey, and was of English descent. After spending several sessions at the Transylvania grammar school, Mr. Carty commenced life, at the early age of fifteen, as deputy of that elegant old Virginia gentleman, Captain John Fowler, then, and for many years after, postmaster of Lexington. Mr. Carty left the post-office to assist Mr. John McCauley, who, at an early day, was one of the extensive grocery dealers of Lexington. In this new capacity, his energy and business talents were so marked, and he exhibited financial sagacity of such a high order, that in a short time he was admitted as a full partner in the establishment. Subsequently, he conducted the same kind of business with Mr. John Dudley and others, but for many years, and up to the time of his death, he was the sole proprietor of the leading grocery house in Lexington, which had also become, under his skillful management, one of the most extensive in Kentucky.

Mr. Carty was one of nature's noblemen, and the seal of a true man was impressed upon all he did. His business was conducted upon the highest principles of truth and honor. Though a patron of learning and of every deserving public enterprise, and the liberal benefactor of struggling merit, yet all was hidden under an extraordinary modesty, which was not the least beautiful of his characteristics. He was a man of remarkable judgment; he weighed everything in his finely balanced mind, and his opinions were rarely at fault and always influential. Mr. Carty was constitutionally incapable of injustice, and his views on all subjects were comprehensive, liberal, and charitable. His most distinguishing mental trait was financial sagacity, and in that respect, in particular, he was one of the most superior men in Kentucky. His old associates will never forget his marvelously black, beautiful, and piercing eyes, the windows of a soul as gentle as it was brave, and as rare as it was exalted. His spotless life and admirable qualities gained him a host of friends. He was universally esteemed and beloved, and few men who have died in Lexington were ever more generally and sincerely mourned. The following notice of his funeral, from a Lexington newspaper, indicates the public feeling at his loss:

"The funeral cortege of Mr. John Carty, on Wednesday last, was probably the largest which ever followed a private citizen of this city to the grave. He was interred with Masonic honors, and the stores along Main street were closed as the procession passed by. This was an unusual testimonial of respect to a private person; but it shows how he had won upon the respect and affection of his fellow citizens."

CHAPTER LXXX.

Christ Church Seminary—Baptist Female College—W. S. Downey.

CHRIST CHURCH SEMINARY, Rev. Silas Totten, principal, was established in 1868.

The first session of the Baptist Female College, on Broadway, between Hill and Maxwell streets, commenced in February, 1868, under Prof. A. S. Worrell. The college buildings are the same used by the Misses Jackson, who for years conducted a female school noted for its fine character and success. Rev. J. C. Freeman succeeded Mr. Worrell. The present president of this flourishing institution is Dr. Robert Ryland, formerly of Richmond, Virginia.

W. S. Downey died at the Phœnix Hotel, in Lexington, January 31, 1868, aged forty-seven.* Major Downey was born near Winchester, Kentucky, and having been bereft of his father at an early age, he was not only thrown upon his own resources, but was left in poverty, with a mother and two sisters to support. He tested freely "the good things that belong to adversity" in his early and youthful struggles. He was educated at St. Mary's College, and studied law with Hon. James Simpson. He was county attorney of Clark county for several years and up to his election as commonwealth's attorney for this judicial district, in 1856, which office he held, by successive elections, at the time of his death.

Major Downey was a self-made man, and rose to position by his own talents and industry. He was distinguished for correct taste and polite accomplishments in literature. His

---

*Observer and Reporter.

fine command of language, arising from an intimate acquaintance with the classics, active, quick, perceptive, and incisive cast of intellect, gave him the power of a formidable and eloquent opponent at the bar.

CHAPTER LXXXI.

Apostolic Times—Hocker School—The Great Eclipse of the Sun—S. S. Nicholas—Farmer Dewees.

THE Apostolic Times, R. Graham and others editors, was established in April, 1869; first office on Main, between Mill and Cheapside.

The Hocker Female School, on Broadway, opened in September, 1869, with Robert Graham as president. The school owes its establishment to donations and loans from liberal citizens.

On Saturday, August 7, 1869, occurred the great eclipse of the sun, and Lexington, being a most favorable point of observation, was visited by many strangers. The crowds, which commenced to gather on the streets at an early hour in the afternoon, grew larger and larger as the momentous period approched, and by the time the great celestial wonder began its sublime, visible work, it seemed that all living Lexington had abandoned shelter and emptied itself out into the main thoroughfares.

The weather all day was beautiful and clear, but cool, becoming even chilly as eclipse time neared. By four o'clock most of the best points had been secured. Every hand held a piece of smoked glass with which to take observations. The first indications to the naked eye of the eclipse was the appearance of a little concave "gap" in the sun, a visible change began to take place in the color of things, and the atmosphere was the least bit hazy. Time passed, and the air took on a coal-smoky hue, the darkening shadows deepened, and our beautiful trees assumed a deeper and deeper green. In a little while only about four digits of the sun's face was yet uncovered, and from this time the circling birds, the domestic fowls and animals, showed most evident signs of uneasiness. The moon moved majestically onward, leaving only two digits unchanged, and the gathering darkness settled in ghastly shadows upon all men and things. The ladies drew their wrappings closer, the edges of the sun glowed strangely with fire, the excitement ran high, and at each advance made by the moon's shadow the intensity increased.

At 5:25 the silence and the darkness awed the expectant multitudes by their strange and mysterious influence. Every eye was upon the sun, the horns of the crescent diminished rapidly, and at last the crescent itself became dissolved into a ball of fire. Rapidly it also diminished in size, and at last disappeared suddenly, like a candle blown out. Still, on the margin of the shadow lingered specks— little globules—two or three, or perhaps five of them, on the moon's northeast edge, like dazzling drops of dew. Suddenly they went out, and the merest golden edge remained a second and flashed out of sight, dropping a sudden darkness on the earth. The stars flashed into the heavens as if they had but that moment been created. On the right was Mercury, on the left Venus, and still further left was Mars or perhaps Saturn.

Time, 5:30. The moment had arrived—such as will not occur again for a lifetime—the sun was eclipsed. And there was something indescribably awful and solemn in this vailing of his face in darkness.

Another has truly said of this moment:

"With the flash of darkness flashed out lines of golden clouds in the southwest and northwest of indescribable beauty. No night clouds, no clouds by twilight, no clouds at sunset, no clouds by day, ever resembled those. The relations of earth and air in color and light had changed night on the earth, twilight in the distant mid-air, and a daylight in the further upper air where the clouds were marshaled. Golden, orange, gray, crimson, lavender, and the tenderest hues of olive were seen mottled and pure in their coloring. They lay in ledges, the lower stratum resting on a bank of rich orange mist that deepened and deepened in color till it reached and disappeared beneath the horizon. In tone these clouds were unlike all other clouds one sees. Rich in color, beyond description of tongue, pen, or pencil, they were not ablaze as are the clouds of day, and appearing and disappearing like the pictures of a phantasmagoria."

Even while the entranced gazers are looking with wrapped eyes and with hearts moved to their deepest depths by the glory of the grandest work of the Omnipotent Creator, there comes a flash and a blinding, dazzling, overwhelming light. It is like nothing else than the breaking loose of great reservoirs that had long been dammed—grateful, warm, genial, blessed light, it came streaming forth, giving life and health and peace. It seemed like a resurrection. It seemed as if the habiliments of the grave had been thrown aside, and in the garments of youth the earth had been decked. The shadow fled away before the sudden burst, the old moon became the new, and once more it began its solemn movement around the earth, and with the earth around the sun. The eclipse was over.

Judge S. S. Nicholas, noted as a profound jurist and publicist, died in Danville, Kentucky, at the age of seventy-three, on Saturday, November 27, 1869. He was born in Lexington, on the corner of Short and Mill streets, read law with R. Wickliffe, Sen., practiced in Louisville, and rose rapidly to a high position. He served in the legislature, upon the appellate bench, and in preparing the revised code of Kentucky. He became particularly celebrated for his able essays on constitutional law. His father, Hon. George Nicholas, was one of the ablest men that ever lived in Kentucky, and was the leading member of the Lexington bar for a number of years.

Farmer Dewees, whose face had been familiar to Lexington for so many years, died at his residence, on Main street, July 28, 1869.* Mr. Dewees was born near Midway, Kentucky, September 15, 1792, but settled in Lexington in early life, and was identified with her banking institutions for nearly half a century. He was teller, at

---

*Kentucky Gazette.

one time, in the old branch of the United States Bank, and was subsequently the first teller of the Northern Bank, with which institution he remained connected until old age crept upon him. Mr. Dewees was distinguished for his gentle manners, amiable deportment, and quiet charity. He filled his allotted part in life with fidelity, and died with the Christian's hopes bright upon him.

CHAPTER LXXXII.

Population—Charter Amendment—Irish Benevolent Association—Fayette National Bank—Lexington Daily Press—David A. Sayre—Fayette Historical Society.

THE census report, and the report of the city assessor of the population of Lexington for 1870, conflict, owing, in part, to the unsettled condition of the negroes. A well-informed citizen estimated the population at seventeen thousand five hundred, which is believed to be about correct. The population of the entire county was twenty-six thousand six hundred and fifty-six.

In January, 1870, the charter of the city of Lexington was so amended as to require elections of municipal officers to take place on the last Thursday in January, 1870, and every third year thereafter.

About the first of March, in this year, the banking office of Headley & Anderson, on Short street, was established.

The Irish National Benevolent Association of Lexington was organized May 13, 1870, with the following officers, viz: J. H. Mulligan, president; J. A. Geary, first vice-president; M. Clark, second vice-president; T. J. Brogan, recording secretary; J. Dowling, corresponding secretary; A. J. Hogarty, treasurer. The objects of the association are to promote the cause of Ireland's independence, to assist distressed Irishmen in Lexington, and to honor the memory of Saint Patrick by a proper celebration of his anniversary. We may mention here, that the first observance of Saint Patrick's day in this city was the occasion of a dinner at Megowan's tavern, in 1790.

The Fayette National Bank, corner of Short and Upper streets, was organized September 8, 1870, by the election of the following directors, viz: R. R. Stone, J. S. Woolfolk, Horace Craig, J. M. Tipton, S. Bassett, J. Hocker, R. McMichael, and J. B. Morton.

The Lexington Daily Press, the first newspaper printed in this city by steam, was established in October, 1870, Messrs. Hart Gibson, H. T. Duncan, Jr., and J. J. Miller, being proprietors. Office on the corner of Short and Market streets. It is now owned by Gibson and Duncan only.

David A. Sayre died in Lexington on the 12th of September, 1870. Mr. Sayre was born in Madison, New Jersey, March 12, 1793. He was a child of poverty, and the hard labor of his youth left him little time for education. He came to Lexington in 1811, a silver-plater's apprentice, walking barefoot all the way from Maysville to this place, with a meager pack upon his back, and only a half dollar in his pocket. The young mechanic was thrifty and shrewd, and while he labored he also saved and watched his opportunities. In 1823, while yet a journeyman, he concluded to add the broker's calling to his regular business, and by dint of close and careful dealing, he achieved great success in amassing money, and in 1829, was enabled to open a banking-office on the corner of Mill and Short streets. He succeeded in his business, and long before his death was known for his wealth; a considerable part of which was devoted to public institutions connected with the Presbyterian Church, of which he was a member, and to the benefiting of his relatives, some of whom he raised from humble life to prosperity and wealth. " Uncle Davy," and his faithful help-mate, " Aunt Abby," sleep side by side in the beautiful Lexington Cemetery. Mr. Sayre was no ordinary man ; he did great good, and the record of his life is full of encouragement to ambitious strugglers with poverty.

The Historical Society of Fayette county was organized in the Lexington Library building, June 7, 1870. The object of the society is to procure and preserve whatever may relate to the history of Fayette county, Kentucky, viz: books, relics, and memorials, and also to collect and publish manuscripts concerning the history of the county and state. The first officers of the society were : President, George Robertson; vice-presidents, James O. Harrison and

Robert Peter; recording secretary, George W. Ranck; corresponding secretary, Joseph D. Pickett; treasurer, John S. Wilson, and librarian, J. B. Cooper. Messrs. Leslie Combs, Benjamin Gratz, S. D. McCullough, Benjamin Kiser, William Swift, Richard Marsh, T. P. Dudley, and others are members of this society.

The writer returns his thanks to the officers and members of the Fayette Historical Society, and to Richard H. Collins, of Covington, (who is now revising and enlarging his father's history of Kentucky,) for the valuable assistance they rendered him in the preparation of this volume.

CHAPTER LXXXIII.

Mission Church—Dollar Press—Broadway Christian Church —Second Church of Christ—Meeting Places and Pastors— Hugh McKee—Knights of Pythias.

THE Mission Church on Boliver street, devoted to the religious improvement of the unfortunate, was dedicated Sunday, January, 1871.

The first number of the Dollar Weekly Press, published by Duncan & Gibson, on the corner of Short and Market streets, made its appearance January 21, 1871.

The Broadway Christian Church was organized, and became independent of the Main Street Christian Church, in July, 1871. (See Christian Church, 1825.) J. W. McGarvey was first regular pastor of the church.

The Second Church of Christ was established in the spring of 1871, by a number of persons who desired freedom and rest from the intolerance and illiberality of certain leaders of the "Main Street Church," with which they had been connected. (See Christian Church, 1825.) The first regular meeting preliminary to organization was held on the afternoon of March 19, 1871, in the upper room of the library building, on the corner of Church and Market streets. Present, Elder G. W. Elley, chairman; J. S. Wolfolk, D. S. Goodloe, J. H. Neville, J. B. Bowman, G. W. Ranck, and others. In addition to these persons, the following were among the earliest movers in the formation of the new church, viz: J. D. Pickett, Mary E. Carty, John Shackelford, A. M. Barnes, Lulie Mays, Marcus Downing and family, Helen C. Ranck, John Curd, Sen., E. D. Luxon, W. S. Lipscomb, N. Prall, John Curd, Jr., Mary D. Bowman, Joseph Wasson and family, Jas. Sullivan and family, E. E. Smith, S. D. Pinkerton, and others.

The establishment of the church was duly perfected, and on Sunday, April 2, the opening sermon was preached in the library building, by Elder Elley.

The first pastors of the church were Elders J. D. Pickett and John Shackelford, who acted jointly. After worshiping in the library building for some months, the congregation fitted up a chapel on the second floor of the Carty building, on the corner of Main and Mill streets. Services were held in this chapel, for the first time, on the morning of Sunday, February 4, 1872, the sermon being preached by Elder R. C. Ricketts, of Harrodsburg. The congregation still worship in the Carty building. The pastor of the church at this time is Elder John Shackelford, a native of Mason county, Kentucky, a graduate of Bethany college, and now a professor in the Agricultural College of Kentucky University. This faithful and earnest minister ably represents the charitable feelings and liberal opinions of his little flock.

The gallant Hugh McKee, who was killed in the attack made by the United States naval forces upon the forts of Corea, Asia, June 11, 1871, was born in Lexington, on the 23d of April, 1844, and graduated at Annapolis, in 1866. He was the first man to reach the fort, within which he died as bravely as did his father, Colonel W. R. McKee, upon the battle-field of Buena Vista. Admiral Rogers, in his report of the fight said: "The citadel has been named Fort McKee, in honor of that gallant officer who led the assault upon it, and gave his life for the honor of his flag." This noble son of a noble sire sleeps in the Lexington Cemetery.

Lodge No. 15, Knights of Pythias, was organized in Lexington, October 25, 1871, with the following officers, namely: J. T. Uppington, W. C.; O. S. Wood, V. C.; Thomas Forman, R. S.; G. C. Snyder, F. S.; C. H. Norris, W. B. The order is a charitable one; its objects, according to its constitution, being to "alleviate suffering, succor the afflicted and unfortunate, and care for the widow and the orphan."

CHAPTER LXXXIV.

Southern Railroad—J. B. Wilgus & Co.'s Bank—Sons of Temperance—B. Gratz Brown—Business Statement—County and City Officers.

In the latter part of January, 1872, the Kentucky legislature granted the right of way through this state to the Southern Railroad, destined to extend from Cincinnati to Chattanooga. The event was celebrated with great enthusiasm by the citizens of Lexington, who regard the road (which is now on the eve of being commenced) as another great means of advancing the growth and prosperity of their city. This important enterprise is not new in its general outlines. Thirty-five years ago, a road from Cincinnati to Knoxville, and thence to Charleston, South Carolina, was projected, and the right of way given by the Kentucky legislature. From that time to the present, the project has always been regarded with favor by Cincinnati and Central Kentucky.

The banking house of J. B. Wilgus & Co. was established February 7, 1872, and commenced business in Hoeing's building, on Main street. The bank now uses an office in the Wilgus building, on Main street, between Mill and Broadway.

Lexington Division, No. 35, Sons of Temperance, was organized on the night of Monday, July 29, 1872, in Kastle's building, on Main street, where the division still meets regularly.

Governor Benjamin Gratz Brown, of Missouri, and now the Liberal Republican nominee for vice-president of the United States, was born on the 28th of May, 1826, in Lexington, at the residence of his grandfather, Judge Bledsoe, who lived at that time on Short street, between Walnut and Dewees streets, in the house now occupied by Mr. Armstrong, and next to the residence of Mrs. Waters. Governor Brown's father, Hon. Mason Brown, was a citizen of Frankfort, and Mrs. Brown was on a visit to her parents at the time of her son's birth.

The character and importance of Lexington, at this time (1872), may be judged by the following:

The city contains eighteen churches, twenty schools, four colleges, one university, eight newspapers, one public library, three railroads, thirty physicians, forty-five lawyers, five hemp and bagging factories, nine carriage factories, twenty livery stables, four planing mills, ten saddle and harness manufactories, eight banking houses, ten hotels, thirty-five drinking saloons, twenty-one boot and shoe establishments, fifteen confectioneries, one hundred and twenty-five groceries, eight sewing-machine offices, twenty-two dry goods houses, sixteen millinery houses, ten drug houses, six blacksmith shops, one woolen mill, four flour mills, ten clothing houses, fifteen dress-making houses, one foundry, one mustard factory, four wagon factories, one soap and candle factory, four mattrass factories, one plaster ornament factory, one hoop-skirt factory, one agricultural implement factory, two pump factories, two broom factories, two cigar factories, three hair ornament factories, five furniture houses, six bakeries, eight restaurants, ten coal yards, one gas company, four dental offices, five hardware houses, two gas and steam-fitting houses, three leather houses, five furniture houses, four agricultural implement houses, ten barber shops, five paint shops, six tin, copper, and stove shops, two machine shops, one cooper shop, three gunsmith shops, two locksmith shops, four lumber yards, one book-bindery, one brewery, three marble works, seven watch and jewelry houses, eight merchant tailor houses, one bath house, one dye house, three photograph galleries, four book-stores, six meat houses, three rag houses, one public laundry, six insurance offices, three nurseries, eight auctioneers, one lottery office, one omnibus line, four builders, four public halls, one sculptor, two portrait painters, four architects, several hundred carpenters, brick-masons, plasterers, and stone-cutters, two quadrille bands, one agricultural and mechanical association, one racing association, one park, one express office, two telegraph offices, one lunatic asylum, one orphan asylum, one female benevolent society, two Bible societies, one musical society, one theater, one work-house, four Masonic lodges, three Odd-Fellow lodges, two Good Templar lodges, one Red Men lodge, one Knights of Pythias lodge, one Sons of Temperance lodge.

The officers of Fayette county at the present time are: Judge of the Circuit Court, C. B. Thomas; Commonwealth's Attorney, J. L. Jones; Circuit Court Clerk, J. B. Rodes; Judge of County Court, B. F. Graves; County Attorney, J. R. Morton; County Court Clerk, A. G. Hunt; Sheriff, R. S. Bullock; Jailer, T. B. Megowan; Assessor, J. D. Sprake; Surveyor, J. F. Slade; Coroner, T. Logwood.

The city officers are: Mayor, J. T. Frazer. Councilmen —Ward No. 1, M. C. Johnson, J. R. Cleary, C. Randall; Ward No. 2, R. A. Gibney, T. W. Foster, J. Hoagland; Ward No. 3, H. Chiles, W. C. P. Breckinridge, J. Laudeman; Ward No. 4, Dennis Mulligan, J. F. Robinson, Jr., Robert Stone. Recorder, J. H. Mulligan; Clerk, J. W. Cochrane; Attorney, John Webster; Physician, J. W. Bruce, M. D.; Treasurer, B. T. Milton; Collector, J. F. Robinson; Assessor, Jesse Woodruff; Marshal, Wm. Tillett; Chief of Police, N. Hendricks.

CHAPTER LXXXV.

Fayette County—Wealth, Population, and Fertility—Soil and Stock—Lexington—Situation, Trade, and Appearance—Characteristics and Geology.

FAYETTE county, the center of the "Blue Grass Region," or "Garden of Kentucky," is situated in the middle of the state, and lies on the waters of the Elkhorn and Kentucky. It is bounded on the north by Scott county, on the south by Madison and Jessamine, on the east by Bourbon, and on the west by Woodford. It is twenty-five miles from north to south, mean breadth eleven miles, and contains 275 square miles, or 176,000 acres. It is fair table land, gently undulating; all the streams rise and flow from the center of the county and empty into their common receptacle, the Kentucky river.

The entire population of Fayette at present, including Lexington, is estimated at nearly 30,000. The taxable property of the county is valued at $14,790,457,* and is second in amount only to Jefferson, including the city of Louisville. The *real* value of all kinds of property in Fayette, not including Lexington, is estimated at $25,000,-000. The proverb, "as rich as Fayette county," is not without point.

There is probably no richer or more productive soil on earth than that of Fayette county. In pioneer days it was a deep mass of rich, black, vegetable mold, the accumulation of ages, which made it a perfect hot-bed for fertility. This gradually changed after the original forests and canebrakes were cleared, and the heat of the sun and the full influence of the atmospheric agencies were admitted to the soil. But then came the rich and luxuriant blue grass, for which this favored locality is noted the wide word over,

---

*Auditor's Report.

and we were still left a region "beautiful as the vale of Tempe and fertile as Sicily, that granary of Europe." The soil of Fayette county now varies from a rich dark brown or mulatto color to a light yellowish or reddish brown in the upper soil, and a light brownish or reddish yellow in the subsoil. The following analysis* exhibits the chemical composition of the soil of Fayette county, viz:

Composition in One Hundred Parts.—Organic and volatile matters, 8.000; alumina, 4.181; proxide of iron, 6.170; sesquioxide of manganese, ——; carbonate of lime, .494; magnesia, .420; phosphoric acid, .460; sulphuric acid, ——; potash, .205; soda, .062; land and insoluble silicates, 79.910; total, 99.882. Moisture, driven off from the air-dried soil, at 400 degrees Fahrenheit, 4.44.

The wheat crop of Fayette is always an abundant one. Of corn she averages more than a million bushels per year, and her last crop of hemp reached the enormous amount of 4,762,300† pounds, or very largely over one-third of the amount produced by the entire state.

But with all this wonderful fertility, Fayette is properly a stock-raising county. The soil and grasses are particularly rich in the chemical elements necessary to the formation of bone and muscle, and has resulted in Fayette's becoming one immense aggregation of breeding establishments. It is the native paddock not only of the peerless "Lexington," that blind old Milton of the turf, whose fame extends throughout Europe and America, but of a multitude of other great and noted coursers. Her blood horses and fine trotters are eagerly and constantly sought after by appreciators of superior stock from every quarter. Droves of mules and splendid herds of thorough-bred cattle browse in her blue grass pastures, and Southdown and Cotswold sheep, and Berkshire and Chestershire hogs, abound upon her farms. It has been said of Fayette county, and without exaggeration, that "the products of the temperate zone and tropic climes here grow as if upon common ground. From the stalk that forms the staple of Russia to

---

*Dr. Robt. Peter in Geological Survey of Ky.   †Auditor's Report.

the vine that blooms in France and Italy, there is scarcely a plant which does not seem indigenous to the soil. From the small grain and blood stock exported from England, to the corn and tobacco leaf known only to the native tenant of the West, there is scarcely an article which is necessary to the subsistence, or which contributes to the comfort of man, to which the soil and climate is not kind and genial."

Lexington, the seat of government of Fayette county, Kentucky, is situated on the headwaters of the town fork of North Elkhorn creek, 25 miles southeast of Frankfort, the capital of the state; 64 miles southwest of Maysville; 77 southeast of Louisville; 85 south of Cincinnati, and 517 from Washington city. Latitude 38° 6' north; longitude 84° 18' west.

The city is located on the extensive table land, on which Cincinnati is nearly centrally placed, formed by an uplift of the lower silurian rock formation, and its elevation taken at one of its lowest points, viz: the depot of the Lexington and Louisville Railroad, is, according to the authority of railroad engineers, 950 feet above the ocean level.

Although originally commenced immediately in what Bancroft styles "the unrivaled valley of Elkhorn creek," and on the springs in which it takes its rise, the city has extended up both the ascending sides of this valley and over a considerable portion of the level grounds above, the natural drainage of the place into the fork of the Elkhorn is therefore excellent.

The population of Lexington at present is believed to be between 18,000 and 20,000. The principal trade of the city, and the heaviest capital invested, is in hemp-manufacture, groceries, dry goods, whisky, and live stock. The taxable property in Lexington amounts to $7,000,000; the real value of all kinds of property is estimated at $15,000,000, and that of the city and county together at $40,000,000.

Lexington for a long time presented more of the appearance of an opulent, stagnant, and contented old English town than the air of a live American city; but this is now changing. The railroads projected and in progress, the growth of an enlightened public spirit, and the encouraging prospects of Lexington have created a new era as well as a new appearance for the city. Large and handsome buildings are taking the place of small and dingy business houses, modern improvements are to be seen on all sides, and the increase of mills and factories indicate the future manufacturing importance of the place. The streets, which are laid off at right angles, are mainly well paved, and are now in a better condition than they have ever been. Fine macadamized roads extend through and from the city in every direction, and constitute the trotting grounds of a multitude of fleet and valuable horses, which are constantly driven over them. Lexington can boast of a large number of exceedingly handsome private residences, beautified by art and taste, and surrounded by extensive grounds luxuriant in flowers and shrubbery. She has long been justly noted for the generous and refined hospitality of her citizens, for her great educational advantages, the skill and standing of her medical profession, and the learning and ability of her pulpit. The Lexington bar, which has ever been distinguished for its strength, is now not surpassed and perhaps not equaled in this country, and there are few places where the young members of the bar constitute a body of such marked promise.

The pre-eminence which Lexington enjoys for elegant society is due to the intelligence, culture, and refined beauty of her women. The striking similarity of Lexington society, in this respect, to that of a European capital, has been more than once remarked by foreigners.

Words can not be found too strong to express the richness and loveliness of the country about Lexington. The landscape is soft, luxuriant, and picturesque; the approaches to the city are beautiful, and the rides and drives in every direction are charming. Noble English-looking homesteads, surrounded by evergreens and magnificent foresttrees, dot velvet lawns of peerless blue grass and clover, the emerald green of which covers every inch of ground, save where the walks and carriage drives are cut through the thick turf. Stone fences and osage orange hedges, or high snow-white pailings, inclose breeding establishments of fine stock on every road. Splendid blood horses and herds of thorough-bred cattle browse in the shade. The land teems with fatness, and the eye is constantly refreshed with scenes of plenty, comfort, and loveliness.

The geology* of Lexington and vicinity is interesting, and is well worthy of careful consideration. The lower silurian rock strata, which underlie the city, are mainly composed of layers, varying in thickness from less than an inch to about two feet, of a dark grayish blue, changing into yellowish gray, granular limestone, usually quite fossiliferous, called by the Ohio geologists the blue limestone, the layers being often separated by seams of marl, generally of a lighter color. This limestone is much used in the construction of the admirable turnpikes and macadamized streets of this locality and city, and is valuable for building purposes, especially in stone boundary walls, foundations, and even walls of houses; the hard light-gray granular layers being quite durable and making quite a handsome structure, even in the undressed state, when skillfully laid up in the wall with good mortar. It also yields very good lime for building purposes, and the more earthy layers, containing much magnesia and silica, might be calcined into hydraulic cement.

This limestone, however, is generally quite shelly and fossiliferous, and hence it readily and continually disintegrates, in place, under the influence of the atmospheric agencies, giving to the celebrated "blue-grass" soil, which it produces, the superior fertility which characterizes it, and keeping up its productiveness under a thriftless culture, in a most remarkable manner.

For the same reason, the water which comes in contact with it is rendered "hard," and deposits, when boiled, a crust on the boiler composed of carbonates of lime and magnesia, with some little phosphate of lime, oxide of iron, etc. The water of all the wells and springs, hence, is more

---

*Analysis by the well-known geologist and chemist, Dr. Robert Peter.

or less hard, causing the inhabitants to resort, very generally, to the use of rain-water collected in cisterns, for culinary and washing purposes as well as for drinking.

The very general use of this hard limestone water is believed to have had something to do with the great prevalence of calculous disease here, in former times, during the early surgical practice of the late distinguished surgeon of Lexington, Prof. Benj. W. Dudley, as the writer has attempted to show, in his publication on the Urinary Calculi of the Museum of Transylvania University; and it may also greatly aid, according to the theory of others, in the very complete development of the bones and bodies of the animals grown in this rich limestone county.

The waters of the deep springs and bored wells of this geological region very frequently contain common salt and other saline ingredients, as well as sulphureted hydrogen, and carbonic acid gases, in greater or less quantity, varying from the celebrated salt-sulphur water of the "Blue Lick" springs down to water containing a mere trace of salts and having only a slight odor of sulphur, such as was obtained by boring at Montmollin's mill, on the town fork, at the lower part of the city, which contains only one thousandth of its weight of saline matters; or that at the bored well of the Lunatic Asylum, sunk one hundred and six feet below the surface, and eighty-six feet through the solid rock, the auger then dropping eighteen inches into a cavity, and the water immediately rising fifty feet in the bore, a soft, very weak, sulphur water, containing about one and one-sixth grain of saline matters to the thousand of the water. Most of the waters of bored wells have a smell of petroleum at first, and in some cases, a considerable quantity of combustible gas (light carbureted hydrogen) has been given out from them for some time.

The irregular disintegration of the limestone layers has caused the formation throughout the whole of this region of extensive caverns, and underground lakes and streams of water, as well as numerous sink-holes. Such lakes and streams doubtless exist under the valley of the town fork of Elkhorn quite extensively, and more than one steam-engine is supplied at the lower part of the city, by tapping them, one of which is the bagging factory of Z. Ward. This gentleman, in boring, also, some eighty or ninety feet for water at his residence, on the high ground, near the trotting track, in the southeastern part of the city, obtained water, which was found, on chemical examination, to be quite impure, it containing not only carbonate of soda and nitrates and other salts, but also a notable quantity of fatty organic matter, smelling somewhat like soap, and becoming quite offensive on exposure, as though he had penetrated into a cavern or stream in the sub-strata into which some of the drainage of the city found access.

Another remarkable instance of the kind, observed by me, was that of the well bored in 1852, by Mr. John S. Wilson, in the cellar of his drug store, on Cheapside, in this city. He obtained water at the depth of forty feet below the level of the street, after boring twenty-six and a half feet through solid limestone, containing hard masses of iron pyrites, and the water was such a strong chalybeate water, sparkling with carbonic acid gas, depositing oxide of iron on exposure to the air, and containing quite a variety of saline ingredients (as detailed in the chemical analysis of it, published in the first volume of the reports of the Kentucky Geological Survey), that it soon became quite popular as a mineral water. Not a long time elapsed, however, before the changed odor of the water gave evidence of the admixture of impurities, and presently it became so offensive from the undoubted presence of town drainage, that Mr. Wilson was obliged to discontinue its use for any purpose, and to plug up the well.

These facts are not at all wonderful, when we know that the whole of the drainage from the extensive State Lunatic Asylum, with its five hundred patients and attendants, situated on the northwestern part of the city, is discharged, through a natural underground channel, probably into subterranean cavities so extensive, under the city, that they never fill up nor become obstructed, notwithstanding the immense and filthy torrent which daily flows into them from the laundry, the water-closets, the culinary department, the bath-rooms, etc., etc.

This may throw some light on the fact that every well bored in the valley of the town fork, below the city, is a *saline sulphur water*, for it is well known to chemists that the spontaneous fermentation of water containing impurities of the kind mentioned, produces, by their decomposition, sulphureted hydrogen, and carbonic acid gases and nitrate. Hence is it important that the origin and source of sulphur waters, found in the line of the drainage of towns, should be carefully studied, more especially as it is the result of experience that the habitual admixture of even very small quantities of town drainage in the water used for drinking is a fruitful source of disease, giving rise to diarrhea, dysentery, and low fevers, and aggravating the mortality of cholera and other epidemics.

A good exposure of the rock strata under the city may be seen on the Elkhorn branch, just below its limits, especially at the old stone-quarry of Van Akin, and that higher up, opposite the cemetery, near the Frankfort railroad. At the first-named quarry, more than twenty feet perpendicular of the rocks are exposed. The layers are from six inches to one foot thick (thicker in the upper quarry). In the lower beds some good specimens of that large *trilobite*, the *isotelus (asaphus) gigas*, have been found; and in those above are to be seen those other characteristic fossils of the lower silurian formation, the *chatetes lycoperdon, leptæna, atrypha, receptaculites;* also portions of small *encrinital* stems, specimens of *modiola, orthis, pleurotomaria*, etc., etc.

In the quarries at the eastern end of the city, the layers are usually thinner and more fossiliferous, containing *atrypha, orthis, leptæna*, etc., etc.

We append, in a tabular form, a statement of the chemical composition of some few of the limestones of this region, as analyzed by Dr. Peter for the late Kentucky Geological Survey, and published in volume two of the reports of that survey, as follows:

No. 507. *Limestone*—forming the thin, shelly upper layer at Van Akin's quarry.

No. 508. *Limestone*—forming a thicker layer below, used for curb-stones, etc., in the city, and containing fossils characteristic of the Trenton limestone of the New York geologists.

No. 511. *Limestone*—an upper layer five inches to one foot thick, at Grimes' quarry, on the Kentucky river; not used for building purposes, but which would probably make hydraulic cement.

No. 512. *Magnesian Limestone*—from Grimes' quarry. A very good and durable building stone, used in the construction of the Clay monument in our cemetery. This material, of a pleasant buff-gray color, was also used in the Clay statue, placed on the top of the column. Its fine granular structure, and its freedom from cracks and fossils, adapt it very well to the chisel of the sculptor.

COMPOSITION, ETC.

	No. 507.	No. 508.	No. 511.	No. 512.
Specific gravity	2.660	2.711	2.716	2.703
Carbonate of lime	92.73	77.63	51.57	55.54
Carbonate of magnesia	.63	10.00	29.33	0.80
Alumina, and oxide of iron and manganese	2.42	3.23	3.57	.96
Phosphoric acid	.86	.70	.37	not est
Sulphuric acid	.34	3.12	.34	.02
Chlorine	.05	not	estima	ted.
Potash	.23	.32	.71	.36
Soda	.28	.15	.82	.22
Silica and insoluble silicates	2.28	4.98	11.58	2.79
Loss	.28		1.71	
	100.00	100.13	100.00	100.69

With these remarks, we close our history of Lexington, the ancient metropolis of the mystic Alleghan; the hunting-ground of the Indian; the first capital of Kentucky; the home of Clay; the center both of the blood-stock region of America, and of the "Garden Spot of the World."

----, Charles 213
ADAIR, General 207 Governor 217 302 335 Major 243
ADAMS, 208 313 316 Daniel 247 George 194 Gus 204 John 216 John Quincy 209 Mr 155 209 229 President 335 Richard 352 S 155 S L 55 Samuel 155 Vice-President 195 Wm 247
AGRICULTURAL Societies, 270
AGRICULTURALISTS of Fayette, 278
AGRICULTURAL and Mechanical College, 60
AKERS, Mr 153
ALCOCK, John 131
ALEXANDER, J W 385 M 149 Mr 148 R A 137 Robert 149
ALLAN, Chilton 371
ALLEN, 250 Celia 25 Chas F 247 Chilton 180 Colonel 254 260 Dr 288 E 395 Edward 395 F J 247 Francis 247 H G 192 Hugh 247 J G 59 J R 288 John 141 174 John G 328 John R 369 Richard 277 Sterling 287 Thomas 152 Thomas M 309 Thos 124 168 W S 365
ALLIN, John 244
ALLISON, Andrew 247 W 161
ALSOP, Alexander 248
AMUSEMENTS, Early 105
ANCIENT, Remains 1 Fortifications 4 Monuments in 1845 9
ANDERSON, 404 Captain 159 George 164 217 Oliver 144 179 R T 384 385 Robert 353 T J 247 Thomas 247 W G 396 Wm 100
APOSTOLIC Times, 400
APPERSON, R A 366

ARDON, Thomas 226
ARGABRIGHT, Alfred 353
ARMANT, Mr 281
ARMSBY, Stephen 124
ARMSTRONG, J L 223 Mr 218 410
ARNOLD, 107 Captain 246 John 168
ARTHUR, John 217
ARTISTS, 144
ASBURY, Francis 152
ASHE, 1
ASHLAND, 60 214
ASHTON, Richard 321
ATER, W W 248
ATHENS of the West, 303
ATHEY, R A 179
ATKINS, Thos 168
ATKINSON, 85
AYER, 115
AYERS, Mary 102 Samuel 119 Sam'l 286
BACON, E 331
BADIN, Father 190 191 Stephen Theodore 190
BAILEY, James 353
BAIN, James 217 P 331 Patterson 248 286
BAINBRIDGE, Dr 334 Eleanor 334
BAKER, Allen 262 I L 247 Issac L 247
BALLARD, Bland 168
BANCROFT, 414
BANK, First in Kentucky 222
BAPTIST, Church 118 Female College 398
BARBEE, Ira 248 Joshua 124 Lewis 161
BARKER, 164
BARKLEY, S L 353
BARLOW, Mr 186 187 Thomas 319 Thomas H 307 Thomas Harris 185 Thos H 262

BARNES, A M 218 392 407 John W
  366
BARNETT, Andrew 130 Mr 129
BARR, Robert 124 194 195 T 195
  245 Thos 262 Thos T 178 W
  331
BARRACKS, 252 269
BARRONE, M 353
BARRY, 73 227 277 334 David
  353 Judge 48 228 229 Major
  229 Miss 326 Mr 227-230 Mrs
  William T 346 Mrs William
  Taylor 227 W T 56 143 178
  179 180 289 William T 43 50
  230 314 346 William Taylor
  226 230 Wm T 228
BARTLETT, President 378 Rich
  168 Rich'd 168
BARTON, Professor 224
BARTOW, A S 289
BASCOM, Bishop 54 154 Dr 54
  Henry B 54 154 Samuel P 352
BASSETT, S 405 Squire 190
BATTERTON, Amor 100
BATTLE of the Blue Licks, 87-
  91
BATTLE of Frenchtown, 253
BAYLES, W W 352 Wm 356 Wm
  W 358
BAYLOR, Walker 72
BEACH, Gabriel 340
BEAN, C Y 331
BEARD, Captain 352 355 358 Col
  306 Henry 247 J H 149 Lowry
  J 352 O P 135 370 Oliver H
  P 352
BEATTY, Adam 160 C 177 Corne-
  lius 160
BEAVER, Henry C 353 Wm 353
BECK, J B 180 James B 62 Mr 62
  145 Mrs 145
BECKLEY, John 247 Mrs 280
BECKLY, John 261
BEKKERS, Father 296 John H 192
BELL, 81 383 Dr 2 G R 385
  Henry 328 368 377 John 177
  219 John W 353 Mrs 280 307
  Superintendent 361 T S 307
  Wm C 247
BENEVOLENT Soc, Female 280
BENJAMIN, Geo W 353

BERKLEY, E F 361 380 Edward
  F 200 370 J W 197 Ludwell
  130 Mr 200 201
BERRY, J W 278 James W 395 N P
  278 S O 352 Wm 168
BERRYMAN, J S 275
BERTRAND, General 215
BEST, Dr 320
BIBB, George M 143 223 Mr 223
BIBLE Societies, 242 299
BIRCH, Miss 367
BISHOP, Purnell 309 R H 281
  283
BITTERMAN, Henry 352
BLACKBURN, E 275 Mr 129 T H
  247
BLAIR, W W 281
BLANCHARD, David 100
BLAND, Charles 169 Chas 126
BLANNERHASSET, 226 Mrs 226
BLEDSOE, 73 Elizabeth 217
  Jesse 43 52 56 143 177 178
  180 217 243 308 Joseph 217
  Judge 217 218 270 409 Mr 218
  Mrs Jesse 217 Richard 248
  Rowan 227
BLINCOE, B W 160 385 Ben 164
BLOCK House, Abandoned 99
  Built 23 Great shot from 74
BLOOD-STAINED Letter, Incident
  189
BLUE LICKS, Battle of 87
BLYTHE, 46 Ebenezer 258 Eliza
  281 J E 159 James 43 44 110
  195 242 James E 247 Presi-
  dent 159 224 250 251
BOBB, John 143
BOBBS, John 142 Wm 164
BODLEY, C S 71 H I 177 Mrs H J
  146 Thomas 50 72 142 160 164
  177 181 217 249 305 313
BOGGS, Robert C 276 Robt C 276
BONDURANT, Joseph 366
BOONE, 26 27 30 86 87 88 91 99
  116 'Squire 126 Colonel 89
  Daniel 16 21 28 42 71 75 85
  92 96 Isaac 86 92 Samuel 86
BOOTH, 205
BOSWELL, B 286 Colonel 261
  George 317 318 Hart 278 J
  130 286 J B 281 Joseph 318

BOSWELL (continued)
  Thomas E 318 361
BOSWORTH, W E 122
BOTANICAL Garden, 304
BOURBON County, created 116
BOWER, Dr 158
BOWMAN, Abraham 176 Col 306
  Colonel 22 Geo H 130 George
  248 J B 62 407 John B 57
  Mary D 57 407 Mr 57 58 59
  Mrs 57 Regent 57 William
  352
BOWMAR, Herman 180
BOWYER, Ezra 248
BOYCE, Dan 274 Mr 274
BOYD, 222
BOYLE, John 43 56 336 Judge
  334
BRADDOCK, 93
BRADFORD, 127 189 Charles 159
  258 Chas 247 261 Dan'l 164
  Daniel 52 143 160 286 322
  Eliza 128 John 42 50 71 72
  124 125 128 164 172 177 194
  195 198 202 217 222 286 305
  Mr 126 259
BRADLEY, 389 O L 383 385
  Thomas 115 148 175 332 W J
  136 William 135
BRANCH Bank of Kentucky, 328
BRAND, Alexander 136 George
  328 George W 369 John 130
  198 217 272 317 318 321 361
  Mrs George 281 W 307
BRANK, Mr 284 Robert G 284
BRASFIELD, W R 136
BRASSFIELD, Capt 249
BRAY, James 114
BREATHITT, Governor 324
BRECHUS, L 385
BRECK, W C 120
BRECKINRIDGE, 383 Colonel 237
  Dr 112 J C 180 John 112 177
  180 181 182 194 206 216 219
  283 302 John C 73 133 148 149
  179 180 183 302 343 357 358
  367 368 378 Jos C 178 Joseph
  C 281 302 Mr 182 183 302 Mrs
  John C 367 R J 73 130 178 277
  301 361 380 Robert 173 Robert
  J 111 361

BRECKINRIDGE (continued)
  W C P 237 411
BREEDERS of Fayette, 135
BRENNAN, 319 E 385 Ernest 71
  277 H C 385 Henry C 197
  John 115
BRENT, Innis B 164 189 190
BRICKBRAT War, 301
BRIGHT, Dr 392 J 385 W 385
BRIGNOLI, 205
BRINK, Daniel 262
BRITTON, Thomas 136
BROADUS, W F 121
BROBSTON, Nicholas 73
BRODIE, F W 385
BROECK, Ten 136 137
BROGAN, T J 404
BROOK, Robert 206
BROOKE, John 100
BROOKS, Ebenezer 124
BROWN, 166 Benjamin Gratz 409
  Dr 44 Edgar A 340 Eliza 150
  George M 353 Governor 410 J
  124 J H 354 James 43 151 173
  194 206 220 227 260 James N
  273 274 Jas 168 John 44 150
  176 180 248 John H 284 358
  Margaret 44 Mason 410 Mr 284
  Mrs 410 Mrs John H 281
  Samuel 38 44 185 223 224
BROWNE, Harry 377
BRUCE, B G 133 Dr 215 J W 411
  John 130 L C 385 Miss 391 S
  D 371 384 Sanders D 71 W W
  197
BRUEN, 204 J 281 Joseph 319
  328 Mrs 326
BRUER, Thos 168
BRUTTON, C H 385 Chas H 377
BRYAN, A C 353 A G 353 E C
  278 395 Enoch 262 353 John
  385 Thomas 352 William 169
  278 395
BRYANT, 28 68 69 70 71 Edwin
  234 235 James 28 Jos Jr 136
  Joseph 28 Judge 235 Morgan
  28 T M 248 W P 248 William
  28 68
BRYANT'S STATION, Settled 28
  Described 77 Seige of 78
  Heroic Women 79 Site of 85

BUCHANAN, Dr 224 225 Joseph 45
  56 185 224 Mr 349
BUCKNER, B F 392 E P 155
  Hubbard 353 Judge 61 R A 60
  150 179 180 357 Richard A
  177 368
BUENA VISTA, Lexington Dead at
  356-358
BUFORD, A 135 149 Abraham 129
  Charles 133 H M 304 Simeon
  129 W 129 Wm 130 131
BULGER, Edward 92
BULLITT, Alexander S 173
  Cuthburt 289 Fanny 148
BULLOCK, 177 E 177 Edmund 177
  179 R S 71 411 Robert 372
  Waller 71 357 Walter 242
BURBRIDGE, Mr 129 Sidney 130
BURCH, James G 353 John 339
  Rev Mr 284
BURGE, Lemuel 199
BURGESS, John 278
BURGOYNE, 107
BURK, Patrick 168
BURNS, Robert 217 262
BURR, 108 Aaron 115 195 226
  244 Colonel 226
BURROWES, 387 N 281 Nathan 184
  Mr 185
BURYING Grounds, Early 38-40
BURTON, Ambrose 353
BUSH, Captain 133 Dr 53 56
  Dudley 384 Elizabeth 148 J
  M 53 55 Joseph H 148 Philip
  148 R W 371 T J 133 384
BUSHART, Mr 194
BUTLER, 281 Father 191 Mann 52
  Percival 176 178 Rev Dr 212
  William O 247 249
BYLES, Samuel 353
BYRD, 36 Colonel 35 36
BYRON, Lord 145
CABELL, 9
CABELLS, 9
CADWALLADER, George 135
CALDWELL, Charles 47 293 318
  Dav 168 Dr 293 294 Moses
  168 Professor 47 T S 307
  Thomas 177
CALEDONIAN Society 217
CALLAGHAN, J B 353

CALLOWAY, Colonel 21
CALVERT, Willis 248
CALVIN, A H 340
CAMERON, John 217
CAMP, E H 284
CAMPBELL, 252 Alexander 120
  308 309 311 Bishop 309 311
  Colonel 280 Dr 111 James 179
  Jn Poage 111 Pres 122 R T
  247 Robert 217 Robt 247 T L
  352 William 176
CANDY, John 340
CANNON, J W 392
CARR, 177 C 275 C D 364 371
  Charles 71 371 Chas 178 249
  275 Judge 215 Mr 71 T D 384
  W 177 219 Walter 176 177
  Walter Jr 248
CARROL, Governor 306
CARROLL, Bishop 190 Dempsey
  353 G A 192
CARTER, G W 352 Landen 262 R G
  366
CARTWRIGHT, Peter 154
CARTY, 408 Henry 102 352 356
  358 John 24 59 100 101 102
  149 328 396 397 Mary Ayers
  102 Mary E 407 Mr 102 396
  397 Mrs John 29 149 156 197
  281
CARVER, John Wise 353
CASS, Mr 369
CASSELL, John L 396
CASTEL, Martin 193
CASTLEMAN, 286 B 353 B T 385
  David 143 281 G 385 H 385
  John B 384 Lewis 262
CASWELL, Henry 199
CATACOMB, Ancient 2
CATHOLIC Church, 190
CEMETERIES, 38-40 Lexington
  260
CHALLEN, James 310 Mr 310
CHAMBERLAIN, Thos 247 261
CHAMBERS, B 281
CHAPMAN, B A 353 Dr 199 George
  T 49 50 199 314
CHARITY, 287
CHARLESS, Lewis 247
CHASSEURS, Lexington, Officers
  and Privates 383

CHEW, S 395 Samuel H 395
CHILES, 115 H 411
CHINN, A B 385 Alfred 248 E
  309 J G 59 310 322 Nathan
  248 R H 178 179 247 Richard
  245 317 William 262
CHIPLEY, Dr 288 Mrs 326 Stephen 154 287 321 W S 55 288
  340 368
CHOLERA of 1833, 325
CHRISTIAN, Thomas 261 Church
  307 Church of Broadway 407
CHRYSTAL, James 136 394
CICERO OF THE WEST, 214
CINCINNATI, Settled 141
CIRCUIT, Judges 177 Clerks 177
CITY, Officers for 1872 411
  Schools 329
CLARK, 26 95 97 189 233 164 A
  385 G Rogers 99 George
  Rogers 22 J 385 John 73 395
  Joseph M 201 M 404 William
  311 Wm 168 262
CLARKE, 64 G Rogers 36 James
  180 Thomas 71
CLAY, 73 213 277 290 336 343
  350 369 377 380 420 Brutus
  180 C M 161 179 353 355
  Captain 353 356 358 Cassius
  M 159 332 351 352 Cassius
  Marcellus 351 Eliza 214
  Green 290 351 H 178 274 H
  Jr 179 Henry 43 60 143 146
  147 154 178 180 196 198 205
  212 218 227 244 250 260 276
  287 303 311 316 317 320 332
  347 356 367 372 374 375 386
  390 394 Henry Jr 214 358 J
  B 161 180 James 215 James B
  214 215 378 390 John 135
  John M 135 214 Lucretia 206
  214 Mr 46 100 148 163 206
  207 209-215 228 229 236 251
  270 323 332 333 335 348 349
  351 368 370 378 379 386 390
  Mrs 206 214 215 307 339 369
  370 Mrs Henry 234 Mrs
  Thomas 145 T H 179 Theodore
  214 Thomas 213 Thomas H 214
  Thos H 378 Young Henry 356
CLEARY, J R 411

CLEVENGER, 332
CLIFFORD, John D 198 201 295
  Mary S 295 Miss 280 Mr 295
CLINES, Hiram 247
CLOUD, C W 313 Caleb W 152 Dr
  153
COBURN, John 108 124 177 Mary
  Moss 108
COCHRAN, J 385 J C 384 J W 197
  365
COCHRANE, J W 197 411
COCK, Jesse 159 247
COIT, Dr 52 53 Thomas W 52
COLEMAN, 203 C 385 D S 278 395
  Horace 262
COLLINS, 204 Elisha 73 247
  Josiah 73 Mr 129 Mrs 98
  Richard H 406 Stephen 73 W
  B 313
COLUMBUS, 12 16
COLUMBUS OF THE LAND, 16
COMBS, 178 Captain 290 General
  133 160 290 291 L 178 179 307
  Leslie 130 131 133 178 179
  196 290 305 313 318 321 368
  406 Lieutenant Col 307 W R
  262
COMSTOCK, L 247
COMING of the White Man, 16
CONNELL, 245
CONNER, M R 366
CONOVER, Sylvester 353
COOKE, John Estin 48
COONS, A 135 Thomas 135
COOPER, 205 J 385 J B 197 406
  Mr 150 197 R W 383 385
  Spencer 154 236 Virginia
  236
COPPAGE, C F 352
CORMAN, Geo 248
CORNWALLIS, 101
COUNTY, Clerks and Officers 71
  Officers in 1872 411 72
  Judges 364
COX, Richard 377 Samuel 159
  247
COYLE, C 286
CRAIG, 29 127 D M 328 331 361
  385 E W 286 Elijah 79 198 H
  G 385 Horace 405 John 124
  Lewis 29 118 Susan 117

CRAIK, James 200
CRAWFORD, Alex 247 261 Alexander 159 George W 366 James 169 W H 209
CREATH, Jacob 119 309
CRITTENDEN, 73 John J 147 223 332 347 Senator 378 T T 178 Thomas T 178
CROCKETT, J 177 Joseph 124 176 177 Robt 272
CROGHAN, George 269 354
CROPPER, E 385
CROPS, of Fayette 413
CROSS, James C 53
CROUCH, Nathaniel 353
CROW, Charles 54
CULVER, John 366
CUMMINGS, Hervey 352
CUMMINS, James 248
CUNNINGHAM, J 179 Mr 110 111 Robert M 110 242 287
CURD, J 179 John 178 John Jr 407 John Sen 407
CURLE, Clayton 179
CURRIE, J C 353
CURTIS, David 353
CLEARY, 245
DAILEY, Captain 313 Lawrence 247
DALY, Lawrence 161 352
DANCING School, First 40
DANDY, W C 155
DANIEL, H 179
DARNABY, G W 179 John 262 W S 179
DARNALL, G W 304
DAVENPORT, John 40
DAVID, Bishop 191
DAVIDSON, Dr 284 J T 331 Mr 283 President 283 Robert 53 54 283
DAVIESS, Annie 244 Colonel 143 243 244 J H 243 Jean 243 Joe 206 Joseph 243 Joseph H 143 146 147 Joseph Hamilton 243 Major 244 Samuel 387
DAVIS, 254 Benj 247 Garret 180 Garrett 348 371 378 James E 322 Jas E 178 Jefferson 56 304 William 159 247 Wm 261
DEACON, Peter 205

DEAN, Julia 205
DECLINE, of Lexington Trade 402
DECOGNETS, Louis 287
DEDMAN, Lewis 276
DELEGATES, to Conventions 106 109 116 123 140 162 170 219 360
DELPH, G W M 353
DEMOCRATIC Society, 181
DENMAN, Matthias 141
DENNY, Richard 205
DERBY, Earl of 48
DESHA, Governor 228 306 346 J R 368
DESYON, Count 306
DEWEES, F 281 Fannie 148 Farmer 402 Mr 402 403 Mrs 326
DICKINSON, Archibald 100 Martin 100 Valentine 100
DIDLAKE, George W 160
DILL, J 385
DILLARD, J W 385 Mr 121 R T 120 121 242
DILLON, J 385
DINWIDDIE, William 113
DISCOVERERS of Lexington, 18
DISHMAN, John 248 352 Rev Mr 194
DISMARIAE, Father 191
DOBYNS, C H 377 Charles 160
DODD, J B 54 Professor 54
DODGE, 148
DOLL, G A 385
DOUGLAS, 383
DOW, Lorenzo 223
DOWDEN, E W 322 368 W W 71 160
DOWLING, J 404
DOWNEY, Major 398 W S 392 398
DOWNING, J L 130 Jos L 275 Marcus 407 R 130 R W 194
DOYLE, William 248
DOZIER, G 385
DRAKE, 204 A S 262 270 Abram 56 B P 55 Daniel 39 45 Dr 45 55
DUCKER, Enoch 262
DUDLEY, 28 103 249 Abraham 71 Ambrose 298 386 B W 45 47 53 56 130 143 223 329 331

DUDLEY (continued)
371 Ben 45 148 Ben W 44 Benj
W 417 Benjamin W 238 368
Benjamin Winslow 238 C W
371 Colonel 103 261-263 Dr
239 288 386 387 E A 179 E L
369 Edward A 357 Elder 298
Ethelbert 387 Ethelbert L 55
386 J G 385 James 270 360
384 Jas 377 John 397 Lieut
Col 306 Mr 237 298 Mrs W A
147 Nelson 357 358 Peter 370
S 385 T P 406 T P Jr 385
Thomas P 298 W A 179 William 103 291 William A 237 368
DUDLEY'S Defeat, 262
DUFF, Mrs 204
DUKE, J K 131 Jas K 130 Mrs Basil 149 W 353
DUMONT, Arthur J 53
DUN, Walter 274
DUNCAN, 407 H T 135 361 368 377 H T Jr 59 197 385 395 405 Henry 275 Henry T 277
DUNCANSON, E S 328 385
DUNKIN, James 18
DUNLAP, 135 293 Col 306 Eve 68 H C 385 J R 178 262 370 John R 368
DUNMORE, Lord 16
DUNN, Philip 247 W 331 Walter 273 274
DUPEE, Aaron 394
DUPUY, Aaron 378
DUQUESNE, 22
DURALDE, Mrs 214
DURHAM, M J 341
DWIGHT Dr 46
EADS, J R 392
EAGLE, E E 133
EALEMAN, Peter 262
EALIER, L W 384
EANES, Wm H 275
EASTIN, A F 261
EATON, H H 48
EAVE, George 261
EAVES, John 248
EBERLE, John 53
ECKLE, 166
ECLIPSE of the Sun, 400

EDGER, Joseph 262
EDMISTON, Miss 326
EDMONSON, Captain 254 John 248 259
EDWARDS, John 174
ELDER, 198 Edward 247 261 G A M 191 Matthew 119 Rev 191 Sam'l 261 Samuel 159 247
ELLEY, Elder 408 G W 407
ELLIOT, Colonel 264 266
ELLIOTT, 256 Captain 157 255 256 J M 197 Mrs 280 William 255
ELLIS, Capt 29 Charles C 353 Lewis 145 Moses 71 Richard L 353 William 29 169
ELLY, Mr 312
ELY, C 385
EPISCOPAL Church, 198
ERWIN, Colonel 306 Jas 275 Mrs 326
ESSEX, William 198
ESTELL, 75 77
ESTILL, 88 Eli 353 W R 278 392 395
EVERETT, 383 Edward 47 Peter 366
FANT, Thos 247 261
FARMERS, Home Journal 394 Club 394
FARRA, Asa 262
FARROW, Asa 286 Thornton 73
FATHER OF HIS COUNTRY, 220
FAULKNER, John C 353
FEAR, James 248
FELIX, W H 122
FERGUSON, 224 A 247 N 385 R 385 W 385
FERRIER, John 217
FERTILITY of Fayette, 412
FICKLIN, Joseph 190 304 Postmaster 149 304
FIELD, Luke 248
FIGG, John 262 John Jr 262
FILLMORE, Mr 150 President 149
FILSON, John 30 42 96 141
FINANCIAL Crises, 292 297
FINCH, John J 353
FINLEY, Samuel 334
FINNELL, J W 235 Mr 235 N L 234 236

FIRE Companies, 164
FISH, Mr 369
FISHBACK, Dr 120 239 309 310
 Jacob 309 James 45 50 120
 178 242 309 326 Mrs 310
 William 244
FISHEL, Michael af 286
FISHELL, Michael 318
FISHER, 286 James 9 Maddox 164
 286 Mr 10
FITCH, John 183
FITZPATRICK, William 353
FLOURNOY, M 71 178 261 Matthias 178 179
FLOYD, John 75
FOLEY, R 385
FORBES, Captain 159
FOREST, Edwin 204
FORMAN, Thomas 408
FORSEE, James W 352
FORT WASHINGTON, 141
FOSTER, T W 411
FOUSCHEE, C W 197
FOWLER, C H 393 Captain 345
 John 123 124 129 156 180
 190 245 305 345 396
FOX, Henry 352
FRANCIS, E 247
FRAZER, Alexander 164 J T 322
 411 Joseph S 395 Mr 147 Mrs
 147 Mrs Warren 149 Oliver
 147 148 149 Robert 286 318
 Warren 149
FREEMAN, J C 398
FREEMASONRY in Kentucky, 142
FRIDAY, J M 353
FRIER, Robert 169 177
FRY, Speed S 341
FULTON, 183 W F 385
FUNERAL, Jefferson 313 Adams
 313 Shelby 313
GAINES, R M Jr 353
GALLAGHER, John 353
GALLEGHER, John 353
GALLOWAY, 106 William 100
GAME, 30 188
GANO, Elder 119 John 118
GARDNER, V N 394
GARDOZNI, Don 140
GARRARD, Governor 42 James 124
 273

GARRETT, Ashton 262
GAS, City lighted by 374
GATES, 107
GATEWOOD, T R 248
GAYLE, Joseph 329 Miss 329
GAYLORD, Henry M 353
GAZETTE, Kentucky (old) 124
 (new) 394
GEARY, J A 404
GEIGER, William 366
GEOHEGAN, Mrs 326
GEOLOGY, of Lexington and
 vicinity 416
GEORGE, Bishop 153
GEORGE, king of England 19
GESS, John 262
GIBBONS, Thomas 154 Z 385
GIBBS, Benj 168
GIBNEY, Alex 309 R A 411
GIBSON, 407 C C 395 Hart 395
 495
GILMORE, F 385 J L 385 W D 385
GILPATRICK, 137
GILPIN, R W 247
GILTNER, Bernard 248
GIRTY, 81 83 84 89 91 James 77
 Simon 77 84
GIST, John 248 Miss 217 Nathaniel 217
GLASS, Wm 353
GOOD Templars, 395
GOODIN, J G 262
GOODLOE, Almira 389 C 385 D S
 407 D S Jr 385 Judge 389 K
 M 247 S S 304 W C 60 177
 392 W Cassius 179 W O 394 W
 Owsley 394 William C 389
 William Cassius 394 395
GOODNIGHT, Michael 248
GORDON, George 124 John 92 Rev
 Doctor 195
GORHAM, George M 353
GOSNEY, Fielding 247
GRAHAM, A 309 R 59 400 Robert
 58 311 400
GRANT, 70 Col 29 John 29 Thos
 148 William 28
GRANT'S STATION, 29 36
GRATZ, B 182 307 331 368 Benj
 59 361 Benjamin 50 62 193 197
 249 277 318 321 328 347

GRATZ (continued)
  360 368 371 377 406 H H 394 M
  B 371 Mr 62 Mrs 326
GRAVES, 189 B F 364 411 Ben
  249 Benj 178 Benjamin 177
  260 Benjamin F 322 363 F B
  363 John 262 John C 363
  Judge 363 364 M E 197 Major
  254-258 Mr 348 Mrs 326 S C
  385 Thos C 262
GRAY, Capt 249 William 262
GRAY EAGLE, 163
GRAYSON, 140 Alfred W 178
GREAT Rain, 315
GREEN, Dr 55 378 Lewis W 55
  Sarah Reed 55 Willis 124
  Willis Reed 55
GREENUP, Christopher 100 124
GREER, Isaac 18
GREGG, James 248
GRIFFIN, 248
GRIMES, 420 John 148
GRINSTEAD, 389 J A 135 149
  James A 71 368
GROSH, Catharine 346
GROSS, Joseph 71 Joseph R 71
  377
GRUNDY, Felix 143 232 243 Mrs
  175
GUNN, J 392 William 155
GUTHRIE, James 378
GWIN, Duke 56
HACKNEY, 166
HAGGARD, 194
HAGGIN, 227 273 James 333
  Judge 334 346 Mrs 334
HALDEMAN, W N 235
HALL, B F 310 Dr 310 311 Mr
  111 Nathan 111 324 S X 155
  T 124
HAMILTON, 6
HAMILTON Capt 249 Captain 262
  James 154 328 John 248
  Thomas 248
HAMPTON, George 352 William
  366
HANNA, John H 289
HANSON, F A 385 Mrs 280 R W
  179 Roger W 379
HAPPY, Josephus 340
HARDESTY, 29

HARD Winter, 36
HARDIN, John 85 Martin D 334
HARDING, Chester 146
HARGROVE, R K 155
HARLAN, James 378 Major 89 Mr
  129 Silas 92
HARMAR, 156 Joseph 162
HARMER, 85
HARNEY, C H 384
HARP, David 396
HARPER, J A 385 Jas A 277 John
  135
HARRIS, Captain 129 James B
  352 L 385 Mr 242 Nathaniel
  152
HARRISON, 259 Benj 175 Gen 279
  General 102 103 168 243 244
  262 267 290 H 177 Hez 177 J
  O 357 368 James O 61 161
  277 329 330 377 405 Mr 61
  Mrs James O 281 T J 340 W H
  251
HARROD, 99 James 96 Samuel 168
HARRY OF THE WEST, 227
HART, 332 Capt 249 Captain 247
  256-258 260 261 Colonel 128
  Eleanor 286 Israel 169 Joel T
  331 John 276 286 Lucretia 206
  Mr 332 333 N S G 156 159 160
  247 Nathaniel G T 260 T P 161
  281 Thomas 194 195 202 206
  Thomas Jr 164 Thomas P 321
  329 Thomas 222 Thomas P
  133
HARTNELL, P C 385
HARVEY, Barnet 247
HAWES, R 180 371 Richard 378
HAWKINS, A F 331 361 D M 385 J
  H 178 John 177 Joseph H 178
  S 385 T 385 Thomas T 353
HAYDEN, J J 395
HAYDON, Benjamin 100 William
  73
HAYES, J 385 S T 26
HAYNE, Robert T 341
HAYNES, C Younglove 379
HEADINGTON, Nicholas 154 155
HEADLEY, 28 404 Charles 135 H
  A 135 278
HEALY, George P 147 Martha 147
HEBARD, S 51

HEBRATI, M 385
HEINER, R 155
HEMINGWAY, T 361
HEMP Manufacture, 184 241
HENDERSON, 29 H A M 155 H P 392 Richard 40 William 73 75
HENDRICKS, N 411
HENGSTENBERG, 55
HENRY, 140 John 322 Patrick 310
HERAN, David 328
HEROIC Era, 34
HERR, L 135
HERRON, D G 61 J L 247
HERVEY, J H 281
HEWITT, J M 242 John M 309
HIBLER, S M 395
HICKEY, Colonel 306 Judge 38 346 Mrs Thomas M 346 T M 177 321 Thomas M 321 346
HICKMAN, Captain 256-258 Jas L 247 357
HICKS, Abram 262 Samuel 248
HIGGINS, James 158 159 247 261 Joel 361 Mrs Wyett R 281 R 119 286 Rich'd 287 Richard 317 318 321 360 361
HILL, H B 368 377 H B Jr 328 385 H B Jr 328 J O 385
HILLOX, Henry H 353
HINES, Bennet 247
HINKSTON, 21 Captain 35 John 35
HISE Elijah 56
HISTORICAL Society of Fayette, 405
HOAGLAN, D J 411
HOCKADAY, E W 275 P B 276
HOCKER, J 405
HODGES, A G 368
HOEING, 409
HOGAN, 69 70 Elihu 179 Elisha 179 James 68 John M 248 John P 248 John T 237
HOGARTH, 301
HOGARTY, A J 404 M 160
HOLDER, 78 81 Captain 78 116 John 116
HOLDING, Samuel 247
HOLLAND, Dr 320

HOLLERGER, F X 385
HOLLEY, Dr 43 46 47 48 49 50 62 147 Horace 46 President 49 Wesley 353
HOLLINGSWORTH, A 61
HOLLY, Dr 293 303 President 307
HOLMAN, William 154
HOLMES, Robert 286
HOOKER, George 248
HOPKINS, General 252
HOPPY, Joseph 161
HOPSON, W H 311
HORD, F T 365 John N 366
HORSES, Noted 134
HORNSEY, T A 394
HOUSTON, Mr 369
HOWARD, Benj 180 Benjamin 103 177 178 180 Margaretta 382
HOWE, Edward 194
HUDGINS, Abner 352
HUDSON, John 275
HUFFMAN, 29
HUGHES, 177 J 177 Jacob 178 179 274 366 392 James 160 177 178 206 Jas 178 Thomas 366 W T 277
HULL, 251
HUMBOLDT, Baron 12
HUME, Will P 274
HUMPHREYS, Charles 43 50 319 351 Mrs Charles 351
HUNT, 135 A G 411 Allie G 71 197 Catharine 346 Charleton 317 321 322 329 338 Charlton 301 F K 34 147 179 346 368 Francis K 54 G D 275 George 122 J W 307 John W 50 190 198 285 289 318 346 390 John Wesley 321 Lewis 152 Mr 346 Mrs J W 326 P B 385 Thos H 133
HUNTER, 215 J J 147 148
HUSTON, General 61 J B 378 James 157 247 John B 61 343 L D 155
IGO, Harrison 353
IMLAY, Captain 31
INGELS, 29
INNES, Charles W 277
INNIS, C W 278 H E 178

INNIS (continued)
John P 278
IMMIGRATION Society, 202
INCIDENTS, Amusing 102 157
Romantic 35 37
INDIAN, Fighters 168 169
Ravages in Kentucky 21 22
Incursions to Lexington 35
68 74 167 Tragedies 34 74
The Great Invasion 77 Steal
Negroes 170 Exterminate the
Alleghan
INFANTRY, Lexington Light 155
204
INFIDELITY, 193 223
INVENTIONS, 183
IRVINE, 167 Wm 124
IRWIN, Dr 254
IRWINE, Mrs 214
JACKSON, 148 269 279 298 316
324 375 Andrew 209 320 323
332 C 353 Dr 212 General 48
208 210 229 270 280 293 323
Henry C 353 James S 353
John 217 Miss 398 President
229
JAIL and Jailers, 163
JAMES, Benj 128 Eliza 128
JANUARY, A J 365 A M 281
Ephraim 73 James 73 Jas B
286 Mr 193 Peter 73 Samuel
100 Thomas 177 194 198 285
Thos 287 Thos 287 281
JAVELL, 167
JEFFERSON, 182 246 313 Governor 71 Joe 205 President
156 174
JEFFREY, Rosa 150 Rosa V 377
JEFFREYS, C B 136
JEREAUME, Jean Baptiste 258
JERRETT, Richie 248
JETER, Bernard 248 Hiram 248 R
H 352
JEWETT, John 124
JEWISH Church, 390
JOHNSON, B H 385 Benjamin 177
C C 385 E P 368 G J 124 H
331 Jas 385 John 385 M C 26
59 179 197 331 357 360 361
368 411 Madison C 60 318
Major 60 Richard M 28 29 56

JOHNSON (continued)
Robert 28 124 Samuel 73
JOHNSTON, James 247
JONES, 204 C 353 Clement 356
358 David C 353 Governor
213 Harry 124 J L 411 Jabez
262 John 164 185 Jos 168 Mr
369 Philip 248
JORDAN, John 190 198 222 John
Jr 164 Mr 189
JOUETT, 148 149 293 303 307
342 A S 352 George P 322
357 Matthew H 146 Mr 147
KALKER, S 247
KASTLE, 395 D 385
KAVANAUGH, Bishop 154 H H 154
KAY, John 247
KEEN, 293 Mrs 306 Sanford 286
KEENE, E 385 J 385 Miss 346
Mrs 130 Oliver 71 346
KEISER, Christopher 164 J G
385 John 262
KELLEY, J E 247 Robert 247
KELLY, Samuel 73 T J 385
KENDALL, Amos 218 270 Mr 270
KENNEDAY, Matt 281 Thos 174
175
KENNEDY, C W 371 377 S P 395
KENTON, 26 99 Simon 18 126 146
KENTUCKY, Racing Association
130 Vineyard 219 University,
Early History of 57 University,
Removal to Lexington 59
University, Donations 59 61 62
University, Officers 59 60 62
District of 37 County Formed
22 First Capital of 170 First
White Native of 116
KENTUCKY SQUAW, 261
KERNSNER, Casper 193
KING, D A 394 John 274 John E
168 T 198 Thomas 247 Thos
261
KING SOLOMON, 374 375
KINKEAD, G B 368 George B 54
357 John P 248 W B 148 278
395
KINNAIRD, J G 278 James 277
KINNEAR, G 385
KINNEY, R P 248
KIRBY, 248

KIRTLEY, Jeremiah 262
KIRTNER, Christopher 100 Widow 100
KISER, 115 Ben 115 189 Benjamin 406 Jacob 193 John 194 John G 384
KNOW NOTHINGS, 376
KOLKER, Solomon 248
LAFAYETTE, 215 G W 306 Gen 305 General 144 305 306 307 Marquis 147 Marquis de 48
LAFON, Nicholas 129
LAKE, Adam 247 262 Richard 217
LAMPHER, P 385
LANCASTER, G L 385 M P 197 281 328 Mrs M P 281
LANCKART, Henry 194 Joseph 340
LANCKHART, G 353 S 353
LANDER, Mrs 205
LANKHART, Joseph 248
LARD, M E 312
LAST Man Killed by Indians, 170
LAUDEMAN, J 411
LAWLESS, J P 385 S 385
LAYTON, 286 Dr 288 T K 154 242
LEARY, Mr 194
LEAVY, Mrs 326 W A 242 331 William 50 286 305 William A 196 197 321 329
LEE, 130 Henry 174 175 J W 385 William 169
LEITCH, David 124
LEMMON, James 305 Joseph 248
LEONARD, James 353
LESLIE, Governor 61
LETCHER, B 385 Dr 55 G R 384 Governor 60 147 278 John W 353 Mrs 183 S 385 S M 55 369
LEVASSEUR, Col 306
LEVASY, J J 353 J W 353
LEWINSKI, Major 147
LEWIS, Charles 247 Colonel 158 249 253 254 260 279 E 385 Enoch 135 General 255 Thomas 72 119 176 177 188 Thos 169 William 157 249 262 Wm 168 261
LEXINGTON, An Indian Camp 21 Appearance of 19 25 30 105

LEXINGTON (continued) 202 220 285 322 Discovered 18 Character and Importance 410 Daily Pres 405 First Native 28 First White Female Settler of 28 First Lot Owners of 73 100 First Trustees of 64 First Brick House in Lexington 193 First Revolutionary Monument at Lexington 20 First Councilmen of Lexington 321 First Schools in 39 First Dry Goods Store in 105 First Session Kentucky Legislature in Lexington 170-174 First Fourth of July Celebration in Lexington 139 In 1872 Described 414 First Methodist Station in 152 First Road Macadamized in 317 First Nail Factory in 222 First Western Railroad in 315 First Western Luncatic Asylum 285 First Western Newspaper 124 First Locomotive 186 319 First Steamboat 183 First Planetarium 185 First Baptist Convention in 119 Incorporated as a City 321 Incorporated as a Town 75 Library 194 Light Infantry 155 Lyceum 303 Orphan Asylum 326 Rifles 377 The Great Race Horse 136 137
LIBERTY Poles, 216
LIFE in the Fort, 33
LIGHT, George C 50 154
LINCOLN, General 101 Mrs 296 President 296 Mrs Lincoln's birthplace 296
LINDSAY, 27 28 James 24 73 Joseph 24
LINDSEY, Joseph 73
LINGENFELTER, D 247
LINGINFELTER, John 247
LINN, J H 155
LINZEN, 385
LIPSCOMB, W S 407
LITTERELL, John 248
LOCKHART, W 385
LOGAN, 22 88 Benjamin 86 C 281 Colonel 86 92 93 David 197

LOGAN (continued)
   General 2 John 173 W B 281
   William 160
LOGSDON, Jos 168
LOGUE, James 197 322
LOGWOOD, T 411
LONG, Edward 352 Hartwell 248
   N P 340 William 248
LORRIMER, G C 122
LOUIS XVI, king of France 354
LOVE, John 159
LOWE, John M 352
LOWELL, R 135 136
LOWNDES, Mr 215
LOWRY, T W 161
LUSBY, 115 H 136 W H 164
LUTHER, H 385
LUTZ, John 51 361
LUXON, E D 407
LYLE, John 110
LYND, S W 121
LYON, Pat 146
M'CALLA, And'w 287
M'CULLOUGH, L 286
M'DOWELL, Jas 168 W 168
M'FARIN, James 169
M'KEE, 77
M'MILLEN, Wm 168
M'MURDIE, F 168
M'NAIR, Robert H 286
MACALESTER, Mrs 326
MACALISTER, Edward 361
MACBEAN, William 164 195
MACCOUN, D 286 J 285 James 195
MADISON, 259 Major 255 President 337
MAFFIT, 154
MAGLONE, W 385
MAGUIRE, Harvey 154 John 191 R 385
MAHONE, S 385
MAHONEY, James 352
MALTA, Sons of 382
MARDIS, John 135
MARKLEY, Jacob 262
MARQUAM, J P 61 W H 61
MARRS, J R 394
MARSH, Richard 406
MARSHALL, 16 355 A K 180 396
   Annie 244 Colonel 96 Humphrey 100 123 124 180 210

MARSHALL (continued)
   339 352 358 Judge 339 Lewis
   347 Louis 53 Mr 348 349 T A
   378 Thomas 71 96 100 107 140
   141 Thomas A 43 100 339
   Thomas F 56 73 347 350 Thos
   F 180 Tom 349
MARTIN, Capt 249 Hugh 73 James
   G 353 John 73 Mr 8 Samuel
   73 William 73
MASON, 140 Geo 353 John T 289
   Miss 227 S T 227
MASONIC Lodges, 142
MASTERSON, 167 Caleb 73 James
   18 24 25 27 73 262 Mrs 98
   Richard Jr 248 Robert 262
MATHENY, W F 384
MATHER, Robt 247
MATTHEW, 198
MATTHEWS, Dr 112 113 F 385 J D
   112 117 John D 284 Mr 284 T
   J 50 Thomas J 50 W M 385
   William M 197
MAUPIN, Thomas 353
MAXWELL, James 247 John Jr 18
   24 26 27 38 71 110 216 217
   247 Sarah 27
MAYDWELL, A 340
MAYER, Daniel 43
MAYES, Daniel 177 351 Judge
   351 Mrs Charles 351
MAYORS of Lexington, 322
MAYS, Lulie 407
MCADAM, 317
MCAFEE, A L 179 Robert 18
MCBEAN, Daniel 217 William 72
   217 Wm 222
MCBRAYER, Miss 334
MCBRIDE, James 73 William 89
   92
MCCABE, B J 385
MCCALISTER, Mrs E 281
MCCALLA, Andrew 111 195 197
   285 286 305 Gen 306 General
   249 John M 159 161 249 313
   324 John W 304 Mr 111
   William L 111
MCCALLIE, Frank 65 68
MCCANN, H 385 Neal 179 R 385 T
   W 385
MCCARTY, 258 Edward 352

MCCAULEY, John 396
MCCAW, T 385
MCCHESNEY, J W 247
MCCHORD, 284 James 52 56 281 282 John 281 Mr 282 283
MCCLAIN, Alexander 73 Daniel 73
MCCLEAR, Joseph 217
MCCLELLAN, H B 374
MCCLELLAND, N H 385
MCCLURE, A 276
MCCONNELL, 21 27 28 38 65 66 67 68 Alexander 24 28 65 73 Col 306 F 248 Francis 73 James 73 248 William 18 19 24 28 73 75 248
MCCOUN, Miles 217
MCCOWN, Professor 354
MCCRACKEN, M W 352 W 385
MCCULLOUGH, Harriet 387 John Lawson 46 L 281 Major 387 Old Mortality 388 R 248 S D 145 146 161 368 406 Samuel D 46 144 160 387
MCDERMID, Francis 73
MCDONALD, Francis 73 Henry 64 73 Hugh 73 James 73 John 73 John M 73 Widow 100 William 73
MCDOWELL, 252 J 177 James 168 175 248 John 100 175-177 195 219 Samuel 124 177 248 Wm 124
MCFADDEN, Mr 135
MCGARVEY, J W 311 407
MCGARY, 88 89
MCGINTY, James 73
MCGOWAN, J R 133
MCGOWEN, T B 321
MCGRATH, H P 135
MCGREGOR, 177 Alexander 142 217
MCGRUDER, Allan B 217
MCGUIRE, Father 383 James 353
MCILVAIN, 254
MCILVAINE, Thos 262
MCINTIRE, W B 385
MCINTYRE, H I 352
MCKEE, H 385 Hugh 408 W R 408 William R 356 Wm R 358
MCKINLEY, John 281

MCKINNEY, 39 99 J G 322 328 J Q 179 John 39 97 Mr 98 99
MCLAIN, Jonathan 248
MCMAHON, Edward 191 Peter 192
MCMAIN, John 353
MCMAKIN, John 247 S 248
MCMANUS, H 385
MCMICHAEL, R 405
MCMILLAN, James 176 177
MCMILLIN, G W 160
MCMULLINS, Samuel 73
MCMURTRY, David 276 G 385 John 368
MCNAIR, John 115 195
MCNEAL, J 385
MCPHEETERS, Margaret 109
MEAD, Captain 254
MEANS, Hugh 366
MEDICAL Society, 223
MEFFORD, Andrew 248
MEGOWAN, 216 404 Capt 249 280 Captain 280 David 317 318 321 James 262 James F 352 James S 288 Joseph R 164 Robert 110 114 160 175 Stewart W 247 261 279 T B 164 411 Thomas B 366 Thos B 164
MELISH, 203
MENIFEE, 73 Richard H 56
MENNIFEE, Mr 343 Richard H 342
MENTELLE, Mr 354 W 145 Waldemarde 102 354
MERCHANT, J L 353
MEREDITH, 9 10
MERRILL, Benj 281 M 326
MESNER, Peter 261
MESSICK, B M 155
MESSMORE, Peter 247
METCALF, Governor 389 Peter 262
METCALFE, Governor 318 335
METHODIST Church, Centenary 185 Independent 153 Morris Chapel 155
MEXICAN War, 352 355
MIKINS, John 100
MILLER, Elizabeth 217 J J 394 405 James H 353 John P 248 John T 115 Reverend Doctor 361 Robert 286 William 217

MILLIGAN, A R 61 President 58
R 59 Robert 58 61
MILLS, Benjamin 177 Judge 335
Zophar 379
MILTON, B T 411
MILWARD, C 385 L P 384 392 W R
392
MITCHELL, 29 85 Alexander 147
David 64 73 James 100
Martha 147 T D 385 Thomas
197 Thomas D 53 Thos 149
392 William 73 75 Wm 248
MONKS, 385 T 161 Thomas 247
MONROE, John 177 President 47
48 215 293 335 T B 322
MONTGOMERY, 254 Miss 280
William 248
MONTMOLLIN, 417 J 385 Mrs 281
W 385
MOON, Jno A 247 John 248
MOONEY, C E 353
MOORE, C C 9 262 C S 262 James
43 44 198 353 John W 275 Mr
199 201 Oscar F 379 S 262 T
R 262 William 248
MOREHEAD, C S 52 56 180 371
Governor 378 380
MORGAN, 95 356 A G 353 356 358
Calvin C 352 390 General
390 391 James 94 John 237
John H 149 352 356 377 390
Louis 146 Mrs 94 Mrs John H
391 R C 377
MORPETH, Lord 215
MORRIS, Bishop 155 J C 385
MORRISON, Archie 261 Colonel
293 James 48 51 142 177 195
289 James H 201 John 25 28
73 175 John C 261 Major 28
147 Mrs 280 R 161
MORROW, James 73
MORTIER, Gilbert 37
MORTON, Abram 324 G W 71 J B
197 405 J H 119 307 J R 304
385 411 John H 178 286 289
Mary S 295 W R 71 130
William 198 222 286 289 295
305 329
MOSS, Mary 108
MOUND, Builders 11 Opened and
Contents 9

MULLAY, W H 353
MULLIGAN, Dennis 411 J H 159
404 411
MUNOS, J 385
MURDOCH, 205
MURPHY, Jeremiah 131
MURRAY, Lindley 348 William
142 206
MUSGROVE, Wm 248
MUTER, George 124 216 217
MYERS, Malcolm 194
NAPPER, Dr 301 James 248
NEAGLE, John 146
NEALE, James 247
NEANDER, 55
NEGROES, 289 338
NEIL, Chas 247
NEMELLY, J 385
NETHERLAND, 90 Ben 100 Benjamin 90 100
NEVILLE, J H 58 407 John H 59
60
NEVIUS, H V D 374
NEWBERRY, W H 340
NEWCOMB, J C 385
NEWTON, Isaac 224
NIBBLICK, William 73
NIBLICK, John 73
NICHOLAS, Colonel 43 George 43
173 206 243 402 L C 385 S S
402 T J 384
NICHOLLS, William T 366
NICHOLS, Thomas 71
NICHOLSON, Lewis H 353
NOBLE, E S 185
NOEL, Silas M 121
NORRIS, C H 408
NORTHERN Bank of Kentucky, 331
NORTON, C C 340 G W 392 George
222 J B 160 177 John 318
Mrs J 326 Mrs John 280 281
NORWOOD, Charles 305 Thomas
Charles 305
NOVEL Trial, 106
O'BANNON, J B 71
O'CULL, James 152
O'FLYNN, F 191
O'HARA, Theodore 230 359
O'HAVER, Thomas 353
OBSERVER and Reporter, 233
ODD FELLOWS Lodges, 340

OFFUTT, M 385
OLD and New Court, 300
OLD HICKORY, 270 323
OLD KING SOLOMON, 149 374 375
OLD SOLOMON, 375
OLDHAM, E 368
OLDHAM, Edward 277 357
OLE BULL, 205
OOTS, H 385
OREAR, Mrs Thos C 281
ORPHAN Asylum, 326
ORR, A D 124
OVERTON, Dr 255 J Jr 124 James 45 249 Major 254 Miss 227 Mr 233 234 Samuel R 233 Waller 227 233
OWENS, Patrick 100
OWINGS, T D 286
OWSLEY, Almira 389 Governor 54 Judge 335 William 389
PAGE, John 152
PAINE, Hugh 262 Thomas 193 223 Tom 106
PAINT LICK Expedition, 123
PALMER, J W 307 Jas W 234 Mr 234 Mrs 280
PARK, Asa 145
PARKER, 127 177 Alex 124 164 285 Alexander 198 281 289 305 J 177 178 James 124 194 Jas P 247 John 177 178 Richard 159 160 Robert 100 114 175 Thomas 248
PARODI, 205
PARRISH, James 29 Timothy 29 W D 248
PARROTT, Henry 352
PARSONS, C B 155
PATRICK, 254
PATTERSON, 99 Captain 26 92 Col 26 27 Colonel 39 91 141 142 J K 56 60 Joseph J 353 Matthew 100 R 177 Robert 18 23 24 26 64 75 110 116 141 177 195 S R 353 Sam'l 168 W D 248 Wm 248
PATTI, 205
PAWLING, William 320
PAYNE, Col 306 D C 366 E 385 Edward 71 119 176 Elder 118 Gen 250 H 178 H C 178 368

PAYNE (continued) Henry 72 177 178 Henry C 277 318 J B 197 John B Jr 59 O F 322 Wellington 197 William 119
PAYTON, Timothy 73
PEERS, Benjamin O 50 51 Mr 51 Mrs 326 President 51
PENDLETON, 140
PENNINGTON, Tobias 248
PEOPLES, John 168
PERKINS, W 385
PERRIN, H P 61
PERRY, 267
PETER, Dr 50 60 419 Robert 10 50 53 146 406
PETERS, B J 366
PETTY, Tom 248
PHELPS, J S 304
PHILLIPS, J J 353 Philip 168
PHYSICIANS of Lexington, 320
PIATT, Salem 248 252
PICKETT, J D 60 407 408 Joseph D 406 Thomas 237
PIERCE, J C 385
PIGG, Samuel 353
PIKE, J M 304 Jas M 313
PILCHER, Beverly 248 Lewis 248
PINDELL, Captain 313 H C 179 368 370 R 368 Rich'd 179 Richard 133 305 320 T H 130 281 322 Thos H 286 Thos S 133
PINKARD, Thomas B 198
PINKERTON, Dr 311 L L 58 311 S D 407
PIONEER Women of Lexington, 93
PLAN of Lexington Adopted, 73
POCAHONTAS, Princess 19
POGUE, Alexander 248
POINDEXTER, 311 James 353 William 119 Wm 308
POLITIÇA, Mr 215
POLK, 350 James K 210 Mr 210
POPE, John 43 143 162 178 180 217 243 286 350 Mr 163
POPULATION, of Lexington and Fayette 220 240 295 363 383 404 412 414
PORTER, Norman 328
PORTRAITS, 145-150

POST Masters, 190
POST Office, 188
POSTLETHWAIT, J 286 307 Sam 195
POSTLETHWAITE, 188 324 Chas 262 G L 159 160 161 385 John 130 160 198 Marshal 371 W 385
POTTER, N S 245
POWELL, Colonel 273 Thos 353
POWERS, Hiram 333
POYTHRESS, Father 152 Francis 152
PRALL, N 407
PRATT, Mr 122 William M 121 368
PRENTICE, 236 350 T B 281
PRENTISS, Nathaniel 164 Thomas M 197 W S 353
PRESBYTERIAN Church, First 108 Second 281
PRESTON, General 278 Mrs Wm 146 William 382 Wm 278
PREWETT, David 384 R H 160
PREWITT, Col 306 David 278 395 Robinson 248
PRICE, Capt 249 Captain 254 Colonel 376 D 135 D L 179 Daniel B 149 General 150 J R 385 Mr 150 Nannette 234 S 135 S W 160 161 190 Samuel 194 W S 149
PRITCHARD, W 247
PRITCHART, Wm 133 281
PROCTOR, 262 280 General 264
PROSPERITY of Lexington, 240 344
PROTZMAN, Edmund 352
PRUDEN, M 386 Mr 386
PUBLIC Spring, 24
PULLUM, A B 385
PURCELL, Archbishop 192
PUTNAM, Mrs 326
PYTHIAS, Knights of 408
QUARLES, Roger 371 Rogers 371
RACING Associations, 128
RADCLIFFE, W D 353
RAFINESQUE, 4 9 C S 1 47 304 Prof 6 Professor 295
RAGIN, Wm 353
RAILROADS, 318 365 366 409

RAINEY, W H 328 William 353
RAISIN Massacre, 255
RAMEY, Nathaniel 356 358
RANCK, G W 61 304 407 George W 406 Helen C 407 Mrs 145
RAND, W S 155
RANDALL, C 411 Thomas G 368
RANDOLPH, John 210
RANKIN, Adam 108 286 Dr 27 Margaret McPheeters 109 Mr 109
RATCLIFFE, Francis 262
READY, Miss 391
REDD, T S 71 177 179 Thomas 190 Thomas S 368
REDMAN, Lewis H 353
RED Men, 394
REECE Hiram 377
REED, J 385 M 385
REES, H 133
REID, David 217 Thomas 217
REILEY, James 247
RELIEF and Anti-Relief, 297
RELIGIOUS, Excitement 220 Revival 328
RENNICK, James 274
REPRESENTATIVES, in Legislature 177 in Congress 180
REPUBLICANS, National and Democrats 316
REYNOLDS, 92 Aaron 84 91 J A 395 396 J W Hunt 135
RHINEHEART, B F 149 Mr 149
RHODES, James C 71 Waller 71
RHOTON, B W 154
RICE, A L 136 David 41 Mr 41 N L 311 Old Father 41
RICHARD, Joseph H 366
RICHARDS, A K 135 149 John W 366
RICHARDSON, J C 71 119 John 72 353 Professor 58 R 58 Robert C 353 W 326 W H 119 278 281 William 242 William H 45 53
RICKETTS, R C 408
RIDDLE, Henry 248 252
RIDGELY, Dr 44 239 F 286 Fred 194 Frederick 44 198 223 Miss 280

RILEY, Jas 261 Jesse 159
ROACH, Fielding 262 Richard 247
ROBB, Joseph 313
ROBBINS, A W 311
ROBERT, Mrs 280
ROBERTS, S E 353
ROBERTSON, Chief Justice 369 Eleanor 334 Geo 378 George 43 54 179 242 311 334 368 371 405 Judge 147 150 238 308 334 336 386
ROBINSON, 115 Governor 236 J F 135 179 411 J F Jr 411 Matthew 169
ROCHE, John 49
RODES, J B 177 411 W 179 William 179
ROGERS, Admiral 408 C C 179 368 Charlton 85 Dr 288 George 247 John I 311 Mr 83 R C 179 Sam E 353
ROLLING, Robert 247
ROLLS, Geo 247
ROSA'S Poems, 377
ROSS, Colonel 144 Eliza 281 Geo G 247 Mrs 280 326 Thomas 322 William 164
ROWAN, Colonel 306 John 56
ROYAL, Thomas 248 William 248
ROYAL SPRING, 18
RULE, 189
RUNYAN, G W 353
RUSH, 293 Professor 224
RUSSELL, Colonel 6 104 251 252 J W 154 James 142 217 Mary O 382 Robert 178 T A 71 385 Thomas A 248 Thos A 179 W 177 Willaim 177 William 103 175 177 251 Wm 178
RUTER, P S 361
RYLAND, Mrs 128 206 391 Robert 398
SAC Legend of Kentucky, 14
SAGE OF ASHLAND, 373 374
ST ANDREW'S Society, 216
ST CATHARINE'S Academy, 328
ST CLAIR, 29 156 169 170 188 General 168 Governor 168
ST TAMMANY Society, 245
SANDERS, 273 G N 275 Geo N 274

SANDERS (continued) Lewis 164 273 285 Mr 233 W 129
SANDERSON, George 248 Jas 248 William 248
SATTERWHITE, 115 304 T P 154 320
SAUNDERS, George 203
SAXTON, H A 377 O 385
SAYRE, Aunt Abby 405 D 317 D A 146 197 300 David A 160 233 277 361 374 405 E 239 E D 197 E K 361 Mr 405 Mrs 326 Mrs A V 281 Uncle Davy 405
SCHOOLEY, James 248 353
SCHULTZ, Charles 160
SCHWING, Jacob 247
SCOTT, 103 125 168 222 250 277 285 Charles 124 167 217 D 385 General 366 Governor 174 250 307 Isaac 149 Isaac W 281 J 273 M T 147 242 281 360 361 368 371 Matthew T 382 Mrs 307 N B 352 Persicles 392 R C 385 T 385 W T 385 Winfield 366
SEAMAN, Charles 73
SEARCY, Reuben 177
SEARLES, 158 Charles 157 159
SEARLS, Charles 247 258 Mr 259
SEELEY, Lyman W 197
SEESILL, Henry 353
SEITZ, John A 72 195
SELLIER, J 385
SENATORS, United States, from Fayette 180 State from Fayette 179
SEPP, J 385
SHACKELFORD, John 407 408
SHALLY, Valentine 247
SHANKLIN G S 180
SHANNON, Geo 178 George 178 Hugh 18 President 57
SHARP, John 100 101 Richard 164
SHARPE, E 217 281
SHAW, Hiram 392 J 385 J P 385 Wm 353
SHAWLEY, V 247
SHEELY, Daniel 198 James 262
SHEEP, Excitement Incident 238

438

SHELBY, 313 314 Colonel 306
  Governor 48 128 156 172-174
  227 267 279 293 310 Isaac
  124 147 171 173 276 277 372
  378 James 272 276 Jas 272
  Major 263 Miss 310 T H Jr
  278 Thos H 276
SHELMAN, T C 155
SHELTON, John 353
SHEPHERD, George 100
SHEPPARD, David 353 Isaac 352
SHERIFFS, List of 71
SHINDLEBOWER, Geo 247 261
  George 159
SHIPMAN, Jacob S 201 Mr 201
SHIPP, Dudley 248 Elizabeth 29
SHIVEL, John 248
SHIVERY, Geo W 248
SHORT, Charles W 48 Mrs 326
  Newton 311 Peyton 179
SHROCK, John 154
SHROPSHIRE, J 372 J H 377
SHRYOCK, Matthew 198
SHULTZ, Christopher 365
SIMPSON, Anderson 248 Captain
  254 George 262 James 398
  John H 353 W W 340
SIMS, W E 180
SINKING Spring, 286
SKILLMAN, A T 361 Dr 56 Elizabeth 299 H M 55 149 308 Mr
  300 Mrs H M 281 Mrs Thomas
  281 Thomas T 300 Thos T 281
SLADE, J F 411
SLAVIN, Duke 392
SLOAN, J R 71
SMITH, 273 Benjamin Bosworth
  199 Bird 276 Bishop 199 200
  Byrd 248 252 Curtis 309 E E
  407 Elijah 261 Elisha 395
  George S 169 Granville 395
  Isaac 352 J B 120 J S 237
  John 193 308 Joseph 62
  Larkin B 179 Lewis H 197
  Miss 233 Mr 234 235 Racoon
  308 S 274 Samuel 262 Samuel
  R 394 Sol 204 Southwood 332
  Speed 311 Stephen 247 261 T
  307 Thomas 161 233 234 247
  272 308 Thos 247 304 W H
  278 366 W Halley 395 Wm 353

SNEDEGER, Chas 168
SNYDER, G C 408 Geo W 353
SOLOMON, William 374
SONTAG, 205
SOUTH, J 177 John 177
SPALDING, Annie 38 328 Archbishop 328
SPEED, James 124 Thos 124
SPENCER, W 385
SPILLMAN, C 385
SPOLEN ,Abram 340
SPRAGUE, G 385
SPRAKE ,J D 411
SPRINGLE, 167 Alexander 217
  Jacob 194
SPRUELL, Mr 155
SPURLOCK, Burwell 152
SPURR, L 385 R J 179 277 278
  369 395 Richard 179
SPYERS, Green 248
STAFFORD, John 353
STALLIONS, Fayette 135
STANDIFORD, D W 322
STANHOPE, A 275 Robert 73
  William 135
STANLEY, Lord 48
STATESMAN, Kentucky (old) 360
  (new) 394
STEEL, David 248 252
STEELE, Andrew 75 100 135
  Robert 110 William 75 76
  100 175
STEP, Geo 353
STEPHENS, B 247 261 Luther 321
  Mrs L 326
STERE, John 262
STEVENS, Luther 318 Mrs 280
STEVENSON, Daniel 392 Edward
  153 242 Mr 393
STEVES, J B 385
STEWART, Abby 383 Armston 159
  Armstrong 247 261 H C 385 J
  H 177
STILES, J C 242
STIPP, George 262
STOCKTON, Mr 369
STOLL, George 340
STONE, Barton 120 308 Barton W
  307 R R 404 Robert 411
  William 119
STONER, Michael 18

STOUT, Benjamin 286 Berry 119
STREETS, Opened and Named 64
   105 219 114 115 203
STROWBRIDGE, George 393
STUART, Gilbert 146 Mr 150
   Robert 43 110
STUCKER, 29
SULLIVAN, 95 Jas 407
SULLY, 148
SUMK, Alexander 353
SURVEY, of Lexington 166
SUTHERLAND, William D 395
SUTTON, G W 361
SWIFT, C H 385 Charles 384 E
   385 Mr 197 S 361 385 Stephen 328 William 197 322
   406
SWIGERT, Daniel 135
SYMMES, Judge 141
TALBOT, W J 370
TALBOTT, Daniel 247 J C 273
   Jesse H 278
TANDY, 286 Gabriel 119 Linton
   248 Willis 249
TANNER, William 248
TAPP, Nelson 248
TARLETON, L P 394
TARLTON, R B 130 275 Ralph P
   130
TARTAR Emetic Treat, 301
TAYLOR, B B 360 Benjamin 317
   318 324 Charles 353 H 272
   Hubbard 169 176 177 Jackson
   353 James 289 James M 352
   353 Zachary 148
TAVERNS, Early 114
TEBBS, S F 392
TECUMSEH, 227 243 266 280
TEGARDEN, 273
TELEGRAPH, 360
TEMPLEMAN, J 247
TEMPY, Christopher 353
TERASSE, Mr 241
THE FIRST NAPOLEON, 279
THE MAN Who Smoked Out the
   Indians, 158
THE PROPHET, 243
THEATERS, 203
THEOBOLDS, S 287
THOMAS, B G 135 C B 177 411
   Charles B 368 General 150

THOMAS (continued)
   George H 149 150 William 353
THOMPKINS, G R 178
THOMPSON, 222 B F 385 C R 179
   Hugh 73 J F 385 Jane 73 M G
   197 Miss 98 Robert 73 S S
   197 307
THOMSON, A 71
THORNTON, Jos 353
THROCKMORTON, A 368
THRUSTON, Buckner 180 Buckner
   177 207 219
THWAITS, William 356 Wm 358
TIBBATS, Thomas 286
TILFORD, J B 368 John 130 145
   281 289 331 361 John B 59
   John W 361 Mrs 326
TILLETT, Wm 411
TIMBERLAKE, R T 340
TINSLEY, Peter 205
TIPTON, Burwell S 366 J M 395
   396 495
TODD, 71 99 Charles S 249
   Colonel 32 37 40 41 87 296 D
   178 David 178 261 286 Dr 258
   General 175 J 286 Jane 100
   John 18 32 40 41 71 73 75 86
   92 262 L B 190 L L 160 Levi
   18 32 33 64 71 72 73 96 116
   123 168 175 247 Levi L 143
   160 178 247 Mary 296 R S 71
   179 247 281 Robert 72 100 101
   116 123 124 174 175 176 177
   179 188 Robert S 296 321 Robt
   S 179 S B 261 Sam'l B 247
   Thomas 181 Thos 124 William
   217
TODHUNTER, J 136 R 136 372
TOLER, Elder 119
TOMLINSON, 81 85 Nicholas 85
TOMPKINS, Grimm R 178
TORRENCE, John 73
TOTTEN, Silas 398
TOULMIN, H 194
TOULNIM, Harry 42
TOWN FORK, 114 162 219 203 242
TOWN, Laid Off 65
TOWNSEND, 247
TRABEIN, A W 394 A W 385
TRACY, B J 136
TRADE and Wealth, 412

TRANSYLVANIA University, Origin of 40 Removal to Lexington 41 Donations to 47 53 54 Library 47 53 Holly's Term 46-49
TRIGG, 86 Stephen 86 92
TRIMBLE, Judge 342
TROTTER, 285 298 Captain 159 252 Colonel 162 Geo 178 Geo Jr 285 Geo R 357 George 178 239 252 267 280 George R 358 J G 160 248 James 50 72 110 116 119 175 176 177 178 179 194 195 281 305 Sam 286 Samuel 238 239 281
TROYE, E 149
TRUE, 178 J 178 J Jr 178 James 178
TRUE American, Removal of 351
TRUMBO, A 366
TURFMEN of Fayette, 135
TURNER, 258 Fielding L 195 Joseph 73 Mr 259 Wm 126
TURPIN, Horace 124
TWAITS, Ezekiel 352 William 353
TWIGGS, 280
TYDINGS, Richard 153
TYLER, 223 348 G 142 Mr 208
UNDERWOOD, Governor 370 Judge 214 Mr 369 R 385
UNITED STATES Bank, 289
UPPINGTON, J T 408
USHER, 115
VALENTINE, R 113
VANBUREN, Martin 215 Mr 208
VANCE, David 73 Joseph 247
VANMETER, Abram 277 I C 278 Isaac 274 J C 179
VANPELT, Derrick 247
VARBLE, Jacob 262
VARDEMAN, Jeremiah 119 120
VARTY, W H 385
VAUGHN, E M 354 356 Edward M 116 358 J A 385 Mrs 116 117 Rhoda 116
VENABLE, John W 341
VENARD, Absalom 249 Thomas 249
VERBRYCK, Mr 149 William 149
VERDEN, T 247
VERTNER, D 371

VILEY, 394 J R 135 278 John R 133 W 131 Warren 135 Willa 130 368
VIRGINIA Town, 181
VONAKIN, 419
VOORHIES, Peter G 190
WAGONER, 163
WAIT, James 352
WALKER, 177 D 177 David 177 H P 155 Matthew 73
WALLACE, 34 Caleb 116 123 124 135 141 195 Judge 334 Thomas 222 William 283
WALLER, Henry 365 Joseph 73
WALLIS, Harriet 387
WALTON, L N 385
WAR 1812, Commenced 246 Incident of 189 Soldiers of 247 261 262 270 Killed of 159 252 254 261
WARD, Jackson B 366 John 199 307 Mr 199 Mrs 280 326 William 123 141 Z 418 Zeb 135
WARE, Abram 262
WARFIELD, B 273 274 Benjamin 272 361 C 385 E 130 272 273 275 286 307 361 368 371 385 Elisha 45 50 135 136 318 L 385 Walter 119 198 223 305 William 392 395 William C 119 Wm 147 197 278
WARNOCK, Michael 64 73
WARREN, William 177
WASH, Colonel 306
WASHINGTON, 37 220 259 George 139 220
WASON, James 73
WASSON, Joseph 62 197 277 407
WATERS, Mrs 410 Simon 248
WATKINS, B P 394 Elizabeth 214 Henry 205
WATSON, Mr 129
WATTS, 109 Dr 109
WAUTE, Stephen 222
WAYNE, 103 108 Anthony 71 102 145 188 General 193 Mrs Anthony 145 Old Mad Anthony 156
WEATHERS, Gran 278
WEBB, Joshua 262

WEBBER, Adam 194
WEBSTER, 336 Daniel 215 J H 304 John 261 411 Larkin 261 Thomas 261
WEIGART, A B 352 Thomas 353 William 352
WEIGERT, David 248 Thomas 356 358
WEIR, Clifton 372 James 318
WEISIGER, Samuel 160
WELLS, 254 General 137
WELSH, James 110 Mr 110
WEST, Benjamin 145 Captain 313 Edward 145 183 184 Edwin 184 F G 161 John B 184 Mr 183 184 Nathaniel 284 R J 385 William 145 William E 145
WHALEY, 117
WHEELER, George 262 Leonard 196
WHIGS and Democrats, 320 350
WHITE, 164 Henry 58 Henry H 59 60 Thomas 353
WHITNEY, 340 351 382 John 247 John W 288 Mrs Dr 149 R P 352 Thomas 164
WICKLIFFE, 72 73 343 C A 56 C H 322 D C 236 368 383 Daniel Carmichael 236 Margaretta 382 Mary O 382 Mr 236 237 364 382 Mrs 326 R Jr 364 R Sen 178 357 402 Robert 33 103 179 318 361 364 366 382 Robert Jr 53 196 Robert Nelson 235 360 Robert Sen 362 364 Robert Sr 301 Robt 130 272 Robt Jr 178 179 Robt N 357 Virginia 236
WIER, James 286
WIES, D K 366
WILGING, P 385
WILGUS, J B 204 339 392 409
WILHOITE, John 249
WILKES, L B 311 Mr 311
WILKINS, C 281 307 Charles 50 164
WILKINSON, 103 151 General 107 108 124 141 168 188 James 106 107 116 156 160 167

WILKINSON (continued) Thomas 152
WILLIAMS, John Augustus 60 Mary D 57 130 Caleb 100 Capt 249 Charles 57 G B 353 J Aug 59 John 73 N 385 S R 374 Zephaniah 247
WILLIAMSON, David 286
WILMOTT, Samuel F 353
WILSON, 115 226 Belle 395 Captain 167 Edward J 178 Isaac 39 42 J S 147 197 John S 197 201 204 406 418 Mr 418 Susie 395 Thos 377 W G 129 William 340
WINCHELL, A 60
WINCHESTER, General 249 250 253-255 290 James 246
WINGATE, Joseph 322
WINN, O D 179
WINSTON, D M 242
WINTER, E J 133 317 Elisha I 50 Elisha J 318
WINTHROP, Edward 200 242
WIRT, John 131 133
WISE, T N 379
WITHERSPOON, J R 178 John R 178
WOLF, D F 392
WOLFOLK, J S 407 Joseph 163 230
WOLVERTON, Mr 152
WOMEN of Lexington, 93
WOOD, Benjamin 262 James 71 177 Noble 169 O S 408 W 385
WOODRUFF, James B 353 Jesse 190 340 353 355 358 411
WOODS, Abel 50 Alva 50 Dr 50
WOODSON, S H 180
WOODWARD, Mrs 146
WOOL, General 366
WOOLFOLK, J S 404 405 Jos S 62
WOOLLEY, A H 146 A K 43 131 177 178 179 196 Aaron K 361 D V 385 F W 304 Major 103 Mrs A K 147
WORLEY, 115 C T 322
WORRELL, A S 398 Mr 398
WORSLEY, Mr 233 234 Mrs 233 W W 307 368 William W 233
WORTHEN, Hiram 248

WYATT, John 198
WYMORE, 34 John 73 Martin 247
WYTHE, Chancellor 205
YANDELL, L P 242 274 Lunsford P 48
YARBOUR, Jackson 353
YATES, Geo 262 J M 384 Wm M 377
YEISER, E 286 George 262 P 2
YOUNG, A 71 Alfred 353 C G 340 Captain 40 Daniel W 340 Dr 283 J D 286 John C 283 John D 71 Leonard 71
ZACH, 248
ZUNWALT, Adam 100 Jacob 100 Stoffre 100

www.ingramcontent.com/pod-product-compliance
Lightning Source LLC
Chambersburg PA
CBHW050324230426
43663CB00010B/1730